CLEAR
IT
WITH
SID!

CLEAR
IT
WITH
SID!

SIDNEY R. YATES
AND FIFTY YEARS OF
PRESIDENTS, PRAGMATISM,
AND PUBLIC SERVICE

MICHAEL C. DORF
AND
GEORGE VAN DUSEN

**UNIVERSITY OF
ILLINOIS PRESS**
Urbana, Chicago, and Springfield

Library of Congress Cataloging-in-Publication Data
Names: Dorf, Michael C., author. | Van Dusen, George, author.
Title: Clear it with Sid! : Sidney R. Yates and fifty years of presidents,
    pragmatism, and public service / Michael C. Dorf and George Van
    Dusen.
Description: Champaign, IL : University of Illinois Press, [2019] |
    Includes bibliographical references and index.
Identifiers: LCCN 2018051408 | ISBN 9780252042447 (hardcover : alk.
    paper)
Subjects: LCSH: Yates, Sidney Richard, 1909–2000. | Legislators—
    United States—Biography. | United States. Congress. House—
    Biography. | United States—Politics and government—1945–1989.
    | United States—Politics and government—1989–1993. | United
    States—Politics and government—1993–2001.
Classification: LCC E840.8.Y38 D67 2019 | DDC 328.73/092 [B] —dc23
    LC record available at https://lccn.loc.gov/2018051408

E-book ISBN 978-0-252-05128-9

To our wives, Maury Collins and Susan Van Dusen:
We would never have met either of you
but for Sid Yates, and we are eternally grateful
that both you and Mr. Yates were part of our lives.

When Abraham Lincoln was a candidate for Congress, he attended a church service conducted by Rev. Peter Cartwright. In the course of his sermon, Reverend Cartwright posed the question, "How many here want to go to Heaven?" After noting the response, he asked, "How many want to go to Hell?" Again, he noted the response. Lincoln, however, failed to indicate a preference for either place, which provoked Cartwright to remark, "Abe Lincoln, you haven't answered at all. If you don't want to go to Heaven and if you don't want to go to Hell, where do you want to go?" "Why," said Lincoln simply, "I want to go to Congress."

—Sidney R. Yates Newsletter No. 233

CONTENTS

Acknowledgments   ix

Prologue   1

PART I. THE CRUSADER, 1949–62

1   The Road to Capitol Hill   5

2   The Class of '49   15

3   "Here Comes This Nice, Good-Looking Guy"   41

4   "The Judgment of Admirals"   55

PART II. DEFEAT AND COMEBACK, 1962–74

5   Yates for Senate   87

6   To the United Nations and Back   109

7   "This Precious Resource"   115

PART III. THE CHAIRMAN, 1975–98

8   America's Committee   133

9   Three Years of the Culture Wars   143

10   "The Last Sanhedrin Met in 70 CE"   183

11   The Final Years   215

Epilogue   219

Notes   227

References   251

Index   259

Photographs follow page 69

ACKNOWLEDGMENTS

In preparing this narrative on Sidney Yates, we have drawn on an array of sources. Although Yates passed away in 2000 at the age of 91, many of his congressional colleagues and other elected officials made themselves available for interviews or correspondence, sometimes both, and provided important insights into the inner workings of the House and of Yates's chairmanship of the House Appropriations Subcommittee on the Department of the Interior and Related Agencies as well as his personal life. They included current and former legislators such as Senator Dick Durbin, and Representatives Nancy Pelosi, Jan Schakowsky, David Obey, and Ralph Regula, former Illinois Governor James Thompson, and former Idaho governor and Secretary of the Interior Cecil Andrus.

The congressman's daughter-in-law and grandson, Debra Yates and Jonathan Yates, provided delightful reminiscences, as did his sister-in-law, Doris Holleb, who gave us insight into Yates's World War II service years and his early forays into politics.

The papers of many of those associated with Yates have been explored, including those in the National Archives and the presidential libraries of all of the presidents from Harry Truman through Bill Clinton. Responding to a Freedom of Information Act request, the Federal Bureau of Investigation provided its files on Yates.

The Research Library of the University of Illinois at Chicago extended us every courtesy in helping us comb through the papers of Mayor Richard J. Daley. The curators at the Paul Simon Center at Southern Illinois University and the Dirksen Congressional Center in Pekin, Illinois, couldn't have been more helpful. Geoffrey Swindells at Northwestern University Library assisted in helping us track down all manner of public documents. The outstanding research librarians at the

Skokie Public Library and the John M. Flaxman Library at the School of the Art Institute of Chicago (SAIC) were unceasing in their help in obtaining even the most obscure publications. The librarians at all these institutions are a resource to the nation in its continuing quest to examine—and re-examine—our history and our perpetually changing democratic institutions.

We owe a special debt of gratitude to Professor Dick Simpson, chairman of the Department of Political Science, University of Illinois at Chicago, who has encouraged us in our work on this project. At the Chicago History Museum, the repository of Yates's papers, Gary Johnson, president; Olivia Mahoney, senior curator; Julie Wroblewski, archivist; and Adam Melville, project archivist, went above and well beyond the call of duty.

We wish also to thank Peter Kovler and the Blum-Kovler Foundation, which provided seed money for this project; Madge Goldman and the Gabriella and Paul Rosenbaum Foundation, who underwrote the professional curating of Yates's papers at the Chicago History Museum; and SAIC, which provided sabbatical support.

Special thanks are due to Vicky Varga, assistant to the mayor of the Village of Skokie, and to the attorneys and staff of Adducci, Dorf, Lehner, Mitchell & Blankenship, PC, who provided ongoing support and encouragement as this work progressed.

We are grateful for the assistance and nurturing provided to us by the editors and staff of the University of Illinois Press and particularly to Senior Acquisitions Editor Daniel Nasset, who encouraged our efforts to bring Sid Yates to a larger audience. We give particular thanks to our copy editor Geof Garvey, and to Faith Brabenec Hart, who provided copy editing and indexing services. Both provided sound critiques and valuable suggestions.

Many others have contributed to this project and are listed in the bibliography. Many of the interviewees listed are not cited for direct quotations in the endnotes but provided valuable background information.

A word about the relationship of the authors to Sidney Yates is in order. Both authors worked for the congressman for several years in his legislative offices in Washington and Illinois and during his election campaigns. We knew him well—warts and all. Many of our observations are retold in these chapters. Over the years, we came to know many of the participants and were told of their first-hand experiences with Yates and the events as they unfolded. Many of the events recounted took place in our presence, and we have sought to corroborate these events through outside sources.

This book would not have been possible without the cooperation of the late Mary Anderson Bain, longtime personal friend and chief of staff, then called administrative assistant, to Congressman Yates. She was present at almost all the important junctures of his career, providing unswerving loyalty and clearheaded advice. Mary Anderson was born in DeKalb, Illinois, on September 19, 1911, attended local schools, and received a bachelor's degree at what is now known as Northern Illinois University in 1931. A staunch FDR liberal, she became chairman of the DeKalb County Democratic Organization, admittedly a small group in that Republican stronghold, in 1932. After a few years of teaching, she became director for the Illinois Northern District of the New Deal's National Youth Administration (NYA), and later, Illinois state director of the NYA, the youngest state director in the nation, and one of only a handful of women directors. During World War II, Mary was deputy director of the War Manpower Commission for Illinois and later Illinois director of the United States Employment Service. During this time, she became close friends with Franklin D. Roosevelt intimate Harry Hopkins; Aubrey Williams, FDR's head of the NYA; and Eleanor Roosevelt, who took interest in the career of the young female liberal, almost six feet tall, slender, and with striking good looks. Mary's stories of all-night poker games with Hopkins as they rode the rails became legendary.

In 1948, Mary, now married and head of her own advertising agency, was making a speech on behalf of Harry Truman when she first met a young candidate with good ideas but a terrible campaign style and not much chance of success. It was, of course, Sid Yates, making his first congressional run. Mary turned to her husband, Herb, and said "Boy, does he need help." The next morning, she showed up to volunteer at Yates's campaign office and ran every one of his campaigns after that. When Yates returned to the House in 1965, she accepted a position as chief of staff, first in Chicago, and later in Washington, where she remained until Yates's retirement in 1999.

Yates and Bain were a team, and for many, Mary was the congressman. Cecil Andrus recalled a time when, as secretary of the Interior, he came to see Yates, chairman of the appropriations subcommittee responsible for his budget, to seek permission for a project. He stopped in Mary's office to describe his request. "Oh, honey," Mary interjected. "There's no need to bother the chairman. I'll take care of it."

With Mary, politics was fun and always captivating. She kept a bottle of good rye and a deck of cards in her desk for times when the House was having late-night sessions, and she invited staff members to tell stories and swap rumors. She was a gourmet cook and invitations to dinner parties that she and Herb threw were eagerly sought. The authors spent many years as Mary's colleagues and friends, sharing her experiences and insights. When Mary retired, we both, together and separately, interviewed Mary, sometimes on the record, but more often on background and deep background. Herb was the love of her life and, after sixty-nine years of marriage, Mary and Herb died within two months of each other. Mary's name is found in many places in this book. Her influence can be found throughout.

Last, and most important, we gratefully acknowledge the loving forbearance of our wives, Maury Collins and Susan Van Dusen, who gracefully accepted our many fits and starts and occasional snags in this enterprise, always ready with encouragement and good counsel. We couldn't have done it without their unfailing support.

PROLOGUE

October 22, 1962

The rear tires of the Air Force VC-137 pounded the tarmac with a thump, the twin tires of its nose hitting a little more gently seconds later, precisely bisecting the center line of the runway reserved for military jets at O'Hare Airport in Chicago. The brakes protested as the jet, over 144 feet long and almost 131 feet wide, wingtip to wingtip, decelerated to a screeching halt, its four Pratt and Whitney jet turbines howling. There was no time for a gentle taxi. The pilot was under orders to get wheels up as soon as the VIPs were aboard.

In 1959, the Air Force had purchased three of these military-transport versions of the Boeing 707 for use by President Dwight D. Eisenhower, replacing the old propeller-powered Columbine III. Whether jet- or propeller-driven, whatever airplane transported the president carried the call sign Air Force One. President John F. Kennedy had been using the VC-137 as his presidential jet, but just weeks earlier, the Air Force exchanged the jet for the newer, longer C-137C Stratoliner. Now the old jet, demoted, had a different mission.

Military airplanes from the Air Force, the Navy, and even the National Guard were landing at JFK's order all over the country on October 22, 1962. The personnel on board had orders to pick up congressional leaders and bring them back to Washington. The summons, by telephone or telegram, to get to Washington immediately took most of the legislators by surprise. They would not learn until they arrived at the White House that the president had decided to blockade, or as JFK put it, to "quarantine" Cuba.

Everett McKinley Dirksen, the sixty-six-year-old white-haired minority leader of the U.S. Senate, waited at O'Hare in the sixty-degree fall afternoon with a military escort, watching the jet, now marked with the logo of the Military Air

Transport Service, approach. He assumed the meeting would be about Cuba. He and other senior Republicans had been speechifying for months against the Soviet buildup on the island only ninety miles from the U.S. mainland. It was a coordinated partisan effort. Just the week before, in fact, the chairman of the Republican National Committee predicted it would be the prime issue of the November elections.

But Dirksen didn't care what the reason was for the trip. He was in the midst of the fiercest reelection battle of his long career. With less than three weeks to go before the election, some polls showed he was going to lose to the liberal Chicago Democratic nominee, Congressman Sid Yates. Yates, charming and combative, seemed indefatigable, attacking the incumbent daily. Dirksen's supporters, in desperation, had tried everything to stop Yates, including spreading anti-Semitic slurs that had been subtly encouraged by the senator's top staff. Yates, an experienced campaigner frustrated by how little his congressional career had advanced after seven terms in the House of Representatives, had gone all in to topple the incumbent senator. Dirksen needed something to halt the congressman's momentum. And JFK was serving it up.

As soon as Dirksen received the call from the White House, he booked a commercial flight to Washington. He was sipping coffee in the passenger lounge at O'Hare with fellow senator Alexander Wiley of Wisconsin, the ranking Republican on the Senate Foreign Relations Committee, when an Air Force officer stopped them from boarding and took them, along with Illinois representative Leslie C. Arends, the House Republican "whip," to the military side of the airport to await the special transport. Dirksen could imagine how the press would report his need to suspend campaigning in order to give the young president the full benefit of his wisdom and experience. He could hear himself reporting back to the people of Illinois upon his return.

Dirksen approached the mobile staircase leading up to the fuselage door. An Air Force officer saluted as he entered. The senator smiled. For the first time since the long reelection campaign had begun, Dirksen knew he would win.

Yates, calling in to his campaign headquarters in downtown Chicago, knew it too. Mary Bain, his campaign manager in all but title, was livid. Even from the public telephone booth he could hear she was almost in tears: "The President's screwed you, Sid. He sent the whole goddamn United States Air Force to pick up that son of a bitch Dirksen from O'Hare and bring him to Washington. It's all over the radio." Yates told her they'd talk after his next campaign stop and hung up the telephone. What was to be his culminating achievement was finished. His life and career would never be the same.

PART I

THE CRUSADER
1949–62

1

THE ROAD TO CAPITOL HILL

The House of Representatives is the only branch of the federal government that has been elected directly by the people since its inception in 1788. Over its long history, "the People's House" has had many statesmen and able politicians, as well as its share of rogues and scoundrels. Some have displayed amazing courage; others have shown crude and narrow self-interest. Regardless, it always has come to represent the dreams, desires, and aspirations of people in the United States. As groups—religious, ethnic, racial, sexual—came to gather political strength, their members sought representation in the House. The first Jewish member was elected in 1840, the first African American in 1870, the first woman in 1916, the first Asian American in 1956, the first openly gay member in 1972, and the first Muslim member in 2006. The House of Representatives truly represents the great diversity of the United States.

In part because of its size and diversity, the House, as an institution, has developed mores, customs, and procedures so that it can get the people's work done in an orderly, if not always timely, fashion.

No man or woman elected to the House is without ambition. Some members see their aspirations fulfilled, some ambitions are rerouted, while others are dashed. For some of them, the House is only a way station, a stepping-stone to perceived greater power and influence. Although nineteen presidents served in the House of Representatives, only one, James Garfield in 1880, ran for president while a sitting congressman. Contrast that to the three senators, seven governors, and thirteen vice presidents who became president directly from their prior position. For those congressmen seeking higher station, the House was not the place to make their name.

But for those who decided to become "men (and women) of the House," the journey could be very rewarding. It was necessary to form friendships, learn the idiosyncrasies of their fellow members and, of course, the rules of the House in order to become an effective advocate for one's district and eventually to advance within the institution.

Unlike the Senate, where a lone senator until just recently could block nominations and delay legislation for substantial periods of time, if not indefinitely, the House of Representatives is dominated by the majority. Through its leadership, the majority party can impose its agenda on the body. The seniority system of Congress, which took root in the House after the Civil War, and continues despite various efforts to reform it, provided the means for members able and willing to accumulate tenure eventually to rise to positions of power and influence. Moreover, the senior members of the minority on each committee, known as the "ranking members," also achieved a measure of power.

While the House, as a branch of our government, has been extensively studied, there have been few biographies of individual congressmen other than Speakers of the House. But as has frequently been observed, the real work of the House is done by individual members outside the limelight, in the hallways, the committee hearings, the mark-ups, and meetings with constituents and special interests. To accomplish anything, representatives must delicately balance personal relationships with colleagues, constituents, and financial supporters. Often getting there is easier than staying there and being effective.

This book is about one such member, Sidney R. Yates, a Democrat from Illinois. During forty-eight years of service between 1949 to 1999, Yates served under ten presidents of the United States and eight Speakers of the House of Representatives. He debated and helped shape many of the major issues that formed U.S. dominance in the postwar world. In particular, through his leadership as a senior member of the Appropriations Committee and chairman of the subcommittee with funding jurisdiction over large parts of the Departments of the Interior, Energy, and Agriculture and all the cultural agencies, Yates became the preeminent legislator on such issues as the environment, the fight against anti-Semitism, and the humanities and the arts. At the height of his influence as one of the congressional "cardinals," House Speaker Thomas P. "Tip" O'Neill would tell members to "clear it with Sid" when certain sensitive policy questions arose.[1]

According to census and naturalization records, Louis and Ida Yatzofsky emigrated to the United States via Quebec from present-day Lithuania in 1899.[2] Initially living in tenements on Chicago's South Side with other Eastern European Jewish immigrants, they soon settled in the Lakeview neighborhood on the city's North Side, where an expanding upwardly mobile Jewish community was establishing roots. Louis, a blacksmith, found a job as a truck driver by the time Sidney

Richard, the sixth and youngest of Louis and Ida's children, was born on August 27, 1909.[3] Sometime between the filing of Louis's petition for naturalization in 1914 and his admission to citizenship in 1915, the family had changed their name to Yates.[4]

Like most children of Jewish immigrants in Chicago, Yates attended his neighborhood public school during the day and his synagogue's Hebrew school in the evening. Tall at six feet, the teenaged Yates was welcomed onto the Lake View High School basketball team. Pictures taken of him at the time show a handsome, smiling, and athletic presence. After graduating in 1927, Yates attended the University of Chicago, placing in the honors program each year. Easily qualifying for the University of Chicago basketball team, at the time a Big Ten member, Yates received an honorable mention for All-American guard. He also joined the school's chapter of Pi Lambda Phi, founded in 1895 and one of the few fraternities that welcomed Jews to its ranks. He graduated from Chicago in 1931 with a bachelor's degree in philosophy.[5]

Yates continued his studies at the University of Chicago School of Law, receiving his degree in 1933, only two years after arriving. At the same time, he pursued his passion for basketball. Yates spent what spare time he had playing for the Lifschulz Fast Freights, a semipro basketball team in the Missouri Valley AAU League that was a frequent championship contender in national AAU tournaments. Yates was paid $5 per game. Formerly known as the Rosenberg-Arveys, the team was sponsored by Chicago alderman Jacob "Jake" Arvey and 24th Ward Democratic ward committeeman Moe Rosenberg, two of Illinois's most influential Jewish politicians.[6] Rosenberg became very wealthy as a business partner of future Chicago mayor Anton Cermak.

Arvey was a product of the Jewish Training School and had received his law degree from John Marshall Law School in 1916 at the age of twenty-one. After a stint in the office of the Cook County state's attorney, Arvey went into private law practice with A. Paul Holleb, a like-minded ambitious Jewish lawyer. In only a few years, Arvey had established himself as one of Chicago's most effective aldermen through attention to the needs of the residents of his ward, the twenty-fourth, on Chicago's West Side. An observer once said, "Not a sparrow falls inside the borders of the Twenty-fourth Ward without Arvey's knowing of it. And, then, before it hits the ground, there's already a personal history at headquarters, complete to the moment of its tumble." Arvey's hard work translated into large majorities on election day. His key moment came in 1931 when Arvey backed the successful election of Cermak for mayor of Chicago. Arvey consolidated his power, becoming Democratic ward committeeman and, in an alliance with Mayor Cermak in 1932, providing critical assistance to elect Henry Horner, a Jew, governor of Illinois. He became chairman of the City Council's Finance Committee, making him one of the city's most important politicians. His ability to produce became legendary when, in 1936, FDR won the 24th Ward with a margin of 26,112 to 974. The president declared Arvey's domain "the No. 1 ward in the entire Democratic party." Arvey described the secret to success in politics: "Let me put it in a crude way—put people under obligation to you. Make them your friends. You don't want to hurt a friend. And that's politics—put a man under obligation."

While Arvey's star was on the rise, Moe Rosenberg was in free fall. He spent twenty months in the federal prison at Leavenworth, Kansas, in 1915 for stealing freight cars. He was again indicted in 1933 for failure to pay $65,000 in taxes from alleged racketeering income but died before he could be brought to trial. Arvey, never one to let sentiment sway a political judgment, replaced Rosenberg as Democratic committeeman and quickly changed the basketball team's name to honor David Lifschulz, a wealthy sponsor and owner of the Lifschulz Fast Freight Company. As part of the deal, Arvey installed Lifschultz's son, Sam, as coach.[7]

Arvey and his law partner Holleb were part of a strong nucleus of Jewish businessmen who built their careers during this period. Several family fortunes, including the Crowns, the Pritzkers, and the Rosenwalds, known for their charitable works as well as good business practices, were created at this time. Most Jews in the 1920s were Republicans in the Lincoln tradition but became converts to the Democratic Party as FDR's New Deal took hold. Arvey and Holleb gladly went with the flow and thrived accordingly.

Yates was admitted to the Illinois bar in 1933 and joined with Holleb's son, Marshall, another young ambitious Jewish lawyer, to create the law firm of Yates and Holleb. Two years later, Yates married Adeline Holleb, Marshall's sister. Yates's marriage to "Addie" would last for sixty-five years.

The practice of law, particularly with A. Paul's help, provided good income but Yates found the work unappealing. Besides, A. Paul would see to it that he and Addie were comfortable even if Yates were not making much money. Not too long after their marriage, A. Paul purchased the young couple a co-op on North Lake Shore Drive.

Yates had been impressed by the speeches of FDR in the 1932 presidential campaign, and he observed with pride and approval the appointment by the president of more Jewish public officials and advisers than any administration in U.S. history. His idealism stirred by the New Deal, he gravitated to government service. Yates told Arvey and A. Paul of his ambitions, and, in 1935, they secured for Yates a political appointment from Illinois attorney general Otto Kerner Sr. as an assistant attorney general. Kerner, a Democrat, and one of the political stars of the influential Bohemian community of Chicago, had founded the Bohemian Lawyers Association of Chicago and had been a close ally of Mayor Cermak, a fellow Bohemian. Cermak had gotten Kerner elected attorney general in 1932, and, in 1934, a year after Cermak's assassination by a bullet meant for FDR, Kerner's son, Otto Jr., would marry Cermak's daughter Helena.[8]

Kerner was glad to do a favor for Democratic committeeman Arvey and wealthy A. Paul, and Yates was soon representing Illinois in transportation and other regulatory matters before the Illinois Commerce Commission. Intellectually challenging at first, the work proved unsatisfying, and Yates resented the anonymity of appointed public service. But politics, with its opportunities for personal recognition as well as good works, was his true vocation. In 1939, with the active support of his father-in-law, he ran for alderman of the North Side 46th Ward in the Chicago City Council. Yates ran as part of an insurgent group allied with Cook County state's attorney Thomas J. Courtney against Mayor Ed Kelly and the 46th Ward machine of Democratic committeeman Joseph Gill. Running in a field of three, including the incumbent, James Young, Yates came in dead last. Yates's slogan during that race was "Smash the Machine." Later, Yates reflected, "I tried to crack the machine and the machine cracked me." On that same election day, a young professor of economics from the University of Chicago, Paul H. Douglas, also running for the first time, won a seat in the City Council from the south side. Unlike Yates, Douglas had aligned against the Courtney crowd and was backed by Kelly.[9]

Discouraged by his poor showing, Yates resumed his work in the attorney general's office. The election of 1940 resulted in a landslide for the Republicans. Republican Dwight Green became governor and C. Wayland (Curly) Brooks took the U.S. Senate seat. Republicans also captured control of the Illinois General Assembly, as well as 18 of 26 seats in the Illinois delegation to the U.S. House. Most relevant to Yates, Republican George Francis Barrett defeated Democratic state senator Harold G. Ward for attorney general. Yates well understood the rules of the game and knew that he soon would be dismissed along with all his Democratic colleagues. He resigned before the end of the year, returning to his law practice with his brother-in-law Marshall.

The experience in the attorney general's office and his unsuccessful race for alderman, however, encouraged Yates to reflect about the role of government in local affairs. In 1941, he published a well-received article, "Design for Chicago Transit: London Style," in the prestigious *Journal of Land and Public Utility Economics*, advocating the unification of Chicago's transit companies into a publicly run utility. Foreshadowing a future date, he even went so far as to urge "upon the suburbs the creation of a metropolitan transit district as an eventual measure." Yates would become an unwavering advocate for public transportation for the remainder of his career.[10]

In 1940, Addie gave birth to their only child, Stephen Richard Yates. The responsibilities and exhilaration of fatherhood would, for a time, tamp down Yates's political plans. When the United States entered World War II, Yates, as a thirty-two-year-old head of household with a young baby, was not on the initial draft lists. But after Marshall was drafted in 1943, Yates enlisted in the U.S. Navy, rising to the rank of lieutenant and serving in Washington, DC, as a lawyer for the Bureau of Ships. No records exist to explain this decision, but it can be presumed that Yates's inherent patriotism, the breakup of his partnership with Marshall, and a candid self-acknowledgment that being a veteran would be essential to any future political career, all played a part.[11]

When the war concluded, Yates and Marshall once again picked up their practice. Yates also became more actively involved in the Chicago Jewish community, both sacred and secular. After Stephen's birth, Yates and Addie had joined Temple Sholom, a reform congregation whose large domed temple, a mixture of Byzantine and Art Deco influences, loomed across the street from their co-op apartment on Lake Shore Drive. In 1947, Yates became editor of the *Bulletin of the Decalogue Society of Lawyers*, a professional organization of Jewish attorneys.

Jake Arvey was also back from the war, and again consolidating his power. He had served as a colonel in the U.S. Army and a judge advocate of the Thirty-Third Infantry Division in the Pacific theater. He resumed his career and by 1946 had become chairman of the Cook County Democratic Party.

Arvey would face a daunting challenge, however. With a string of successes in the elections in 1940, 1944, and 1946, the Republican Party had gained dominance in Illinois. They controlled most of the statewide offices, including governor and both houses of the General Assembly. The elections of 1946 had been especially crushing for the Democratic Party. William G. Stratton defeated Emily Taft Douglas, Paul Douglas's wife, in her bid to win reelection to an at-large seat in the U.S. House. Stratton took 92 of 102 counties with a wide margin of 367,469 votes. The Republicans captured an advantage of 15 to 1 in downstate congressional seats, exceeding their margins only two years previous. The Democrats suffered defeat in Chicago as well. The Republicans took five congressional seats, including electing businessman Robert Twyman on the North Side of Chicago along the lakefront. In all, the tally was decidedly against the Democrats, with the Republicans holding an advantage of 19 seats in the House to only 7 for the opposition. One bright spot was the reelection of Adolph Sabath, the dean of the Jewish members of the House. Nationally, the Republican Party swept into power by taking control of both houses of Congress. This major defeat resulted in calls from many corners for Mayor Ed Kelly to step down and not run for reelection in 1947 for a third term.

Insisting on being called colonel, Arvey set about unifying the well-to-do Jews of Chicago's lakefront with the disadvantaged Jews of the West Side, using Israeli statehood as the common cause. Many have credited Arvey with using his influence as the boss of the Cook County machine to convince President Harry S. Truman to recognize the State of Israel.[12]

After consolidating his Jewish base, Arvey turned to a constituency that had felt neglected for years. A machine politician through and through, the Colonel had an uncanny ability to understand and to work with the liberal reform element of the Illinois Democratic Party. As Paul Douglas reflected, "Arvey was polished, lucid, and conciliatory in manner, but underneath the surface he had a will of steel. His sympathies were basically on the side of the poor, and his acquaintances with the educated Jewish community had given him an insight into liberal movements that the average politician lacked."[13]

Arvey encouraged many liberals to seek higher office. A wily chairman, he understood that the so-called good government advocates, "goo-goos" to the professional politicians, had political value to the machine. Placing them at the top of the party's ticket would benefit the machine candidates at the lower end of the ballot. Besides, it would get them out of Chicago and out of the local machine's patronage affairs.

Arvey's talents were put to the test in the mayoral election of 1947. Mayor Kelly had worn out his welcome and increasingly came under attack from the city's newspapers, especially after the disastrous elections of 1946. Good government advocates like Douglas opposed Kelly's continuation in office and threatened a tough race if he didn't step down. The city's ethnic groups had soured on Kelly and strongly opposed his open-housing proposals. They let their aldermen and committeemen know their unwavering opposition to Kelly and his ideas on housing. After a poll conducted by a friendly source indicated the difficult reelection effort, Arvey finally persuaded a reluctant Kelly not to seek reelection.

In Kelly's place, the machine, with Arvey's guidance, chose a successful businessman, Martin Kennelly, who possessed all the characteristics Arvey was seeking. Blessed with classic features and a mane of silver hair, he looked the part of a mayor chosen out of central casting. He had established credibility through his association with the American Red Cross. For Arvey and the Democratic ward committeemen, Kennelly had one other indispensable attribute—he knew little or nothing about government or politics. In fact, he did not like machine politics and opposed "spoil politics," as he put it. It didn't hurt that the Republicans chose a party hack, Russell W. Root, as its candidate. Kennelly won with a nearly 300,000-vote majority, and Arvey's strategy for preserving the machine by running a reform candidate seemed vindicated.

In 1948, Yates, now thirty-eight, interviewed before the Democratic committeemen of the 9th Congressional District for the party's nomination to oppose the incumbent congressman, Republican Robert Twyman, a naval veteran of World Wars I and II. Unfortunately, two of the most important committeemen, the notorious Charlie Webber and Paddy Bauler, considered the seat to be German. Arvey was asked to help but declined to intervene in a matter of ethnic privilege. As a result, Yates was passed over by the party for German-American John Haderlein, who had run unsuccessfully for Congress in 1946 in the 10th Congressional District.

The election prospects for Democrats in 1948 did not look favorable and, when Chicago's postmastership became available, Haderlein eagerly accepted the appointment and withdrew from the campaign. Looking for an attractive war veteran, and the Germans having been taken care of, the Democratic committeemen, now with the encouragement of party chairman Arvey, chose the young former navy lieutenant as their new candidate, but not without a few final complications. A. Paul Holleb wanted his son, Marshall, for the spot first, but Marshall, fortunately, declined.

Committeeman Joe Gill, whose 46th Ward included much of the 9th District, didn't want Yates as the candidate. Even though Yates had by now joined his Democratic organization, Gill remembered Yates's opposition in 1939. Gill approached Alex Resa, a former congressman who had lost reelection in 1946, and Irwin Walker, who had unsuccessfully run in 1942, but both turned him down. "Finally," Gill said later, "I offered it to Yates. He was a live wire and by now a member of the organization."[14]

Despite the mayoral victory in 1947, Yates was thought to have little, if any, chance of beating the popular Twyman in the Republican-leaning 9th District in what promised to be a national Republican sweep in 1948. Hoping to save the party, Arvey joined the movement to draft the popular retired General Dwight D. Eisenhower, currently president of Columbia University, for the Democratic presidential nomination. Arvey was "certain that Truman could not win."

The Eisenhower boomlet was an odd concoction of ideological liberals, like Americans for Democratic Action (ADA), and pragmatic big city bosses such as Arvey, Mayor William O'Dwyer of New York, and Mayor Frank Hague of Jersey City. There was good reason for Democrats to be pessimistic about Truman's prospects. A Roper poll taken in late spring revealed that Eisenhower would defeat both Truman and the likely Republican nominee, Governor Thomas Dewey of New York, by sizable margins—and he hadn't even done anything to launch a campaign. But their hopes were dashed in July, just before the Democratic convention, when Eisenhower declared that he would not accept the nomination of any party. Arvey, the ADA liberals, and other big city bosses reluctantly turned back to President Truman. Compounding Truman's mounting problems, the Democratic Party split, as Governor Strom Thurmond of South Carolina led the so-called Dixiecrat segregationists out of the Democratic convention over the issue of civil rights and Henry Wallace, FDR's former vice president, formed the Progressive Party, contending that the president wasn't sufficiently liberal.

In Illinois, the Democratic Party, at Arvey's urging, endorsed two liberal reformers to top the state ticket, Adlai E. Stevenson II for governor and Paul H. Douglas for senator. Both Douglas and Stevenson desired the Senate seat but Arvey felt Douglas would have the better chance at winning. He had given up his aldermanic seat and, at age fifty, enlisted in the Marines, where he was severely wounded in battle. Arvey knew that he needed a veteran to run against the incumbent senator, Wayland Brooks: "In 1946, Douglas came to a mass meeting in uniform. He did not make a speech but he waved a greeting to the crowd. I saw his withered hand. Brooks never made a speech without saying, 'I got shrapnel in my back at Chateau-Thierry [World War I] and I'd learned what it means to serve our country.' I knew the shattered hand would dispose of that." Stevenson, on the other hand, had not served in the military during the war but, then, neither had Governor Green. The party leaders had additional reasons. Stevenson, like Kennelly, knew little about government internal operations and would be compliant. Douglas, they knew from their experience with him as an alderman, was stubbornly independent-minded. A seat in the Senate would get him out of Illinois with a position that had little if any real patronage, the coin of the local political realm. Yates, of course, filled the bill and, by accident, became part of the "blue ribbon" ticket.

Governor Green decided to run for an unprecedented third term, even though he had stridently criticized FDR for doing the very same thing in 1940. Senator Brooks also decided to seek reelection. Both Green and Brooks vigorously campaigned against the New Deal and as isolationists opposed to Truman's Marshall Plan and other foreign policy initiatives. Adding fuel to the political fire, there was widespread speculation that Green was being seriously considered for the vice-presidential nomination.

Yates campaigned with gusto. He developed a special appeal to his audiences by taking up his guitar and entertaining his audiences with various popular songs of the day. He had long loved Broadway musicals. To assuage those who still thought a German-American should have the seat, he became especially adept at singing German folk songs. As a youngster, Yates had become acquainted with the theater through his older brother, Charles, a vaudeville talent agent whose clients would include Bob Hope and America's first openly transsexual entertainer, Christine Jorgensen. Yates worked as an office boy for the Keith-Albec-Orpheum vaudeville circuit during his teen years. Later, while at the University of Chicago, Yates's roommate brought Gilbert and Sullivan to his attention. He promptly memorized the scores and never forgot them or, for that matter, many of the others he'd learned during his vaudeville experience. Yates put these talents to good use during the campaign of 1948. He campaigned as a defender of FDR and Truman on domestic and international policies.

While the experts, including the famous (or infamous) Gallup Poll and the *Chicago Tribune* ("Dewey Defeats Truman") predicted an overwhelming Republican victory, Truman retained the White House in a dramatic upset over Thomas Dewey. Truman campaigned relentlessly, hammering the "do-nothing Republican congress," including two whistle-stop visits to Illinois. Truman won Illinois's crucial 28 electoral votes by only 30,000 votes, 84,764 fewer than FDR four years earlier. Fortunately for the president, the Dixiecrat and Progressive Parties were kept off the ballot in Illinois through successful legal challenges that went all the way up to the state supreme court. Nationally, the president captured nearly 50 percent of the vote, with Dewey getting 45 percent and third-party candidates Thurmond and Wallace each approximately 2 percent. But the Democratic ticket in Illinois swept into office with the elections of Stevenson and Douglas, by 572,000 (57%) and 401,000 (55%) votes, respectively. Yates defeated Twyman by a little more than 15,000 votes (54.5%). Yates's victory that year was the largest percentage of any candidate for the House in the 9th Congressional District in the decade. Years later, when young people would ask him for the secret to winning a seat in Congress, Yates would recall the victory of '48 and say, "Find a ticket with Truman, Douglas and Stevenson at the top and go along for the ride!" The careers of Yates, Douglas and Stevenson would continue to intersect in important ways.

The immediate question, however, was whether Yates could hold the seat and succeed as a legislator. "There is no test of a man's ability in any department of life more severe than service in the House of Representatives," James G. Blaine, Speaker of the House and nominee for the presidency once explained. "There is . . . no place where so little consideration is shown for the feelings or the failure of beginners. What a man gains in the House he gains by sheer force of his character; and if he loses and falls back he must expect no mercy, and will receive no sympathy. It is a field in which survival of the strongest is the recognized rule, and where no pretense can deceive, no glamour can mislead. The real man is discovered, his worth is impartially weighed, his rank is irreversibly decreed."[15]

Few would have believed, or even imagined, in 1948 that Sidney Yates would hold this congressional seat for almost fifty years.

2

THE CLASS OF '49

New Year's Day 1949 fell on a Saturday, and, in Washington, DC, except for the thunderstorms that threatened all day, there was little incentive for revelers to shorten the festivities that had started the previous evening, as there was still all of Sunday to rest up. The members of the new Congress, the 81st in the history of the United States, were to be sworn in on Monday, January 3. Its predecessor, nicknamed the "do-nothing Congress" by an angry and frustrated President Truman, would go out of business at noon. Both branches of Congress had switched from Republican to Democratic majorities, and expectations were high for change, particularly in the House of Representatives, which Truman hoped, at last, would enact his progressive agenda.

In what would today be called a "wave election," the Democrats picked up 75 seats in the House, sweeping the Republicans out of power and changing the balance from 246 Republicans, 188 Democrats, and 1 American Labor member in the 80th Congress to 263 Democrats, 171 Republicans, and 1 American Labor representative in the 81st. This was the largest reversal of fortunes for either party since FDR's 1932 landslide, when House Democrats picked up 97 seats previously held by Republicans. While Republicans would get their own wave elections in later years, particularly those in the 1994 and 2010 elections, they would not beat the 1948 numbers.

In addition, of those Democrats elected to the 81st Congress, 104 were freshmen, almost 40 percent of the new majority. They were joined by 14 freshman Republicans who had survived the tide. The 114 men and 4 women of the freshman class of '49, which counted 22 former members as freshmen, would produce many who would become household names, for better or ill, in later years.

- Gerald R. Ford Jr. of Grand Rapids, Michigan, the most prominent of them, would go on to become Republican House leader, vice president, and president.
- Eugene J. McCarthy of St. Paul, Minnesota, would run for the Democratic Party's nomination for president in 1968 against Lyndon Johnson as head of an antiwar movement and would be a major factor in LBJ's decision not to seek reelection.
- Lloyd Bentsen of McAllen, Texas, who jumped freshman seniority by getting elected in a special election on December 4, 1948, to fill a vacancy in the 80th Congress, would be the Democratic vice presidential nominee in 1988, where he would memorably tell Hoosier senator Dan Quayle, his Republican opponent at the vice-presidential debate, when Quayle equated his congressional experience to John F. Kennedy's when JFK ran for president, "Senator, I served with Jack Kennedy. I knew Jack Kennedy. Jack Kennedy was a friend of mine. Senator, you're no Jack Kennedy."
- Abraham Ribicoff of Hartford, Connecticut, would become governor, senator, and secretary of the U.S. Department of Health, Education and Welfare but would gain his greatest national attention from his speech at the 1968 Democratic convention in Chicago, where he accused Mayor Richard J. Daley of using "Gestapo tactics" to suppress the antiwar protests in Grant Park, as a red-faced Daley shouted back "You f--ker" (as most of the television audience could lip read) or "You faker," as Daley later asserted.
- Peter W. Rodino Jr. of Newark, New Jersey, would, as chairman of the House Judiciary Committee, lead the Watergate impeachment proceedings that led to the passage of three articles of impeachment and the resignation of President Richard Nixon.
- Wayne L. Hays of Flushing, Ohio, described by Representative Phil Burton as "the meanest man in Congress," would become chairman of the House Administration Committee, rewarding friends and punishing enemies through his control of office space and committee budgets, until a thirty-three-year-old staff member confessed to the *Washington Post* that she was paid $14,000 a year by the committee to serve as Hays's mistress, forcing Hays's early retirement in 1976.

Both official and unofficial Washington awaited the change in power and new personalities. Mary Mundt, wife of former House member Karl Mundt, who was now a freshman senator from South Dakota, advised the wives of freshman representatives, through a column in the *Sunday Star*, that they would soon be receiving letters from "the leading hotels and department stores of Washington, telling her how honored they would feel to secure her patronage." The wife of

Leon Chatelain Jr., president of the Washington Board of Trade, invited the fresh-man wives to tea that Tuesday, while the Board of Trade invited their husbands to dinner later that evening at the Shoreham Hotel, where the Honorable Bolitha J. Laws, chief judge of the District Court of the District of Columbia, was scheduled to welcome the freshmen and outline their responsibilities as the "city council" for the District."[1]

But before the swearing in could occur, there were partisan organizational mat-ters to be taken care of, leadership posts to be decided, and for the new majority, rule changes to be debated and strategies to be discussed, all of which would be ratified when the new House met for the first time. The dispirited Republicans held a short caucus on New Year's Eve, voting to make Joseph W. Martin Jr., the soon-to-be former Speaker, minority leader. Martin, putting the best face on a disaster, pledged to assemble a "young and vigorous" new leadership team.[2] The Democrats, however, scheduled their caucus for Saturday evening, giving their members a chance to celebrate and recover before the serious business of gov-erning began.

Yates was eager to get started. Unlike many of the other eight freshmen in the Illinois delegation, six Democrats and two Republicans, who were still finalizing living arrangements in the capital, Yates had rented a house on Van Ness Street in northwest Washington soon after the election.[3] The sky was overcast and dark in the late January afternoon when he reached the Capitol for his first meeting of the Democratic caucus, meeting in the House chambers. But he had one stop to make first. Walking past the House wing, he crossed over Independence Avenue and entered the lobby of the New House Office Building. The building wasn't really "new," having opened fifteen years earlier, except in comparison to the adjacent Old House Office Building, the Beaux-Arts monstrosity whose cornerstone had been laid by President Theodore Roosevelt in 1906. It would not be until 1962 that the buildings, along with a third, known as the "Additional," were given their permanent designations, named after House Speakers Joseph Cannon, Nicholas Longworth, and Sam Rayburn, respectively.

Showing his identification to the attendant Capitol police officer, who had not yet memorized the faces of the new members, Yates walked quickly down the marble floor to Room 1136, the spacious suite of Adolph Joachim Sabath of Illinois, the dean of the House, a title given to the longest continuously serving member, and the once and future chairman of the Rules Committee. Sabath had summoned the twelve Democrats of the Illinois delegation to a precaucus.

Yates liked and admired the stocky, cigar-chomping Sabath, a fellow Chicagoan and the senior Jewish member of Congress. First elected in 1906, he represented the large Jewish immigrant community in the city's Lawndale and Pilsen neigh-borhoods on the West and Southwest Sides. Sabath had emigrated to Chicago from Zabori, Bohemia, in 1881, and sixty-eight years later still had a thick accent. He became a U.S. citizen in 1887 and ascended a familiar immigrant ladder, going to business college and law school and establishing successful real-estate and law practices. Moving smoothly into Democratic politics, he became a ward committeeman, justice of the peace, police magistrate, and finally congressman for the 5th Congressional District and chairman of the managing committee of the Cook County Democratic Central Committee. When Yates's mentor, Jake Arvey, joined the Chicago City Council in 1925, Sabath was already a political powerhouse and the preeminent Jewish political leader in the state. Friends and colleagues called him Judge, from his days on the bench.

By 1948, many of Sabath's West Side Jewish constituents had moved to Chicago's North Side, mirroring Louis and Ida Yates's own migration from the South Side, and were now living in the 9th Congressional District. Sabath became close to the rising West Side politicians Cermak and Arvey. Observers of the West Side politicians of the era commented that they were a breed apart from the rest of the city. "It is doubtful whether another neighborhood ever has produced as many legendary characters and persons of achievement as the old West Side"[4]

Friends of both Arvey and Yates's father-in-law, A. Paul Holleb, Sabath welcomed Yates upon his election and established an easy, fatherly affinity with his new colleague. It is tempting to conjecture that the childless Sabath saw in Yates the opportunity to create the same type of paternal relationship that he had seen play out in the House between his friend, Speaker Sam Rayburn, and Congressman Lyndon B. Johnson, a relationship about to move to a new stage now that Johnson had been elected to the Senate. As with the two Texans, the two Chicagoans had much in common, sharing religion, constituents, friends, and political allies. Sabath looked forward to tutoring Yates in the workings of the House.

A round of handshaking took place as Yates entered the chairman's inner office. He took a seat near the back. When Sabath, seated at his desk, saw that everyone had arrived, he quickly came to the point. He wanted to be sure that the Illinois delegation would vote as a bloc in caucus on two matters important to Speaker Rayburn and President Truman: the election of members to the Ways and Means Committee, and the liberalization of the Rules Committee.

Ways and Means was important for two reasons. Not only was it the committee with initial jurisdiction over all revenue bills, but its Democratic members acted as the Committee on Committees, with the power to appoint the Democratic members of all the other House panels, subject to final approval by the caucus. Six Democratic vacancies had opened up as a result of the changed Democratic-Republican ratio in the House. Sabath pointed to Tom O'Brien, sitting directly opposite, and said that a deal had been struck to return O'Brien to the Ways and Means Committee; O'Brien had been on that committee before the Republican takeover. O'Brien nodded.

Yates looked at the seventy-year-old O'Brien with interest. O'Brien, a West Sider, was first elected in 1932 and was a close friend and ally of Rayburn. O'Brien took credit for getting Rayburn chosen Democratic majority leader in 1937 by unifying a divided Illinois delegation in Rayburn's favor, all but assuring Rayburn's subsequent elevation to speaker. But after only three terms, O'Brien suddenly left the House, choosing not to run in the 1938 election. Patrick A. "Paddy" Nash, boss of the Cook County Democratic machine, wanted O'Brien to run for Cook County sheriff instead. The move surprised O'Brien's Washington colleagues but raised few eyebrows back home. O'Brien was known to be a friend of Murray "the Camel" Humphreys, an enforcer for Al Capone, now sitting in Alcatraz. Known as the Chicago Outfit's fixer, and for a time, Capone's successor as head of the syndicate, the Camel specialized in the labor and government relations side of the Outfit's work. In and out of trouble with the law, Humphreys was assessed $74,617.77 by the IRS in income taxes, interest, and penalties for failure to declare, among other illegal income, $50,000 received as ransom income from the 1931 kidnapping of Robert C. Fitchie, president of Local 753, AFL Milk Wagon Drivers' union.[5] Humphreys was never charged with the actual kidnapping, however, as the statute of limitations had run out.

Easily elected sheriff, O'Brien pledged to be a crime buster, sending his deputies on frequent raids of illegal slot machines, bookmaking, and other gambling run by Humphreys and his associates. Somehow, however, his underlings could never find any evidence. The *Chicago Tribune* soon labeled him, in editorials and news stories, "Blind Tom" O'Brien, and the moniker stuck. It is almost certain that O'Brien received a regular percentage of the take from the Camel's establishments. When Yates made his unsuccessful run for alderman in 1939, during O'Brien's tenure as sheriff, he had been backed by the Cook County state's attorney, Thomas J. Courtney, who had himself run as a reformer and was an enemy of both the sheriff and Boss Nash. In the 1939 municipal elections, Courtney had challenged Mayor Edward J. Kelly, Nash's political partner, and lost by over 280,000 votes.[6]

The heat was on O'Brien after one term as sheriff, and he returned to the House in 1942, going on the Appropriations Committee until March 26, 1946, when he transferred to Ways and Means, gaining influence and remaining a reliable vote for the Speaker. The Republican takeover of the House in the 1946 election had knocked O'Brien off Ways and Means, but now, with the Democrats back in control O'Brien would be back on the committee and would be one of the members deciding who would take his place on Appropriations. Yates wondered whether O'Brien was aware of his Courtney connections, and whether any lingering hostilities would rub off on him.

Yates refocused his attention as Sabath continued his remarks. For Truman to succeed, the Rules Committee had to be reformed. Yates had been elected as a staunch Truman supporter. He listened closely.

In the House, the Rules Committee is the ultimate gatekeeper of legislation. Bills can't be brought to the floor for a vote without getting a "rule" from the Rules Committee, which establishes the length of time permitted for debate, the types of points of order that would be allowed or denied, restrictions on amendments, and even whether any amendments could be offered at all. Powerful chairs of other committees were required to appear before Rules and plead for permission to bring their bills, which may have undergone months of hearings and negotiations, up for consideration by the full House. Under the control of the Republicans in the 80th Congress, the Rules Committee had frequently refused to allow votes on legislation backed by Truman. Even bills such as the Wagner-Ellender-Taft Housing bill, addressing the post–World War II housing shortage, and including provisions for public housing and slum clearance, which had passed the Republican-controlled Senate with bipartisan support, were killed because the Rules Committee wouldn't allow them to come to the floor.

The Democrats would be in control of the Rules Committee now, and Sabath would be chairman, but the party still had a problem. Truman had run on a strong civil-rights platform, and Rayburn and Sabath knew that the southern members of the Rules Committee, many of whom had backed the segregationist Strom Thurmond's Dixiecrat party in the 1948 elections, would ally with Republicans to prevent any chance of a civil rights bill ever being debated, let alone pass, the House. It was not that Republicans, who still proudly called themselves the Party of Lincoln, were opposed to civil rights. It was more that they were opposed to margarine.

The freshmen listening reacted with surprise. Yes, margarine. To dairy farmers dependent on income from the manufacture and sale of butter, this cheap butter substitute was a threat that had to be eliminated. Congressmen from dairy states like Wisconsin, Minnesota, and Iowa, most of them Republicans, did their best to keep margarine off the grocery shelves and out of the refrigerated aisles. Through their efforts, federal law required special licensing for margarine's production and sale and imposed oppressive taxes, which were multiplied if the makers put any butterlike coloring in the margarine to make it more appealing. Instead, margarine makers were forced to include a packet of yellow dye with the spread. Standing at the kitchen sink, the unhappy homemaker had to dump the shiny white vegetable fat into a bowl to soften it. Then, after adding the dye, it took energetic stirring with a long spoon to try to get a semblance of an even color throughout the congealed blend. After being shaped into a relatively smooth mound on a butter dish, it could be presented at the dinner table next to the bread. When efforts were made in Congress to eliminate the taxes on margarine or to allow a precolored product, the Republican leadership inserted amendments on those bills to ban lynching and the poll tax, thus ensuring that the southern Democrats would kill the entire measure.[7] Now the southerners could reciprocate, and, in exchange for Republican votes against consideration of civil rights bills, they would make sure no margarine bills reached the floor, despite the fact that much of the cottonseed oil used to make margarine came from southern farmers.

Sabath knew that there was a lot of sentiment among the more liberal Democrats to punish Dixiecrat congressmen, particularly Edward Eugene Cox of Georgia and William Colmer of Mississippi, who had supported Thurmond over Truman, and keep them off the Rules Committee.[8] Colmer was a rabid segregationist who would later call the Civil Rights Act of 1957 " the tragedy of the beginning of the downfall of the Republic."[9] "Goober" Cox, who was second in seniority to Sabath on Rules, had opposed the New Deal and was expected to oppose Harry Truman's Fair Deal as well. But the Democratic leadership wanted to offer an olive branch and bring them back into the party. Sabath confessed that Rayburn had doubts, but both Cox and Colmer were friends of Rayburn. Rayburn thought that the risk of continuing obstructionism within the party was outweighed by the risk of a permanent schism between Democrats and Dixiecrats. In addition, Cox and Colmer were poker pals of John W. McCormack of Massachusetts, the incoming majority leader, and Cox had managed McCormack's first election to that leadership post in 1940. McCormack said that "Gene Cox jumped up to lead the fight for me . . . As long as I live I will never forget it."[10] McCormack was confident he could keep Cox and the other southerners in line.[11] O'Brien agreed that, as a member of Ways and Means, he would vote with the leadership to seat Cox and Colmer on the Rules Committee.

As a safeguard, just in case the Dixiecrat-Republican alliance held, Rayburn was also proposing a change to the House rules that would permit committee chairmen to bypass the Rules Committee. Under the new procedure, if a bill had been approved by a legislative committee and had not been granted a rule within three weeks of its presentation to the Rules Committee, the chairman of that legislative committee had the right to ask the full House for an up or down vote to place the bill on the House calendar for debate as "a matter of the highest privilege," taking precedence over other deliberations. Sabath admitted that he was not happy with this diminution of his own powers, but he was fed up with the southerners and their continual obstruction.

So, said Sabath, are we agreed? None of the freshmen spoke. But one of the delegation veterans, William Levi Dawson, one of only two blacks in Congress, leaned forward and, in a soft but intense voice, said, no, there couldn't be peace with those bigots.[12] Dawson, known as "Big Bill" or "the Man" on the South Side of Chicago, was about to make history in the 81st Congress as the first African American ever to become chairman of a standing congressional committee, and he wasn't afraid to speak his mind. Dawson's Committee on Expenditures in

Executive Departments, later named the Committee on Government Operations and, later still, the Committee on Oversight and Government Reform, was the investigative arm of Congress, reviewing how appropriations were spent, and in charge of reorganizations in the Executive branch and intergovernmental relationships.

Born in Albany, Georgia, Dawson had worked as a porter and waiter to get through Fisk University in Tennessee and the Kent College of Law and Northwestern University law school in Chicago. A World War I veteran, he entered Chicago politics as a Republican and twice unsuccessfully ran for Congress under the GOP banner, in between winning election as an alderman in the Chicago City Council. Like many other African Americans, however, Dawson deserted the party of Lincoln, the traditional political home of black voters, pulled to the Democrats by the gravitational force of FDR and the New Deal. Dawson's conversion was encouraged by the political patronage offered by Mayor Kelly, who made Dawson the Democratic Committeeman of the 2nd Ward. Now able to dispense—or withhold—favors and jobs, Dawson built an army of precinct workers, extending his influence well beyond the 2nd Ward and controlling most of the African American vote in the city. It was "the best machine—white or Negro—in this country," he told a reporter.[13] From this solid base, Dawson made a third run for Congress, winning with 53 percent of the vote. At the time he took his seat in 1943, Dawson was the only African American then serving in the House, and only the third elected in the twentieth century.

Dawson had grown up with the likes of Cox and Colmer. He knew they would never change. The other returning members of the delegation, Martin Gorski and Tom Gordon from Chicago and Mel Price from East St. Louis, spoke up. Yates listened to the arguments with fascination. Finally, Dawson agreed to Sabath's request and said he would raise no objection in caucus. It is likely that he recognized that as a committee chairman he was obligated to support the leadership. In addition, he knew that he owed that chairmanship in large part to John McCormack, and that letting a racist like Colmer back on Rules was part of the deal.[14] The delegation meeting ended and the members put their coats on to walk over to the House chamber.

But Yates still had one more place to visit. Leaving Sabath's office, he bypassed the mostly unmanned elevators, striding up six flights of marbled steps to Room 1620, where, in the dim light of a far-off corridor, he saw the polished wooden door with the simple sign "Mr. Yates, Illinois." The assigned two-room suite was tiny and the location not particularly desirable, but he was thrilled. It would be his on Monday, open for business. He ran down the steps and back across to the House chambers.

Francis E. Walter, congressman from Easton, Pennsylvania, and chairman of the caucus, called the meeting to order. The first votes were perfunctory. The caucus unanimously nominated Sam Rayburn and John McCormack to return to their respective positions as Speaker and majority leader. Next, as Sabath had foretold, O'Brien and Cecil R. King of Inglewood, California, were unanimously restored to the Ways and Means Committee. A vote was then held as seven other Democrats vied for the remaining four spots.

Sabath then called for the vote on the reformation of the Rules Committee. The Democratic caucus voted 176–48 in favor of the proposal; 38 Democrats did not vote. Chairman Walter told the Democrats that this vote bound them all to support the change when it came up for ratification by the full House on January 3. But Howard Smith of Virginia, a member of the Rules Committee, speaking for many of the southerners, stated that he did not feel bound by the caucus's decision and would vote with the Republicans.[15]

The caucus had also planned to discuss the abolition of the Committee on Un-American Activities, which Truman despised and, at one point, declared dead.[16] HUAC, as the Committee was known, had spent the last two years investigating the loyalty of Hollywood actors, directors, and writers, as well as suspected communists in the Roosevelt and Truman State Department. The committee's hearings on accusations against Alger Hiss, a former senior government official, by *Time* editor, and admitted communist, Whittaker Chambers, had run right through the presidential election. But after more than four hours of caucusing, the Democrats had no stomach for another fight. The caucus adjourned, and Yates went home.

Precisely at noon on Monday, January 3, in accordance with Section 2 of the Twentieth Amendment to the Constitution of the United States, the 81st Congress convened. The glare of television and newsreel lights bounced off the steel girders that had been installed a few years earlier to reinforce the unstable roof. Rayburn would, within six months, move the entire House into the Ways and Means Committee Room for almost a year so that the roof could be fixed and the chambers modernized. The galleries were packed with friends and family of the members, including Addie Yates and eight-year-old Stephen. Jake Arvey was also in the Capitol, but on the other side, there to celebrate Paul Douglas's swearing in as senator. Arvey said, however, that he expected to have dinner with Douglas and the new 9th District congressman while he was in town.

The chaplain of the 80th Congress, Rev. James Shera Montgomery, DD, led the members-elect in the Lord's Prayer. It is not known whether Yates joined this New Testament recitation. The roll of the House was then called by state and district, and to this, when Yates's name was called, he did answer with a loud "Present."[17]

Rayburn was elected Speaker on a straight party-line vote of 255 to 160. Next, Sabath, as dean of the House, along with McCormack, Joe Martin, Robert Doughton, and Leo Allen, the congressional leadership, escorted Rayburn to the chair. Sabath administered the oath to Rayburn, who in turn administered the oath of office to the remaining members en masse. Each member would later individually sign a written oath, which would be retained by the clerk of the House. The House quickly wrapped up its remaining organizational matters, filling in the spots for clerk of the House, sergeant-at-arms, doorkeeper, postmaster, and chaplain.

Next, the House resolved a disputed election, voting again on party lines to seat Democrat John C. Davies of Utica, New York, who had defeated his Republican opponent, Hadwen C. Fuller, by 138 votes in an election Fuller contended was riddled with fraud.

But party solidarity soon dissolved as Rayburn recognized Sabath and his motion to reform the Rules Committee and to give Truman's legislative agenda a chance for passage. The motion was structured in two parts. First would be a test vote prohibiting debate on the reforms. The success of that vote would determine whether the second, substantive, vote, would be presented. Sabath's motion passed 275–142. Thirty-one Democrats, all from the former Confederacy plus Kentucky, voted against the motion. Surprisingly, forty-nine Republicans, including freshman Gerald Ford, broke with their leadership to support the reform. The Dixiecrats, led by Goober Cox and John Rankin of Mississippi, tried to prevent the final vote. Yates wondered whether Dawson had been right after all. But Goober was unable to get past the parliamentary barriers Sabath had set up, and his motion was defeated on a point of order. The rules change then passed on a voice vote. The House adjourned until January 5, when President Truman would present his State of the Union Address, formally laying out his Fair Deal program.[18]

Yates was impressed by the parliamentary command that Sabath had shown in structuring his motion. He understood that a mastery of the House's often arcane and complicated procedures, the niceties of points of order and degrees of priority in motions, would give him an advantage over those too lazy or uninterested to bother. Sabath encouraged him to sit nearby during floor debates so that he could watch the rules put into practice. Yates would set aside time to pore over Thomas Jefferson's manual of parliamentary practice and Cannon's *Precedents of the House of Representatives*, the Bible and Talmud of House Rules. He would frequently walk over to the office of the House parliamentarian, with questions or just to chat, and developed a close rapport with the staff.

Cox resented his defeat. Later in the year, feeling that Sabath had slighted him in the allocation of time to debate the public housing bill, the sixty-nine-year-old Cox slapped the eighty-three-year-old Sabath on the nose, sending his glasses flying across the House floor. Sabath immediately responded with right and left jabs to Cox's face, a "pair of beauties," as Congressman Walter later proclaimed. They went after each other until pulled apart by the two-hundred-pound congressman James Delaney. Although the two later apologized to each other and even shook hands for newspaper photographers, their mutual distaste never waned.[19]

It was now time for Yates to get on a committee. The Ways and Means Committee Democrats, now constituted as the Committee on Committees, would meet to prepare recommendations for the full Democratic caucus scheduled on January 17. Many members had been lobbying for weeks in hopes of receiving preferred assignments.

Yates had not thought much about the Appropriations Committee. "I didn't know anything about Appropriations," he later confided, "never having been in a legislature before."[20] But many of his friends, including Arvey and Sabath, as well as his father-in-law, A. Paul, encouraged him to be on the committee that gave out the money. The chairs of the appropriations subcommittee wielded such power that they were known as the "Cardinals." Congressmen got reelected by bringing federal projects back home. To get those dollars, they had to come hat in hand to Appropriations. The members of the committee accumulated a lot of chits from other representatives, which could be exchanged in many ways. A fourteen-term congressman who befriended Yates told him, "Son, if you want to stay in Congress a long time, get yourself a project for your district. During my first term here I struck it lucky, because I got a river dredging job that lasted 14 years."[21] The members of the Appropriations Committee were the ones who decided whether and where those projects would be funded.

Tom O'Brien understood that too. He had been the only Illinois Democrat on Appropriations when he was asked to return to Ways and Means, and he wanted to ensure that someone remained on the committee who would keep the federal spigot open for Illinois, particularly Chicago. He made a condition of his transition that Illinois would retain a fist in the purse.

There were twelve Democrats in the twenty-six-member Illinois delegation. Six of the twelve were freshmen. Sabath told Yates that, if none of the Democrats senior to him wanted Appropriations, he would get O'Brien's support to give Yates the seat. Sabath, of course, was remaining as chairman of Rules, and Dawson was becoming chairman of Expenditures. O'Brien was creating the vacancy in the first place, so that left three other Illinoisans to take a pass on the committee.

Thomas S. Gordon, representing Illinois's 8th Congressional District, didn't want it. A "quiet, pleasant man of Polish descent," Gordon represented a heavily Polish constituency and made few waves. He had been Chicago city treasurer and the business manager of *Dziennik Związkowy*, the *Polish Daily News*, founded by his late uncle. Paddy Nash made Gordon a congressman in 1942 after dumping the incumbent for supporting antilabor legislation. Gordon was quietly accumulating seniority on the Committee on Foreign Affairs and would, in fact, become chairman a few years later. He had no interest in switching committees. His main interest, in fact, was photography, and he kept a small darkroom in his congressional suite.[22]

Martin Gorski, congressman from the 5th District, was born in Poland, grew up in Chicago slums, and also represented a heavily Polish district. The epitome of the Horatio Alger hero who worked his way out of poverty into success, Gorski had been an assistant state's attorney and a master in chancery in the Cook County court system before coming to the House. Now he was happily ensconced in the Judiciary Committee, where he accepted special assignments to provide legal opinions to his colleagues and burrowed into the obscure minutiae of bankruptcy law. There was also the question of his health. Gorski, sixty-three years old, would be dead by the end of the year.[23]

Finally, Sabath checked with Charles Melvin "Mel" Price, of East St. Louis, representing the 25th District just across the Mississippi from Missouri. Price, a former baseball writer and sports editor, had been serving as an enlisted man at Camp Lee, Virginia, when he was first elected in 1944. Price had been appointed to the Joint Congressional Committee on Atomic Energy, set up to oversee the work of the Atomic Energy Commission in all its military and civilian applications. Many considered this committee, which would determine the future of both nuclear weapons and electricity-generating nuclear reactors, and also influence the locations where massive public works projects would be situated, to be one of the most powerful committees of the Congress. Price took a pass. The spot was Yates's.

If any of the other new representatives in the delegation resented Yates's selection, they kept it to themselves. Four of the five, Neil J. Linehan, James V. Buckley, Chester A. Chesney, and Peter F. Mack Jr., had never run for office before. Linehan, an electrical engineer, and Buckley, an auto worker, were both union officials. Chesney was a former center for the Chicago Bears, a member of the famous Bears team that beat the Washington Redskins 73–0 in the 1940 National Football League championship game. Mack, only thirty-two, was a pilot and naval air navigator and worked in his family's automobile dealership in downstate Carlinville.

The only one of the five who might have had a superior claim was Barratt O'Hara, a well-known figure in Chicago and Illinois politics. He laid claim to being the youngest U.S. soldier at the siege of Santiago, Cuba, during the Spanish-American War and was an infantry officer in World War I. He was elected in 1913 as the youngest lieutenant governor in Illinois history. For several years in the

'30s, O'Hara had a weekly fifteen-minute slot on radio station WCFL, the voice of the Chicago Federation of Labor, where he praised the New Deal and organized labor and attacked big business and the "servile press."[24] In a succession of failed candidacies, he had run for United States senator, governor, and congressman-at-large, before finally winning the 2nd District seat.

Yates got along well with O'Hara. They had crossed paths professionally in 1939 when O'Hara was a traction attorney for the City of Chicago, handling cases involving the Chicago transit system, the trains and trolley cars of which were powered by electric traction motors, and Yates was an assistant Illinois attorney general assigned to the Illinois Commerce Commission as a traction attorney. He thought O'Hara might oppose him for Appropriations. But as a sixty-six-year-old freshman legislator, O'Hara could see that the leadership had struck a deal, and it was in his interest to go along.

On January 18, 1949, the House confirmed Yates's appointment to the Appropriations Committee.[25] He was immediately greeted with stern disapproval by its chairman, Clarence Cannon. The chairman didn't like freshmen, and particularly didn't think that freshmen belonged on Appropriations. He resented that the House leadership, particularly Sabath, had foisted Yates on his committee.[26]

Cannon was first elected to the House in 1922, representing a rural district in Missouri. "I live on a farm. I'm a dirt farmer," he told people.[27] He was a master of the rules of the House and for five years prior to his election had been the House parliamentarian, writing the compilation of House procedural rulings, *Cannon's Precedents of the House of Representatives*.

With the exception of two terms when the Republicans controlled Congress, Cannon had led Appropriations since 1941. Perhaps ironically for someone charged with overseeing the federal budget, Cannon hated spending the taxpayer's money. He had no use for urban liberals like Sid Yates.

Cannon was in charge of appointing the Democratic members to the various Appropriations subcommittees. He put Yates on the permanent subcommittee responsible for funding the District of Columbia and the special subcommittee on Foreign Aid, established to implement the post–World War II Marshall Plan for the economic reconstruction of Europe, administered by the Economic Co-operation Administration.

The DC Appropriations subcommittee had been in continuous existence since 1879, the first year that the Appropriations Committee created formal subcommittees.[28] Article I, Section 8, Clause 17, of the U.S. Constitution gave the Congress authority "to exercise exclusive legislation in all cases whatsoever" over the District. Except for a few brief experiments in home rule, Washington was directly ruled by Congress through a three-member board of commissioners, two members appointed by the president after approval by the Senate and a third member selected from the U.S. Army Corps of Engineers. Although residents of the District paid taxes, they had no representative in Congress and their budget depended on the subcommittee's will.[29]

Cannon assured DC residents that "The District subcommittee of our appropriations committee in my opinion, will be one of the most important subcommittees in the House."[30] Insiders, however, knew full well that the DC subcommittee was frequently a dumping ground for freshmen members, a committee assignment where they could get trained in the culture of appropriations without affecting the welfare of the constituents of any of their colleagues. Yates, along with fellow freshman Foster Furcolo of Springfield, Massachusetts, were two of the three Democrats on the subcommittee, the third being Chairman Joe B. Bates of Kentucky. Bates was one of the southerners who had voted against the Rules Committee reform, and the District of Columbia in 1949 still permitted official racial segregation.

Yates didn't mind the assignment, and wasn't going to let his freshman status keep him from being an active participant. Even before the official appointment, he had joined five other representatives at a press conference sponsored by the American Veterans' Committee to endorse both home rule and a seat in the House for the District.[31] At the subcommittee's first hearing on January 26, 1949, questioning the DC commissioners, he modestly admitted, "As a new member, I wonder whether you would educate me a little bit"[32] and then plunged in with his questions. Both he and Furcolo would take an active role, both inside and outside the hearing room, to try to use the subcommittee to eliminate, or at least alleviate, the rampant racial discrimination in the nation's capital. Yates worked to improve the conditions of the "colored" schools in the District and was instrumental in the desegregation of the Capitol police force, issues not of much help to his reelection needs in Chicago, but which he later confided were among the most important accomplishments of his congressional career.[33]

Unlike DC appropriations, Yates considered the Foreign Aid Appropriations subcommittee a plum assignment. He would have a major role in implementing the Marshall Plan to rebuild Europe, of crucial importance to his many constituents with relatives still living in postwar devastation. He would also be able to direct funds to support the new state of Israel, and the relevance to his Jewish constituents could not be overstated.

Foreign Aid was headed by yet another southerner, J. Vaughan Gary, of Richmond, Virginia, but Gary had sided with Rayburn on the Rules Committee vote and was ready to support Truman. In his initial year on the subcommittee, Yates participated in his first worldwide travels, flying to London, Paris, Brussels, Frankfurt, Berlin, Stockholm, Rome, and Athens to investigate and report on the postwar situation in Europe. While in Frankfurt, Yates met the U.S. high commissioner for Germany, John J. McCloy, who succeeded a series of military governors, and discussed with him the de-Nazification of West Germany. Yates challenged McCloy on the efforts being made to combat anti-Semitism in the ruins of the Third Reich.

Through the subcommittee, Yates also made the first of what would be dozens of official trips to Israel. There he had meetings with Prime Minister David Ben-Gurion, who offered him tea and cookies in the Knesset, and with Mrs. Goldie Mayerson, then minister of Labor and Housing, who would later become Prime Minister Golda Meir. She also offered him tea and cookies in her office.[34] Seeing the devastation from the first Arab-Israeli war, Yates asked Ben-Gurion about Israel's future. Ben-Gurion smiled and replied, "We will win. This is the land of miracles. The miraculous we do today. The impossible takes a little longer."[35] The Jews of the Ninth District "kvelled" with pride to have a congressman with such influence.

He also sparked attention for one of his favorite pastimes, golf. Yates was almost a scratch golfer and had been four times champion of his home course, the Bryn Mawr Golf Club in Lincolnwood, as well as a former golf champion of the Chicago Bar Association.[36] In July, he volunteered to be part of the Democratic team in a match-play tournament against Republican members of the House and Senate. He was paired against the legendary senator Robert Taft of Ohio, the son of the late president and chief justice William Howard Taft. The senator was an isolationist, an opponent of the New Deal and a bitter foe of FDR, Truman, and organized labor. His namesake Taft-Hartley Act, which was passed over Truman's veto in 1947, severely restricted the rights of unions and was called the "slave labor" act by John L. Lewis and other labor leaders.[37] Called "Mr. Republican" by the press, he had unsuccessfully sought his party's nomination for president in 1948 and blamed Thomas Dewey, who had bested him at the convention on a platform of "Taft can't win," for Truman's upset victory. Taft was feared and respected as a master of the Senate rules and the architect and guidestar of conservative thinking.

Yates was slightly apprehensive as his 1:30 tee time at the Burning Tree Country Club approached, but he relaxed as the Ohioan, dressed in khaki shorts, a faded blue T-shirt, gray woolen socks embellished with green elephants, and an old fishing hat with a green sun visor worn backward, walked over to shake hands. Over the next three or so hours, the forty-year-old liberal freshman and the sixty-year-old conservative icon were deadly serious as they chose their clubs and planned and executed their shots, but they chatted amiably as they strolled the fairways and greens. At one point, a brief rain began to soak the two. Taft, who, following his conservative instincts, had brought an umbrella, beckoned Yates to join him under it. Taft laughed when Yates, heads almost touching, told

Taft that he expected this to be the closest he would ever come to Taft's position.[38] Yates won the match that afternoon, and the Democrats beat the Republicans by a final score of 30–6. The leadership delighted in the symbolic victory and noted the talent of the likeable Chicagoan. And, at least as important an accomplishment, Yates had made a new friend on the other side, both literally—the House versus the Senate, Democrat versus Republican—and philosophically, one with whom he would seldom agree, but a fellow legislator with whom he could work in a professional and mutually respectful manner.

Yates developed a reputation as one of the best golfers in the Congress. In the second session of the Congress in 1950, he was invited to participate in the annual National Celebrities Charity Golf Tournament sponsored by the *Washington Post* to raise funds to combat juvenile delinquency in the District of Columbia. He mingled at the Army Navy Country Club with Hollywood and television stars such as Bob Hope, Danny Kaye, Milton Berle, and Arthur Godfrey, as well as golf and sports legends such as Ben Hogan, Gene Sarazen, Babe Didrickson Zaharias, Jim Thorpe, and Chick Evans.

He was particularly pleased to see Hope, who remembered Yates. Charlie Yates, the congressman's older brother, had been Hope's first booking agent in the star's vaudeville days in New York, and the two were still close friends. Almost six years later, Charlie, in fact, would die of a heart attack while sitting with Hope in a golf cart, playing in Palm Springs.[39] But for now, Yates was delighted to be seen by Hope as a peer, and not just as Charlie's little brother. It was even sweeter when Yates shot a 76, winning the Official Washington Division, while Hope and Danny Kaye tied with scores of 78 to share the trophy in the Celebrity Division. Babe Didrickson led the women's division with a 69, and Ben Hogan won overall with a five-under-par 65. The Associated Press sent the story out and Yates's accomplishment ended up in hundreds of papers around the country.[40]

The 81st Congress was a heady time for Yates, joining Democratic members for dinners with President Truman and the cabinet, conferring with national and international leaders, rubbing elbows with movie stars and famous athletes. Dinners hosted by Yates and his wife, which included songfests and guitar playing, were featured in the *Washington Post*.[41]

Sabath warned him not to lose his connection back home. From the first days after being sworn in, he encouraged Yates to spend his freshman term keeping his head down, doing his homework on the two subcommittees, and watching and listening. Yates agreed and did all of that. But he wasn't going to hide his light under a basket either. He dropped his first bill into the House hopper on January 13. Designated H.R. 1444, it was designed to eradicate racial restrictions in immigration and naturalization laws for the Japanese. He would file two more bills later that month, H.R. 1736, to establish labor extension courses in the Department of

Labor, similar to the agricultural extension courses offered by the Department of Agriculture, and H.R. 1851, to extend the existing rent-control laws to April 20, 1951. None of the bills got out of the committees they were assigned to, nor did any of the other eight bills and resolutions he offered during the 81st Congress. Still, each bill was an opportunity for a floor speech, which could be republished and sent to his supporters.

Yates spoke in the House for the first time on February 16, 1949, concurring with a remark made by his fellow DC subcommittee colleague, Foster Furcolo, about the benefits of continuing subsidies to the Tennessee Valley Authority.[42] He made his first floor speech on March 1, 1949, in support of a bill to extend naturalization privileges to all legal immigrants and to end naturalization restrictions against Asians.[43]

Yates grew more comfortable in seeking recognition on the floor, and members soon grew to appreciate his relevant comments and classical allusions. On a bill about pensions for veterans, he stated, "Mr. Chairman, it seems to me that if the ghost of Diogenes had been in this Chamber last night he would have been very frustrated; if Diogenes were in this Chamber today with his lantern he might have some difficulty finding his honest man. But we could certainly use his light because right now we are groping in darkness."[44]

He made sure to take to the floor to praise the Irish, and their "faith in righteous causes," on St. Patrick's Day, and the heroism of the Jews on the first anniversary of the State of Israel.[45]

He stayed active in his subcommittees, and in summer 1949 participated in his first conference committee, the meeting of the House members of the Foreign Aid Appropriations subcommittee with their counterparts in the Senate to work out the differences between the bills passed by the two bodies. It was the Senate's year to host the conference, and, as was tradition, Yates and the House conferees, led by subcommittee chairman Gary and full committee chairman Cannon, walked together across to the Senate side of the Capitol. There, in Room S-127, Senate conferees, already seated, awaited them in a large hearing room decorated with flying cupids, eagles, and Constantino Brumidi's large-breasted frescoes of Venus, the Roman goddess of love, sex, and victory, and of Amphitrite, the wife of Neptune and queen of the sea.[46] The House conferees took their seats at the other side of the table. The room was closed to the public and members were forbidden to disclose the negotiations. Yates observed the "polite parliamentary parlance" that disguised the deep stubbornness of the two sides, as, painstakingly, the conferees considered each difference between the two bills, attempting to come to agreement on a unified appropriations measure that could be returned to their respective houses for passage. The divisions were deep, but unlike the pugilistic Cox and Sabath, there seemed to be a shared culture among the appropriators that distinguished their committees from the others. The work would get done. Just as he had made friends with Bob Taft, conference was an opportunity to work with other senators, other Republicans, find common ground, and become known.

Yates kept an eye on 1950, when he would face his first reelection. He actively participated in floor debates over rent-control legislation, a major concern of his urban, largely apartment-dwelling district. He organized the first Small Business Conference in his district, bringing representatives from federal agencies to Chicago to meet with local businesses to provide information on applying for federal procurement contracts.[47] The success of this conference led many of his colleagues to copy his model.[48] And, on March 17, 1949, he began what would become one of the signatures of his twenty-four terms in Congress, the authorship of a periodic newsletter sent to his constituents.

The newsletter was initially designed to do away with the necessity of personal correspondence with a small group of around one hundred friends and supporters.[49] Newsletters had been used as a means of communication between congressmen and constituents since at least 1920, but only a few members kept up a regular correspondence.[50] Most newsletters were laundry lists of votes and personal accomplishments with little analysis and even fewer insights. Yates aimed for something more. In what would be the first of more than five hundred newsletters, he wrote, "I believe you are entitled to know of the impressions of your Representative on legislation which affects you. I intend to address a letter to you every week, if that is possible under the pressure of business here, and I hope you will send me your reaction."[51]

He went on to describe the House debate on the rent-control act. In what would be a continuing theme, he went on to describe the "unholy alliance" between the "reactionary" southern Democrats and the Republicans to oppose civil rights in exchange for the southerners' opposition to Truman's social legislation program. Later newsletters explained the intricacies of the committee system, seniority, and the tensions between the House and Senate, Republicans and Democrats, the Congress and the president. They were filled with anecdotes, detailed character studies of the major players, and his personal experiences.

True to his word, Yates sent out sixty-six weekly newsletters between March 17, 1949, and September 15, 1950 in the 81st Congress, almost every week when Congress was in session.[52] The weekly newsletters would continue until the second session of the 83rd Congress, in 1954, when he switched to a semimonthly format, and later, in 1962, to a monthly schedule, with occasional extra newsletters as events dictated. As the years passed, the newsletters received national attention. Russell Baker, in the *New York Times Magazine*, described them as "literate, sophisticated, informative and as incisive as many a professional syndicated column."[53] Allen L. Otten, in the *Wall Street Journal*, called the newsletters "a literate labor of love by a man who clearly cares about words and ideas. . . . Anecdotes about Lincoln or Harry Truman mix with ones about George Jessel or Thomas Edison; there are references to Greek mythology, quotations from Shaw and Shakespeare, Mark Twain and Anatole France, Lewis Carroll and Ogden Nash."[54]

By fall 1949, the newsletter mailing list had grown from one hundred constituents to more than fifteen hundred.[55] The list continued to grow with individual names, and Yates actively solicited readers, sending out invitation letters with postage-paid return postcards. Finally, Yates availed himself of U.S. Post Office regulations in effect since 1924, which permitted congressmen to use the franking privilege to send mass mailings to each person within a congressional district simply by addressing the letter "Postal Patron—9th Congressional District, Illinois."[56] Now the newsletter could go by franked mail to hundreds of thousands of constituents, as well as persons outside the district who specifically requested copies.

Yates sought additional ways to increase his name recognition. For this, he looked to the example of his fellow freshman, Barratt O'Hara. O'Hara had convinced radio station WCFL to resume the radio show he had voiced in the 1930s. Now called "Quorum Call," the spot allowed O'Hara to hold forth each week on the latest congressional controversies. It was a great platform for the former lieutenant governor.

Yates went to Marshall Field III, grandson of the founder of the iconic department store bearing his name, and publisher of the recently merged *Chicago Sun* and *Chicago Daily Times*, now the *Sun-Times*, the city's progressive rival to the *Tribune*. Field also owned radio station WJJD, a 50,000-watt station originally owned by the Loyal Order of Moose. The station was known for its sports coverage and its broadcasts of recorded music.[57] Field wanted the station to broadcast a progressive viewpoint to complement the *Sun-Times*. He started "Negro Newsfront," the nation's first black daily radio newscast, headed by journalist Vernon Jarrett and future composer Oscar Brown Jr.[58] He was the only local broadcaster to carry a speech made by former vice president Henry A. Wallace on May 14, 1947, at the Chicago Stadium criticizing President Truman's anticommunist foreign policy, which was sponsored by the far left Progressive Citizens of America.[59] Yates could provide a youthful progressive voice.

At 9:55 AM on Saturday, May 7, 1949, between the 9:45 AM "Take It from Here" news report and the 10:00 AM "Songs You Remember," Yates gave his first "Washington Story." The format and script Yates and Field agreed on was straightforward:

> ANNOUNCER: And now THE WASHINGTON STORY . . . a weekly re-
> port from the halls of Congress by Congressman Sidney R. Yates of the
> Ninth District of Illinois. Congressman Yates is one of the hardest work-
> ing Congressmen in Washington. This weekly radio report direct from
> Washington D.C. is his summary of Congressional news . . . and now
> Congressman Yates, what's THE WASHINGTON STORY for this week?
> YATES: A PREPARED STATEMENT . . . HARD HITTING . . . HUMAN
> . . . WITH HUMOR . . . TO READ EXACTLY 3 MINUTES
> ANNOUNCER: Thank you Congressman Yates. Each week at this time
> Congressman Sidney R. Yates of the Ninth District of Illinois presents
> The Washington Story . . . a radio report to you, the people, of the weekly
> happenings in the Halls of Congress. Listen again next week to another
> chapter in The Washington Story.[60]

The shows were rebroadcast later in the week on a smaller FM sister station, WMOR-FM. Yates used the broadcasts to expand on his weekly newsletters, most weeks tracking the last newsletter topic. Occasionally he varied from the format, inviting other Illinois congressmen such as O'Hara and Mel Price as guests, and appearing on O'Hara's show in exchange, gaining increasing recognition over the airwaves, and more and more comfort in front of a microphone.

As the April 11, 1950, primary election approached, Yates evaluated his chances. Joe Gill and Jake Arvey had cleared the Democratic field, leaving Yates to run unopposed for the party's nomination. On the Republican side, former repre-sentative Robert Twyman declined to try to take back his seat, citing the pres-sures of his manufacturing business.[61] The Republican ward committeemen of the 9th District couldn't come to consensus, splitting between two candidates, John E. Babb and Maxwell Goodwin, and forcing a bitter primary fight.[62] Babb was a longtime member of the Republican organization. Goodwin was a sales representative for a Michigan truck-equipment manufacturer. The primary cam-paign was marked by histrionics as each tried to out-patriot the other. Goodwin said he was running in "a last ditch fight to save what is left of America's liberties and living standards from those creeping socialists and welfare staters who have sacrificed our heritage for a mess of votes." Babb called Truman "a discredited and inadequate President" and lauded the Senate's investigation of homosexu-als in the State Department, which resulted in the discharge of ninety-one men "because of a loathsome abnormality which automatically disqualified them as good security risks" and demonstrated "the New Deal-socialistic conspiracy to wreck this government."[63] Despite expectations to the contrary, Goodwin, who had only recently changed his voting registration from Michigan to Illinois, de-feated Babb by more than two thousand votes.

As an individual opponent, Goodwin did not trouble Yates. His chief worry about the 1950 election was one shared by most of the Democratic freshmen who had been swept into office in 1948. Did the Truman upset signify a lasting change in the makeup of the Congress or would the midterms bring buyers' remorse by the voters? Americans had accepted Truman's challenge to throw out the "do-nothing" 80th Congress. Would they do the same to the 81st? As the summer progressed, the unleashed fervor of anticommunism was stretching into the North Side of Chicago. On June 25, 1950, 75,000 soldiers of the North Korean People's Army crossed over the Thirty-Eighth Parallel to invade South Korea, stoking doubts about the ability of Truman, and by extension his Democratic Congress, to contain communism. The patriotic litmus test for representatives was their position on the Internal Security Act of 1950, also known as the McCarran Act.

The McCarran Act, named for Nevada senator Pat McCarran, was premised on the existence of a "world Communist movement . . . whose purpose it is, by treachery, deceit, infiltration, . . . espionage, sabotage, terrorism, . . . to establish a Communist totalitarian dictatorship in the countries throughout the world." Not only did this movement work through openly communist entities, but also "on a secret, conspiratorial basis [through] 'Communist fronts,' which . . . conceal the facts as to their true character and purposes and their membership."[64] To protect the United States from this danger, the act required all communist organizations, including communist-front organizations, to register with the attorney general. Members of such organizations were subject to employment, travel, and other restrictions. They were also forbidden to use the mail or airwaves to disseminate their views unless a statement was included affirming that they were sponsored by "a communist organization." The determination of whether an organization was communist was given to the five-person Subversive Activities Control Board.

Civil libertarians were appalled by the bill. Under its provisions, any organization that expressed any progressive views could be labeled a communist front and be subject to sanctions if even one of its planks was shared by the communists. But in the midst of waging a "hot" war against the communists in Korea and a Cold War everywhere else in the world, members of Congress were terrified of the consequences of being labeled soft on communism. Yates was opposed to the bill but didn't know how outspoken he should be. His labor friends in the AFL and the CIO, along with his progressive allies from the Americans for Democratic Action, an organization of which he was a member, urged him to vote against the act. Meanwhile, Joe Gill and some of the other political regulars urged him either to go along with what was clearly going to be an overwhelming majority in favor of the legislation, or at least lay low in his opposition.

As it turned out, Yates was absent with the flu on the date the House version of the bill was debated and passed by a vote of 354–20 and sent to conference with the Senate version. Yates was paired as a no vote with the absent Republican Wilson Gillette of Pennsylvania, but the pairing would provide little political ammunition to Goodwin. But neither did it give any pleasure to the liberals whose support he needed in November. In his September 1, 1950, newsletter, written three days after the vote, Yates mentioned his flu but conspicuously omitted any discussion of the missed debate and vote, instead focusing on his support of a bill making appropriations for military preparedness and national defense.

The House recessed for ten days in September and Yates returned home, meeting with constituents and consulting with friends about the campaign. When he came back to Washington, he resolved to take a more public stand in opposition to McCarran. His opportunity came when the conference report was brought to the House for approval on September 20, 1950. The conference version of the bill had made the restrictions even more onerous, adding a Senate provision for the emergency internment of any person who the president believed might "engage in, or probably will conspire with others to engage in, acts of espionage or of sabotage."

Yates rose and requested time from Congressman John Stephens Wood of Georgia, chairman of the Un-American Activities Committee and the manager of the conference report. Unlike the Senate, which has few limitations on the amount of time a senator may consume in speaking, House debate is usually strictly limited, the time allocated between proponents and opponents of any given measure. As a stark sign of how few members were willing to oppose the conference report, when Yates rose to speak, instead of being allotted the customary one, two, or five minutes usually granted, Chairman Wood yielded Yates "such time as he may desire" for his remarks.[65]

Yates needed to hit two targets with his speech. He had to preempt and block any charges of communist sympathies. He also had to satisfy his progressive supporters. For the first, he invoked the politically unassailable FBI director J. Edgar Hoover, who opposed the bill on the grounds that the registration provisions would drive the communists underground. Yates gave other examples of counterintelligence experts who called the bill amateurish, "designed to catch headlines, but not spies." He concluded the first phase of his oration with the charge that "the McCarran bill is not only ineffective; it is actually harmful to our best interests, if we want to protect ourselves from commie sabotage."

Having asserted his anticommunist bona fides, Yates turned to the civil liberty aspects of the legislation. In much more personal and passionate terms, he stood up for the right of U.S. citizens to express unpopular views. "No, Mr. Speaker, America will cease to be the land where different opinions bring progress. Fear and shame are powerful gags, and I do not want to tape up the mouths of those who want to think and speak differently, even in unpopular opinions. It is the

Communist we must beware of—the international plotter, the saboteur, the spy. . . . Let's do it effectively—not by an un-American act of this type." The conference report passed by a vote of 313–20. Of the Illinois delegation, Yates was joined only by Bill Dawson, Barratt O'Hara, and Adolph Sabath.[66]

The Senate passed the report 51–7 and sent it to President Truman, who promptly vetoed the bill, calling it "the greatest danger to freedom of speech, press, and assembly since the Alien and Sedition Laws of 1798." The House immediately took up the vote to override the veto. Debate was not allowed. As Yates went up to cast his vote to sustain the veto, he was approached by Richard Bolling, a fellow freshman from Kansas City, Missouri. Bolling supported the bill when it first came to the floor and later voted for the conference report. But even though he had been elected by opponents of Missouri's Prendergast machine, the political patrons of Harry Truman, he would not oppose his fellow Missourian's veto and prepared to join Yates against the override. Bolling extended his hand to Yates and said, "Well, I guess neither of us will be back next year." Yates returned the handshake, but his face went pale, as the full significance of the vote hit him. The House overrode Truman's veto 286–48, well above the two-thirds required by the Constitution. Ninety-five members, including Sabath, who was absent, did not vote. Yates, rattled by Bolling's comment, went back to his office and vomited.[67] He then went to his desk and prepared a final newsletter for the 81st Congress, explaining his vote to his constituents. He didn't know whether it would be the last one of his career.

Writing quickly, he quoted legendary Irish nationalist leader, Daniel O'Connell: "Nothing is politically right which is morally wrong." He would not sacrifice his beliefs for the sake of reelection. Somewhat fatalistically, he ended the newsletter with the story of the World War I Marine sergeant who waved his men over the top with the cry; "Come on, you so-and-sos—do you want to live forever?"[68]

Yates returned to the district and campaigned hard. Senator Douglas stumped with him throughout the streets of the North Side in an old station wagon equipped with a sound system. National leaders sent endorsements, including Majority Leader McCormack ("Seldom have I known a [freshman] more conscientious, hard-working and fair-minded than you. . . . You also enjoy the respect and confidence of Speaker Rayburn and the President."), his subcommittee chairman Joe Bates ("If his political success in the future is to be in any manner commensurate with the ability he has shown on this subcommittee, then he shall have a long and successful career."), and Senator Hubert Humphrey ("The hardest working Congressman I know"). He reprinted commendations from national newspapers such as the *Washington Post* ("one of the able, dynamic and courageous new members in the House") and the *St. Louis Post-Dispatch* ("Yates is part of a new force in Congress made up of young war veterans who are making themselves felt in the House.").[69]

But as Yates had feared, the Republicans weaponized his vote on the McCarran Act and other pro-civil-liberties votes into a picture of Yates as a communist tool and sympathizer. Goodwin charged that a vote Yates had cast against deportation without due process had allowed "3,000 . . . anarchists and subversives . . . most scheduled for deportation to Russia and her satellites, [to] have complete freedom of movement here."[70] He labeled Yates and the Truman Administration "Commiecrats"[71] while Goodwin's campaign manager, Lakeview *Times* editor Robert Reese, charged that Yates was a left-winger whose voting record was identical to Representative Vito Marcantonio, the sole congressman of the American Labor Party, whom the *Tribune* described as "Communism's spokesman in the lower house."[72] The *Tribune* portrayed Yates's votes against the conference report and to uphold Truman's veto as offering aid and comfort to subversives, while his support of Truman's plan for a Department of Health, Education, and Security was called pure socialism. "Yates, judging from his record, apparently is for protecting subversive elements in our country and for furthering crackpot socialistic schemes."[73] The *Tribune*, unsurprisingly, endorsed Goodwin, drily stating that Yates's "pink record is exceeded only by that of the ancient and disreputable Adolph Sabath."[74]

Yates put on a public show of indifference to the charges. "Am I a Red?" he asked his audiences. "Did you ever hear of a Communist that could break 75 on the golf course?"[75] But he knew he would have to offer a more substantive answer. He reserved broadcast time on WCRW, a 250-watt AM radio station operating only five hours a day and airing from a bungalow on top of the Embassy Hotel at Pine Grove and Diversey, in the heart of the Ninth District. Known as the Gold Coast Station, as the neighborhood was called, it shared its frequency with two other local stations, but its signal could be heard loud and clear by Yates's constituents. On October 27, 1950, taking the studio microphone, he made his formal response.

He began by describing the 9th District, "a true meeting ground of the peoples of the world—of various cultural backgrounds, of different viewpoints and opinions—all living and working together." Describing his governing philosophy, he returned to Daniel O'Connell and added "the advice given by Polonius to Laertes in *Hamlet*: "This above all—to thine own self be true, and it must follow as the night the day that thou canst not then be false to any man."

He challenged his constituents: "Do you believe in Social Security? Do you believe that we should provide the opportunity for decent living for . . . people who are too old to work and too young to die? . . . Do you believe that the vast numbers of our people who are now living in slums and cannot afford to leave the filth and degradation in which they must bring up their children should be given a lift by their government, so that they might live in decent surroundings? . . . Do you believe that there should be a minimum wage, a basic standard establishing a reasonable base in order that people may be protected in decent living? . . . Do you believe that minority groups are entitled to the same civil rights as other Americans?" The Democrats, under Harry Truman, stood for those programs. The Republicans did not.

Finally, he addressed communism and his votes on the McCarran Act. Again stating that the McCarran Act was more anti-American than anticommunist, he declared that he and the Democratic Party were "determined to halt the spread of communist imperialism abroad. . . . We are equally determined to check communism in this country. [Democrats] seek to eliminate from our midst the causes upon which communism flourishes—ignorance, poverty, disease, discrimination and filth—the conditions used by communists as a base for their challenge. The way to meet the challenge of communism is to let the people know that their government belongs to them; that it is a government which takes an interest in their problems and is seeking to help solve their problems on a realistic and practical basis."[76]

Yates was reelected 51.8 percent to 48.2 percent. His margin was 5,147 votes, less than a third of his plurality over Robert Twyman two years earlier.[77] Four of the other five freshman Democrats, O'Hara, Linehan, Chesney, and Buckley, were not as fortunate and were rejected by the voters after their single term.[78]

An unnamed Democratic Party leader—likely Joe Gill, who enjoyed putting Yates down and could never resist recalling Yates's 1939 loss against his 46th Ward machine—boasted that he had ensured Yates's election by helping Goodwin defeat Babb in the primary. "You don't think we wanted Babb running against Yates, do you?" he told the Tribune. Babb, following his primary defeat for Congress, had been overwhelmingly elected Cook County sheriff in 1950, filling in as a last-minute entry upon the death of the nominated Republican candidate. But Babb's Democratic opponent was Daniel A. "Tubbo" Gilbert, a Chicago police captain under investigation by the Senate's Kefauver committee on organized crime, and Babb's success against Tubbo cannot be so easily inferred as auguring his unrealized prospects against Yates.[79]

3

"HERE COMES THIS NICE, GOOD-LOOKING GUY"

The Wisteria Tea Room, on the near north side of Chicago, was one of only a handful of Japanese restaurants in the city in the late 1940s. Its neon sign flashed "SUKIYAKI," and Mrs. Okimoto, the owner, boasted that the restaurant was the only one in Chicago that did a tableside preparation of this one-pot national dish of thinly sliced meat, vegetables, soy sauce, and spices. Catering to those of the general public who enjoyed the exotic cuisine, it was also a favorite destination for Japanese immigrants and "resettlers," those Japanese Americans who had left the hostile atmosphere and painful memories of the West Coast for the more welcoming Midwest.

Shigeo Wakamatsu was a frequent diner at Wisteria. His friends called him Shig. Born in Tacoma, Washington, in 1914, Shig had been taking premed, biology, and chemistry courses at the College of Puget Sound when he was swept up by the army and deposited at the Tule Lake concentration camp in Newell, California, as part of the government's Japanese-American internment program. Released from camp in 1943, he resettled in Chicago, where, with the help of friends, he had taken a number of jobs, finally being hired as an industrial chemist at Lever Brothers. Wakamatsu usually brought his wife with him to Wisteria, but on this evening in 1948 he was there with Tom Masuda, Noby Honda, Dick Yamada, and Dick Akagi, founding members of the Chicago chapter of the Japanese American Citizens League (JACL), to meet with Yates, who had requested a meeting to seek the support of the Japanese community. The JACL was founded in 1929 as a civil-rights organization for the benefit of Asian Americans. Shig had been a member back in Tacoma and actively worked to get the Chicago chapter established.

The men were astonished that Yates wanted to talk to them. "Back home on the West Coast," Shig said, "what candidate would ever come to a Japanese-American group to ask for support? We never got that kind of recognition." They waited for Yates to arrive, but they were apprehensive. On the West Coast, they were second-class citizens at best, forbidden to own property and practice their professions. Would it be different in Chicago?

Ever since the Japanese attack on Pearl Harbor on December 7, 1941, the status and safety of Japanese Americans had been in doubt. President Roosevelt had vowed that "this form of treachery shall never again endanger us."

In a near-unanimous vote, the Congress passed the declaration of war against Japan and, two days later, the United States was at war with Germany and Italy. For the first time in its history, the United States was in a two-front war in the Pacific and Atlantic Oceans.

The future of the residents of Japanese ancestry on the West Coast was then a matter of grave concern. In the first weeks after the attack, political and media leaders, such as California Governor Culbert Olson, a Democrat, and the state's attorney general, Earl Warren, a Republican, urged their residents to be restrained and calm. The *San Francisco News* reflected this sentiment: "A large proportion of them are natural-born Americans. They must not be made to suffer for the sins of a government for whom they have no sympathy or allegiance." Similar sentiments were expressed in Oregon and Washington.[1]

Nevertheless, within hours of Pearl Harbor, the FBI began arresting suspects of Japanese heritage, regardless of their immigration or citizenship status, and 1,212 Japanese immigrants were displaced. Lists had been compiled of people of Japanese descent prior to the attack in anticipation of possible war in the Pacific and the FBI on orders from Washington apprehended anyone who might be suspected of supporting the emperor of Japan.[2]

As reports of the Japanese army's brutal conquering of the Philippines, Burma, Hong Kong, Malaysia, and the Dutch East Indies reached the West Coast, hysteria took hold and toleration vanished. White farmers and merchants in California saw an opportunity to eliminate their Japanese competition and joined in the calls for forced evacuation and internment of anyone of Japanese ancestry. One leader of the Grower-Shipper Vegetable Association of Salinas Valley was forthright: "We're charged with wanting to get rid of the Japanese for selfish reasons. We might as well be honest. We do. It's a question of whether the white man lives on the Pacific Coast or the brown man."[3] The fear on the West Coast quickly spread nationally.

Racist prejudice against people of Asian ancestry wasn't anything new in the United States. It had been enshrined in the Chinese Exclusion Act (1882) and most recently in the Immigration Act of 1924, which severely restricted immigration from southern and eastern Europe and prohibited citizenship for immigrants from Japan. Japanese immigrants, called Issei, also could not own property under

California state law. The children of Issei, called Nisei, born in the United States, were U.S. citizens under the Constitution.

Governor Olson, fearing a challenge by Attorney General Warren in the election of 1942, joined in the anti-Japanese chorus. In a statewide radio address, Olson threw gas on the flames: "It is known that there are Japanese residents of California who have sought to aid the Japanese enemy by way of communicating information or have shown indication of preparation for Fifth Column activities." Warren matched the rhetoric. "Unless something is done it may bring about a repetition of Pearl Harbor," he warned.[4]

Throughout December 1941 and January of the following year, a fierce debate raged within the Roosevelt Administration over what to do about the Japanese Americans. First lady Eleanor Roosevelt met with Nisei women soon after Pearl Harbor and expressed strong support for toleration and the observance of democratic rights in her nationally syndicated column, "My Day." Attorney General Francis Biddle opposed internment of Japanese Americans as unconstitutional. FBI Director J. Edgar Hoover also opposed internment, assuring the president that his agency had the situation well in hand without any need for evacuation. Support for evacuation and internment derived substantially from Assistant Secretary of War John J. McCloy, and Lieutenant General John DeWitt, commander of the Western Command. McCloy's attitude was typical: "If it is a question of the safety of the country and the Constitution . . . why the Constitution is just a scrap of paper to me." The president was aware of the differences of opinion but was preoccupied with more weighty matters in the days after the declaration of war. The leading newspapers and service organizations such as the Lions and Elks clubs followed the politicians in anti-Japanese hysteria. Even Edward R. Murrow, the legendary journalist for CBS News, was caught up in fear of Japanese Americans. "I think it's a problem," he observed menacingly, "that, if Seattle ever does get bombed, you will be able to look up and see some University of Washington sweaters on the boys doing the bombing."[5]

Secretary of War Henry Stimson and President Roosevelt discussed the situation on the West Coast by telephone, and the president simply delegated responsibility of the situation to the secretary with the admonishment to "be as reasonable as you can." A few days later, on February 17, 1942, the president instructed Stimson and McCloy to prepare an executive order for evacuation and internment. Roosevelt cautioned them not to tell the attorney general about the order.

When Biddle did learn that an executive order was in the works, he warned the president: "The last advice from the War Department is that there is no evidence of imminent attack and from the FBI that there is no evidence of planned sabotage." In mid-February, however, the California, Oregon, and Washington congressional delegations wrote the president recommending "the immediate evacuation of all persons of Japanese lineage."[6]

Executive Order 9066 gave the secretary of war and his military commanders the authority to execute a program of evacuation and internment of "any or all persons" living in "prescribed military areas." The order did not specify the Japanese, but there was no doubt toward whom it was aimed. The following day, Stimson promptly issued DeWitt the orders he had lobbied for.

General DeWitt wasted no time using the full force of his command. Japanese Americans were given only a few weeks to dispose of their property and report to assembly centers for transportation to one of the ten relocation centers in California, Arizona, Colorado, Wyoming, Utah, or Arkansas. In all, 120,000 Japanese Americans were interned. At least two-thirds of the internees were citizens of the United States. They never were convicted or even charged with any crime. In fact, no one of Japanese ancestry was ever convicted of sabotage or treasonous activity of any kind. Their only crime was their ancestry. DeWitt got to the point in his explanation to the House Committee on Naval Affairs: "A Jap is a Jap! There is no way to determine their loyalty."[7]

The relocation centers were in out-of-the-way areas, far from urban centers but close to railroad lines for easy transportation.[8] The camps were bleak, military-style barracks with barbed wire surrounding them. Photographers Dorothea Lange and Ansel Adams documented the plight of the internees, as well as their attempts to normalize their situation by forming communities with schools, ball teams, even scout troops.

Most of the Japanese Americans complied with the army's orders and went quietly. A few did not. Fred Korematsu, a twenty-three-year-old U.S. citizen, defied the order to report to an assembly center and was arrested and convicted for violating Civilian Exclusion Order 34. In 1944, the Supreme Court heard a challenge to the constitutionality of Executive Order 9066 brought by Korematsu and others similarly detained. In a divided decision, 6–3, the court upheld the order and convictions as "a military necessity." Justice Robert Jackson's dissent would live on as he acknowledged the racism of the executive order: "Korematsu, however, has been convicted of an act not commonly a crime. It consists merely of being present in the state whereof he is a citizen, near the place he was born, and all his life he has lived. . . . His crime would result, not from anything he did, said or thought, different than they, but only that he was born of different racial stock." Substantial evidence indicates today that General DeWitt and the U.S. solicitor general suppressed critical evidence in the case.[9]

Many Japanese Americans volunteered for service in the U.S. military during World War II and served honorably. The 442nd Regimental Combat Team, composed entirely of Nisei, earned citations and medals, including the Congressional

Medal of Honor, than any comparable fighting unit in U.S. history. They were made honorary citizens of the state of Texas for their valor in rescuing the Texas Lost Battalion of 200. The 442nd rescued all two hundred but took losses in excess of that amount themselves.

Toward the end of the war, the federal government created a program to relocate the internees inland and to assimilate them into U.S. society. Nearly twenty-five thousand evacuees settled in Chicago, where they took jobs with the city's light manufacturing companies. Most, like Shig Wakamatsu, settled on the South Side, but others migrated north to the Uptown and Edgewater neighborhoods in the 9th Congressional District.[10]

Yates knew that Chicago had a large population of resettled Japanese Americans and that the JACL's Chicago chapter was one of the largest in the country. Like any good Democrat, he was an admirer of Franklin Roosevelt, but Yates felt strongly that internment was a tragic mistake and needed to be righted. Wakamatsu lived outside the district and couldn't vote for Yates, but as the chairman of the chapter's membership committee, he had the ability to influence hundreds of voters who could. Yates suspected that many of them were Republicans. A Japanese-American friend of his explained, "It was that damn Democrat, FDR, who put us in the camps!" But, running as an underdog in 1948, Yates couldn't afford to overlook any possible constituency and actively solicited the JACL's support. This was probably not the time to sing his old German songs, he thought, as he walked into the Wisteria Tea Room for the meeting.

For Shig Wakamatsu's part, his own suspicions soon melted. "But anyway, here comes this nice, good-looking guy—tall, athletic," Wakamatsu recalled of their initial meeting. "He's asking for our help in his candidacy for the 9th District. Both principals, we, as well as Sid, were genuine, that's how the relationship got started."[11] Over the tableside sukiyaki, a lifelong alliance and friendship began between Yates and the JACL.

Yates was deeply touched by the stories he had heard from the JACL leaders and others about the experiences in the internment camps. The stories of two Japanese Americans, Jean Mishimi and Ross Harano, especially affected him. Jean Mishimi was only six years old when she and her family, including grandparents and extended family, were driven from their home near Fresno, California, and interned in the Gila River Camp in Arizona. Her father had been a truck farmer and they lost everything when they were removed. She attended school at the camp taught by a Caucasian teacher. The experience had a profound effect on her father, a proud Japanese man who expected to provide for his family. The feeling of ultimate failure followed him for years after the family's release. Ross Harano was born in the Fresno Assembly Center in mid-September 1942 and relocated to a permanent camp in Jerome, Arkansas. The Harano family lived in the camp for approximately a year. After the war, the Mishimi family relocated to Chicago's South Side and then moved north into the Fullerton Avenue area, where her father took a job with International Harvester. Young Jean attended six different grammar schools, the only child of color in each. The Harano family left the Jerome Camp in August 1943 to move to Alton, Illinois, where the father worked in a greenhouse. Several years later, the family moved to Chicago. Ross Harano's family had four members who served in the 442nd Regimental Combat Team and three others who were in U.S. intelligence. Jean Mishimi married and became a special education teacher. Harano became a banker in Chicago and was very active in the JACL's effort for redress and in Chicago politics. His parents had been Republican but he became a prominent supporter of Yates after being introduced to the congressman in 1964 by Mike Masaoka, the lobbyist for JACL. "He started off by saying that he knew that I was a Republican," Harano remembers. "I told him that both Japanese American Republicans and Democrats always have supported him because he was our community's champion in Congress." Harano later became chairman of the Japanese Americans for Sid Yates Campaign Committee.[12]

In one of his first acts as a congressman in 1949, Yates introduced HR 1444, a bill "to provide the privilege of becoming a naturalized citizen of the United States to all immigrants having a legal right to permanent residence, and to make immigration quotas available to Asian and Pacific peoples." It would overturn the discriminatory immigration policies of the United States created by the Immigration Act of 1924 and permit Issei eligibility for citizenship. "I never knew a more hard-working, thrifty, honest group," Yates wrote.

The 1924 immigration law, also known as the Johnson-Reed Act, was one of the most xenophobic laws ever passed by the Congress, aimed at liberalizing the entry of persons of British and Western European descent while tightening quotas on those from other countries. In particular, it targeted the Japanese. Previous immigration laws had already prevented Asians from naturalizing but allowed them to come to the United States. Johnson-Reed extended the restrictions to exclude from entry into the United States any alien who would otherwise be ineligible for citizenship. Calvin Coolidge signed the bill into law over the protests of the Japanese government.[13]

Yates's bill contained many of the provisions included in H.R. 199, a similar measure introduced by Congressman Walter H. Judd of Minnesota, a former medical missionary in China and one of the House's leading foreign policy experts on China and Japan. Although a Republican, Judd's seniority and expertise convinced the leadership to make his bill, which was progressing through the Judiciary Committee, the primary legislative vehicle for immigration reform. Judd had offered a similar bill during the Republican-led 80th Congress. Yates was disappointed that his own bill would not be debated. He was encouraged, however, to support Judd's version by Judge Sabath, who, as chairman of the Rules Committee, had worked out the procedures for the bill's debate, and by Emanuel "Manny" Celler of New York, chairman of the Judiciary Committee, who would manage the bill on the floor. Celler had been in the House since 1922, representing an overwhelmingly Jewish district in Brooklyn. Celler hated the 1924 immigration act, and along with Sabath, vehemently opposed it when it was first debated in the House. Its repeal had become a crusade and an obsession. Celler resolved to establish a quota system devoid of discrimination based on race or national origin. Now, as Judiciary chairman, he thought he had a chance. Using Judd's version would provide a measure of bipartisanship, which might bring enough Republicans over to offset the nativist Democrats from the South who were opposed to giving rights to any people of color. Both Sabath and Celler saw the anti-Semitism that had afflicted them and their families repeated in the racism and discrimination burdening the Issei.

Celler promised Yates that the *Congressional Record* would reflect that Yates had introduced a bill substantially identical to H.R. 199. Yates understood and, on March 1, 1949, the freshman congressman made his maiden speech on the floor in support of Judd's bill. He began thus:

> Mr. Chairman, I take great pride in supporting this legislation. I believe it will end a wrong against a fine segment of our national community, a wrong which had no foundation in fact at its inception, and which certainly now has no excuse for existence.
>
> I have many Japanese within my district, the parents who are aliens, and their children born in this country who are citizens of the United States. I never knew a more hard-working, thrifty, social-minded group. They contribute generously of their time and money to the charity and welfare drives of the community, and participate in every respect with its best elements. . . .
>
> It is a cynical paradox that these people should be designated aliens. They are Americans. Too long have they carried the unwarranted and discriminating burden of being a people apart from the remainder of the country. Just as they assumed the obligations of citizens by giving their blood, their lives, and their substance to protect our democratic ideals, so, comparably, are they entitled to the benefits which citizenship bestows. They are entitled to take their place in the community; to practice the professions which in many States are now denied to them because of their alien status; to vote, which is the ultimate recognition of citizenship, and to own property, which in many States as aliens they cannot do.[14]

Judd's bill passed the House overwhelmingly but died in the Senate. In the meantime, however, Yates won the admiration of the Chicago Japanese community, as well as the national leadership of the JACL. During this period, Yates and Mike Masaoka, the lobbyist for the JACL, formed a lifelong friendship. Masaoka had served in the 442nd, receiving the Bronze Star, the Legion of Merit, and the Italian Cross for Military Valor.[15] He was described by friends as "cocky, aggressive, bursting with enthusiasm and ideas."[16] Shortly after passage of the naturalization legislation in the House, Masaoka expressed his "heartfelt appreciation" for Yates's efforts. The sentiment was reciprocal; as Yates commented several months later, "Mike wears the Purple Heart, as do most of his Japanese comrades of the 442nd. A grateful country gave him this decoration for the blood he shed for the cause of liberty and freedom. But Mike wants no medals. He wants only that his people shall be accorded the rights of citizens of the land they fought for and which they love." Yates and Masaoka would work together on a series of private bills to prevent the deportation of married Issei women and the breakup of their families.[17]

In an unfortunate twist of political fate, Yates's support of Japanese-American civil rights became entangled with his opposition to the McCarran Act and its successor legislation. In addition to its other anticommunist sections, the act had a provision (Title II) reminiscent of the internment camps, called the Emergency Detention Act. It authorized the president to "apprehend and detain" each person "as to whom there is a reasonable ground to believe that such person probably will engage in acts of espionage or sabotage." It was as though the lessons from Japanese-American internment had left no mark.[18] The JACL applauded Yates's decision to oppose the McCarran Act and to support Truman's veto.

Two years later, however, the Congress passed the McCarran-Walter Immigration and Nationality Act of 1952. The McCarran-Walter Act put Yates in a tight spot. The act abolished the racial restrictions of the Johnson-Reed Act and finally allowed Issei citizenship, which Yates had championed for so long. But Yates thought it was a bad bill, and he had serious reservations about the overall impact of the legislation. "[The bill] endorsed a closed door policy," he wrote, "exhibiting the type of philosophy sponsored by organizations such as the 'Know-Nothings' who achieved a powerful position in public thinking and political life during the 1850's by preaching the superiority of native born Americans over naturalized Americans."[19] Reluctantly, Yates told Masaoka and Wakamatsu of his intention to vote against the bill and to vote to uphold the president's expected veto when the bill passed. "He was very pained with that, I remember," recalled Wakamatsu. This bill, like the previous McCarran legislation, was enacted over the president's veto, but, at long last, the Issei were granted their right to U.S. citizenship. Yates rejoiced in passage of at least that part of the legislation.[20] But his opposition to McCarran-Walter meant that, once again, Yates would have a reelection campaign focused not on issues, but on his patriotism.

As the election of 1952 approached, Yates threw himself into the Draft Adlai Stevenson for President campaign. The popular one-term Illinois governor was the favorite of progressive Democrats, but he resisted running for the nomination, preferring at least publicly to be seeking reelection as governor. Stevenson's allies conveyed his reluctance to party leaders and allies. Truman, having chosen not to seek reelection, offered his endorsement and was alternately annoyed and infuriated that Stevenson refused it, an endorsement that the president felt would be tantamount to the nomination. Senator Paul Douglas was incredulous. Douglas and Stevenson met privately at a friend's cottage in the Indiana Dunes in October 1951 to discuss the nomination, and Douglas went away convinced that Stevenson would not seek the presidency. Likewise, Jake Arvey, now former chairman of the Cook County Democratic Organization, came away disappointed, reporting "I did my best to draw the Governor into the race, then I gave up." Assuming Stevenson was out, Truman encouraged Vice President Alben Barkley to run, while Douglas promised his support to fellow Senator Estes Kefauver, a Democrat from Tennessee, who had become popular with the public for his televised congressional hearings highlighting organized crime in the United States.

The progressives refused to give up, however, and continued to push for a draft. It was a movement without an active candidate, hardly the formula for success in modern U.S. presidential campaigns. In one sense, though, playing the reluctant suitor gave Stevenson an advantage over his rivals. He could avoid the nasty primaries and interparty fighting. It also would be hard to attack him as the candidate of the machine. This plan, if that's what it was, suited Stevenson just fine. He was a patrician who had come from a long lineage of involvement in Illinois politics. Jesse Fell, Stevenson's great-grandfather, had been Lincoln's friend and campaign manager in 1860. The first Adlai Stevenson, Stevenson's grandfather, had been Grover Cleveland's vice president in his second administration and ran as William Jennings Bryan's running mate in 1900.

Journalist and historian David Halberstam wrote that, when Stevenson ran for governor in 1948, he "was bright, funny, and literate, and he seemed incapable of uttering a sentence that did not sound polished." His writing and delivery were described by many commentators as simply "elegant." The governor's admirers thought he was the ideal torchbearer for the legacy of FDR, despite Truman's dramatic drop in popularity over the Korean War and McCarthyism.

Yates, a founding member of the reform-minded Independent Voters of Illinois, joined the Executive Committee of the draft organization, along with his brother-in-law and law partner Marshall Holleb; Leo Lerner, publisher of a local chain of newspapers; and Hubert Will, later a federal judge of great distinction. The campaign was cochaired by Walter Johnson, a University of Chicago history professor, and attorney George Overton. During the Democratic National Convention, held in Chicago's International Amphitheatre, Yates and Holleb occasionally used their law offices for meetings when the group wanted to get away from their hotel headquarters for some privacy to discuss strategy. Few observers gave the draft effort much chance. Yates's campaign manager, Mary Bain, temporarily left her small public relations business to handle publicity for the draft movement. At the convention, Yates, using his floor privileges as a congressman, was the delegate hunter and counter. The "amateurs" proved more skillful than they were given credit for. On the first ballot, Kefauver had the largest number of committed delegates, but Stevenson won the nomination on the third round. It was the last true draft of a candidate by a major party in U.S. history.[21]

Working on the Stevenson draft had been satisfying and exhilarating. But it was time to turn to his own campaign and Yates had good reason to be concerned. His district was a tossup at best, and he had a formidable opponent, Bob Siegrist, a very determined thirty-two-year-old conservative radio news commentator, who had no primary opposition. Siegrist broadcast from WGN, the 50,000-watt clear channel station owned by the *Chicago Tribune*. Siegrist's message matched the *Tribune*'s anticommunist screed, in which liberals like Yates were one small step away from the Kremlin. In 1950, Yates had prevailed, but the continuing drumbeat of Commiecrat charges cut his victory margin by more than half from 1948.

Yates took Siegrist seriously and campaigned vigorously. The incumbent sought to portray Siegrist's conservatism as extremist, outside the mainstream. A speech, called "The Destroyers," made before the JACL in mid-October, was representative of Yates's tactics. He defended his votes on the McCarran Act and its successors and charged that "another group of destroyers who, wrapped in patriotic phrases and disguises, are jeopardizing our constitutional rights." He went on to take direct aim at Siegrist: "He would destroy the fundamental freedoms of every American. He would destroy the right of every American to think and speak freely and to worship God in his way."

Siegrist attracted attention by touring the 9th Congressional District in his "rolling office," called the Bob Siegrist Freedom Mobile. The mobile campaign office attracted thousands of interested constituents to his message. Yates countered with his own sound truck, often accompanied by Paul Douglas, who, as in 1950, campaigned hard for his House colleague. Siegrist was unimpressed, describing the senator and the congressman as "Big Pinko" and "Little Pinko."[22] Generally, Siegrist attacked Yates as a Truman–New Deal liberal who was failing the country in the face of the communist menace. It is not surprising that Yates countered by attacking Siegrist for his isolationism: "Isolationism simply means the abandonment of the rest of the free world to Godless Communism. It would move us closer to war."

Siegrist was clever and knew how to get under Yates's skin. He turned the tables on Yates's civil rights record, daring him to defend Adlai Stevenson's running mate, the racist Alabama senator John Sparkman, chosen to balance the ticket and bring back the Dixiecrats. "[Yates] and his political bedfellows speak loftily about civil rights. . . . Now his party's ticket is offering as Vice President one of the bigoted southern senators who have taken bold pride in sabotaging the civil rights bills brought before congress by Republicans." He impugned Yates's own motives for running. "Make no mistake about it, Yates votes for Yates," Siegrist charged. "My opponent rode in on Truman's coattails four years ago, and will ride out on them next November 4. . . . He's going down the administration's left wing in the hope that President Truman will reward him with a federal judgeship."

The *Tribune* summed the race up in its own inimitable style. It editorialized, "Sidney R. Yates . . . not only votes for all administration measures but seems to believe all of the New and Fair Deal nonsense. . . . All who are in favor of crushing taxes and enlargement of the Washington burocracy [*sic*] should by all means vote for Mr. Yates. . . . Those who want to reduce taxes and halt the march of socialism should vote for Mr. Siegrist."[23]

In spite of the electoral sparks, Yates again narrowly won reelection, carrying four of the five wards in his district and increasing his margin of victory slightly over the previous election. It was still a tossup district, but slowly Yates was making it safe. There was one warning sign, however: Dwight D. Eisenhower carried the 9th Congressional District over Adlai Stevenson.[24]

In 1956, Yates took up a new cause, the burgeoning ownership of switchblade knives by teenagers. It was a surprising issue for Yates. Certainly, it was a serious concern in the city of Chicago where switchblades were considered an increasing menace used by youth gangs. His motivation may have originated from a letter sent to him by Valerie Long, the managing editor of the neighborhood Lerner Home Newspapers, and the publisher of the *Booster*, which frequently ran friendly stories about Yates, with a wide circulation in the district. "The other issue will explain our (switch blade) campaign which, by the way, has already been commended by the mayor, police commissioner, and our local police captains," Long explained in urging Yates to introduce legislation. "The campaign in the Booster was commended over radio and television." Yates responded by telling Long that he "prepared and introduced a bill banning the shipment of switch blade knives in interstate commerce." Yates and the publisher of the newspaper chain, Leo Lerner, were close personal friends. They were members of the Independent Voters of Illinois and had been on the Executive Committee of the Draft Stevenson effort.

Once the congressman decided to support the issue, he devoted his full attention to the effort. Members of the House and Senate lined up to support the
legislation. It made for good political fodder. The newspapers couldn't get enough
of it. In testimony before the Interstate and Foreign Commerce Committee, Yates
was unusually graphic: "Vicious fantasies of omnipotence, idolatry . . . barbaric
and sadistic atrocities, and monstrous violations of accepted values spring from
this cult of the weapon and the switch blade knife is included in this." He went to
add that "newspapers and magazines are filled with descriptions of gang fights,
holdups and stabbings, committed by teenagers, and running through almost all
such stories is the switch blade knife."

With support from Mayor Richard J. Daley, the City Council, and the City
Club of Chicago and with the cosponsorship of fellow Illinois representative
Peter Mack, a member of the critical Commerce Committee, Yates's legislation
went to the House floor. Eisenhower's administration was split. The Justice and
Commerce Departments objected while the Department of Defense endorsed the
legislation. Ironically, the National Rifle Association supported the bill while the
Izaak Walton League of America opposed it. On the floor, Yates did not invoke
the descriptive language he had earlier but, with an attention-getting flourish,
brandished a six-inch switchblade knife he'd secured from the Washington, DC,
Police Department. "The switch blade knife has become the symbol, as well as
the weapon of the teen-age gang," Yates charged. "You can see from the weapon
that I hold in my hand that this is not the type of a knife that we used when we
were boys or that the Boy Scouts now use." The House passed the legislation, the
Senate a month later, and it was signed into law by President Eisenhower. Years
later, that legislation became the prototype for Yates's gun-ban efforts, a crusade
not nearly as successful.[25]

The 1956 presidential election was a repeat of the previous one. Stevenson had
shed his Hamlet-like ambivalence and was again the Democrats' nominee. The
Republicans renominated President Eisenhower without opposition.

By now, Yates was established as a strong supporter of civil rights and he was
chosen to represent the Democrats at the annual convention of the National
Association for the Advancement of Colored People in late June in San Francisco. Representative Hugh Scott of Pennsylvania spoke for the Republicans.
Yates criticized Eisenhower for neglecting African-American civil rights and
for failing to enforce the order of the Supreme Court to integrate public schools.
Scott responded that the Democrats wouldn't do anything for civil rights as long
as southern chairmen could prevent legislation from getting to the floor.[26] The
following year, however, Congress passed the Civil Rights Act of 1957, the first
such legislation since Reconstruction. Even though the law was watered down,
Yates proudly supported it as an important first step.

Yates continued to pursue justice for Japanese Americans throughout his career. He was one of the first representatives of non-Japanese descent to sponsor Japanese redress legislation and legislation to undo the McCarran Act, including the abolishment of the Subversive Activities Control Board and repealing the Emergency Detention Act. His efforts to eliminate funding for the Subversive Activities Control Board failed but, after years of persistence, Congress overwhelmingly agreed to repeal the Emergency Detention Act in 1971. Mike Masaoka, Representative Spark Matsunaga, and Ross Harano expressed their gratitude for his consistent support over the years.[27]

The issue of Japanese redress was more complicated. Originally, Yates introduced legislation to directly confer reparations on internees but he changed his mind, to the consternation of some of his Japanese-American friends, and instead supported the formation of a national commission to hold regional hearings and report back to Congress.[28] Yates agreed with those members who felt it was necessary for the people of the United States to hear about the experiences of the internees before taking up the question of reparations. Few in the United States were even aware that these camps had existed. In 1980, thirty-one years after Yates introduced his first Japanese-American immigration bill, Congress established a bipartisan Commission on Wartime Relocation and Internment of Civilians to "review the facts and circumstances surrounding Executive Order Number 9066," to "review directives of United States military forces requiring relocation, and in some cases, detention in internment camps of American citizens" and to "recommend appropriate remedies." The commission held hearings in ten cities, including Chicago, on September 22, 1981, at Northeastern Illinois University Alumni Hall in Chicago. Ross Harano and the Yates staff helped organize the hearings and the *Chicago Tribune* and *Chicago Sun-Times* devoted extensive coverage and commentary. Jean Mishimi's mother, Kimiye (Doris) Matsumoto, testified about her experiences in the internment camps. Yates submitted a statement in strong support of reparations.

In February 1983, the Commission on Wartime Relocation and Internment of Civilians issued its unanimous report, *Personal Justice Denied*, expressing severe criticism of the government's conduct. "Careful review of the facts by the Commission has not revealed any security or military threat from the West Coast ethnic Japanese in 1942," the commission concluded. "The record does not support the claim that military necessity justified the exclusion of the ethnic Japanese from the West Coast, with the consequent loss of property and personal liberty." After an exhaustive recitation of the losses suffered by the Japanese, the commission, with one member dissenting, recommended the establishment of "a special fund" to provide "personal redress to those who were excluded." Subsequently the Congress, on a strong bipartisan vote, passed the Civil Liberties Act of 1987, signed, after some hesitation, by President Ronald Reagan, whose years as governor of California had sensitized him to the impassioned feelings on both sides of the issue. The act provided for reparations for the former internees. "It's a measure of our maturity as a nation to be able to admit to this (injustice) and provide a remedy," William Hohri commented approvingly for the National Council for Japanese American Redress.[29]

4

"THE JUDGMENT OF ADMIRALS"

Yates felt pretty good about himself after the 1952 election. He had beaten Siegrist despite a voter backlash around the country which allowed the Republicans to retake both Houses of Congress on Eisenhower's coattails. He had won despite the fact that Illinois had rejected its own favorite son Adlai Stevenson in the presidential race and, in the 1950 contest for U.S. senator, had elected former congressman Everett McKinley Dirksen, throwing out Senator Scott Lucas, the majority leader. Yates was also delighted that his friend Barratt O'Hara had swum against the tide, returning to office after his defeat in 1950. And he was particularly pleased to have played a role in getting his friend, Congressman John F. Kennedy of Massachusetts, elected to the Senate.

Yates and Kennedy were part of a small group of young World War II veterans who had been elected to the House in 1946 and 1948 and met regularly to strategize in the daytime and socialize at night. Kennedy asked Yates to use his influence with Jewish voters in his campaign against Senator Henry Cabot Lodge for the upper house. There was a widespread, and for the most part accurate, belief held by Massachusetts Jews that Joseph P. Kennedy, the patriarch of the Kennedy clan, was anti-Semitic and had even been pro-Nazi during the war. Joe Kennedy ranted to Jack's campaign advisers that the Jews were working against his son in the campaign.[1] The Kennedys were deeply concerned that a backlash from those voters could make the slim difference in what was already an uphill race against the three-term Lodge. Yates, along with several other well-known congressional Jews, such as Emanuel Celler of New York and Abraham Ribicoff of Connecticut, made multiple appearances before Jewish organizations and provided the support necessary to cool down the concerns of Jewish voters and bring them to Kennedy. It was natural that Celler and Ribicoff, from states neighboring Massachusetts, would be asked to help. But when Jack Kennedy sought Yates's assistance, it was a sign that the Chicagoan had become a national leader in the Jewish community. Yates was confident that his and the others' work made a difference, providing a large portion of the 70,737 vote margin, out of 2,353,231 votes cast, by which Kennedy defeated Lodge.

On the other hand, Judge Sabath, Yates's mentor and friend, would no longer be there to watch his back and provide counsel. Not because of defeat. Adolph "Judge" Sabath had breezed to reelection with 70 percent of the vote. But just two days after his victory, the eighty-six-year-old dean of the House, his health failing for months, finally succumbed to old age at the Bethesda Naval Hospital. Some critics and historians would evaluate Sabath as a weak Rules Committee chairman, particularly when compared with earlier chairmen, such as Thomas Brackett "Czar" Reed and Joseph Cannon in the late nineteenth and early twentieth centuries, both of whom used the position as a springboard to becoming two of the most powerful Speakers in House history. But neither Reed nor Cannon had had to deal with the racist obstructionism of men like Goober Cox and the other Dixiecrats, who sought to use the Rules Committee to thwart their own party's congressional leaders and their own party's president. Sabath and Rayburn had used the tools available to them to further the progressive agendas of Roosevelt and Truman, while still trying to hold the Democratic Party together. Moreover, Sabath had provided a moral touchstone for Yates and many of the younger members. He told them, "The rich and the strong can take care of themselves. It is the poor and helpless who rely on us and need our help. It is to them that we owe our loyalty."[2] Yates already missed the old Bohemian. He thought the Judge would have enjoyed knowing that Cox had died on Christmas Eve, seven weeks after Sabath, and he smiled at the thought that they might be continuing their halted fist fight in another place.

The 83rd Congress held an additional implication. Yates would be a congressman in the minority party for the first time. Speaker Reed had famously said that the best way to operate the House was to have one party govern and the other party watch. In Reed's opinion, the right of the minority was to draw their salaries and their function was to make a quorum. The new Speaker, moderate Republican Joe Martin of Massachusetts, was no Czar Reed, but Yates had no illusions that the Republicans of 1953 would be any different from the ones Reed led in 1889 when it came to allowing the opposing party to help run the show.

Yates had enjoyed the small perquisites that even junior members of the majority party received. He liked the occasional opportunity to chair one of his subcommittees when Vaughan Gary or Joe Bates was absent, asking the questions that most interested him without worrying about the time consumed. Bates had also appointed Yates to head the delegation of House conferees on the DC appropriations bill and manage the passage of the conference report when it came back to the House.[3] Speaker Rayburn even gave Yates the privilege of chairing the Committee of the Whole House on the State of the Union, the procedural device through which the entire House membership sits as a single committee to debate legislation. Yates described the experience of sitting in the Speaker's chair, presiding over debate, and guiding a bill to final passage, as "thrilling." Moreover, Rayburn told him that he was one of only three second-termers ever to be accorded the honor.[4] But now, as a backbencher in the minority, with little power or influence, there would be few chances to accomplish anything.

On December 29, 1952, Yates was sitting in his downtown Chicago law office at 33 N. LaSalle, where he practiced with his father-in-law and brother-in-law, pondering his next two years in the wilderness. Congress was in recess and, like many congressmen who were lawyers, and as was permitted then, the suite doubled as his 9th District local office. Senator Douglas had written in a personal note to him the previous year that he had included Yates's name on a list of potential nominees for one of several new federal judgeships that had been created for Chicago. Because of some local political infighting among Douglas, Arvey, and Sabath, President Truman never got around to making the appointments before his term ended. Yates had not sought the bench and, in fact, had had no interest in leaving Congress, but now, as he considered his opportunities in the 83rd Congress, he wondered whether he should have been a little more aggressive about switching to the judiciary.

Yates's thoughts were interrupted by the unexpected arrival of Irving Berman, a local lawyer and longtime friend. Berman was in an agitated state. His brother-in-law, naval captain Hyman G. Rickover, was the officer who had envisioned and designed the USS *Nautilus*, the first submarine to be powered by atomic energy, currently being built at Electric Boat's shipyard in Groton, Connecticut. Rickover headed the Nuclear Power Branch of the Bureau of Ships, and had been cited by the secretary of the navy for being responsible "more than any other individual" for the development of the nuclear-powered-ship program. But Rickover had been passed over twice for promotion from captain to rear admiral by the Naval Selection Board, and, as a result and according to regulations, was about to be cashiered from the navy at the age of fifty-two. Berman was blunt about his in-law's personality: "There's no question that the admirals do not like Rickover. He is brusque and argumentative. He shouts, he disputes. He doesn't socialize. His superior officers don't like him because he doesn't bow and scrape to them. . . . All he wants is to get his work done and he fights anyone who gets in his way. But in his line of work, he is a genius, the best in the Navy and the Navy needs him. The fact that the admirals don't like him isn't enough reason to kick a man of his talents out of the Navy."[5]

Berman said that Senator Hubert Humphrey had gone to see President Truman about Rickover but Truman didn't want to get into a fight with the navy just as he was leaving office. "Sid, I hope you can find some way to help him." Yates told Berman he'd try, but had little expectation that he could do anything. Then he began digging in.

By all accounts, Rickover was, as Berman described, stubborn, arrogant, ambitious, and insensitive to the feelings of others. But he also was acknowledged to be a brilliant engineer. Yates never disclosed whether Berman addressed it directly, but it is clear that when he told Yates that "the admirals don't like Rickover," it involved more than the captain's abrasive attitude. It was code for anti-Semitism.

Rickover was a Polish Jew, born in the village of Makow, Poland, in either 1898 or 1900.[6] His father, Abraham, a tailor, left Poland for New York soon after Rickover's birth, planning to establish a business there. Eventually, Abraham sent word to his wife, Ruchal, and their two children, Rickover and his younger sister Fanny, to join him in Chicago, and, in 1904, they settled in Lawndale, known as the "Chicago Jerusalem" for its large Jewish population. Working as a Western Union messenger during high school, he became a frequent visitor of Congressman Sabath, whose district office was in the heart of Lawndale. As Rickover biographers Norman Polmar and Thomas B. Allen described it, "the young hardworking Western Union messenger from Lawndale was introduced to Adolph Sabath as a fellow Jewish immigrant. Thus began a long relationship between Rickover and the 'Jewish Congressmen of Chicago.'"[7] In 1918, Sabath used one of his five allocated slots to nominate Rickover for admission to the United States Naval Academy in Annapolis, Maryland. Rickover easily passed the entrance examination and entered Annapolis on June 29, 1918.[8]

Rickover was one of seventeen Jewish midshipmen in the class of 1922. There is some debate about the extent of anti-Semitism at Annapolis. According to Polmar and Allen, however, "there is no doubt that anti-Semitism was at times strong enough to exile Jewish midshipmen at least to a psychological ghetto and ultimately to Coventry," a situation wherein other midshipmen would refuse to talk to or even acknowledge their existence.[9] One fellow Jewish midshipman, Leonard Kaplan, was a particular target of prejudice. His biographical page and picture in the 1922 *Lucky Bag*, the Annapolis yearbook, was printed on an unnumbered, perforated page, so that it could be easily removed by his non-Jewish comrades in arms. Although Rickover's page did not suffer such a fate, it is clear that he was hazed throughout his Annapolis years as a result of his religion.

Graduating 106th in a class of 509, Rickover was commissioned as an ensign on June 2, 1922. After a succession of sea duty assignments, including duty as engineer and electrical officer of the submarine S-48, and several on-shore educational tours at the Naval Postgraduate School at Annapolis and Columbia

University, where he earned a master of science degree in electrical engineering, Rickover found his interests lay on the engineering rather than the command, or line, side of the navy. In 1937, he requested classification as an engineering duty officer, which would effectively remove him from consideration for command.

Rickover became an expert in the science of ship powering and propulsion, particularly in submarines, where the need to recharge batteries limited the hours in which a submarine could remain submerged. As early as September 1939, the potential of nuclear fission as a means of running submarines was being explored. The Manhattan Project stopped the navy's efforts until the completion of the atom bomb. In 1944, however, development of postwar uses of atomic energy, including nuclear-propelled submarines, was again encouraged.[10] In 1946, Rickover, now a captain, was assigned to Oak Ridge, Tennessee, where a nuclear pile, or reactor, project was being initiated, with both military and industry participation.

By 1949, Captain Rickover had taken over the Nuclear Power Branch of the Bureau of Ships, known as BuShips, and had been appointed to a parallel position as head of nuclear propulsion in the civilian Atomic Energy Commission. In 1950, planning began for the construction of the *Nautilus*, the first nuclear-powered submarine, to be built by Westinghouse and Electric Boat.

In July 1951, Rickover became eligible for review by the Naval Selection Board for promotion to rear admiral. If passed over twice for promotion, a navy captain was subject to compulsory retirement.[11] The deliberations of the board were private and no minutes were kept. When the navy released the promotion list on July 11, 1951, Rickover was not among thirty-two captains raised to rear admiral. Among the reasons informally given to Rickover was that "he could not get along with people."[12] Further, he was "a loner and a nonorganization man. And, to those around him, he seemed to have believed he had got the Navy's payment for that behavior: no promotion."[13]

The next review board would be the following July. On February 9, 1952, Rickover met with President Truman, at Truman's request, to brief him on the status of the *Nautilus*. At Rickover's suggestion, the president was invited to the keel-laying ceremony for the submarine, which Truman gladly accepted.[14] When the invitations went out for the June 14, 1952, event, both naval and civilian allies of Rickover discovered that the navy had not included Rickover on the invitation list. He was finally included on the guest list of Electric Boat. During the ceremony, Chairman Gordon E. Dean of the Atomic Energy Commission stated that if any single person should be honored, "such an honor should go to Captain H. G. Rickover."[15]

On July 7, 1952, Secretary of the Navy Dan A. Kimball issued the following citation to Rickover: "Captain Rickover, more than any other individual, is responsible for the rapid development of the nuclear-powered ship program. His efforts have led to the laying of the keel of the world's first nuclear-powered ship well in advance of its original schedule. . . . Rickover has accomplished the most important piece of development work in the history of the Navy."[16]

One day later, the Naval Selection Board again rejected Rickover for promotion to admiral, apparently ending his career. Under U.S. Navy guidelines, Rickover would be allowed to serve an additional year before being forced to retire. The Naval Selection Board would send its recommendations to the president, who would in turn send them on to the Senate for what would be a pro forma confirmation. On August 4, 1952, *Time* published a story entitled "Brazen Prejudice," strongly implying an anti-Semitic motive in the Selection Board's decision.[17]

Yates knew that if Sabath had not been so ill in 1952, he would have taken up the cause of the man he had appointed to Annapolis so many years earlier. Sabath's death made Yates the only Jew in the Illinois delegation, and one of only ten then in the Congress. Moreover, Yates had been a lieutenant in BuShips during the war. While he had not experienced, or at least had never complained of, anti-Semitism while serving, he knew firsthand both the bureaucracy and the WASP culture of the navy and BuShips. He remembered that FDR had found "the Navy Department as frustrating as any agency in government. 'To change anything in the Navy,' he said, 'is like punching a feather bed. You punch it with your right hand, you punch it with your left hand, until you are exhausted. Then you find the damn bed just as it was when you started.'"[18]

After Berman left, Yates called Mary Bain for advice. He told her that it sounded like an "impossible mission." Should he take it on even if it was probably doomed to failure? Bain thought it was a great idea.[19] Paraphrasing the Daniel O'Connell quotation he had used throughout his campaigns, she told him that helping Rickover was morally right as well as politically right. It was also a great story. Rickover was single-handedly dragging a hidebound navy into the new age of nuclear power, allowing our submarines to travel farther and stay submerged longer than any ships in history. The atom bomb had changed warfare forever. Now that power could be harnessed to defend our country. Yet, instead of honoring Rickover and giving him the authority necessary to complete his mission, a group of admirals, for contemptible reasons, were preparing to fire him. For Yates, this would not be an impossible mission, but a noble crusade, one that would give him a national platform as a champion of our nation's defense as well as a fighter against anti-Semitism and discrimination. She urged him to get started before January 3, when the Republicans would take over Congress.

Fortunately, there was still time. The Senate Armed Services Committee had not finished its work on the Naval Selection Board's recommendations prior to recessing for the election. As a matter of courtesy to President-elect Eisenhower, the committee returned the promotions list to the White House for resubmission to the new Republican-controlled Armed Services Committee, which would be led by Leverett Saltonstall, former governor of Massachusetts and a senator since 1944.[20]

As soon as Yates returned to Washington for the Democratic caucus meetings, he visited Congressman Carl Vinson, a Georgia Democrat and longtime chairman of the House Naval Affairs Committee, now the House Armed Services Committee since the creation of the Department of Defense. A strong supporter of the navy, Vinson was called "the Admiral" by his colleagues and staff. Vinson heard Yates out, then shook his head slowly and drawled, "There's nothing you can do, Sid. Rickover is a good man, but so are the others who were promoted. The Navy can't promote them all." Yates then went to Speaker Rayburn, who was similarly dismissive. "Carl's right. There's nothing you can do."[21]

Yates told Berman that he needed to meet with Rickover, and the captain came in January to Yates's new office in Suite 1740 of the New House Office Building, a slightly better size and location than the rooms he had occupied for the previous two terms. The captain was unsmiling and embarrassed to seek help in this way. "You told my brother-in-law that I should come and see you," he said abruptly. "I am here."[22] He insisted that he not be directly involved in any effort to overrule navy procedure. "While I appreciate what you are trying to do, you must know that I cannot help you. I cannot fight my superior officers." Moreover, he was adamant that Yates make no charges of anti-Semitism on his behalf. First, Rickover argued, there was still a possibility, if small, that he could get his promotion through normal channels without having to tarnish the navy. Second, Rickover said that he truly believed that anti-Semitism played less of a factor than his having fought the admirals on technical aspects of the nuclear-powered ship program. And, finally, he did not want to give Russia any ammunition for propaganda against the United States based on anti-Semitism.[23]

It can be fairly speculated, however, that the real reason Rickover did not want to make his religion the centerpiece of his strategy is that he had spent a good part of his career trying to escape being a Jew. In 1928, Rickover met Ruth Masters during his studies at Columbia University, where she was doing graduate work in international law. Three years later, they were married by an Episcopal priest in Litchfield, Connecticut. From that time forward, Rickover described himself as Episcopalian. Soon after the wedding, he wrote a letter to his parents describing his decision, which led to years of silence and resentment. Rickover tried never to appear Jewish. To Ruth, he was always George. Other intimates and colleagues called him Rick. He signed correspondence "H. G. Rickover." Friends knew never to call him Hyman, the Americanized version of his given Hebrew name Chaim.

But within the navy, Rickover would always be looked at as a Jew. Admiral James L. Holloway Jr., chief of Personnel, referred to Rickover as "a little Jew," even while helping him in his career. Admiral Ruthven E. Libby, commander of the First Fleet and a classmate of Rickover at Annapolis, remarked, "I know Hyman, too. When they circumcised him they threw the wrong end away."[24] The indignities that had started at Annapolis never receded.

Yates didn't like the idea of removing a potent weapon from his efforts, but he appreciated Rickover's sentiments and agreed he would not raise the specter of anti-Semitism on the captain's behalf. Politically, however, he knew that horse had already left the barn. Julius Klein, a retired army brigadier general and former national commander of the Jewish War Veterans (JWV), had been contacting senators about Rickover since fall 1951. Klein, head of a public relations firm in Chicago, was chairman of the JWV's National Defense Committee and a consultant on national defense to the Republican National Committee. Klein's involvement would leave no doubt that the Rickover crusade was also a Jewish one. Klein contacted Yates soon after Berman's visit. Yates was wary. Klein, a Republican, lived in the 9th District only a few blocks from Yates's own home, and they had known each other for years. Yates didn't want to become too close to the general, an open foe of both Harry Truman and Adlai Stevenson. In July 1951, Stevenson deactivated the Illinois National Guard's 109th antiaircraft artillery brigade, housed at Chicago's Broadway armory on the North Side, and commanded by Klein. Klein charged that Stevenson acted because Klein had criticized Truman's firing of General Douglas MacArthur, and because Klein objected when a senior officer refused to allow Klein's troops to fire a salute at a MacArthur celebration in Soldier Field. In response, Klein approached Republican congressman Edgar Jonas, who introduced a resolution calling for an investigation of the deactivation. Yates did not support the resolution, and Bob Siegrist used that refusal as fodder in his 1952 campaign against Yates.[25] Klein was a Taft delegate to the 1952 Republican National Convention and was looking forward to the change in administration and control of the Congress. Klein would praise Yates for his "brilliant speeches" in support of Rickover, but both men realized that this was a strategic alliance only.

Although Rickover refused to participate actively in his case, Rickover's associates displayed no such recalcitrance. Three civil engineers who worked for Rickover at the Atomic Energy Commission—Robert Panoff, Harry Mandil, and Theodore Rockwell—called Yates's office in early January 1953 and were astonished when Yates asked them to come by that afternoon.[26] The three decided not to tell Rickover, calling his secretary to say that they were out running some personal errands. Meeting with Yates, they provided technical information and offered to draft remarks that he could use in his floor speeches. "Rickover is key," they said. "He is the only one able to keep the nuclear submarine project going."

According to Rockwell's recollection of the meeting, Yates was pleased to accept their assistance but told them their efforts needed to be directed to the Senate. While they waited, Yates telephoned Henry "Scoop" Jackson, a Democrat from Washington, who had just moved over from the House to the Senate. As a representative, Jackson had been on the Joint Committee on Atomic Energy, and during a long flight earlier that year to the Pacific to observe nuclear tests, he had sat next to Rickover and had become a supporter and friend. "Scoop," Yates said, "I'm flattered that you still deign to talk with your old friends in the House, now that you are settled in the Other Chamber. Scoop, I have a couple of young men here who are concerned about Captain Rickover's situation . . . and they'd like to talk to you about it." A meeting was set up for the weekend and Yates sent the trio on their way.[27]

Now armed with technical facts and statistics, Yates called upon members of the Senate Armed Services Committee, charged with ratifying the decision of the board upon submission of the promotion list to it by the president, and forwarding the list on to the full Senate for confirmation. The senators were sympathetic but told him "No chance to win."[28] Yates next wrote to President Eisenhower, who, like Truman, replied that he did not believe that a president should intervene in military personnel matters.[29]

Having gone as a supplicant to the Senate and the White House, Yates decided that it was time to make use of the platform afforded to him by the Constitution—the House floor. On January 22, 1953, he sought permission from Speaker Martin to address the House: "Mr. Speaker, we are moving into an atomic age. We are engaged in a desperate race with a deadly enemy for the discovery of secrets of nuclear power, the control of which may well determine our fate and the fate of other free nations. At such a time it is unthinkable that service politics played by a branch of the Armed Forces should be permitted to throw into the discard knowledge which is essential to our well-being. Yet that is exactly what Navy brass proposes to do." Describing the Naval Selection Board's secret deliberations in the rejection of Rickover, Yates charged "only God and the members of the Naval Selection Board" knew why Rickover had been passed over. . . . [R]ank discrimination must have been present, for six officers in the engineering branch junior to Rickover received promotions to rear admiral." Attaching the *Time* article "Brazen Prejudice," he called on the Senate Armed Services Committee to investigate.[30]

The speech attracted some attention. Lloyd Norman of the *Chicago Tribune* called for additional comments. He also wished Yates belated congratulations on his reelection, but said that, because of the editorial position taken by his paper during the campaign, those congratulations needed to be unofficial.[31] Yates also wrote a newsletter to his constituents describing his speech but knew that he needed a broader audience. On February 9, 1953, he requested permission to make a thirty-minute address to the House the following week. That same day, Irv Berman wrote Yates that "I received a communication from the Captain advising me that 'the Navy is *absolutely determined* not to promote him and will resist it by every means.' He would like to speak with you and suggests that you call him when you have some free time." Yates responded the following day, February 10, that "As it happens, I called the Captain yesterday and am seeing him today."[32]

Consulting with Bain, he prepared and distributed a press release, with an embargo request for release after delivery of his speech, scheduled for Thursday, February 12. The release contained excerpts of the remarks he intended to make. Refining his previous address, he included a variation of the line he had used the prior month, "Only God and the nine admirals on the board" knew why Rickover was rejected, and added a new one. Rickover's rebuff was due either "to an admiral's stepped on toe with a long memory," or to "convoy mentality," wherein the speed of all the vessels in a convoy was restricted to that of the slowest vessel. "Apparently the admirals have transferred that rule of the convoy to the field of officer selection. . . . They demand uniformity of thinking. They want a Navy of yesmen. Rickover is not like that."[33]

Yates received permission to extend his remarks on February 12 to sixty minutes. He cited the opinions of scientists, military officials, and members of Congress extolling the work of Rickover. He inserted analyses from the *New York Times*, the *Christian Science Monitor*, and even *Life*, which wrote that Rickover "may be destined to go down in naval history as the man who exerted as much influence on naval shipbuilding as Robert Fulton," the inventor of the steamboat. Mocking the secrecy of the Naval Selection Board, Yates charged, "for all that we know—for all that even the Commander-in-Chief of the Navy, the President of the United States knows, the standards for promotion employed by the selection board may be those recommended by Admiral Joseph Porter in Gilbert and Sullivan's 'Pinafore' when he sings

> I cleaned the windows and I scrubbed the floor
> And I polished up the handle on the big front door
> I polished up that handle so carefulee
> That now I am the ruler of the Queen's Navee."

Yates called for a full overhaul of the officer selection process, adding civilian scientists and engineers to the Selection Board, ensuring that at least three of the admirals on the board were engineering admirals, and making a civilian, the assistant secretary of the navy, chairman of the board. To end the secrecy of the board, he demanded stenographic reports to be made of proceedings and sent to the president, the secretary of defense, the secretary of the navy, and the Senate Armed Services Committee chairman. Finally he asserted the right of the secretaries of the navy and defense to recommend officers not selected by the board.

Fellow Illinois congressman Mel Price, who, as a member of the Joint Committee on Atomic Energy, knew Rickover's achievements, added his support. "By passing over Captain Rickover we are further destroying morale within the Navy for these specialist assignments." Herman Eberharter, Democrat from Pennsylvania and another member of the Joint Committee, seconded his remarks. Minority Leader John McCormack also joined in, questioning the impartiality of selection boards in general. "If they can give a break to someone who is a friend of theirs, can they not give somebody else a bad break sometimes?" "That is correct," Yates responded. Only Republican William Cole of New York, chairman of the Joint Committee, expressed reservations. "While I deplore the fact that Captain Rickover was not selected for the rank of admiral, if for no other reason than for the great work he has done, I do not think the fault lies necessarily with the system of selection."

This time, Yates's speech, aided by the press release, drew national attention, receiving lengthy write-ups in the *New York Times*, the *Washington Post*, and the *Boston Globe*, among others. As the *New York Times* reported, "The Navy's system of promotion for the higher grades was attacked today by Representative Sidney R. Yates, Democrat of Illinois, as antiquated, unfair and a product of 'convoy mentality.' . . . [Yates] declared that there had been an effort to 'hush up' Captain Rickover's retirement because 'it is a case in which the admirals disposed of a naval officer who wouldn't conform.'"[34] The *Washington Times-Herald* headlined "Yates Blasts Navy Again on Capt. Rickover." A leading columnist, Bob Considine, wrote, "The Navy's upper brass has never looked worse than during its deplorable treatment of Capt. H. G. Rickover."[35]

General Klein and other officers of the JWV praised Yates for his speech, urging him to charge anti-Semitism, but Yates demurred.[36] Meanwhile, Rickover, his protestations of uninvolvement notwithstanding, quietly permitted Rockwell, Mandil, and Panoff to continue their efforts to provide Yates and others with information, while making sure that he had deniability if they were questioned. Klein continued to pursue his Republican connections on the Armed Services Committee, particularly focusing on Chairman Saltonstall and pointing to the reaction to Yates's speeches.

Yates continued his efforts, leading one of Rickover's biographers, Clay Blair Jr., to describe them as "an all out attack on the Navy."[37] On February 18, 1953, Yates provided further evidence that the navy was attempting to "hush" unflattering stories on its actions concerning Rickover in *Time* and the *Washington Post*.

He noted that President Eisenhower had not yet re-sent the Selection Board's recommendations to the Senate and revealed that Saltonstall, in response to a letter from Yates requesting that the committee withhold confirming the July 1952 recommendations, promised that the committee would specifically address Rickover's promotion when the list was sent to them for confirmation.[38] Saltonstall publicly announced that he would hold up all thirty-nine captains recommended for promotion until the committee's investigation was finished.[39]

A week later, retired major general Verne D. Mudge, staff director of the Senate Armed Services Committee, called Yates at Saltonstall's request to invite him to attend, and if he wished, to testify at an Armed Services Committee hearing on the Rickover case scheduled for March 5. Yates eagerly accepted. Yates met with Mandil, Panoff, and Rockwell, and together they agreed that Yates should give one more floor speech before his testimony, summarizing what had gone before and putting Rickover and the nuclear program in the larger context of U.S. defense strategy. Yates reserved ninety minutes of floor time for March 2. Panoff prepared the documents from which Yates would quote in his remarks. Once the speech was ready, Yates again prepared and distributed a press release embargoed until after delivery. Copies were sent and follow-up calls were made not only to reporters at the *Chicago Sun-Times*, *Chicago Daily News*, and *Chicago Tribune*, but, in recognition of the national attention Yates was getting, to the *New York Times*, the *Washington Post*, the *Christian Science Monitor*, *Time* and *Life*, the wire services and to influential columnists such as Stewart Alsop.[40] On March 2, joined again by Mel Price, and with the support of Democratic representatives Louis Heller of New York, who was one of the Jewish members, Cleveland Bailey of West Virginia, and Overton Brooks of Louisiana, a member of the House Armed Services Committee, Yates made his final case for Rickover. The chambers were only half full, but the press gallery was packed. He decried the deliberate failure of navy admirals to credit Rickover for his work in the conception and development of the atomic submarine, in contrast to the praise given him by the secretary of the navy. He declared "laughable" the navy's suggestion that Rickover retire and then be rehired by the navy as a civilian consultant. "This offer is the usual smoke screen laid down by the admirals as they beat a hasty retreat from an obvious and colossal blunder. In one breath they said that Rickover doesn't merit promotion and we can get along very well without his services. In the next breath, they say that his talents are so vital to the success of the atomic project that they urge him to retire and come back on active duty." He criticized the secrecy of the Naval Selection Board. "Today there is no protection under the law and regulations for officers who are eligible and not promoted. The Rickover case is only one example of flagrant errors that must have happened in many other instances, but nobody knows about them or takes the trouble to investigate." To prevent future wrongs, Yates stated that he had introduced a bill containing the reforms in Naval Selection Board membership and transparency that he had described in his earlier speeches.[41]

On March 5, 1953, Yates testified for the first time in front of a Senate committee. Unlike many congressional hearings, where only a few members attend, twelve of the fifteen senators on the committee were present. For more than an hour, in a methodical, lawyerly manner, Yates laid out the Rickover case, drawing on the technical facts prepared by Mandil, Panoff, and Rockwell, and repeating many of the statements and "money quotes" he had made in his House speeches. "The judgment of admirals," he concluded, "is not infallible merely because they are admirals."[42]

Scoop Jackson also testified. He had previously urged Rickover to meet informally with some of the committee members, but the captain refused. Jackson made the case in his absence. "I am sure that it is the drive, the energy and leadership of Captain Rickover" that put the nuclear submarine program so close to fruition. "If Captain Rickover hadn't stuck his neck out, we wouldn't have this program, and I can cite chapter and verse over a long, long period of time in that connection."[43]

One day after the hearing, on March 6, 1953, Secretary of the Navy Robert B. Anderson wrote Saltonstall to advise that he was calling for the convening of two special selection boards. The first, to be convened immediately, was to "recommend engineering duty captains for retention on active duty for a period of one year with the requirement that one of those recommended for retention be experienced and qualified in the field of atomic propulsive machinery for ships." The second, to be convened in July 1953, required that the board select for promotion to rear admiral "one engineering duty captain experienced and qualified in the field of atomic propulsive machinery for ships."[44]

Saltonstall released the Anderson letter on March 9, 1953. John Harris of the *Boston Globe* called Yates to see whether he had a statement. It was evident to the press corps, he said, that the slots described could be filled only by Rickover. "The consensus seems to be that the Navy has thrown in the sponge."[45] Yates agreed. The first of the naval selection boards convened on March 10 and a week later confirmed Captain Rickover's retention, thus revoking the automatic retirement it had forced on him. Senator John Stennis of Mississippi, a member of the Armed Services Committee, wrote Yates "to congratulate you most heartily on your splendid presentation of the Rickover matter to our Committee . . . and on the results obtained."[46]

While Yates waited for the July board to meet, allegations of anti-Semitism continued to simmer below the surface. Eisenhower was warned that if the Rickover matter were not resolved, it could become another Dreyfus affair, the famous example of political anti-Semitic persecution in France,[47] although many others, including Senator Richard Russell, said it more closely resembled that of Billy

Mitchell, the World War I general court-martialed for being too outspoken about the need for military aviation.[48] Yates received a message from Milt Freedman, a reporter from the Jewish Telegraphic Agency, calling from the House press gallery. Freedman said that when Adlai Stevenson was working for Secretary of the Navy Frank Knox in 1942, Stevenson discovered that the Naval Selection Board was not recommending Jews for promotion from captain to admiral, and in fact enforced a quota of Jewish officers. According to Freedman, Stevenson turned the information over to the Anti-Defamation League.[49]

On March 16, 1953, the *Cleveland Plain Dealer* editorialized that "the real haggle is the fact that Rickover is Jewish. . . . [I]t is time to cut out such nonsense."[50] Will Maslow, director of the Commission on Law and Social Action of the American Jewish Congress, sent Yates a copy of the editorial, asking "whether you think [the AJC] ought to keep quiet." Yates wrote back, stating, "a number of organizations addressed the same question. After conferring with Rickover, I respected his belief that the charge of anti-Semitism should not be raised."[51]

The second selection board met in mid-July and on July 24, 1953, announced that Rickover was among the captains recommended for promotion to rear admiral. On July 30, President Eisenhower formally nominated Rickover and included him on a list of nominations sent to the Senate, which confirmed his nomination on August 3.[52]

On April 20, 1956, Yates saw the fruit of his labors when he, along with twelve other congressmen, boarded the *Nautilus* for a day-long undersea cruise. Yates, as a navy veteran, was offered the opportunity to take the controls, steering the submarine and operating the diving rudders. "For me, the occasion had special meaning. I saw the Nautilus as the symbol of a man's dedication and devotion to a dream—a dream of harnessing the atom for the United States Navy—of utilizing it in the cause of peace, as well as war. It was a dream which came true for Admiral Rickover only after he had overcome almost insuperable obstacles."[53] Rickover was less prosaic. "The nuclear reactor is a device for splitting atoms. As the atoms split, they strike against other atoms. The friction produces tremendous heat which boils the surrounding water and converts it into steam to drive the steam turbines and the submarine's propellers. That's all there is to it."[54]

Yates and Rickover corresponded frequently over the years. Yates assisted when possible in Rickover's subsequent promotions to vice admiral in 1964 and full admiral in 1973. The navy tried several times to force Rickover to accept mandatory retirement, but presidents from Johnson to Carter, with bipartisan support from Congress, extended the admiral's active duty status.[55] Yates discussed Rickover in eleven of his constituent newsletters, sometimes devoting the whole newsletter to him, including a final letter following Rickover's death on July 8, 1986. In deference to Rickover's wishes, he never openly referenced anti-Semitism. In later years, Yates would use the Rickover battle as an example of fighting for justice and applied it to discussions of the recalcitrance of other branches of the armed services.[56] He devoted a newsletter to Rickover's call for better education programs in engineering, science, and mathematics, calling the gap between the education programs of the United States and the Soviet Union "American's Achilles' Heel," and foreshadowing the National Defense Education Act and other education programs that would follow the launching of Sputnik and the fear of Soviet supremacy in the sciences.[57] He expressed his outrage, and that of his colleagues, at the disclosure that Admiral Rickover had not been invited to a White House ceremony celebrating the *Nautilus*'s successful submerged crossing of the North Pole in August 1953.[58]

Rickover would write or telegraph Yates from each of the dozens of nuclear-propelled attack submarines, strategic missile submarines, missile cruisers, and aircraft carriers commissioned during the admiral's tenure as head of the nuclear navy. Many were perfunctory typed letters addressed to "Congressman Yates," and clearly prepared for general distribution to important members of Congress. But Yates treasured the handwritten note, marked "Personal" received from Rickover and dated January 24, 1955: "I have just returned from the first surface and underwater trials of the Nautilus. The ship has been at sea for six days, and all on board consider her performance to be outstanding. My real purpose in writing is to thank you for what you did when the road was rough. Many people and organizations are responsible for what has been accomplished. However, you deserve my special gratitude for what you did; you gave help when help was needed. In this way you contributed to the success of the Nautilus just as significantly as those who were more directly concerned with the design and building of the ship. With many thanks, Sincerely, H. G. Rickover, Rear Admiral, U.S.N."[59]

Yates would later describe the Rickover victory as his greatest accomplishment in Congress. Clay Blair wrote that Yates, more than anyone else, "can take credit for saving Adm. Rickover and his atomic program."[60] It had also given him national exposure as a congressman who had taken on the navy and won. His position as a national Jewish leader solidified. And he was a hero at home. The *Booster*, always his most ardent newspaper champion, splashed the headline "YATES WINS BATTLE; NAVY UPS RICKOVER!"[61]

The year that Yates had dreaded as a minority party congressman had instead turned into an adrenaline-charged triumph with unbounded prospects. Morris R. DeWoskin, a prominent Chicago hotel owner and operator, wrote to congratulate Yates on his victory: "I think that the successful fight puts you in line for the candidacy for Senator from the State of Illinois." Yates quickly wrote back. "I haven't thought about the Senate, but now that you mention it, when do we start?"[62]

Sidney Yates, junior, is regular forward on the

Yates, in his junior year on the 1930 University of Chicago basketball team, was named an honorable All-American as a guard. (Special Collections Research Center, University of Chicago Library)

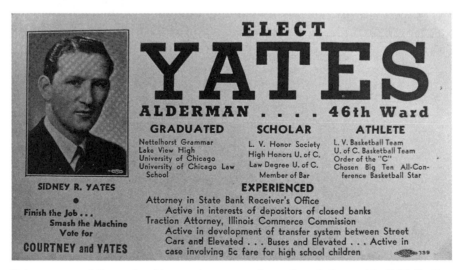

ELECT

YATES

ALDERMAN . . . . 46th Ward

GRADUATED
Nettelhorst Grammar
Lake View High
University of Chicago
University of Chicago Law
School

SCHOLAR
L. V. Honor Society
High Honors U. of C.
Law Degree U. of C.
Member of Bar

ATHLETE
L. V. Basketball Team
U. of C. Basketball Team
Order of the "C"
Chosen Big Ten All-Conference Basketball Star

EXPERIENCED
Attorney in State Bank Receiver's Office
Active in interests of depositors of closed banks
Traction Attorney, Illinois Commerce Commission
Active in development of transfer system between Street
Cars and Elevated . . . Buses and Elevated . . . Active in
case involving 5c fare for high school children

SIDNEY R. YATES

•

Finish the Job . . .
Smash the Machine
Vote for

COURTNEY and YATES

Yates unsuccessfully ran for alderman in 1939, vowing to "smash the machine." (Collection of Debra Yates)

Mary Bain, following appointment as Illinois state administrator of the National Youth Administration (1940), was at twenty-eight the youngest woman state director. (ACME photo. Collection of the authors.)

Yates joined the navy in 1943, serving as a lieutenant in the Bureau of Ships in Washington, DC. (Sidney R. Yates Papers, Chicago History Museum)

An early official photograph of Yates, taken soon after his 1949 swearing-in. (Abraham Lincoln Presidential Library and Museum. Collection of the authors)

Yates at a 1950 charity golf tournament with film star Danny Kaye (center) and radio and television host Arthur Godfrey. Yates shot a 76, winning the Official Washington Division. (Sidney R. Yates Papers, Chicago History Museum)

Congressman Adolph J. Sabath was first elected in 1906 and served until his death in 1952. He was Admiral Rickover's sponsor to Annapolis and Yates's mentor in Congress. (Abraham Lincoln Presidential Library and Museum. Collection of the authors)

Undated picture, c. 1950. Comedian Bob Hope called Yates his "favorite congressman." Yates's brother Charlie was Hope's first agent from his vaudeville days. (Sidney R. Yates Papers, Chicago History Museum)

Yates accompanies then-governor Adlai Stevenson on congressional visits in 1952. Yates would help lead the Draft Stevenson for President campaign later that summer. (Associated Press photo. Collection of the authors)

Yates participated in an undersea cruise of the USS *Nautilus* in 1956. The success of the nuclear navy was in large part due to Yates's battle for Admiral Rickover. (Official United States Navy photograph. Collection of the authors)

Yates successfully led a two-year crusade for a law banning the sale of switchblade knives in interstate commerce. He brandished the knives on the House floor in 1958. (United Press telephoto. Collection of the authors)

Campaigning for reelection in 1958 with Senator Paul Douglas (far left) and Adlai Stevenson (near left). Stevenson and Douglas would remain Yates's most loyal allies. (Pauer, *Chicago Sun-Times*. Collection of the authors)

1958 Reelection victory party with Mary Bain (right) and Addie Yates. (William Knefel, *Chicago Sun-Times*. Collection of the authors)

Conferring with Senator Paul Douglas as Representative Thomas O'Brien looks on, Yates testified before the Senate Public Works Committee in support of a 1959 bill allowing Chicago to divert more water from Lake Michigan. (Sidney R. Yates Papers, Chicago History Museum)

Vice President Johnson with Senators Mike Mansfield (left) and Everett Dirksen, the Senate Democratic and Republican leaders. LBJ and Mansfield worked behind the scenes and sometimes openly to help Dirksen defeat Yates for Senator. (UPI telephoto. Collection of the authors.)

Yates in deep thought as he begins his campaign for senator. (UPI photo. Collection of the authors)

Yates with President Kennedy on Air Force One in 1962. Yates assumed that JFK would actively support his Senate race. (Sidney R. Yates Papers, Chicago History Museum)

President Kennedy's preference of Dirksen over Yates was common knowledge throughout the state as this editorial cartoon by Les Immer for the *Peoria Journal Star* demonstrates. (Sidney R. Yates Papers, Chicago History Museum)

The Senate race gave Yates the opportunity to travel the state. Here he meets with a farmer in downstate Illinois. (Sidney R. Yates Papers, Chicago History Museum)

Yates was a longtime supporter of organized labor and received their support during the Senate race. (Sidney R. Yates Papers, Chicago History Museum)

Yates seeks votes from sunbathers at Oak Street Beach on Labor Day weekend, 1962. (Larry Nocerino, *Chicago Sun-Times*. Collection of the authors)

President Johnson with Mayor Richard J. Daley at a Cook County Democratic fundraiser. Daley and Paul Douglas told LBJ he was unwelcome unless he made a strong speech for Yates over Dirksen. (Item RJD_04_01_0048_0015_009, Richard J. Daley Collection, University of Illinois at Chicago Library, Special Collections and University Archives)

A family portrait at son Stephen's wedding, with Addie, Steve, and new bride Debra, 1973. (Sidney R. Yates Papers, Chicago History Museum)

Yates and Gerald Ford were freshman congressmen together, and President Ford regularly sought Yates's views on Middle East matters. (Courtesy Gerald R. Ford Presidential Library)

As President Jimmy Carter sought to bring peace to the Middle East, he frequently invited Yates, now the senior Jewish member of Congress, to the White House. Carter wrote in his diary that "everyone trusts [Yates]." (Courtesy Jimmy Carter Presidential Library)

Yates worked closely with African American Members of Congress to defuse black-Jewish tensions. Here he meets with fellow Chicago congressman (and later mayor) Harold Washington. (Sidney R. Yates Papers, Chicago History Museum)

Yates loved to tell stories about taking his guitar to campaign stops in 1948. Here, in a 1981 snapshot in his office, he sings some of the old songs. (Collection of Donald and Judith Fisher)

Yates's formal photograph, used in his final few terms of office. (Collection of the authors)

President Bill Clinton awards the Presidential Citizens Medal to Yates for his work on behalf of the arts and humanities. Yates chided Clinton for not being sufficiently liberal. (White House photo. Collection of the authors)

At the time of her retirement in 1999, Mary Bain was the last remaining New Dealer still in the federal government. (Courtesy of Chuck Kennedy. Collection of the authors)

PART II

DEFEAT AND COMEBACK
1962–74

5

YATES FOR SENATE

September 21, 1960. It had been a very good week for Yates. First, he had just won (for the seventh time in the last twenty years, as he reminded everyone who congratulated him) the golf championship at his home course at the Bryn Mawr Country Club in Lincolnwood, Illinois.

Second, the *Chicago Tribune*, whose editorial page was no friend of Yates, had reported favorably on a speech he had made earlier in the week at the Sheraton-Blackstone Hotel in support of John F. Kennedy's presidential campaign. His remarks had followed appearances on the same stage by Kennedy's two sisters-in-law, Ethel and Joan, the wives of Bobby and Ted, respectively. The women had assured him they would report back to JFK on how he had attacked the Eisenhower-Nixon administration for its "anti-intellectualism," calling for a renewed appreciation of "the value of the person with the mind," meaning, of course, the senator from Massachusetts.[1]

Yates was doing a lot of campaigning for Kennedy. Next week, he was scheduled to speak at the Sheraton Towers to the annual leadership training session of the Conference of Jewish Women's Organizations, which represented three hundred separate groups. His Republican colleague from Evanston, Congresswoman Marguerite Stitt Church, also would be speaking, but Yates was not worried about being shown up. Marguerite, who had taken over her husband Ralph's seat after his death ten years earlier, had turned down a spot on Appropriations to serve on the Foreign Affairs Committee. She had famously said, when criticized by the State Department that her overseas travels were no place for a lady, "I'm no lady, I'm a Member of Congress."[2] But she had no taste for the political warfare that Yates was planning to launch against Richard Nixon, and he knew that his more political remarks, would be the ones remembered. Illinois, which had spurned its favorite son, Democrat Adlai Stevenson, in both the 1952 and 1956 presidential elections in favor of General Eisenhower, was going to be a battleground in 1960. Yates wanted to make sure that Kennedy won the state and also wanted to be sure the Kennedys knew how much he had assisted in getting it done.

Best of all, he had just received word that Prince Preston, the racist and segregationist congressman from Bulloch County, Georgia, had finally conceded defeat in last week's Democratic primary for Georgia's 1st Congressional District.[3]

Preston's defeat, while it meant one fewer racist in the House, was not going to bring civil rights into the South. In fact, at that same primary election, the Georgia Democrats had passed a nonbinding referendum permitting its delegates to the Electoral College to refuse to vote for Kennedy, sending a signal that the deep South was not going to go along with the liberal leanings of the Bay Stater.[4] But Preston's loss meant that Yates would finally get an Appropriations Subcommittee chairmanship.

Since Reconstruction, the seniority system had ruled without exception in the House of Representatives. But unlike other committees, Appropriations ranked seniority on the basis of the time served on the subcommittee, rather than the member's seniority on the full committee. The rule testified to the power wielded by Appropriations Subcommittee chairmen, equivalent to that of full committees for other matters. Preston had been chairman of the Appropriations Subcommittee for the Department of Commerce for the past six years. And although two subcommittee members were senior to Yates on Commerce, Albert Thomas of Texas and John J. Rooney of New York, each of them already had a subcommittee that they chaired. Under the Rules of the Appropriations Committee—and assuming, of course, that Yates was reelected and the Democrats retained their majority after the 1960 general election—Yates would take over Commerce as soon as the new Congress was organized in January 1961.

But Yates had not counted on the hostility, and long memory, of the Appropriations Committee chairman, Clarence Cannon, who, even after all these years, still harbored resentment against Yates.

Everything about the Illinois congressman aggravated Cannon. He didn't like Yates's inclination to support government programs, particularly foreign aid. Vindictively, he took Yates off the subcommittee that was funding the restoration of postwar Europe because Yates supported the Marshall Plan and Cannon didn't. He refused to put Yates back on the subcommittee even after Speaker Sam Rayburn tried to intervene.[5] Cannon was furious that Yates had even tried to get the Speaker to usurp Cannon's prerogative as chairman to allocate subcommittee membership.

And that would not be the last time Cannon believed that Yates was challenging his authority. While Yates was serving under Albert Thomas on the Independent

Offices Subcommittee, Cannon tried to remove some of the subcommittee's jurisdiction. Thomas complained and demanded a vote of the full committee membership. Yates voted with his subcommittee chairman, Thomas, rather than with
Cannon. Yates saw Cannon's expression when he cast his vote. Their relationship, never warm, turned ice cold.[6] Thomas, however, appreciated the gesture
and would reward Yates with earmarks designating specific appropriations on
legislation, including a new federal building in Chicago.[7]

And finally, Yates committed what for Cannon was the cardinal sin of filing a
dissenting report on an Appropriations bill. Cannon was outraged: "I told [my
committee members] we should have a united front. If there are any objections or
charges, we ought to hear it now, and not wash our dirty linen out on the floor. If
we don't have a bill that we can all agree on and support, we ought not to report
it out. To do that is like throwing a piece of meat to a bunch of hungry animals."
But even though the issue involved the matter of funding a nuclear reactor for
military aircraft, an issue Yates had become expert on through his work on behalf
of Admiral Rickover, Yates had indeed "washed the dirty linen," not only in full
committee, but in front of the entire House. Yates knew he had crossed a line, but
he was tired of having his expertise ignored, and his frustration won out. When
asked about his relationship with the chairman, he replied, "Oh, he's polite and
smiles at me, but when I ask for things, I don't get them."[8]

But Yates could not imagine that Cannon would violate the sacred seniority
rules of the Appropriations Committee. Any qualms he might have had about
the chairman were put aside as he spent the rest of the fall campaigning for Kennedy, and for his own reelection. His opponent that year was Republican Chester
Emanuelson, a former assistant U.S. attorney for the Northern District of Illinois
and the regional counsel for the Small Business Administration. Yates trounced
Emanuelson with more than 60 percent of the vote.[9] Kennedy, of course, as has
become legendary, won Illinois, and ultimately the election, by only 9,000 votes,
some of which were suspiciously part of a sudden influx of late-reported votes
from Cook County. Nevertheless, JFK was in, and Yates eagerly prepared to return
to Washington to support the president-elect's domestic agenda. As chairman of
Commerce appropriations, Yates would be the gatekeeper of a large slice of the
new administration's budget requests. Even more, as one of the cardinals, Yates's
influence would extend to all aspects of Kennedy's agenda, and his opinion would
be sought on foreign as well as domestic matters.

Clarence Cannon had other plans. When the Democratic caucus met to organize the committees for the new Congress, the Commerce Appropriations Subcommittee had suddenly vanished. Cannon had eliminated the subcommittee
and merged it with the Subcommittee on General Government Matters, chaired
by George W. Andrews of Alabama, another unreconstructed conservative and

segregationist. Andrews and Yates could not have been more different. Andrews, in fact, would become famous in 1962 for his response to the Supreme Court's decision, in *Engel v. Vitale* (1962), to ban state-sponsored prayer in schools: "They put the Negroes in the schools," he complained, "and now they've driven God out."[10]

Yates was now the third ranking Democrat on the newly named Subcommittee on Commerce and General Government Affairs, with a subcommittee chairman he detested. To make the humiliating lesson even more evident, Andrews was given a second subcommittee to chair, the Special Subcommittee on Permanent Appropriations. It was clear to Yates that his career in the House had hit a wall.

Yates was frustrated and restless, even resentful, throughout the 87th Congress. He wondered whether he still had a future in the House. Now fifty-two and completing his seventh term without a chairmanship, he would have to decide whether to stay in his comfortable seat or take a chance on moving to the most exclusive club in the world—the U.S. Senate—as the Democratic Party decided who should take on the incumbent Republican senator, Minority Leader Everett Dirksen. Yates decided he wanted the job.

Yates was clear-eyed about his chances for nomination, as he and his campaign manager, Mary Bain, sent out feelers among his political and financial supporters from past campaigns. He particularly sought out the support of the network of liberals he had cultivated from the University of Chicago and from his days as a leader of the group that had first drafted Adlai Stevenson for president in 1952. And, of course, he spoke to his old mentor, Jake Arvey, still influential, but no longer preeminent. From Arvey, Yates was disappointed but not surprised to learn that he was not first on the nomination wish list of the Illinois Democratic Party's power brokers. In an early poll of newspaper editors in the state, Yates wasn't even included among the potential Democratic nominees.[11]

Back home in Chicago, Yates had established a satisfactory, if not warm, relationship with Mayor Richard J. Daley, Arvey's successor as the city's dominant politician. "The Boss" and Yates had an arrangement. As long as Yates brought home the bacon, and didn't stick his nose too much in ward politics, Daley didn't interfere with Yates or his social-issue politics in Washington.

But Mayor Daley's Senate choice was Paul Powell, Speaker of the Illinois House.[12] Powell had beaten Daley's candidate for Speaker, Joseph De La Cour, just a year before. Daley would be glad to get Powell out of the state capital and put his own man back in. But Powell decided his political future lay in Springfield, not Washington. Five years later, Powell would be elected Illinois secretary of state and die of a heart attack five years later than that. Powell would be the source of posthumous scandal ten years after he died.[13]

Adding to Yates's problems, Senator Paul Douglas felt the party's candidate needed to be a downstater, both for regional balance and to contest Dirksen on his home turf in central and southern Illinois. Douglas also argued that a nationally known challenger was required to counteract the national support that Dirksen would surely get from Republican colleagues in the Senate.[14] Yates, who had counted his fellow Chicagoan Douglas a close friend and ally, was deeply hurt.

Douglas let it be known that Adlai Stevenson, now serving as Kennedy's ambassador to the United Nations with cabinet rank, was his top choice. Daley was agreeable. Stevenson had saved Daley's career from extinction years earlier when, as governor, Stevenson appointed Daley his state director of revenue. Pollster Lou Harris confirmed Douglas's and Daley's thinking in December 1961: "The results show clearly that as of this time, Stevenson is the strongest Democrat and the only one within striking distance of achieving victory." But Daley suspected that Stevenson, having run three times for president, receiving the nomination twice, would not want the job, and he quickly tried to confirm Stevenson's interest, urging him to run. Both he and Arvey said they would support the ambassador.[15]

Stevenson was coy. His longtime friend and biographer, Porter McKeever, later revealed that Stevenson never seriously considered running for the Senate and, indeed, had previously written that his "tastes" were "executive, administrative and creative—not legislative or representational." But Stevenson realized he could use the possibility of his departure from the administration as a lever to bolster his standing with Kennedy. A few well-placed remarks to columnist Max Frankel in the *New York Times* led to a column implying a lack of respect by the Kennedys and their inner circle for Stevenson and, by association, for the liberal wing of the Democratic Party.

President Kennedy was hooked. He made strident public efforts to keep Stevenson in the New Frontier. "I told [Adlai] we needed him at the UN and that I counted on him to stay on," Kennedy explained to an aide. With an alacrity previously unseen in the notoriously indecisive Stevenson, which must have both surprised the president and made him suspect that he had been played as well, Stevenson agreed to remain at the UN.[16]

Front-runners Powell and Stevenson out of the way, Yates redoubled his efforts to woo Stevenson supporters and the rest of the liberal wing of the party. But Douglas continued to argue for a downstater and, in what Yates took as deliberate offense, turned his attention to a trio of possible candidates, all of whom were more favorable to him than the North Side congressman: Paul Simon, the downstate owner of a series of newspapers and a state legislator; Irving Dillard, former editor of the *St. Louis Post-Dispatch*; and Congressman Mel Price, whose congressional district encompassed the downstate Democratic stronghold of East St. Louis.

Simon, thirty-two years old, took the speculation seriously enough that he initiated a campaign committee and made no secret of his interest in the nomination.[17] Dillard and Price, although flattered by Douglas's attention, decided to stay where they were. Speculation continued for still more candidates. Representative Peter Mack Jr., a Democrat from Carlinsville, near East St. Louis, was eyed as a possible candidate inasmuch as it appeared he might lose his current seat through redistricting. There even was a brief suggestion that Sargent Shriver, director of the Peace Corps and a brother-in-law of the president, might be interested in the race. Shriver had a legitimate claim to represent Illinois. After his military service in World War II, he had been sent by Joseph P. Kennedy to Chicago to run the Kennedy-owned Merchandise Mart, and, after his 1953 marriage to Eunice Kennedy, the couple settled in the city. Shriver quickly became a prominent figure in Chicago, chairing both the Catholic Interracial Council, an organization established for the desegregation of schools, and the Chicago Board of Education.[18]

Further complicating Yates's attempts to secure not only Daley's endorsement but his Jewish base, a wealthy Jewish industrialist, Arnold Maremont, announced that he, at the suggestion of Daley, planned to tour southern Illinois in search of support from the Democratic county chairmen. Some speculated that Governor Otto Kerner preferred Maremont as the candidate and had appointed him to the Board of Trustees of Southern Illinois University as a sign of his support. Maremont, naive to a fault, thought his reports back to Daley describing his meetings with the downstate bosses would win the day for his candidacy. When he did not become the Democratic nominee, Maremont grew embittered, feeling—correctly this time—that Daley had used him simply as a stalking horse.[19]

Finally Daley, still smarting from the belief that he, along with JFK, had been used by Stevenson, resolved that Yates would be the nominee. Daley, many reasoned, decided that Yates would help carry the local machine candidates in Chicago in November. Nothing was more important to Daley than generating support for the local slate. Daley also considered the long-term advantages of moving Yates out of the House. Yates's absence would give Daley the opportunity to advance his protégé, two-term representative Dan Rostenkowski, as leader of the Illinois delegation. By virtue of his seniority and committee position, Yates was acknowledged as the head of the delegation. By congressional tradition, he had an informal veto over legislation affecting Chicago. Having the loyal Rostenkowski, rather than the cooperative but ultimately independent Yates, as head of the delegation would be of great benefit and help the mayor further consolidate his power.

As soon as Daley made his support of Yates known, Paul Simon withdrew his candidacy. Paul Douglas finally agreed to endorse his old friend.[20] Once committed, Douglas jumped into the race full throttle for Yates. He campaigned throughout the state from that date forward until the election in November. Douglas's wife, Emily Taft Douglas, a former congresswoman and noted politician in her own right, campaigned statewide with Addie Yates before women's groups. By all reports, they were a great hit. The Yates-Douglas combo made a formidable political force. With only token opposition, Yates easily won the Democratic primary election, and prepared to face Dirksen, now the nation's highest-ranking Republican in the Senate.

Dirksen, the son of German immigrants, was born in Pekin, Illinois, a small town about ten miles from Peoria, in 1896. He had served in World War I with the 19th Balloon Company in Toul, a city on the Moselle River and the primary base of the U.S. Army Air Service, the forerunner of the Army Air Corps and later the United States Air Force. From 1927 to 1931 Dirksen had served as finance commissioner on the Pekin city council, during which time he had unsuccessfully sought a seat in the U.S. House of Representatives. In 1932, on his second try, he had been elected to Congress. He had served seven terms from the south-central 16th District, getting a law degree in the meantime, and had launched an ill-fated campaign in 1944 against Wendell Willkie for the Republican nomination for president. In 1948, he had retired from the House because of an eye condition. Two years later, fully recovered, he decided to challenge Democratic incumbent Scott Lucas, the majority leader of the U.S. Senate.

Like Dirksen, Lucas was a downstater, from Havana, Illinois, a community along the Illinois River. Although Lucas had been widely praised for his work in the 1948 Truman victory and had been credited with bringing nine new Democrats into the Senate that year, the political winds had shifted sharply to the right by the time of Dirksen's challenge in 1950. Lucas became an early opponent of Wisconsin senator Joseph McCarthy's anticommunist witch hunts, causing McCarthy in turn to target Lucas and to raise support for Dirksen.

In addition, a financial scandal was raging at the time around the Democratic candidate for Cook County sheriff, Dan "Tubbo" Gilbert. Tubbo was being described by the tabloids as "the world's richest cop" and was associated with well-known mobsters like Roger Touhy and Jake Guzik. Senator Estes Kefauver's anticrime committee subpoenaed Tubbo in its investigations of corruption, gambling, and mob affiliations. But, as a courtesy to the Chicago machine, Kefauver heard Tubbo's testimony behind closed doors.[21]

Lucas had nothing to do with Tubbo Gilbert, but he could not avoid being tarred with the same brush. Adding additional insult, Stevenson, whom Lucas claimed to have brought into electoral politics, initially declined to campaign for him and finally offered only a lukewarm endorsement. Stevenson told a furious Paul Douglas that he'd had Republican support for his campaign in 1948 and didn't want to alienate it. More cynical observers noted that Lucas had expressed interest in seeking the nomination for vice president in 1952, and Stevenson sought to eliminate a possible rival for national office.[22]

While Yates survived the Republican onslaught, Lucas lost the 1950 election by 285,000 votes, as Democrats nationally lost 6 seats in the Senate and 29 seats in the House. Locally, Republicans won control of the Illinois General Assembly and won most of the races in Cook County. Because the Lucas-Dirksen matchup had been followed nationally and interpreted widely as a referendum on President Harry Truman's policies, Dirksen received considerable national exposure.

In that 1950 midterm election, Congressman Richard M. Nixon won a seat in the Senate from California and Senator Robert A. Taft of Ohio was reelected. On the evening of the election, Dirksen told Taft in a telephone conversation: "I guess we broke their backs this time."[23] Dirksen became a firm Taft loyalist, fighting in support of Taft and against the nomination of General Eisenhower at the 1952 Republican convention, and he opposed the Eisenhower Administration for being too liberal for much of the president's first term.

By 1956, as Dirksen prepared for his first reelection campaign, the ground had shifted. Taft was dead and McCarthy, after his censure by the Senate, had been rendered powerless. Having lost his main supporters on the Republican right, Dirksen quickly pivoted to make peace with President Eisenhower. Riding the president's reelection wave, Dirksen easily dispatched his Democratic foe, Richard Stengel, a little-known state representative from Rock Island in northwest Illinois on the Mississippi. Here, too, Dirksen enjoyed some luck, as he benefited from the continuing intraparty jealousies of the Illinois Democratic Party. Stengel had been recruited by Paul Simon and Adlai Stevenson over the vehement objections of Scott Lucas, who argued that he deserved a rematch against Dirksen. Lucas certainly would have made a stronger candidate. But the state party would not countermand the desires of Stevenson, the 1952 standard-bearer who would likely be leading the national ticket again in 1956, although one hopes the party also did not fail to see the irony of Stevenson's own need for another try against Eisenhower.[24] For Stevenson, only one rematch on the ticket was allowed.

Three years later, the Senate Republicans chose Dirksen as their leader. Dirksen had established a reputation as a politician who could keep his caucus unified and yet work with the White House on certain foreign policy issues. As he got ready for the 1962 Senate race, Dirksen recognized that, unlike his 1956 opponent, Yates would be a strong challenger. Dirksen remembered well the 1950 election and was not about to let happen to him what had happened to Lucas.

For despite his national reputation, Dirksen saw troubling signs that he was vulnerable. His 1956 victory margin of more than 375,000 votes was impressive, but it was only half the margin by which President Eisenhower defeated Stevenson in Illinois. Moreover, there was some speculation that Dirksen might be facing serious opposition even among Republicans in the primary election. George Tagge of the *Chicago Tribune* revealed that Charles H. Percy, the millionaire wunderkind CEO of Bell and Howell, was considering a challenge to Dirksen for the nomination. Percy, seeking to enter politics, had received widespread attention in 1959 when President Eisenhower asked him to chair the Special Committee on Program and Process to examine the future of the Republican Party. Soon after, with both Eisenhower's and Nixon's blessing, Percy had been appointed chairman of the Platform Committee for the 1960 Republican National Convention. Percy had crafted a platform that he thought connected both the moderate and conservative wings of the GOP. But his work had been undone by the infamous "Compact of Fifth Avenue," a revised platform negotiated between Nixon and New York Governor Nelson Rockefeller. Eisenhower had denounced the compact, viewing the policy revision as a personal attack on his administration. Equally outraged from the right was Arizona senator Barry Goldwater, who had derided it as the "Munich of the Republican Party."

Despite that setback, or perhaps because of the uproar from it, Percy emerged as a national voice and fresh face for the GOP. Meanwhile, many back at home thought Dirksen had "gone Potomac" and hadn't paid enough personal attention to Illinois. But after a few months of pulse taking by Percy, and advice that he wait for two years and run for governor instead, Percy dropped his bid and endorsed Dirksen. The intraparty conflict resolved, Dirksen, like Yates, faced only nominal opposition in the primary, and got ready for the main event in November.[25]

Dirksen certainly was acutely aware that the Democrats had made significant gains in the recent elections. The off-year congressional elections of 1958 had proved especially profitable for Democrats as the party substantially increased its margins in both the House and the Senate. In 1960, Kennedy had defeated Richard Nixon narrowly and Paul Douglas had won reelection in Illinois by a comfortable margin. The Democratic majorities in Congress remained significant: 64–36 in the Senate and 261–176 in the House.

That Dirksen took the race seriously was further indicated by a testimonial dinner arranged for the senator by his Republican friends on September 15, 1961, at McCormick Place in Chicago. A star-studded affair, it included Senator Barry Goldwater, representing the national Republican Party's conservative wing, his new bedfellow Charles Percy, representing the party's moderate wing, and Phyllis Schlafly, president of the Illinois Federation of Republican Women and a rising conservative activist. The guest speaker was former president Eisenhower. In his speech endorsing Dirksen, Ike warned, "Looming in the background is a grim reality. Nuclear-tipped missiles place all of us—even in Chicago—but 30 minutes from Armageddon—tonight, every night and every hour of every day. There is no spot on earth assured of safety from obliteration. The maximum warning time is measured in minutes." The audience of more than two thousand attendees understood the message—we need Dirksen in the Senate at a time of grave nuclear peril. This would become one of the dominant themes of Dirksen's reelection campaign.[26]

Voters watching the Yates-Dirksen matchup beginning to gel could not have seen a clearer choice between political and personal opposites. Yates came from Chicago and Dirksen was from central Illinois and was thought of as southern in his roots. The fifty-two-year-old congressman was Jewish, urban as well as urbane, and a lover of the arts and humanities, while the wily sixty-six-year-old Republican leader exuded southern charm and folksiness mixed with a touch of quirkiness. Dirksen was referred to as "The Wizard of Ooze" by news reporters because of the flights of rhetorical flourish he often delivered in his speeches. A reporter for the *Chicago Sun-Times* admiringly described Dirksen as "an American artifact" and "the undisputed master of old-fashioned American oratory." Dirksen had used his appealing personality to effectively establish a national reputation as part of the popular "Ev and Charlie Show," an entertaining news conference that the Republican congressional leaders, Dirksen and House Minority Leader Charles Halleck, held frequently. Dirksen was a much-sought-after orator for national Republican causes. Yates, on the other hand, despite his growing national reputation, was hardly known outside Cook County.[27]

The differences extended to their ideologies as well. Yates was an ardent believer in the principles of the New Deal and the New Frontier while Dirksen was a fiscal conservative and a self-described Eisenhower balance-the-budget Republican. Even here, though, Dirksen could be elusive and difficult to pigeonhole politically. When news reporters would point out his changes in positions on major issues, as well as his flip-flop on Eisenhower himself, Dirksen was ready with a quip, explaining, "I am a man of principle, and one of my basic principles is flexibility."[28]

Yates, however, heralded his own constancy to his beliefs and his principles. Yates pointed out that he had supported President Kennedy's New Frontier by voting for the president's proposals 97 percent of the time while Dirksen voted for them only 27 percent of the time. Yates labeled Dirksen "just a chronic againster," and was relentless in attacking Dirksen on economic issues. "He is the original 'no' man," Yates contended. "On medical care under Social Security, on the minimum wage, on federal aid for depressed areas, on emergency public works, on aid to education, on housing—and you name it, he voted no, no, no and no again."[29]

Consistent with his previous positions advocating programs for senior citizens, for example, was Yates's strong and steadfast support of President Kennedy's plan to extend Social Security to a national health-care system for retirees, called Medicare. Dirksen labeled Medicare "socialized medicine," just a heartbeat away from communism. Anyone who supported Medicare must be a commie, too.

Yates had endured years of being called a communist, and he was not deterred. On May 20, Yates addressed a rally in Chicago organized to express support for the president's Medicare legislation. Yates ridiculed and rebuked Dirksen and the Republicans: "Here it is—30 years after Franklin D. Roosevelt, giving this country a new level of living thru the New Deal, and there still are those who are fighting programs such as social security for selfish reasons."[30]

For all their differences, Yates and Dirksen had one thing in common. Practiced in the skills necessary to remain in office, they were both effective communicators with their constituents. Each had regularly written narrative newsletters to their residents, Yates since his first week in Congress, Dirksen while he was in the House, discussing the issues of the day and giving his insights on them.

Dirksen also took full advantage of his skills as a radio and television personality. In 1961, he had a weekly show on fifty radio stations and nine television stations across the state. Yates, on a smaller scale, had enjoyed a five-minute spot on a Chicago radio station for several years.

Unafraid of Dirksen's prowess as a communicator, and confident in his own oratorical skills, Yates proposed televised debates between the two of them reminiscent of the Kennedy-Nixon presidential debates of 1960. Undoubtedly, Yates considered the debates to be a route to increasing his name recognition. Dirksen, however, perhaps also remembering the way Kennedy had gained parity and stature by sharing the stage with the better-known Richard Nixon, did not take the bait and the proposed debates never came off. Yates would have to garner attention on his own.[31]

In July, Yates received the results of an extensive poll that he had commissioned from Louis Harris and Associates, the firm that had done the political surveying for Kennedy in 1960. The results confirmed that, indeed, Yates had an uphill battle. Nearly 45 percent of the respondents indicated they favored Dirksen over Yates. In addition, a similar percentage gave Dirksen an "excellent" or "pretty good" rating for the job he was doing as senator. The senator's rating on "standing up to communism" was similarly impressive. Dirksen was perceived by a solid majority as "working for Illinois." The one area where Dirksen did not fare as well was on the issue of extending Social Security to medical care for the elderly. Almost two-thirds of the respondents gave Dirksen a "poor," "only fair," or "not sure" rating on Medicare. On other domestic issues too, such as civil rights, unemployment, and federal aid to education, Dirksen appeared vulnerable. Harris, who would become a close friend of Yates, advised that if Yates were going to make the race competitive he'd need to hammer home those social issues. And he would need the expected help from the local and national Democratic Party and its respective leaders, Mayor Daley and President Kennedy. Little did Yates anticipate that there he would be betrayed.[32]

Yates thought he had a right to expect the president's support. First, he was the Democratic nominee and a loyal and consistent vote in Congress for JFK. But on a more personal level, Yates recalled how he had answered the call when Kennedy requested his help in 1952 to secure the Jewish vote in Kennedy's Senate race. He expected the president to reciprocate.[33] Admittedly, Yates had been a Stevenson man during Adlai's initial attempt to run again for president in 1960, but he had immediately come over to Kennedy once Stevenson dropped out.

For Kennedy and the Senate Democratic leadership, however, Yates's challenge to Dirksen presented a dilemma in congressional relations. Dirksen, as Senate minority leader, generally supported Kennedy on foreign policy and opposed him on domestic spending. If he were to lose the race to Yates, Dirksen's probable successor as Republican leader would be Bourke Hickenlooper of Iowa, a staunch ideological conservative hostile to the White House. Hickenlooper's anti-Kennedy activities as chairman of the Republican Policy Committee presaged years of intransigent opposition to the New Frontier legislative agenda should he become leader. Kennedy had a weak legislative record and, looking to his reelection campaign two years hence, realized his only chance for significant legislative victories rested to a large extent on Dirksen, not Hickenlooper.[34] At the same time, Kennedy, who had narrowly won Illinois in 1960, could ill afford to alienate Democrats in the 1962 senatorial contest. A difficult balancing act confronted the president.

Senator Douglas got an inkling of Kennedy's waffling support in 1960 when the new president confided that he didn't think he could do any better than Dirksen as minority leader among the Republicans.[35] In addition, Dirksen and the young president seemed to have formed a personal relationship. "John Kennedy was easy to talk to," Dirksen said smugly. "When he had difficulties, he had no hesitation about calling me up for help. He always felt free to talk to me." There is, in fact, little dispute about JFK's courting of Dirksen. For example, on the morning of the 1962 Illinois primary, newspapers prominently featured a photo of Dirksen, who had not felt it necessary to remain in Illinois, instead sitting with Kennedy in Washington and enjoying the opening day of the baseball season with him. Theodore Sorensen noted in his memoir that "by 1962 [JFK's] relations were so good with Dirksen—whom he had always found entertaining and at times movable by invocations of patriotism (or patronage)—that both men had to reassure their respective party members that each had not embraced the other too much."[36]

This interparty sentiment for Dirksen extended to the Democratic leader-
ship of the Senate. They also feared Hickenlooper's possible ascension. Senator
Mike Mansfield, the Democratic majority leader, had a cordial relationship with
Dirksen and obviously preferred working with him. In August 1961, for example,
Mansfield sent a laudatory letter to the chairman of a Dirksen testimonial dinner
in Pekin. While declining to attend the event because of "prior commitments,"
Mansfield went on to heap praise on his Republican colleague, saying, in part,
"As my counterpart in the U.S. Senate, I have nothing but words of praise for his
understanding, his tolerance, and his cooperation in seeing to it that the Senate
functions as a legislative body in its true meaning and as a man in whom I have
the utmost confidence." Dirksen later thanked Mansfield for his letter: "Never has
anyone written a more glowing letter than did you addressed to the chairman of
the testimonial dinner in my home town. I cannot thank you enough."[37]

The intentions of the White House soon became apparent. Douglas learned
that Kennedy, without consulting him, intended to nominate Bernard Decker,
a Republican judge from Lake County, Illinois, as a U.S. District Court Judge.
Douglas was outraged. Nor was this the first time Douglas had clashed with the
Kennedy administration over presidential nominations to the bench. Early in
the administration, when Robert Kennedy, the president's brother and attorney
general, informed Douglas of his intention to nominate two Republicans from
Illinois to the federal bench, the senator furiously objected. "I told him that this
was intolerable," Douglas recounted in his memoirs. "We Democrats in Illinois
had won the state for John Kennedy against heavy odds, and by so doing we had
probably saved the election for him. To repudiate us now would be base ingrati-
tude." Inasmuch as Decker's nomination came as a surprise to Douglas, he, along
with Mayor Daley, persuaded Kenneth O'Donnell, the political assistant to the
president, to delay the nomination until after the election. Douglas told Lawrence
F. O'Brien, special assistant to the president, "The Republicans are still making
capital on Senator Dirksen's alleged pull at the White House in comparison to
Yates." Regardless, the harm had been done and it was widely speculated that
Kennedy wanted to help Dirksen.[38]

And, apparently, so did Vice President Lyndon B. Johnson. Daley and Douglas
were aghast when they read prepared remarks that the vice president planned
to deliver at a fundraising event for the Cook County Democratic Organization. Johnson's remarks contained no "real" endorsement of Yates. Douglas, with
Daley's support, informed Johnson's office that the vice president was unwelcome
unless the speech contained strong support for the congressman's victory.[39] But
Johnson and Dirksen had been friends for years in both the House and the Senate,
a relationship that had deepened almost to intimacy during the years in which
they were opposing party leaders. As Dirksen later recalled, he and Johnson "fully

understood each other (and) got along exceptionally well." The speech was revised with a paragraph in which Johnson gave Yates a mild endorsement reciting some of the domestic issues that Yates and the administration supported.[40] The White House almost certainly cleared Johnson's remarks. For the Yates camp, it was small consolation that at least the speech didn't hurt the campaign.

In fact, Johnson was actively working for Dirksen. In a telephone call made by Johnson to Dirksen from the Oval Office after Johnson's succession to the presidency, Johnson informed Dirksen that, when President Kennedy had asked his advice about whether to support Yates, Johnson told JFK that "the day [Dirksen] weren't there [in the Senate] would be a sad day for Kennedy." Johnson also told Dirksen that Mayor Daley "liked you too."[41]

With most of the Kennedy administration pulling for Dirksen, only Adlai Stevenson, from his suite at the Waldorf Astoria a few blocks from the UN, continued to lobby for his old friend and supporter. Behind the scenes, and sometimes not very behind, Stevenson helped arrange for political fundraising for Yates both in New York and in Illinois. Through his son, Adlai E. Stevenson III, a rising political star in his own right, the ambassador kept up with events in Illinois and wrote letters of support and supplied names of potential donors to the campaign. Stevenson also consulted with Mayor Daley about the race. On May 17, 1962, he wrote to Daley, "I share your view that there is nothing for Sid to do but to ignore the gossip about Dirksen and the Administration. I have no doubt that after Congress goes home we will get more positive sounds from this direction."[42]

Mayor Daley was so impressed with Adlai III that he considered slating him for the 9th District congressional seat that Yates had vacated. He went to Adlai II with his plan. Adlai told the mayor, however, not to offer the position to his son, perhaps because he thought his son wasn't ready, or perhaps because he secretly thought Yates would lose to Dirksen and would be seeking his old seat. He never told Adlai III about the opportunity.[43]

Labor Day marked the beginning of the final push for the campaign. According to Lou Harris's polls, Yates had caught up with Dirksen and was in fact leading by a small but significant number. Harris called Bain: "Mary, put all your money on Sid."[44] Explaining the surprising support for Yates in traditionally Republican downstate counties, Harris speculated that voters might be associating the congressman with Richard Yates, Illinois's Republican governor during the Civil War. Perhaps in response, several of Dirksen's supporters began a smear campaign, alleging that Yates was trying to hide the fact that he was Jewish and instead was deliberately representing that he was related to Governor Yates. One such supporter wrote to Howard Rainville, Dirksen's campaign manager, that Yates had changed his name from "Yackevitch" solely to run for office. Rainville responded that Yates had used his current name well before running for office. He did not, however, discourage his correspondent from continuing to spread the misrepresentations.[45]

The stench of anti-Semitism continued to seep from the Dirksen campaign. With Rainville's approval, a group called the German-American Committee for Senator Dirksen sent out a series of four letters on Dirksen for Senate stationery to a thousand persons whose names were chosen from membership lists of 235 German societies in Illinois. The letters denounced the "rapacity of the victors" of World War II and said that "it was not the Republicans who were responsible for the first World War, nor for the second. . . . Both these wars were conducted against the German nation and everything German." The letter concluded by urging a vote for "our man," Senator Dirksen. Responding to the media uproar that ensued after publication of the letters, Rainville said that he was sure that Dirksen was unaware of the letter and would have no comment.[46]

Yates tried to keep the campaign's focus on Medicare, budget and taxes, and domestic issues, where he had a sizable lead. But throughout 1961 and 1962, Yates was dogged by the persistent rumor in published reports that he didn't expect to win. Instead, the pundits suggested, he had agreed to run in exchange for a federal judgeship following a likely loss to Dirksen. John Dreiske of the *Chicago Sun-Times* continued the speculation into August 1962 despite Yates's vehement denials. The rumors reinforced the question about the White House's support for Yates. The rationale for the rumors was that Illinois needed to reduce its congressional delegation after the census of 1960 and Yates's candidacy would solve that dilemma. The *Chicago Sun-Times* editorialized as early as July 16, 1961, "But putting judicial robes on him [Yates] to solve the reapportionment dilemma would be promoting a good man for bad reasons." Despite repeated denials, the rumors could not be finally put to rest.[47] Legendary political journalist David S. Broder, then a thirty-three-year-old staff writer for the *Washington Evening Star* assigned to cover the campaign, was convinced that there was no truth to the story. "If [Yates] is 'running for a judgeship'," Broder wrote, "he is running a lot harder than anyone would have thought necessary."[48]

In the last weeks of the campaign, however, there was another blow from alleged friends. This time it was on the floor of the U.S. Senate. Senate Majority Leader Mike Mansfield led a parade of colleagues in tribute to Dirksen, celebrating the thirty years since Dirksen's first election to Congress. Mansfield echoed the sentiments he had expressed at the testimonial dinner in honor of Dirksen the previous August: "Everett, I am honored and grateful that you sit across from me. You are a tower of strength as a collaborator in the leadership of this body. For thirty years you have served your party faithfully and brilliantly. But for thirty years you have served your country more." Senator Douglas reported to the White House that Mansfield's speech "has done immeasurable damage to Congressman Yates." Even liberal senator Hubert H. Humphrey paid his respects to the Republican leader. These tributes, of course, were reported throughout Illinois and served to further weaken the morale of Yates's supporters.[49]

More was to follow. Two national magazines ran glowing articles on Dirksen. In late September, *Time* published an adulatory story on Dirksen featuring the senator on its cover striking a statesmanlike pose. The article emphasized, among other things, Dirksen's relationship with and importance to the Kennedy administration. An anonymous Democrat, later identified as LBJ aide Bobby Baker, was quoted as saying, "I like Sid Yates. But my party would be in a hell of a mess—the Kennedy Administration would be in a hell of a mess—if Dirksen got defeated." This sentiment was seconded by a White House aide, likely Lawrence O'Brien: "Who could dislike Dirksen? He gets his arm around your shoulders and, well, he is a total pro, able, cute, and clever." In early October, the *Time* feature was followed up with a fawning article on Dirksen in the *Saturday Evening Post*, similarly lauding the senator. Referring to Yates as "a militant Democrat," the *Saturday Evening Post* article described Dirksen as an effective leader, repeated the "powerful rumor" of White House support, and quoted one important Republican senator as saying "Esprit de corps has never been higher" among Republicans in the Congress. Dirksen's campaign understood the value of the *Time* and *Saturday Evening Post* articles and had two hundred thousand copies reprinted and distributed to Illinois voters.[50]

It was left to the president, however, to administer the coup de grâce. After all the speculation about the nature of his support, Kennedy had finally agreed to a trip to Illinois to campaign for Yates. Kennedy's trip was scheduled for Friday and Saturday, October 19–20. An extensive itinerary with joint appearances had been planned for Springfield and Chicago. Daley expected that Kennedy's appearance would help with the Democrats' get-out-the-vote effort, particularly in Cook County and some downstate precincts where the president's rural electrification program was popular.[51]

Kennedy addressed a crowd of five thousand in Chicago on Friday evening at the invitation of the Cook County Democratic Organization. But the president's endorsement of Yates consisted simply of a recitation of the congressman's support for the New Frontier domestic agenda. Significantly, JFK did not criticize Dirksen. Robert Kennedy explained later that "the President did not want to become so personally involved that it would antagonize Dirksen." The following morning, Kennedy abruptly canceled all further political appearances, pleading illness with a cold. The president had been informed by Robert Kennedy that the special committee JFK had put together to address the Cuban missile crisis was ready to present its recommendations.

Before leaving Washington to deliver the Friday speech, the president had been informed by his staff that there was preliminary evidence of Russian missiles in Cuba. Kennedy instructed his national security staff to confirm the buildup in Cuba and to provide him a report outlining his options. Abruptly abandoning his political trip and returning to Washington, the president immediately conferred with his brother and met with his national security staff.

Two days later, on the evening of Monday, October 22, 1962, the president spoke to the nation on radio and television about the crisis in Cuba. "Within the past week, unmistakable evidence has established the fact that a series of offensive missile sites is now in preparation on that imprisoned island," he announced. Kennedy continued: "The purpose of these bases can be none other than to provide a nuclear strike capability against the Western Hemisphere." Eschewing more dangerous options and adopting a cautious approach, the president announced that he was initiating a "strict quarantine on all offensive military equipment" to Cuba. He assured the U.S. people: "We will not prematurely or unnecessarily risk the costs of worldwide nuclear war in which even the fruits of victory would be ashes in our mouth—but neither will we shrink from that task at any time it must be faced."

Finally, the president predicted that the affair would be long and drawn out: "Many months of sacrifice and self-discipline lie ahead—months in which both our patience, and our will, will be tested—months in which many threats and denunciations will keep us aware of our dangers. But the greatest danger of all would be to do nothing."[52]

Emotions ran high as the public faced the very real threat of nuclear warfare between the world's two superpowers. The Cuban missile crisis was the latest, and most ominous, in an ever-escalating series of developments between the United States and the Soviet Union: the Suez Canal crisis of 1956; the Soviet launch of Sputnik in 1957, beating the United States into outer space; Nikita Khrushchev's "We will bury you" speech before the National Press Club in 1959; the U-2 incident in 1960; a tense summit between a new young president and a defiant Soviet premier; and the Bay of Pigs fiasco in 1961[53]—culminating in this nuclear faceoff. A Gallup poll published the day after Kennedy's speech reflected this anxiety. One in five Americans believed that a naval blockade of Cuba would mean a third world war. Over the next thirteen days the world sat wondering if nuclear war was about to devour them.[54]

Kennedy had consulted with congressional leaders a few hours before his national address to let them know of developments. He telephoned Dirksen and other congressional leaders and summoned them to Washington from their states and districts for consultations. To emphasize the gravity of the situation, he sent special airplanes to escort them back to the nation's capital. A photo of

Dirksen at O'Hare airport in Chicago waiting for the presidential airplane appeared throughout Illinois the day after Kennedy's address to the nation. The message to the public was clear—in a time of national emergency, Kennedy needed Dirksen.

The president opened his meeting with congressional leaders by saying to Dirksen, "Tonight you're going to get reelected." To which Dirksen could not resist responding: "That was a nice little speech you gave for Sid Yates in Chicago. Too bad you caught that cold making it." Kennedy did not reply. During the meeting, Dirksen and Halleck supported the president's blockade strategy while Democratic leaders, J. William Fulbright, chairman of the Senate Foreign Relations Committee, and Russell Long, chairman of the Senate Armed Services Committee, proposed an invasion of Cuba. The meeting was testy. At one point, Halleck is said to have "glared" at Fulbright, saying, "I'm standing with the President."[55]

But while pledging his support to the president, the Cuban missile crisis fit perfectly into Dirksen's campaign theme. From the beginning of the campaign, he had relentlessly criticized Kennedy for the Bay of Pigs fiasco. For example, only a few days before the president's national address, Dirksen told an Illinois audience that there were dire consequences from the Bay of Pigs: "And now what do we see? That bearded dictator [Fidel] Castro and his Russian motor torpedo boats, with launching pads on them. And they have builded [sic] missile sites on the land. Oh, I know whereof I speak. I know because they told me so at 1600 Pennsylvania Avenue."[56]

And now Dirksen took full advantage of the missile crisis. He told his wife in a loud voice near a local news reporter that the president thought that he had his reelection secured. According to the report, broadcast on WIND radio in Chicago, as he was leaving the White House after a second meeting on October 24 on the status of the blockade, Dirksen told the president that he was returning to Illinois to "report to the people." To which Kennedy retorted, "Why, Ev? You know you've got it in the bag." When asked about the accuracy of the reported conversation, Dirksen simply replied that he considered his conversations with the president private. An infuriated Yates labeled the alleged exchange "an outright and contemptible lie." Regardless, the story had its intended effect. Douglas reported that when the White House didn't deny Dirksen's story, it "further demoralized our workers."[57] Privately, however, Yates and Bain believed it to be true. Yates told Bain that "Kennedy told me it would be unpatriotic to go at Dirksen anymore."[58] Lou Harris, tracking the election, made a second call to Bain: "Mary, cover your ass, he's going to lose." As Yates later said, "I could feel the campaign going out from under me."[59]

The political implications of the crisis were very much on the mind of the president and his advisers with congressional elections only three weeks away. During one of the meetings of the special committee on the missile crisis, Treasury Secretary Douglas Dillon, a Republican, passed a note to Ted Sorensen: "Ted—Have you considered the very real possibility that if we allow Cuba to complete installation and operational readiness of missile bases, the next House of Representatives is likely to have a Republican majority? This would completely paralyze our ability to react sensibly and coherently to further Soviet advances."

Adding salt to the wound, the day before the election, Senate Majority Leader Mike Mansfield announced that he and Dirksen would make a trip to international hot spots after the election and report back to President Kennedy.[60]

But despite the national humiliations, Yates always counted on the vote-getting power of the Cook County Democratic machine to pull him through, as well as Daley's own self-interest that his hand-picked candidate succeed. But here, too, he was mistaken. The week before the election, Yates asked Daley whether he should use the final days to campaign in Cook County or go downstate. Daley reportedly told him, "Leave it up to me in the county. Go downstate. That's where you need to pick up support." Against the advice of Bain, Yates followed the mayor's direction. Bain always and Yates eventually suspected the motivation behind that advice. Had White House aides—O'Donnell or O'Brien, for example—asked Daley to manipulate the outcome in Cook County?

After the election, Yates and Bain were convinced that Mayor Daley had shaved votes in some of Chicago's select machine wards in order to help Dirksen at the urging of the White House. Paul Douglas, despite his sometimes rocky relationship with Daley, did not seem to agree with this appraisal. In a letter to William P. Roberts, a Chicago lawyer who had written him questioning the Decker nomination and the party's support for Yates, Douglas noted that Yates "will be supported by the party right up to the top. No one is tossing him to the wolves." The senator then added a handwritten postscript: "Daley really is behind Yates."[61] On the other hand, former Chicago alderman William S. Singer reported years later that Daley had confided to Alderman Tom Keane, his floor leader, that Kennedy had personally requested that he "lay down" on Yates's candidacy.[62]

It is interesting that the three Democratic candidates up for Illinois statewide office in 1962 (senator, treasurer, and superintendent of public instruction) were separated by only 30,000 votes from each other. Of the three, Yates received the lowest count at 1,748,007. It is significant that Yates, the other two statewide candidates, and seekers of local office ran roughly equal in the ten "river wards" in Chicago, the wards most directly under control of the Daley machine. If, indeed, Daley had suppressed the vote, he must have done so at the expense of all statewide and local Democratic candidates. In the end, Yates won Chicago by approximately 300,000 votes but lost the suburbs and downstate by 500,000.

Yates lost the election with 47 percent of the vote—by only 213,195 votes out of 3,709,209 votes cast, a very respectable showing considering all the havoc that had surrounded the campaign. It was the closest Dirksen came to losing in his senatorial career. Yates was not alone among Democrats in his defeat, however. It was a Republican year in Illinois. William J. Scott became state treasurer, Ray Page was elected superintendent of public instruction, and the GOP retained control of the state senate and won a slim majority in the Illinois House of Representatives. In Cook County, Richard B. Ogilvie, a World War II hero, stunned the local political world by defeating the Democratic machine candidate for sheriff of Cook County. Businessman Donald Rumsfeld, only thirty years old, won a seat in the U.S. House from a north suburban district.[63]

Across the country, however, the results were much different. Eight new Democrats were elected to the Senate in 1962, among them liberals Abraham Ribicoff (Connecticut), Gaylord Nelson (Wisconsin), George McGovern (South Dakota), Birch Bayh (Indiana), Daniel Inouye (Hawaii), and Edward M. Kennedy (Massachusetts), the president's younger brother. Senator Barry Goldwater, a leading light among conservative Republicans, reflected on the political effect of JFK's handling of the Cuban missile crisis: "We were Cuber-ized."[64] Because of the White House's actions, Cuba helped all the Democrats except Yates.

Kennedy and Dirksen each got what they wanted as a result of the 1962 campaign. After the Cuban missile crisis was resolved peacefully and Americans could breathe a little more easily, Kennedy's prestige increased, culminating in ratification of the 1963 Nuclear Test Ban Treaty. Dirksen voted for the treaty and garnered Republican votes for it. The nomination of Dirksen's candidate for circuit court judge, Bernard Decker, was sent to the Senate for confirmation.

Senator Douglas was incensed with the White House and the Senate Democratic leadership. Shortly after the election, he dispatched a letter to the president with a sharply worded memorandum in which he castigated the Senate Democratic leadership and strongly objected to the Decker nomination. "The appointment of Judge Decker at this time would certainly give the appearance that there really was a deal for Dirksen and against Yates," Douglas said. "On top of all of the things that have happened, to reward Dirksen with a personal appointee will not only give the appearance of a deal but would dishearten our people who did so much for you and for Sidney Yates in the last two campaigns. It would take the heart out of our loyal people to see something like this happen." The Decker nomination was confirmed regardless. No reply to Douglas's letter appears in the records.[65]

Yates learned some tough lessons during the campaign. Chief among them was that loyalty was a hard commodity to come by in politics. Past service does not ensure future loyalty. During the campaign, the two leaders of the Democratic Party, his president and his mayor, had, one way or another, deserted him. To Yates's reckoning, only Douglas and Stevenson, two old friends who had been through a lot of political wars with him, had remained steadfast to him. If the 1948 election had taught him something about luck, he learned another valuable lesson about politics and loyalty in 1962.

The close and hard-fought election left wounds on both candidates. In Dirksen's case, he attributed the unprecedented closeness of the race to the loss of some expected loyalties. Although Dirksen has been rightfully lauded for his crucial and decisive support of the Civil Rights Act of 1964, his initial inclination was to oppose it out of pique. Clarence Mitchell, civil rights leader and director of the Washington bureau of the NAACP, recalled bringing an Illinois constituent with him to a meeting with Dirksen to seek his support for the bill. "When he got in the office the Senator was very brusque and said, 'Clarence, you are through. I don't want to have anything to do with you at all because you haven't done your homework.' He said, 'None of these Negroes voted for me up there in Illinois and I'm through with them.' And I said, 'Well, Senator, here is a Republican who is with me, and I'm sure he must have voted for you.' Well, that mollified him a little bit but he still remained very belligerent and very ill mannered. So when we left his office, this Republican who was along with me said, 'That Senator'—he called him Senator Dirksten, not Senator Dirksen, he said, 'That Senator Dirksten is a very difficult man,' he said. 'I'm sure glad I voted for Sid Yates!'"[66]

Yates likewise never forgave the Kennedys. Hal Bergan, a former aide to Yates, recounted the depth of this resentment. Yates was known for having an obsessive pride of authorship in his speeches and letters. Staff members were asked to provide drafts to assist Yates in his thinking, but the final product would be completely rewritten by Yates after lengthy consideration and soul-searching. In all the years that Bergan worked for Yates, he said, only one draft statement was accepted without review or comment. It was when Bergan was asked in June 1968 to write a eulogy for the just-assassinated Robert Kennedy for insertion in the *Congressional Record*. Bergan completed his task and handed it to Yates. Yates barely glanced at the paper as he signed his name and told Bergan, "Take it to the floor and get it thrown in the hopper."[67]

6

TO THE UNITED NATIONS
AND BACK

Yates was not without a job for long. When Jonathan Bingham transferred to the UN Economic and Social Council, President Kennedy nominated Yates as his replacement as representative to the United Nations Trusteeship Council, with an enthusiastic recommendation from Ambassador Stevenson. The appointment carried with it the rank of ambassador.

The White House ordered the FBI to rush through their investigation of Yates's background prior to the formal appointment. Agents throughout the country interviewed friends and colleagues, including many members of Congress, Republican and Democratic. Clarence Cannon, no doubt glad to see Yates leave the Appropriations Committee, said he was "very fond of Yates" and that Yates was "my hard fighter for any cause he personally backs." Dirksen conceded that Yates had a "certain amount of native ability." Dirksen said he had no reason to question Yates's loyalty but would have no further comments to make about Yates. All those interviewed testified to Yates's patriotism and character.[1]

Yates appeared for confirmation hearings before the Senate Committee on Foreign Relations on March 5, 1963, to endure some good-natured needling. Chairman J. William Fulbright of Arkansas asked him whether he knew what his salary was going to be, and whether it would be paid by the government or the United Nations. Senator John Sparkman of Alabama quizzed him on his foreign languages. In words more positive than those he had given the FBI, Dirksen briefly testified that "in the true spirit of friendship I . . . say that he has my unreserved endorsement."[2] The nomination sailed through the Senate without controversy. Even Dirksen voted for the Yates nomination. The new employment gave Yates an opportunity to see some of the world, particularly developing countries like India and Africa, and to learn about the inner workings of the United Nations and the U.S. Department of State. Yates would remain a strong proponent of the United Nations for the remainder of his political career.

After the election, speculation continued among Chicago's political observers that Yates had accepted the post at the United Nations as a stopping-off point en route to a federal judgeship. George Tagge of the *Chicago Tribune* reported in his column "Political Outlook" that Yates was in line to take the vacancy created by the death of federal Judge Julius Miner of the Northern District of Illinois in March 1963. According to the columnist, the Department of State objected to Yates's appointment to the bench so soon after his confirmation to the UN post. Yates reportedly agreed with this assessment and declined the judgeship.[3]

While at the trusteeship council, Yates became involved in one high-profile conflict over the sovereignty of the United Nations and the laws of its host, the United States. Captain Henrique Galvão, a longtime outspoken opponent of Portuguese colonization of Angola, hijacked a Portuguese ship, the *Santa Maria*, on January 22, 1961, and sought refuge at Recife, Brazil. The Afro-Asian delegates to the United Nations supported the Angolan independence movement and voted overwhelmingly to have Galvão appear before the United Nations to make the case against Portugal's "shameful outrages," particularly its forced-labor system. Yates warned the delegates in lawyerlike fashion that the United States had an extradition treaty and thereby might be compelled to turn over Captain Galvão to Portugal. "The United States has never objected to any petitioner coming here," Yates noted. "If Capt. Galvao comes here, it is possible Portugal might start a suit in court to bring about extradition. The Secretary of State has no power to stop extradition except in cases of immunity." The Soviet delegate and the Afro-Asians disagreed, citing a clause in the UN charter giving the charter precedence over the laws of the United States. In the end, a compromise was made. Galvão appeared before the United Nations. Portugal requested extradition, but the processing of the request by the U.S. Department of State wasn't completed until after Galvão had left the country and was safely back in Brazil.[4]

After a year at the United Nations, Yates was restless and decided to reclaim his seat in the House. Conveniently, Representative Edward Finnegan, a loyalist of Mayor Daley, withdrew from the race after having been nominated to run again and Yates was selected to replace him. Yates's track record led the party to take it for granted that Yates would add strength to the Democratic ticket. Yates won the 1964 election handily, winning 63.9 percent of the vote, which exceeded President Johnson's 59.47 percent Illinois total.

His two-year absence had sent Yates back to the bottom of the seniority ladder, but he soon let the leadership know that, at least in some areas, he wasn't going to be treated as a newcomer. The House Administration Committee tried to stick him in the Class of 1965 with other freshmen when allocating office space, putting him behind three hundred other congressmen to choose his suite. The fact that he'd already served fourteen years in the House didn't matter to the committee. It allocated seniority according to consecutive, not aggregate, service, along with an obscure formula that gave former governors and senators additional priority. Yates raised hell with Omar Burleson, chairman of House Administration, and went to Speaker John McCormack and Majority Leader Carl Albert. He created enough noise that they established what became known as the "Yates Rule," which defined seniority for office space purposes by aggregate terms served in the House.[5]

He couldn't pull that trick off with respect to committee service, however. Even though he had been returned to the Appropriations Committee, he understood that as thirty-third among thirty-four Democrats on the committee he'd need to rebuild his seniority before he could exert real influence, unless, of course, he found an issue of national importance he could commandeer. Yates suspected that his Appropriations assignment was due, more than likely, to the growing influence of Representative Dan Rostenkowski, now the head of the Illinois delegation, and to Mayor Daley's assistance. Daley always wanted at least one Democrat from Chicago on the Appropriations Committee, and Yates had been helpful representing the city's interest in his previous service. There was no reason to think Yates wouldn't continue to help advance Chicago's national agenda.[6]

Yates was relegated to the second-tier Appropriations Subcommittee on Treasury, Post Office, and Executive Offices, an assignment that only compounded his restlessness and desire for an issue to tackle. He needed to raise his profile. A hopeful sign was that his nemesis, Appropriations Chairman Clarence Cannon, had died while Yates was at the United Nations. In his place was George Mahon of Texas. He and Yates were not particularly friendly, and they had never served on the same subcommittee, but they had worked together over the years on the full committee and Mahon didn't bear the animus that Cannon had toward Yates.

Yates had discovered with the Rickover controversy that "David versus Goliath" issues (with Yates as David, of course) worked best for him. He reveled in mastering a complex subject, championing the cause in committee and then taking the fight to the floor of the House. This tactic had been one of the many things that peeved Cannon, but he might get some leeway with Mahon. Yates respected members who, like the late Judge Sabath, knew the House's complicated parliamentary rules and used them to advance their own causes. They were the work horses, not show horses, of the Congress.

Yates also decided to make some changes to the way his congressional office operated. Constituent casework had always been part of a member's duties. John Quincy Adams, who served in the House in the 1830s and 1840s after his presidency, wrote in his diary how he had helped one constituent correct a military pension certificate and assisted another with a Post Office appointment.[7] The twentieth-century increase in government programs, obligations, and benefits and the need of bewildered citizens to have a liaison to the federal bureaucracy brought constituent services to the forefront of a representative's job. Yates opened his first district office, specializing in assistance with Social Security, veterans affairs, immigration, and a host of other problems. He hired Bain, who had never been on his congressional payroll, to head the Chicago operation.

Bain put together a casework team who understood both the workings of government and the political benefits that would result from efficient services provided to 9th District residents. Under Bain's direction, the district office became an essential component of Yates's work and a key element in his reelection efforts. Later, when Bain relocated to Washington and took full control of Yates's offices, she insisted that all staff, including those on the legislative side, take a turn responding to constituent mail. It was important that the Washington staff be reminded that their ability to work on great national issues depended on the constituents who returned their boss to office every two years.

Occasionally, Bain and her staff clashed on the appropriate way to answer a letter. National Public Radio journalist Scott Simon, who years earlier interned for Yates, once criticized Bain for her proposed response, over Yates's signature, to a youthful letter writer. Bain had addressed the writer by his first name. "When you're writing to a young person," Simon admonished, "Don't use their first name, because it's denigrating. Use 'Mr.' or 'Miss.'" For years afterward, whenever Mary called Simon, she would ask for "Mr. Simon. And tell him Mary's calling."

His office organized, Yates awaited the swearing-in of the 89th Congress on January 4, 1965. Several members of the class of 1949 still served. Only one member of the Illinois delegation originally elected that year was still in office, his old friend Barratt O'Hara, who was moving up in seniority on the House Committee on Foreign Affairs. Two classmates were now senators. Abe Ribicoff, who had joined with Yates in supporting Kennedy in his 1952 Senate campaign, had first become governor of Connecticut and then JFK's secretary of the Department of Health, Education, and Welfare. In 1962, Ribicoff had won a Senate seat. Unlike Yates, however, Ribicoff ran for an open seat, and Kennedy gave his full support. Eugene McCarthy was elected senator from Minnesota in 1958. McCarthy and Yates were close, and the Minnesotan was a strong supporter of Yates's bid in 1962, part of a small group led by Adlai Stevenson and including former New York governor and senator Herbert H. Lehman, who raised money among liberals for Yates.[8]

Still others had remained in the House, accumulating seniority and influence. Peter Rodino of New Jersey was moving up on the Judiciary Committee. In a few years, he would become chairman, gaining national recognition during his oversight of the impeachment proceedings of President Nixon. Yates's old Appropriations committee seatmate Gerald Ford rose in leadership and became minority leader in 1965. Finally Wayne Hays, an Ohio Democrat, was well on his way in 1965 to becoming a committee chairman. In 1973, Hays would become chairman of the Democratic Congressional Campaign Committee and later chairman of the House Administration Committee.

As he stood with the members at their seats in the House and raised his hand for the en masse taking of the oath of office, Yates was already considering another race for the Senate. Back in Chicago, rumors lingered of Yates's interest in a federal judgeship. The rumors took on added life when Judge Michael Igoe went on senior, or semiretired, status in August, opening up a slot on the federal bench in the Northern District of Illinois. According to the *Chicago Tribune*, "Yates received the strongest early backing" among House Democrats from Illinois. As the state's lone Democratic senator, Paul Douglas would normally control the nomination, and presumably he would recommend Yates. But in 1961, Kennedy had ignored Senate prerogatives, giving Dirksen the opportunity to appoint a Republican. Douglas suspected that LBJ, who had never been close to Douglas, would do the same thing. *Tribune* reporter Philip Warden observed that Yates, "a longtime candidate for appointment for federal bench, was passed over four years ago when vacancies were filled."[9]

Any interest Yates might have had to be a judge had long since dissipated, and he moved quickly to squelch the rumor, telling the *Tribune* "that Mayor Daley, Gov. Kerner, and other party leaders may prefer to have him in Congress rather than on the federal bench." He left open, however, which branch of Congress and wasn't secretive about his continuing ambition for the Senate. It was generally accepted that Yates would be the Democratic candidate should Douglas not seek reelection in 1966. In a speech before the Tazewell County Democrats in downstate Illinois, a long way from the 9th District, Yates said he was interested in another senatorial race but only if his good friend retired. Once Douglas, now seventy-four, decided to run for a fourth term, Yates abandoned the quest and filed for reelection to the House.[10] Douglas ultimately lost to forty-seven-year-old Charles H. Percy, the former president of Bell and Howell, who had been an unsuccessful candidate for governor in 1964. Percy's youth, good looks, and moderate Rockefeller Republicanism sharply contrasted with the rumpled, aging Douglas. In addition, progressives were upset at Douglas's unwavering support of LBJ's Vietnam policies. Finally, Percy garnered a huge sympathy vote as a result of the brutal, unsolved murder of his daughter Valerie in the midst of the campaign.

Yates won his own 1966 reelection easily with 60 percent of the vote. He was certain that he would have beaten Percy. He would have run a much more vigorous campaign than Douglas, neutralizing the age comparisons. Since he was at the United Nations when Congress had passed the Gulf of Tonkin Resolution, which gave Johnson broad authority to expand the war in Southeast Asia, he had no voting record on Vietnam to challenge. There was no countering Percy's personal tragedy, of course, but Yates was certain that his electoral margin would have been sufficient.

Dirksen was up for reelection in 1968, but Yates had no taste for a rematch, anticipating that his opposition to the Vietnam War would reinforce LBJ's determination to see Dirksen reelected. With the Senate no longer an option, and a judgeship no longer an interest, Yates determined to focus all his energy on the 9th District and his career in the Congress. He became more strident in his opposition to LBJ's foreign policy and continued to be a reliable vote and voice on liberal issues, earning a 100 percent rating from Americans for Democratic Action, a 92 percent rating from the AFL-CIO's Committee on Political Education and a 0 percent rating from the conservative Americans for Constitutional Action. In the November 1968 elections, Nixon narrowly won Illinois over Vice President Humphrey, but Yates cruised in with 64.4 percent of the vote. As Yates expected, Johnson, who had chosen not to run again for president, undercut Dirksen's Democratic opponent, Illinois attorney general William G. Clark. Reporters invited to talk to LBJ in the Oval Office were shown an autographed color photograph of Dirksen "prominently propped up on a table" next to the president's desk. It was signed "To my long time colleague, my steadfast friend, President Lyndon Johnson, with esteem and warm personal wishes." LBJ handed the picture around. Clark, who was supported by both Yates and Adlai Stevenson III, Adlai's son, and was handpicked by Mayor Daley to run, conceded that he had neither LBJ's nor Daley's endorsement and hadn't seen the president in months. Dirksen beat Clark by 6 percent.[11]

7

"THIS PRECIOUS RESOURCE"

By 1969, Yates had moved off the Treasury, Post Office, and Executive Offices Subcommittee onto the newly formed Appropriations Subcommittee on Transportation, with his good friend Massachusetts congressman Edward Boland as chairman. The subcommittee had been established as a special subcommittee in the prior Congress to oversee the Department of Transportation, which had begun operations on April 1, 1967. The Transportation subcommittee would be the springboard for Yates's next crusade and make him a national champion of environmental issues.

Yates saw that a transformation in thinking was occurring about the environment. The conservation movement created by Gifford Pinchot and Theodore Roosevelt earlier in the twentieth century was no longer restricted to protecting the nation's great treasures like national parks and forests from developers and even from public uses like hydroelectric dams. The publication of *Silent Spring* in 1962 by Rachel Carson, an environmental scientist, had revolutionized politics and policy by declaring a public health emergency caused by the dangerous use of pesticides, particularly dichlorodiphenyltrichloroethane, better known as DDT. Protection of the environment now had a wider scope to include the whole life cycle and every living thing. Essentially, Carson, "the nun of nature" as many followers called her, contended that human actions had dire unintended consequences leading to a crisis in the entire ecosystem. *Silent Spring*, serialized in the *New Yorker*, and chosen as a Book-of-the-Month Club selection, was a best seller and provoked fierce opposition from the pesticide industry and the Department of Agriculture. After all, how dangerous could DDT be if it had been used during World War II to combat typhus and malaria? Dr. Paul Herman Muller was awarded the Nobel Peace prize in 1948 for his research in the use of DDT. But

President Kennedy's Science Advisory Committee followed up with a report on May 15, 1963, mostly verifying Carson's science and conclusions.

Within a decade, Carson won the ensuing debate with the public and Congress in dramatic fashion. The Environmental Defense Fund was founded in 1967 as a nonprofit advocacy organization, the Environmental Protection Agency was created by President Richard Nixon in 1970, and a phased-in ban on DDT was signed into law in 1972. The EPA was a special victory for Carson. She had contended there was a need for an independent arbiter on environmental matters inasmuch as the Department of Agriculture had the twin conflicting responsibilities of regulating the use of pesticides and, at the same time, promoting agriculture. The EPA gave environmentalists an independent voice. Yates was extremely well prepared to become one of the leading independent voices on the environment in the House, particularly on the Appropriations Committee.

One of the first clashes of technology and the environment after the *Silent Spring* revolution was the development of the supersonic transport airplane, nicknamed the SST. A civilian application to supersonic travel had been under discussion and study since the end of World War II. The mission of the project was to design a commercial aircraft that could fly 250 to 300 passengers at an altitude of 60,000 feet across the country, or the Atlantic, at the speed of sound. Conceptually, the SST was designed to be approximately 300 feet in length, with a wingspan of 142 feet and a height of 50 feet. With a little research and development funding, it seemed perfectly doable. If the military could achieve transportation at the speed of sound, it was reasoned, civil aviation could do the same, especially if the United States wanted to maintain its dominance in the world aviation marketplace. The National Advisory Committee on Aviation, the predecessor to NASA, was given the responsibility for conducting the initial studies on the feasibility of an SST.

In the meantime, the Soviets were engaging in their technological competition with the United States: exploding a hydrogen bomb; launching Sputnik, the first satellite in space; and developing and preparing to install intercontinental ballistic missiles. They also were looking into supersonic travel, as were the French and British. French president Charles de Gaulle, in particular, viewed the development of a French SST as a matter of French pride, a part of rebuilding his country after the physical and psychological devastation of World War II. When the French and British reached an agreement to jointly study and develop this new aviation phenomenon, the race was on.[1]

President Eisenhower was aware of some of the problems the military had encountered during the war with its aviation program and had misgivings about the economics of a civilian SST. He decided to go slow despite the activities of the Soviets and U.S. allies. Kennedy's election, however, reenergized the push for the SST. The new president, who had campaigned as a Cold Warrior, feared the loss of American prestige if the Soviets' version of the SST, called the TU-144, or even the French-British joint venture, now called the Concorde, were to beat the United States for superiority in civilian aviation. Some in the administration, particularly Defense Secretary Robert McNamara, a former president of the Ford Motor Company, seriously doubted the technological and economic viability of the SST. But Kennedy could not let either Charles de Gaulle or the Soviets get the best of him. On June 5, 1963, soon after the British and French announced their intention to move forward with the Concorde, Kennedy declared that "the United States will commit itself to an important program in civilian aviation." Significantly, Kennedy added, "Neither economics nor politics of international air competition permits us to stand still in this area." He went on to tell his audience, the graduating class of the Air Force Academy, "this Government should immediately commence a new program in partnership with private industry at the earliest practical date, the prototype of a commercially successful supersonic transport superior to that being built by any other country in the world." Kennedy sought to assure the public, "If these initial phases do not produce aircraft capable of transporting people and goods safely, swiftly, and at prices the traveler can afford and the airlines find profitable, we shall not go further."[2]

While supporters of the project were encouraged by the president's pronouncement, cautionary notes persisted. The president's green light was not a full-throated endorsement. Perhaps bearing in mind McNamara's warnings as the Federal Aviation Administration moved forward with NASA's assistance, certain stipulations were made for the project to proceed. Kennedy was lending his support to the SST, but he was not championing it as he had the space program. His address left open questions about the potential effect of the SST on the environment.

The Kennedy proposal became the basis for proceeding with development of an SST prototype. The administration sought to induce industry to buy into the partnership with a generous financial incentive. The Federal Aviation Agency (renamed the Federal Aviation Administration in 1967 when it became part of the Department of Transportation), which had taken the lead in promoting the project within the Kennedy administration, originally proposed that the federal government contribute half the funding for the development of an American SST, the other half to come from industry. When this proposal fell on deaf ears, the Kennedy administration upped the ante with new incentives under which the government would contribute 90 percent of the funding with industry matching with only 10 percent. Kennedy set the limit of government investment at $750 million. The administration required one payback stipulation in return for its investment. Industry would reap the profits from the first three hundred airplanes sold. Thereafter, the taxpayers would begin to recoup their money, and if five hundred airplanes were sold, the government would recapture all of its investment plus interest.

Secretary of Defense McNamara continued to have serious reservations and adopted a strategy of stalling advancement of the project for as long as he could. It was the economics of the project that McNamara questioned. While there was little public opposition, the *Wall Street Journal* consistently questioned the SST as an unwise expenditure of public funds. Finally, however, Boeing and General Electric won the competition for developing prototypes of an airframe and engine, respectively. The project was marching forward, slowly perhaps, but forward nonetheless.

For the remainder of the 1960s, Congress went along with the program with little dissent on the Appropriations Committees. One senator, William Proxmire of Wisconsin, regularly objected to the program. Proxmire argued that the SST should be developed solely by the aerospace industry and not with taxpayers' money. He was considered something of a crank and few colleagues paid much attention to him. And the project didn't receive much scrutiny by outside interests, either. The leading conservation groups, including the Sierra Club, Wilderness Society, and the Izaak Walton League, didn't consider this project their fight and confined themselves to their historic battles of protecting the wilderness.

In Yates's first tour in the House, his domestic interests had largely been urban, appropriations, and economic issues, and he had little involvement with environmental debates aside from supporting passage of the Federal Water Pollution Control Act in 1960. He responded to Eisenhower's veto of that act by writing, "The shortage of clean, usable water seems certain to become one of our greatest sources of worry for the future—and should be for the present, too, because we are rapidly running out of this precious resource."[3] But when he returned in 1965, he took a larger role and began to express himself in terms of the new thinking on air quality, clean water protections, and threats to the environment from modern technology, the new environmentalism.

In September 1966, Yates joined forces with Paul Douglas in an effort to preserve the Indiana Dunes along Lake Michigan by giving this pristine territory the status of a national lakeshore. He explained, "We must be concerned with the appearance and disappearance of America's irreplaceable national scenic treasures. They should be a part of the American heritage for all generations to come." Yates and Douglas overcame opposition from Indiana congressman Charles Halleck and successfully passed the act designating the Indiana Dunes National Lakeshore. Douglas was dubbed "the third senator from Indiana." The side of the border on which one lived determined whether it was a term of endearment or derision.

The following year, Yates took on the SST. The project had been moved to the Department of Transportation, and, as a member of the Transportation Appropriations subcommittee Yates had an opportunity for the first time to study the budget justifications presented by the Johnson administration. He was appalled at the cost, the environmental impact, and the decision of the White House to place the SST over priorities such as education, urban housing, and air and water pollution programs. While he labeled it "an adventuresome, imaginative program," he announced his opposition to the airplane. Yates could not have wished for a better opportunity, and the slowly forming opposition movement could not have wished for a better ally.[4]

Opposition to the SST had been slow to form. William Schurcliff, a research scientist from Harvard University, published *The SST and the Sonic Boom Handbook*, the first critique of the project by a source outside the government. It received little attention at the time but would soon become the bible of the anti-SST movement. In 1967 Schurcliff founded the Citizens' League Against the Sonic Boom. Another activist, Ken Greif, who was independently wealthy, joined in the fight. A high school science teacher, Greif read Schurcliffe's handbook and enlisted in the cause. A significant development was when the Sierra Club hired David Brower as its executive director in 1966. Brower recognized that the time had come for the Sierra Club to expand its reach beyond the narrow fights over wilderness preservation and into a larger sphere, as Rachel Carson had suggested, if it were going to maintain its leadership role. The brewing fight over the SST was about the larger environmental consequences of the airplane and the issue demanded the support of the new environmental movement sweeping the country. The group, ably assisted by Larry Moss and George Liebmann, an attorney hired by Greif, decided it needed an organized plan of action, which would include members of Congress to help lead the fight on the appropriations front.

The SST was not enough to keep Yates fully occupied, however. On a parallel track, he also undertook a leadership role on another issue of both local concern and national consequence, the antiballistic missile system (ABM). President Johnson had proposed that an antimissile system, the Sentinel, be developed to prevent the Chinese from attacking U.S. cities. Congress authorized $5 billion for deployment of the plan. When it was revealed that the army intended to site Sentinel missiles near major urban areas, an uproar arose among members representing densely populated areas. Yates was vocal in his opposition, submitting a minority report, neutrally titled "Additional Views" to the Military Construction appropriations bill for fiscal year 1969. He recalled how Clarence Cannon had penalized him years ago for filing a dissent to an appropriations bill, airing, as Cannon put it, the "dirty laundry" of the Appropriations Committee. This time,

however, Yates was joined by two colleagues on the committee in a lengthy ex-
position of their opposition. They argued that the Sentinel system was likely to
be ineffective against an attack, would be too costly, and would only aggravate
the arms race.[5]

Between January and June 1969, Yates devoted four monthly newsletters to
his opposition to the ABM. Yates pointed out that the army planned an ABM in
nearby Libertyville, Illinois, which, coincidentally, was Adlai Stevenson's hometown, in order to protect the Chicago area from attack. Like other congressmen
from urban areas, Yates was concerned about one of the ABMs exploding near
a densely populated area: "Although the chance for an accidental explosion of a
warhead either in or above the site is extremely small—the Army says it is 'essentially nil'—so long as there is even an infinitesimal chance of an accidental
nuclear explosion, it must be a source of great concern."[6]

The new Nixon administration got the message. The president halted the
Sentinel program and directed his secretary of defense, Melvin Laird, a former
congressman, to study the ABM program and report to him on its future. Laird
understood the mood of his former colleagues. He wisely recommended that
deployment of the new system, now called Safeguard, be in spacious areas of
the country, far away from population centers. The revised policy quieted much
of the opposition, though not Yates.[7] In June, he got into a letter-to-the-editor
debate in the *Chicago Daily News* with Dr. Edward Teller, a famous nuclear scientist and a strong supporter of Safeguard. Among other points, Yates questioned
the prioritization of military spending: "Our national security is of paramount
importance; but does it require that we continue to spend billions of dollars for
military hardware that is at best marginally relevant to our defense needs when
domestic programs for health, education, antipollution, housing, to mention only
a few, are gasping for funds?"[8]

Following up on his minority report, Yates continued his opposition on the
floor when the bill came up for vote in October 1969. In his speech, he took an
interesting tack. Proponents of the ABM had painted Yates and his allies as completely opposed to the system. Instead, Yates noted that he was not opposed to
the ABM but only to the plans for its deployment: "There is a time for research.
There is a time for deployment. As far as I am concerned we have not yet reached
the time for deployment. I support the efforts of the ABM proponents to continue
research to try to find a system that will resist incoming missiles. We have not yet
reached that position."[9] Over Yates's objections, the House approved funding for
Safeguard, accepting Nixon's argument that he needed the ABM as a bargaining
chip in his negotiations with the Soviets over an overall nuclear disarmament
agreement. In the Senate, the vote for approval was much closer than in the House,

51 to 50, with the vice president providing the tie-breaker. Nixon was aided in the Senate by the yea vote of Yates's friend, Scoop Jackson.[10]

Yates was not deterred and continued to express grave concern about nuclear warheads near urban areas, particularly those associated with the Nike-Hercules long-range, high-altitude antiaircraft missile system, which struck especially close to home. When Yates asked Secretary Laird whether the Nike-Hercules site situated in the 9th District at Belmont Harbor in Lake Michigan was armed with nuclear warheads, he was met with "stony silence." Yates demanded deactivation of the Belmont site. While he was unsuccessful in scrapping the ABM in the House, he was eventually successful in getting the Belmont site removed in 1971. His efforts were well received back home. As an editorial published by the widely circulated Lerner Home Newspaper chain concluded, "As we have said before about Yates, even though he sometimes is on the losing side, he is seldom on the wrong side. We congratulate him for once again serving the public interest."[11]

Five weeks after the Senate narrowly approved the ABM appropriations, the SST issue resurfaced. President Nixon announced that his administration would proceed with development of the SST. The president emphasized the need to remain competitive in aviation, where the United States presently had a decided edge but could lose it to the Europeans and the Soviets. The forces supporting Nixon's decision were formidable—congressional, business, and labor. The leadership in the Congress—across the board, Republican and Democratic—supported the project. The proponents in the Senate were led by Washington State's two Democratic powerhouses, Scoop Jackson and Warren Magnuson, dubbed "the Senators from Boeing."[12] Both were committee chairmen, Magnuson of Commerce, and Jackson of Interior and Insular Affairs. Each one was influential in his own right but, taken together, it was estimated they had control over the immediate interests of at least half the Senate. It didn't go without notice that Jackson, in particular, had delivered for the president on the ABM. Jackson also had a reputation as a supporter of conservation and was considered a friend of the Sierra Club and similar environmental organizations. In the House, the Speaker, the chairman of the Appropriations Committee, and their Republican counterparts were united in support of the SST. Boeing and General Electric had secured the contracts to develop the airplane and exerted economic muscle. It was estimated the SST would produce as many as fifty thousand jobs. The International Association of Machinists and Aerospace Workers took an aggressive stand in supporting the project. The industry had been losing jobs as the airline industry was in a recession and the machinists needed this project desperately.

For good reason, the supporters saw victory as inevitable. Not only were the supporters well positioned, experienced, and influential, but the opposition appeared especially weak. In the Senate, Proxmire led the opposition with Maine's Ed Muskie and Proxmire's Wisconsin colleague Gaylord Nelson. In the House, Yates and Henry Reuss took on the fight. They were joined by Silvio Conte, a moderate Republican and ranking member of the Appropriations Subcommittee on Transportation. None of the opponents chaired a major committee or even a subcommittee. A Department of Transportation official summed up the sentiment well: "All along we'd been fortunate in our opponents. Yates and Reuss are not exactly powerhouses in the House. And Proxmire—being Proxmire—was never able to mount any kind of support for his position."[13] Besides, the environmental lobby had not, as yet, coalesced and mobilized on the issue. The perseverance and intelligence of the congressional opponents were greatly underestimated.

Yates and Reuss targeted one of Nixon's great vulnerabilities—his penchant for secrecy. The president had commissioned four studies on the SST from several groups, including a subcabinet-level interdepartmental Ad Hoc SST Review Committee and a committee of outside technical experts headed by Dr. Richard L. Garwin, one of the world's most eminent physicists, who had designed the world's first hydrogen bomb and was a member of the president's Science Advisory Committee. In December 1969, the congressmen demanded the release of the studies. The White House, citing executive privilege, initially refused. Yates had previously attacked the SST Ad Hoc Review Committee's report and when Nixon finally bowed to public and congressional pressure and released the report, Yates expressed "amazement" that "President Nixon approved the request for the SST." "The committee," he said, "which consisted of many of the ablest people in the administration, recommended overwhelmingly in favor of suspending work on the project." The report disputed the administration's major arguments in support of the SST—that it was economically viable, that the private sector would invest in it, and that there were few, if any environmental concerns, including sonic booms. Finally, Yates summed it all up: "With the appropriations proposal for this year expenditures on the project will very nearly reach the limit set by President Kennedy, and if the appropriations scheduled to be made over the next 5 years are added, this airplane will cost more than one half billion dollars more than the amount Mr. Kennedy established. I believe this is the logical time to call a halt to the program and I shall try to strike the appropriations in committee."[14] Yates proceeded to have the report published in the *Congressional Record*. Meanwhile, Reuss appealed to the House Committee on Freedom of Information to enlist its support in getting the administration's other reports on the SST.

The effort did not go without notice. Alan L. Otten of the *Wall Street Journal* took note: "For his valuable warning the public is indebted to Democratic Representative Sidney Yates of Illinois, who has somehow caused the Department of Transportation to make public a full record of the deliberations of President Nixon's SST Ad Hoc Review Committee."[15] Otten explained that the report's conclusion in support of continued funding did not follow the content of the report. The *Wall Street Journal* would be the only major business news outlet to consistently oppose future development of the SST.

In the midst of this fight, Yates found that his membership on Transportation Appropriations gave him other opportunities to challenge Nixon's priorities and enhance his environmental credentials. Yates led a successful effort in November 1969, for instance, to kill a proposed airport on the outskirts of Everglades National Park six miles north of Miami, Florida, which, if built, would have had severe environmental consequences.[16]

Despite Yates's efforts in the Appropriations Committee and Reuss's ongoing public barrage, Congress, in December 1969, approved Nixon's request for $96 million to continue the SST project. Republican Thomas M. Pelly of Washington summed it up succinctly: "The issue before us is whether we support a policy which would contribute to the economy of Russia and the economy of Britain and France by turning down the U.S. SST progress; or rather if we want to provide for many thousands of jobs in America for Americans in practically every state."[17]

Yates realized that the environmental movement had been slow to understand the SST's impact. For example, the week before the SST vote, Gary Soucie, executive director of Friends of the Earth, telephoned Richard Wegman, Proxmire's legislative assistant, asking what his group could do to stop the SST. "Where were you when we needed you?" Wegman bluntly responded. He told him to be better prepared next time.[18] The environmental groups accepted the advice, stimulated in large part by Lawrence Moss, who had been a White House fellow at the Department of Transportation (DOT) in 1969. Moss entered DOT as a self-described " SST enthusiast," had been in the meetings of the president's Ad Hoc Review Committee, and had left convinced that the project was an environmental travesty. Moreover, the Sierra Club and Friends of the Earth had concluded the time had come to organize. On March 24, 1970, a group "interested in organizing opposition to the SST appropriations bill" met at the Occidental Restaurant in Washington, DC. Attendees included representatives from the Sierra Club and Friends of the Earth, scientists and engineers, and staff representing Yates, Reuss, and Senator Clifford Case. The National Wildlife Federation and the Consumer Federation of America joined the coalition shortly afterward.[19]

Yates's designee was a young staffer, Harold Bergan, a Chicago native and a constituent. As a graduate student at Georgetown University, Bergan had taken an interest in the ABM debate, written a paper on the subject, and dropped off a copy at Yates's office. When two weeks passed and he'd not heard anything, Bergan returned to Yates's office and inquired about the congressman's reaction to his thoughts. Janet Schnitz, who ran Yates's Capitol office, told Bergan she'd not seen the paper but asked whether he'd like to work for Yates. Surprised, he immediately accepted the offer. Now he was attending a strategy meeting with environmental heavyweights on an issue of national consequence.

It was agreed that, in light of Yates's position on the Appropriations Subcommittee on Transportation, he'd lead the opposition. Bergan was assigned responsibility for lining up and preparing the witnesses who would testify in opposition to the SST funding. The group formally organized as the Coalition Against the SST.[20]

The day after the Occidental meeting, the Concorde made its maiden flight at 700 mph. The competition now was for real.

Events moved quickly. On April 22, 1970, the First Annual Earth Day, a momentous event in the history of the emerging environmental movement, took place. Environmentalists were no longer sequestered in their classrooms or offices but were taking direct political action. The Earth Day event drew an estimated 20 million participants with ten thousand schools and two thousand colleges and universities joining in organized events. Speakers around the country urged a more robust environmental policy guaranteeing protection from air, land, and water contamination. Speakers at the rallies were cheered as they emphasized preservation of the "ecosystem," not just parks but all of life.

The success of 1970 Earth Day caught the attention of politicians. To highlight the opposition to the SST and to relate it to Earth Day, Proxmire held hearings of his Subcommittee on Economy in Government over three days, May 7, 11, and 12, and intensified his efforts on the SST. Yates and Reuss testified before the Senate, as Yates had in the Rickover fight, but an unusual step for Reuss. For the most part the hearing went according to script until the third day, when Dr. Garwin and Russell Train, chairman of the Council on Environmental Quality, testified. Garwin speculated that the SST at takeoff would generate as much noise as fifty 747 jumbo jets and Train added that the SST proposal posed "environmental problems" that he described as "exceedingly serious." Train was concerned about the effect of a fleet of SSTs on the ozone layer in the atmosphere.

Although Train had made a distinction between a fleet of SSTs and the few prototypes being proposed, the distinction was lost on the reporting of his testimony. Train's words got everyone's attention, including that of the Department of Transportation and Yates. Train later attempted to clarify his testimony but it was too late. Their analysis confirmed what Yates had been saying all along. In future congressional hearings and floor debate, Yates continually used the hearings to buttress his case and to appeal to members whose districts were situated near airports.[21]

When the Transportation Appropriations bill came to the floor for debate, Yates was ready. The committee's recommendation was $289,965,000 for the SST. The debate was contentious but polite. At one point, Silvio Conte said, "This is a very tough problem. How to vote is going to be a tough decision for everyone here today," to which Yates promptly replied, "Not for me." The opponents emphasized noise at the airports and the sonic booms that would be generated by the SST. Some questioned the economic viability of the project and cited studies showing the estimated cost of the project at $1.3 billion with cost overruns already estimated at $76 million. Supporters argued that the United States needed to remain competitive in the international market or lose out to the Soviets and the British-French Concorde collaboration. The administration conceded the sonic boom argument, agreeing that the SST would not fly across the United States until the problem was solved. Perhaps the most compelling argument was over job growth. There was no denying that the U.S. aerospace industry had lost jobs and that the SST would provide a significant boost to the industry.

Yates imaginatively tried, toward the end of the debate, to derail the SST on a technical point of order by questioning whether DOT even had the legal authority "to develop an aircraft for a private company." Congressman Edward Boland, the manager of the bill, challenged Yates's contention, maintaining that "the funds sought in the appropriations bill go only toward Government's share of the SST prototypes." The point of order was overruled. Next Yates offered an amendment to strike all funds for the SST. After a short continuation of the debate, the Yates amendment lost 176–162. It had been closer than ever. The organizing of the environmentalists and their congressional allies was beginning to show signs of progress.[22]

A *Chicago Sun-Times* editorial commended Yates on his efforts, declaring the SST "a boondoggle." Soon thereafter, Senator Charles Percy became the first Republican to break ranks and oppose the SST, foreshadowing a more sympathetic response on the other side of the Capitol.[23] The Senate voted down the appropriation 51–41 on December 3, 1970, requiring that the SST's future be settled in conference.

Members were eager to adjourn for the Christmas recess but couldn't leave a $7 billion transportation bill hanging. As the House prepared to appoint conferees, Yates made a strategic error. As a subcommittee member, he would automatically be a conferee. Instead of quietly working within conference to uphold the Senate's position, he moved that the House instruct the House conferees to do so. The motion awakened the White House and its allies in the Senate. On December 5, President Nixon, who to that point had been preoccupied with foreign policy concerns, strongly declared for the SST, labeling the Senate's vote "a devastating mistake." He noted that the government had spent $700 million and it would cost an additional $278 million to close out the project if the Senate prevailed. "It would be like stopping construction of a house when it was time to put in the door," Nixon concluded. The House voted 213–174 to table Yates's motion. On December 10, the conferees compromised and cut the appropriations for the SST to $210 million, an $80 million reduction.[24]

Buoyed by the narrowness of the vote in the preceding session, Yates got ready for the next round. He particularly threw himself into preparations for the committee hearings in the new Congress. Bergan reached out to prospective witnesses before the Appropriations Subcommittee on Transportation. He and Yates discussed strategy as they walked briskly between Yates's office in the Rayburn House Office Building and the Capitol. It was heady stuff for the young staffer as the witness list began to grow. Yates, in the meantime, steeped himself further in the details of all aspects of the SST.[25]

Yates recognized that he needed more public support. Hearings of the Appropriations Committee had traditionally been held in executive session, with outside attendance strictly limited. Yates proposed an exception to open the hearings to the public and the press. The committee agreed. Now Yates needed to make sure that the show lived up to the hype. He sought the support of the foremost living U.S. aerospace pioneer, Charles Lindbergh. Now sixty-eight, Lindbergh was a celebrity and a legend. The first aviator to fly nonstop from New York to Paris, the recipient of the Congressional Medal of Honor, the grieving father of the most famous kidnapping in American history, and in FDR's (and Yates's) view, a Nazi sympathizer, Lindbergh would ensure media attention. On the eve of the hearings, Lindbergh, currently serving as a member of the Board of Directors of Pan American World Airways, which in fact had signed a purchase option for the Concorde, announced his opposition to the SST. He wrote Yates that the SST was "within the state of the art technically but not economically or environmentally."[26]

Reporters from radio, newspapers, and television swarmed to cover the SST hearings. To emphasize the leadership's support for the project, Representative George Mahon, chairman of the full Appropriations Committee, attended much of the hearings and even questioned one of the witnesses, William Ruckelshaus, the first administrator of the Environmental Protection Agency. Mahon wanted the administrator's assurance that the EPA would limit its review of the SST to matters of the environment and wouldn't step into the economics of the project or any other matter. He got his assurance, but Mahon's presence made an even stronger point. It was unusual for the chairman of the full committee to participate in a subcommittee hearing unless he was a member of that subcommittee.

The hearings were chaired by John J. McFall, who had lined up his own stellar cast of supporters, which included John Volpe, secretary of Transportation, and William Magruder, the administration's point man on the project. Probably no one in government knew more about the SST than Magruder. He had all the details at his fingertips and was well prepared. To blunt Yates's questioning of the economics of the project, Magruder promised, "You will get all of the money back. This is a loan. The taxpayer will put up $1.3 billion and starting with the sale of the first airplane when 300 airplanes are sold in a successful production program all that money will come back." Back and forth, Yates sparred with Volpe and Magruder, and all other administration witnesses. The dialogue involved details on trade statistics, science, and even projections on how many passengers there would be on the SST.

Opposing the machinists union was particularly uncomfortable for Yates. He had always championed organized labor but could not support the SST, despite the jobs it would create. When Floyd Smith, international president of the International Association of Machinists and Aerospace Workers, testified about the lifeline the SST would provide to his members, seriously hurt by the dramatic downturn in the aerospace industry, Yates tactfully replied, "I am sorry I find myself on the opposite side."

Next came the economists' turn. There wasn't much that the likes of Paul Samuelson and John Kenneth Galbraith, both liberal economists, and Milton Friedman, a noted conservative leader of the famous University of Chicago school of economic thought, agreed about, but, in the case of the SST, Yates submitted statements from both schools of thought expressing their opposition. The reasons were different, of course, but their unified opposition was referred to several times during the hearings and the subsequent floor debate.[27]

Not unexpectedly, the subcommittee voted 7 to 2 to continue funds for the SST, acceding to the administration's request. Republican Silvio Conte voted with Yates. As he had done on the ABM, Yates submitted a "Separate Views" statement summarizing his reasons for dissenting. After reviewing the environmental dangers—noise, sonic boom, consequences for the atmosphere—and the dubious economics, Yates took direct aim at Boeing: "Mr. Wellington, Vice President of the Boeing Company, admitted last year that he doubted Boeing could obtain the necessary financing after the prototype phases because the

company's net worth was not adequate for the purpose." He then quoted Friedman's statement that the economic arguments for the SST "have no economic
validity whatsoever" and Samuelson's description of the program as "an economic and political disaster." Indeed, Yates continued, "The Administration,
which has flooded the [Congressional] Record with the views of every authority it could find in support of the SST, apparently could discover no economist
willing to challenge his colleagues." Yates could not resist noting: "Every opinion poll in the country, without exception, shows the American people do not
want government financing of the SST." He concluded by contending the SST
would be an airplane for the elite. "Only 10% of American air travelers would
use the plane," he added, and "they do not want to fly supersonically if they
have to pay a premium fare." Five members of the full Appropriations Committee concurred with Yates's statement.[28]

Yates introduced an amendment to overturn the Appropriations Committee's
decision and end funding for the SST. The floor debate promised to be most unusual. Floor debates ordinarily are predictable and poorly attended. Leadership
rarely brings a bill to the floor for a vote unless they know there is a majority to
pass it. Such was not the case with the SST. Quite the opposite. Over two days,
March 17 and 18, 1971, the House of Representatives debated the future of the
SST.[29] It attracted attention across the nation. Congressman Teno Roncolio from
Wyoming summed it up: "Mr. Chairman, the supersonic transport plane has
generated more response from Wyoming than any other national issue, and it
is nearly unanimous in opposing another cent for the SST at this time." He continued, "There is no way to characterize the mail from Wyoming. It came from
medical doctors, ranchers, laborers, housewives, students, retired persons, from
a genuine cross section of the population."

The congressional leadership, Republican and Democratic, knew they had a
fight on their hands. Both Mahon and Representative Gerald Ford, the Republican minority leader, started out the debate making clear that this was a strong
bipartisan effort. More than fifty members engaged in the debate on both sides.
At one point, on the second day of debate, Mahon took to the floor again: "Mr.
Chairman, there is a mood of expectancy and excitement in the House of Representatives today which we seldom find." Yates was front and center during the
entire debate, sparring with opponents and strategically recognizing allies to
speak in support.

Finally, time on debate expired. Yates demanded that the vote on his amendment be counted by "tellers with clerks." This was a new form of voting instituted
by the House only the past March. Previously, votes in the Committee of the
Whole, where legislation was debated before final passage, were not recorded. If

the vote was contested, members were appointed as "tellers" to walk down the aisle and count which representatives were standing. By demanding "tellers with clerks," the name of each member supporting or opposing a measure was taken down and made public. Although electronic recording machines were contemplated and would later be installed, for now the tellers would walk with House staff to record the votes.

Tellers with clerks were ordered and four members of the subcommittee, Yates, Jack Edwards of Alabama, McFall, and Conte, were appointed as tellers. The tellers reported there were ayes 217, nays 204, not voting 12.[30]

Against all the odds, Yates had won. He smiled broadly at the announcement of the vote, happily receiving the congratulations of his allies on the floor. Up in the visitors' gallery, Magruder, who had attended the debate, slumped in his seat, a glum look on his face.

Shortly thereafter, Yates analyzed the victory in one of his monthly newsletters. He attributed the result to two procedural changes: "For the first time, the hearings of the appropriations subcommittee were open to the public and open to the press, something for which I had been fighting for years." He added: "The second procedural change was contained in the Legislative Reform Act passed last year, which provided for a recorded vote during debate on the floor." Yates commented wryly: "Members are most attentive to a recorded vote." This had been the first major piece of legislation using the new tellers with clerks reform.[31]

Yates did not mention in the newsletter his mastery of House procedure and the substance of the subject. He didn't need to. Yates's leadership on the SST was noted by news commentators in Chicago and nationally. John Madigan of WBBM radio in Chicago, for example, opined: "But Yates was in there fighting the SST . . . just as he was on the anti-ballistic missile issue . . . long before the down-with-pollution kick . . . and the cry for more relevant priorities . . . became good political issues to which a candidate might hitch his rhetoric. And it's his bill that has now scored a direct hit on the SST." David Broder of the *Washington Post* saw the vote as a test of the new transparency: "Last Thursday's vote on the Yates amendment to delete funds for the SST . . . provided the first real test of that reform (recorded votes), and it checked out on all points."[32]

On May 20, 1971, Boeing canceled the SST project. There had been speculation for a year or so beforehand that Boeing had lost enthusiasm for the project, particularly after it had launched its newest entry into air travel, the 747 "jumbo jet," the previous year. One of the selling points of the SST had been its ability to move more passengers, since it could go back and forth so quickly. The 747, however, with its much larger seating capacity and far lower per-passenger expense, took away much of that argument.

Yates's successful leadership on the SST made him a hero to the Sierra Club and other environmental organizations. In particular, the Sierra Club became a major supporter and would, in February 1982, during a particularly nasty primary election campaign, give Yates the club's first political endorsement of a federal candidate in its history.[33]

On a wider scope, the SST controversy marked a new era in U.S. politics. For the first time, the Congress rejected a technological advance in favor of environmental considerations. Yates reflected on this change in attitude in his testimony in August 1970: "We no longer are willing to accept the concept that anything which is bigger or more faster [*sic*] or will earn a dollar is automatically progress."[34] Rachel Carson's message had been received and acted on.

PART III

THE CHAIRMAN
1975–98

8

AMERICA'S COMMITTEE

Yates enjoyed his participation on the Transportation Appropriations Subcommittee, but he was ready for a new assignment. At the start of the 92nd Congress in 1971, he had made the Appropriations Subcommittee on the Department of the Interior and Related Agencies, known informally as the "Interior Appropriations Subcommittee," or just the "Interior subcommittee," his second subcommittee, and in 1973, at the urging of both the Chicago leadership and national Jewish leadership had added Foreign Operations, the main source of Israel's foreign aid, as a third subcommittee.

In 1975, upon the retirement of Interior Appropriations chair Julia Butler Hansen, and the decision of David Obey, whose position on the subcommittee was senior to Yates's, to move to another subcommittee, Yates decided to bid for the chairmanship, spurning the pleas of many of his important Jewish supporters to keep his seniority on the Foreign Operations Subcommittee and to seek its chairmanship instead in another term or so.[1]

Yates's desire to take the chairmanship betrayed a keen understanding of the process and the potential of the Interior Appropriations post. Members called it "America's Committee." He would be first chair of this subcommittee representing urban areas. All the previous chairs were from rural and mostly western districts dependent on the departments overseen by the subcommittee. The panel controlled the budgets for land use departments like the U.S. Forest Service, the Bureau of Land Management, and the National Park Service, as well as Indian affairs and fossil fuel development and energy conservation within the Department of Energy, among others. Yates, however, saw great potential to assist urban areas of the country as well. He had been a strong supporter of regional parks, like the Indiana Dunes National Lakeshore, and was an advocate of the slowly emerging urban parks and forestry movement. He believed in the work of the National Endowments for the Arts and Humanities, which he saw as culturally beneficial but also as engines of economic development for urban and rural areas alike.

The chairmanship had one additional important immediate benefit. It meant admittance to that most important club of all, the College of Cardinals, as the chairmen of the appropriations subcommittees were called. As a cardinal, Yates would have a seat at the table with the other twelve chairmen when decisions were made and could use his new position to help Chicago and Illinois secure funding for transportation and other necessities that the governor or mayor might need.

The chairmanship was not assured. He had been robbed of a similar opportunity when Clarence Cannon thwarted his promotion by eliminating the subcommittee. This time would be different. On August 9, 1974, Nixon became the first and only president to resign from office. On the heels of Nixon's departure, the autocratic chairman of the House Ways and Means Committee, Wilbur Mills, was caught in a titillating scandal when police stopped his Lincoln Continental early in the morning of October 7, 1974, and one of Mills's passengers, Annabelle Battistella, jumped into the Tidal Basin near the Jefferson Memorial. Battistella, a thirty-eight-year-old stripper known as "Fanne Fox, the Argentine Firecracker," was grist for the newspaper mills. The chairman shortly compounded the scandal by appearing on stage at a strip club in Boston with Fox. Despite his assertion that "this won't ruin me . . . nothing can ruin me," Mills ended up resigning his chairmanship and entered an alcoholism treatment center. Mills became the poster boy for congressional reform.[2]

Revulsion at the Watergate scandal that engulfed the Nixon administration came swiftly in the 1974 congressional elections. Republicans suffered a massive defeat at the polls, losing 49 seats in the House and 5 in the Senate. In the House there was a turnover of 92 new representatives, of which 71 were Democrats, known as the "Watergate babies." Congressman Tip O'Neill, a keen observer of the House's membership, described the new members as "highly sophisticated and talented . . . and independent, and they didn't hesitate to remind you that they were elected on their own, often without any help from the Democratic Party."

The new class of freshmen was bent on making reforms in the way the House functioned. A major change was to diminish the role of seniority in selecting the chairmen of the Committees and the Appropriations Subcommittees. Yates had long supported such reforms vocally and with his votes. He had chafed since first being elected to the Congress under the rigid seniority system and had made his views well known. Yates's first newsletter, dated March 17, 1949, discussed the defeat of legislation he had helped sponsor and he described the southern Democrats as "reactionaries" and speculated about "talk" then circulating around the Capitol about "a sub-rosa deal (that) has been made between the twin blocs of reaction": Republicans opposed to social programs and southern Democrats opposed to President Truman's civil rights program. Nothing in the interim had happened to change Yates's mind. In January 1969, Yates, Phil Burton, and a few like-minded reformers challenged John McCormack's reelection as Speaker. For Yates, it wasn't personal. He had a cordial enough relationship with McCormack but felt the time had come for a change in the way business was conducted. Yates seconded Representative Mo Udall's nomination. Even though Udall lost, the reformers' point had been made. Upon taking office, McCormack began to schedule more meetings of the House Democratic caucus so the reformers could have a forum for expression.

Yates's reputation as a champion of reform was growing. His reputation was enhanced when, in August 1974, William Shannon in the *New York Times* included Yates as one of the Democrats "deserving of serious consideration" for the Democratic presidential nomination in 1976, as far-fetched as that may have seemed.[3]

After meeting for a few days in January 1975, the Watergate babies were ready to do battle. Burton and Obey, admirers and supporters of Yates, were advising them on strategy. Startling the old barons on Capitol Hill, the freshmen demanded that all the chairmen, including Appropriations subcommittee chairmen, submit to formal interviews before getting their votes in the Democratic caucus to continue their chairmanships. This was a direct challenge to the authority of the southern Democratic members and, for a few of them, the interviews went poorly. The "unbelievably uppity" freshmen challenged them on their tight-fisted use of authority and on policy issues, like the war in Vietnam and civil rights. Four southern congressmen lost their chairmanships, including F. Edward Hébert, longtime leader of the Committee on Armed Services. Hébert, according to David Obey, a frequent target of Hébert's scorn, treated younger members, particularly liberals and progressives, like "pond scum."[4] He was contemptuous of the few women and minorities on his committee, notably Congresswoman Pat Schroeder of Colorado and Congressman Ron Dellums of California, an African American. Hébert deliberately arranged the seats on the committee dais so that the two liberals were required to share the same chair. When Hébert opened his interview with the freshman caucus with the words "Well, boys and girls," his fate was sealed. The caucus removed Hébert from Armed Services. Yates didn't mind seeing another segregationist ousted. And he was pleased when his friend and ally, Henry Reuss, became the new chairman of the Committee on Banking.[5]

Yates was nervous as he went for his interview, but, unlike the autocratic chairmen, the meeting was almost a love fest. The congressman's opposition to the Vietnam War, support for the Great Society antipoverty programs, and support for reforming the seniority rules stood him in good stead with the Watergate class.

Leaving the room, he joked to his colleagues, "My chairmanship came quickly . . . overnight, in fact. All I had to do was wait twenty-four years for it."[6]

Aside from gaining the chairmanship he had desired, Yates also protected the subcommittee's jurisdiction. It had been rumored that George Mahon, chairman of the Appropriations Committee, would try to transfer control of the fossil fuel and energy conservation programs of the Department of Energy from Yates's Interior Appropriations Subcommittee to the subcommittee on Natural Resources, with a chairman more amenable to Mahon's Texas politics. The freshmen revolt and the warm reception that Yates received put an end to Mahon's plans.

In the period when Yates took over, the membership of this subcommittee, both in the House and in its counterpart in the Senate, came primarily from states with significant natural resources, particularly the Western states. That part was not a surprise. The federal government owns approximately 28 percent of all the land in the United States, the greatest percentages in the West. The government owns, for example, 61.2 percent of Alaska and 61.6 percent of Idaho. It followed that senators such as Ted Stevens of Alaska and James McClure of Idaho each fought to be on, and ultimately chaired, the Senate Interior Appropriations Subcommittee. Similarly, on the House side, members from states such as Washington (28% federally owned), Utah (65% federally owned), and Oregon (53% federally owned)—Julia Butler Hansen and Norm Dicks, Gunn McKay, and Bob Duncan and Les AuCoin, respectively—bid for participation on the subcommittee. The United States not only managed and regulated most of the federally owned acreage, through agencies such as the Bureau of Land Management, the Fish and Wildlife Service, the National Park Service, and the Forest Service, but also, through a program known as "payment in lieu of taxes," reimbursed the Western states for the property taxes and other fees the states would have been able to impose had the public lands been held privately.

Congressmen from those states needed to make certain that their constituents, who were affected by the rules and regulations of these federal instrumentalities, had a voice, and no voice spoke louder to an agency head than the committee that appropriated the funds for its operations. When federal dollars were allocated to the West, these Western representatives wanted to be sure they had a seat at the table.

Urban congressmen were rarely interested in the Interior Appropriations Subcommittee. The 9th District of Illinois, anchored on Chicago's lakefront, had no national parks, national forests, or coal mines. The closest national park was the Indiana Dunes National Lakeshore, across Lake Michigan in Indiana, which Yates and Douglas helped create in 1966. And Illinois's sole National Forest, Shawnee, was hundreds of miles south at the tip of the state. But Yates knew that the Interior Appropriations Subcommittee's apparent distance from his constituents' interests would make it all the more valuable.

Since 1949, Yates had been watching the ways other appropriations chairmen ran their committees and their staff. Interior was going to reflect his idea of how a subcommittee should be run. His subcommittee clerk, Dave Wilson, chosen by Chairman Mahon, was not happy. Wilson had been Julia Butler Hansen's clerk and had been with the subcommittee a long time. The professional staff of the Appropriations Committee had a saying, "Chairmen come and go. The staff stays forever." Wilson had his own way of doing things. Yates had other ideas. He had been waiting too long and was planning to make up for lost time.

Yates's first action was to move the subcommittee offices out of the Capitol and into larger quarters in the Rayburn Building. Appropriations committee rooms were deliberately cramped, to discourage public and press attendance, and the members sat at an elevated dais, looking down at the witnesses. Yates wanted more seats available for the public. In addition, instead of a dais, he wanted hearings held around a conference table, so that he could have conversations with witnesses rather than interrogations. Wilson was furious, as an office in the Capitol was a status symbol, and he had a huge fight with Yates over the move. But Mahon sided with Yates, partly to support his subcommittee chairmen, but more likely because he was delighted to have another room in the Capitol for his use.

Next, Yates changed the way the subcommittee's proceedings were published. At the beginning of each year, the administration presented its proposed budget to Congress, which was then divided among the jurisdictions of the various subcommittees. These budget justifications were eventually published in printed volumes along with the transcripts of the subcommittee's hearings. The practice of the Appropriations Committee was to wait until all the hearings were held and the bill passed, before publishing the justifications. This had the effect of preventing public witnesses from seeing the budget before testifying in favor of or in opposition to particular programs. Yates wanted to reform the process. He consulted Bob Wolf, a professional forester who had become assistant chief of the Environment and Natural Resources Division of the Congressional Research Service. Wolf suggested that the justifications be published immediately as volumes 1 and 2 of the subcommittee record, and that public witnesses be scheduled at the end of the hearing season, so that they would have an opportunity to comment on the administration's proposals. Yates readily agreed and sent Dan Beard, a member of his personal staff who covered the Interior Appropriations Subcommittee, to tell Wilson to implement the change. According to Beard, "Wilson just about had a heart attack. 'If we do that,'" Wilson told Beard, "'everyone will have a copy of the budget.'" Wilson refused and went to see Yates. Another fight ensued, but Yates again prevailed with Mahon.

Finally, before each hearing, Wilson would provide Yates with a set of questions. The questions were soft, on the assumption that the agencies that appeared before the subcommittee would never lie to a subcommittee clerk and the real work would be done in private negotiations between the clerk and the agency staff. Yates refused to accept the questions, preferring to use a combination of his own questions and those prepared by Beard in consultation with Yates.

By the end of Yates's first year as chairman, he and Wilson were barely speaking to each other. Beard was the go-between, hearing Wilson say "I can't do this," and Yates saying "We are going to do this." Finally, Yates went to Mahon and demanded a replacement clerk. Mahon agreed, and Fred Mohrman was assigned. Morhman, an Illinois native and professional budget analyst, worked with Yates for the next ten years, until he was appointed chief clerk of the full committee. Despite some initial misunderstandings, Mohrman appreciated the difference between elected representatives and permanent staff and assisted Yates in his continuing reforms of the subcommittee.[7]

The subcommittee finally under control, Yates wasted little time advancing his agenda of including urban areas, for the first time, in his subcommittee's appropriations. In November 1978, President Jimmy Carter signed into law the Urban Park and Recreation Recovery Act (UPARR), legislation that Yates and Phil Burton, the primary author of the bill, had long sought, authorizing $725 million in federal matching grants and technical assistance for economically distressed communities. In the statement accompanying the president's signing, Carter noted that UPARR "addresses the primary need to improve recreational opportunities in our urban areas" and offered to work with Congress "to assure swift implementation." Yates now had his vehicle and, indeed, moved swiftly.[8]

On February 10, 1979, Yates gaveled his subcommittee to order at the Broadway Armory at 5917 North Broadway in the 9th District. On only three previous occasions since its creation in 1865 had the Appropriations Committee ever held a hearing outside Washington, and for the first time in its history the Interior Appropriations Subcommittee was holding a "field hearing." The purpose of the hearing was to highlight the importance of UPARR and to give a vivid example of the need for its funding. The Broadway Armory was a facility under the direction of the Illinois National Guard that was greatly underused and offered an opportunity for conversion into a neighborhood recreation center, as President Carter had envisioned in his signing statement. Yates recalled that the armory was also the former headquarters of the National Guard regiment of General Julius Stein, his ally in the Rickover fight so many years earlier.

Two local leaders, Neil Hartigan, the Democratic Committeeman of the north side's 49th Ward, and state senator Arthur Berman, in whose district the armory was located, had approached Yates in 1978 seeking federal funds. After hearing the details of the project and touring the armory, Yates, seeing a great opportunity, told the two leaders that he expected UPARR to be passed and signed by the president. He advised them to begin organizing the Edgewater and adjacent communities and assured them of his support.[9]

The hearing was attended by senior leadership of the Department of the Interior, including the assistant secretary for Fish and Wildlife and Parks, the assistant to the secretary of the Interior, the Interior Department's director of the budget, and the director of the Heritage Conservation and Recreation Service, with direct responsibility for administering UPARR. Several dignitaries of the City of Chicago, including Mayor Michael Bilandic, and several local activists and community organizations took part in the hearing. The principals of the local schools also attended to support the project. The U.S. Conference of Mayors, represented by the mayor of Toledo, Ohio, participated and testified to the growing national need for UPARR.

Opening the hearing, Yates described how he had watched the Chicago Bruins play professional basketball at the armory in the 1920s and later, in the following decade, he had played semipro ball there "when 2-handed shots were in style." He observed that the surrounding area had grown in population, but recreational opportunities were "minimal" and that "the new law which we are discussing today presents the opportunity to provide recreation for the people of the area as a necessary part of their lifestyle."

The staff from the Department of the Interior then explained the background to enactment of the legislation and its intent: "The opportunity posed by the Urban Park and Recreation Recovery Act is to restore some of our aging facilities and therefore brings additional vitality and activity into urban recreation programs. Indeed, Chicago would be unique among American cities if its recreational system were not suffering the effects of the past decade's crisis in local financing." After the department's representatives concluded their remarks, Mayor Bilandic testified in support and thanked Yates for all his previous assistance to the city. Subcommittee member Robert Duncan, who had flown in that Saturday morning, described the change in direction of the subcommittee's work: "May I also say that this chairman that you people have sent to Washington, D.C., is an Easterner and the Interior Committee has traditionally been Western oriented, but Mr. Yates has shown a great deal of empathy and understanding for the problems all over this country. He has a truly national approach to the legislative problems of this country and it has engendered a reciprocal feeling, indeed eagerness, on the part of his colleagues from out West to want to take a similar approach to the problems of the big cities. So you owe him a lot."

Yates was in his element, enjoying the proceedings. When the principal of Edgewater's Senn High School appeared, Yates engaged in some friendly banter. "Mr. Martin, can you tell me whether or not Lakeview High School still beats you in basketball, as they did when I played on the team?" Yates inquired. With pride, Martin replied: "No, Lakeview is still a fine educational institution, however last time we played basketball about 10 days ago we were victorious." The hearing went on. Martin, a former Latin teacher, and Yates were comparing their language proficiency when Representative Duncan broke in: "He (Yates) translated that Latin for your benefit. I assume because we speak Latin fluently in the Northwest."

As planned, the hearing caught the attention of the Chicago media. Television, radio, and print outlets all provided coverage. The hearing was the talk of the local community and expectations were high.

The City of Chicago, the Chicago Park District, and the local leaders put together a cooperative application and filed it with the Department of the Interior. As a result of Yates's leadership and influence, the Department of the Interior awarded a UPARR matching grant for the conversion of the Broadway Armory into a community recreation center, and today it remains a thriving magnet for the neighborhoods of Edgewater, Uptown, and Rogers Park.

Yates did not forget his old friend Senator Douglas and the Indiana Dunes National Lakeshore. In July 1978, his amendment to rename the lakeshore in Douglas's name passed the House by a voice vote but encountered strong resistance in the Senate. The Indiana delegation firmly opposed the renaming after an Illinois senator. At one point, the Indiana members suggested renaming Chicago "Hartkeville" after Indiana senator Vance Hartke, but later they accepted Yates's compromise proposal by authorizing the building of the Paul H. Douglas Center for Environmental Education at the Indiana Dunes National Lakeshore. Funding for the center and the expansion of the lakeshore from its original size of 8,330 acres to 15,000 acres was provided by Yates's subcommittee.[10]

Yates's subcommittee also had jurisdiction over the Department of Energy's conservation programs. On March 10, 1984, Jay Lytle, Republican mayor of Evanston, Illinois, along with the president of Northwestern University and the trustees of its Corporate Advisory Board, including renowned attorney Newton Minow and industrialist and philanthropist Lester Crown, presented to Yates a detailed concept for developing a research park in the city. Yates was impressed with the quality of detail and thought that had gone into the presentation and, after additional meetings, he responded positively. The City of Evanston viewed the project as a crucial element in its plan for redeveloping the downtown. It was also hoped that the cooperation between the university and the city would begin to heal some of the wounds resulting from the town-and-gown disputes that had plagued the two for years.

The 9th District had been reapportioned in 1982 and Evanston was new to Yates's district. The research park was a prime opportunity to help his new constituents and, once again, use the resources of his subcommittee to give new direction to a federal department that had ignored a growing problem. What appealed to Yates was the potential for the transfer of academic research to practical conservation of energy in manufacturing, a program Yates had long thought was lacking at the Department of Energy. "The benefits of such research and training to basic industry," explained David Mintzer, vice president for research and dean of science at Northwestern University, in a letter to Yates, "will include improved quality and lower cost manufactured products, reduction of environmental problems and increased competiveness and international markets." The Department of Energy operated research laboratories around the United States studying various methods of energy conservation but did not have one looking into advances in energy conservation in manufacturing as would befit the Midwest.

In late October 1984, to great fanfare in Evanston, Republican governor James Thompson and the leadership of the City of Evanston and Northwestern University honored Yates at the announcement that the Department of Energy's Basic Industry Research Laboratory would anchor the new Northwestern University/ Evanston Research Park.

Governor Thompson was so complimentary of Yates that, on the eve of the congressional elections, his remarks could have been taken as an endorsement. When an aide to Yates pointed this out to Thompson's assistant, the reply was, "It's a public meeting. I hope you're taping this ceremony." Yates's assistant said that everything was being recorded, to which Thompson's aide responded drily, "Just get the wording correct. It's a free country." Both aides smiled, shook hands, and went their separate ways. Over the next few days of campaigning, Yates consistently pointed out the governor's comments—taking care to quote him exactly, of course.

The initial federal money for the project, $15 million, was contained in the Interior Appropriations Bill for fiscal 1985.[11]

Both these projects—the Broadway Armory and the Basic Industry Research Laboratory—demonstrated how Yates responded in a direct, positive way to the needs of the nation and of his district. But "cardinals" have an added benefit that comes with their status. They often accord each other mutual respect on projects affecting their respective districts or states. One such case involved pesticides containing the carcinogen toxaphene.

In 1977, the Environmental Protection Agency (EPA) initiated a study of the effects of toxaphene when tests indicated that the pesticide might be a cancer threat to humans. Two years later, studies in mice by the National Cancer Institute confirmed the EPA's suspicions. Toxaphene was substituted in the production of cotton after the pesticide DDT had been banned. It was a mobile substance that traveled from the South through the wind currents to northern areas, like Chicago. Yates warned his constituents that the Fish and Wildlife Service "finds toxaphene residues significantly contaminating Great Lakes fish such as lake trout and whitefish." He pledged to offer an amendment to ban the use of the substance. Easier said than done.[12]

Fortunately, Yates was able to prevail on his colleague, Representative Ed Boland, now chairman of the Appropriations Subcommittee on HUD and Independent Agencies, which had jurisdiction over the budget of the EPA. As a courtesy to a fellow cardinal, Boland agreed to allow Yates to submit an amendment banning use of toxaphene to Boland's appropriations bill even though Yates was not a member of the subcommittee. The amendment was accepted and included in the bill as reported on August 10, 1982.[13]

The amendment, however, presented a jurisdictional dilemma. Authorizing committees, which create programs, are very sensitive to encroachment on their turf by appropriators, who fund programs, and vice versa. Such was the case with Yates's amendment. To mollify the Committee on Agriculture, the authorizing committee, Yates offered his amendment when the Federal Insecticide, Fungicide, and Rodenticide Act Amendments of 1982 came to the floor. Resistance to Yates came from fellow liberal and California Democrat George Brown. Brown, a respected member of the Agriculture Committee, offered a substitute to the Yates's amendment proposing that the EPA be "required under the present law within 30 days" to complete its review of toxaphene. Yates did not accept Brown's substitute amendment, insisting that EPA had had more than sufficient time and it was time for Congress to take action. Yates's Republican colleague, Silvio Conte, with whom Yates had worked in opposing the SST, then rose to make a poignant statement in support of the Yates amendment. Yates's wife, Addie, had been diagnosed recently with cancer and Conte made this appeal: "In the 24 years that I have been in Congress I had the opportunity to become very closely acquainted with Sid Yates. I have been on trips with him and his lovely wife, Addie. I have never seen a greater, a finer partnership and marital relationship than Sid Yates and Addie and our hearts go out to her and we wish her well." Conte then went on to explain his substantive support for Yates's amendment. Brown's substitute amendment was rejected and Yates's amendment was accepted. While the House-Senate conference committee dropped Yates's amendment from the final bill, the debate had its desired effect. The EPA got the message.[14] The *New York Times* announced on October 17, 1982, that the EPA would restrict the use of toxaphene.[15]

9

THREE YEARS
OF THE CULTURE WARS

June 1989. The two 8x10 glossy photographs, reproductions of recently exhibited works of art, lay side by side on the round, leather-inlaid conference table in Yates's personal office. The one on the left seemed innocent enough. A blurred image of the Crucifixion, with Christ suffused with an orange light, his pierced body illuminated in yellow as if by a sunbeam from heaven. If it weren't for the title of the work, *Piss Christ*, or the fact that its creator, Andres Serrano, had explained that he had submerged a thirteen-inch crucifix into a container of his own urine to get the right effect for the camera, it could have been displayed on the wall of any parochial school classroom. The black-and-white picture on the right, *Jim and Tom, Sausalito*, photographed by the late Robert Mapplethorpe, was less subject to multiple interpretations. A lanky bare-chested man, wearing a leather hood secured by a metal-studded leather collar and chain, stood on one side, holding his exposed penis in his leather gloved right-hand, urinating into the unresisting open mouth of a kneeling, bearded second man.

Yates hunched over the table and sighed. He was turning eighty later that summer, and for a brief moment, he felt his age. "Jesus, Sid," said Bain, looking at the photos over his shoulder. "How the hell are you going to defend the Endowment on this one?" Call slips from angry members, goaded by a morality campaign instigated by the American Family Association, were already piling up. The National Endowment for the Arts, whose appropriations came from the subcommittee that Yates chaired, had awarded $15,000 to the Southeastern Center for Contemporary Art in Winston-Salem, North Carolina, which used it to exhibit *Piss Christ* and works by nine other artists in an exhibition. The NEA also had given a $30,000 grant to the Institute of Contemporary Art at the University of Pennsylvania, which used it to organize a Mapplethorpe show, including *Jim and*

Tom, Sausalito. Even supporters of the NEA were calling Yates, some looking for cover, others demanding that the chairman go on the attack.

Yates smiled at his assistant's remark. "Pretty impressive," he said, pointing at the exposed genitalia. "I've seen better," Bain retorted. She was seventy-eight, and after working with "the Boss" for more than forty years, knew she could say anything she pleased. "We'd better start calling the troops," Yates said. They would have to go to the defense of the NEA once again. It was not the first time. It would not be the last.

The NEA had started in the early '60s with a legendary entrepreneur, Roger L. Stevens. Almost every mention of Stevens referred to him as "the man who once owned the Empire State Building," as if that, more than anything, set him apart from other people. He was also a highly successful theatrical producer, bringing now-legendary productions such as *Bus Stop*, *Cat on a Hot Tin Roof*, and *West Side Story* to Broadway. But what brought him to the attention of President John F. Kennedy was his skill in raising enormous sums for Democratic candidates. Kennedy asked him to help establish and chair a National Cultural Center in Washington, knowing Stevens had the Rolodex to raise vast amounts of money. The President, of course, had no idea that the center would later bear his name.

Lyndon Johnson always sought political rainmakers and kept Stevens in his administration as chairman of what is now titled John F. Kennedy Center for the Performing Arts as his special assistant for the arts and, once the NEA was enacted, as the first chairman of the National Endowment for the Arts. When Stevens was asked how the new NEA would differ from private foundations in funding arts projects, Stevens replied, "We do more daring things than they can do."[1]

Yates was at the UN during the initial congressional deliberations over the creation of the NEA. Nor was Yates an active participant when, on March 10, 1965, two months after he returned to the House, President Johnson sent Congress proposed legislation creating independent government agencies for the support of the arts and the humanities.[2] However, after the enactment of the National Foundation on the Arts and the Humanities Act of 1965 and creation of the two endowments (arts and humanities), Yates would become the foremost congressional champion of government support for the arts and the humanities.[3]

The relationship of government to the development of arts and culture has been a source of controversy since the origins of U.S. government. Advocates of direct government support for the arts frequently quote John Adams's letter of May 12, 1780, to his wife Abigail that "I must study Politicks and War that my sons may have liberty to study Mathematicks and Philosophy . . . in order to give their Children a right to study Painting, Poetry, Musick, Architecture, Statuary, Tapestry and Porcelaine."[4] They use this statement, written from Paris as the future president bemoans his inability to enjoy the city because of his official duties, as an affirmation of the arts as an ultimate goal of a civilized society, and a mandate for government to actively work toward that goal.

The Congress, however, was not as receptive as Adams to this idea. It argued for more than eighteen months in 1835–36 whether to accept a $500,000 bequest from the estate of James Smithson for the establishment of the Smithsonian Institution, and finally only did so upon the eloquent pleas of Congressman John Quincy Adams, who had returned to the House of Representatives after his presidency. President James Buchanan appointed a National Art Commission in 1859, but it closed down in 1861 for failure of Congress to appropriate funds in light of wartime priorities.[5] The few federal arts programs of the early and mid-twentieth century all had significant, if not primary, non-arts agendas. The federal arts projects of the New Deal, such as the Public Works of Art Project of the Civil Works Administration, the Federal Art Project and the Federal Writers' Project of the Works Progress Administration, were primarily jobs programs, and in fact were criticized for being little more than "make-work relief."[6] The Cold War brought a new surge in arts funding, as President Eisenhower created a Program for Cultural Presentations Abroad, which between 1955 and 1961 spent $16.2 million to send U.S. artists on overseas tours. Operated through the State Department, this program, which did not support any artists' activities in the United States, was part of the administration's overall propaganda effort, as the United States attempted to counteract the Bolshoi Ballet and other cultural programs heralded by the Soviet Union to demonstrate that the arts, and hence a high level of civilization, could flourish under communism.

In the meantime, several members of Congress, usually either those representing states or districts with significant commercial arts constituencies, or those for whom the Adams father and son's philosophy resonated, introduced bills providing for direct federal subsidy of the arts. These included attempts by Representative (and later Senator) Jacob Javits to create a national theater in 1948,[7] and by Senator Hubert Humphrey in 1953.[8] These plans failed, however, for lack of congressional and presidential support.

Meanwhile, on a parallel track, members of the university and other academic communities had been pushing for federal support for the humanities, citing the establishment of the National Science Foundation in 1950 as a precedent for federal subsidies for academic research.[9]

As further motivation, the employment potential of the arts made organized labor one of the chief influences lobbying for a direct federal subsidy. The Department for Professional Employees of the AFL-CIO, under the leadership of Jack Golodner, had jurisdiction over the white- and pink-collar unions. These unions included not only such associations as the nurses and teachers unions, but also most of the art-related unions, including the American Federation of

Musicians, Actors' Equity, the Screen Actors Guild, and the entertainment craft unions of the International Alliance of Theatrical and Stage Employees, which included locals of carpenters, electricians, costumers, and box-office workers, as well as virtually all the crafts working in the theater, film, and television industries. DPE's constituents had lobbied for years for federal money that could be directed to their industry.[10]

Kennedy's election in 1960 brought to government a much more sympathetic environment for both the arts and the humanities. The efforts of Jacqueline Kennedy to bring culture to Washington played a large part in President Kennedy's issuance of an executive order in June 1963 establishing an Advisory Council on the Arts, although the council never was convened.[11] President Johnson picked up on the idea, however, and with the support of organized labor and the academic community, pushed through the legislation to create the two endowments.

Congressional leadership in both the House and the Senate assigned the two endowments, along with the Smithsonian and other cultural agencies, to the Interior Appropriations Subcommittee, now under Yates's chairmanship. It seemed a strange choice. The subcommittee's primary responsibility was deciding the amount of money to be spent on the Department of the Interior, the fossil fuel programs of the Department of Energy, the Forest Service of the Department of Agriculture, and all the Native American programs.

In his first years as chairman, Yates, a collector of abstract expressionist paintings and a frequent concert and theatergoer, downplayed the cultural issues under his jurisdiction. He focused instead on energy and environmental matters. Hearings on the Bureau of Indian Affairs and the Indian Health Service, and the fact that the 9th District had one of the largest Native American populations of any urban congressional district, also piqued his interest in Native American issues. Yates tested his constituent's interest in the arts by including a question in a survey asking whether cultural institutions should receive federal funding.[12] The response, 44 percent to increase funding, 36 percent to keep it at current levels, and only 20 percent to reduce funding, reassured Yates that the 9th District, which included many arts organizations, as well as wealthy arts aficionados living along the Chicago lakefront, would not resent greater attention to cultural issues.[13]

He followed up by writing a newsletter about the activities of the Smithsonian Institution, and the tensions arising from the ability of the Smithsonian not only to receive congressional appropriations, but also to solicit private donations. The Smithsonian's Board of Regents felt that congressional approval was not necessary for actions taken with private funds, to which Yates responded by calling hearings that would examine "the Smithsonian's total operations."[14] This lack of deference by the Smithsonian to Congress would be a continuing irritation to Yates. He had, in fact, been named by the Speaker of the House as a congressional regent of the institution in 1975, but he resigned as regent when he determined that his chairmanship created a potential conflict of interest, particularly as he grew more inquisitorial about the operations of the Smithsonian.

In a subsequent newsletter, dated June 19, 1987, he described how he had killed a $5 million gift the Smithsonian was ready to accept from the government of Saudi Arabia on the grounds that the Smithsonian was going to cede control over its publications to a foreign government. "We do know, however, that the Saudis are hard-headed investors," he wrote. "They rarely make contributions purely out of friendship or from the goodness of their hearts."[15]

Yates also embraced the issues of the humanities. He wrote his constituents about the problem of brittle books, the "slow fire" that was destroying historic "manuscripts, documents, maps, papers," and all books printed on acidified paper, the standard type of paper used for printing in the late nineteenth and most of the twentieth centuries.[16]

> The world was horrified in 1966 when floods in Florence, Italy destroyed many treasures of the Renaissance. A few weeks ago a fire in the Leningrad Library, which was built by Czar Peter the Great in 1713, consumed 400,000 volumes and damaged another 3.5 million. These losses are irreparable, but they can only be designated as minuscule when compared to the enormous catastrophe caused by the "slow fires" burning the books and papers in our libraries and depositories. Of the estimated 300 million volumes in our nation's research libraries about 77 million are now brittle. At least 25% of the 18 million volumes in the Library of Congress, the nation's permanent library, are being eaten away as though by a plague.
>
> We appropriate hundreds of millions of dollars every year to fight the fires that consume our national forests. We will have to do the same in order to extinguish the slow fires destroying much of the record of earlier civilizations and our own.

Yates brought a new attitude to arts and humanities funding. He was more comfortable championing a cultural agenda. He recognized that the key to protecting the interests of the arts community was to utilize the Interior subcommittee's programs as a bargaining chip for cultural programs.

The question was often raised why NEA and NEH were under the jurisdiction of the Interior Appropriations Subcommittee. The easy answer was because that was where the Smithsonian Institution had been placed decades earlier. As time went on, however, proposals arose to move all the cultural agencies into the subcommittee responsible for funding education programs, which many thought was a closer match. Yates fought successfully against each such attempt. The nation's artists and arts organizations, he argued, were no less natural resources of our country than its mountains and rivers. This appeal resonated strongly in the arts community and also earned support in the Congress.

But Yates also understood that constituencies whose primary interests were education were likely to support the arts. Congress had imposed increasing restrictions on the appropriations subcommittees to prevent them from exceeding budget targets. These constraints made the subcommittees' recommendations equivalent to zero-sum games; that is, given an aggregate amount that the subcommittee could spend, in order for one program to get more, another had to get less. Forcing arts funding to compete with education would pit natural allies against each other. Requiring the arts to split the pie with timber cuts and grazing rights would force the supporters of those programs, both on his own subcommittee and on their counterparts in the Senate, to make an accommodation.

In seventeen out of twenty years, between 1979 and 1998, for example, the Senate appropriated more for the Bureau of Land Management—the Department of the Interior agency that managed the payment in lieu of taxes (see chapter 8) and other land programs—and less for NEA and NEH, than their House counterparts. In almost every case, each side of the Capitol gave something back in conference. More times than not, the House got its NEA and NEH money restored.[17]

Yates's ability to barter for the arts with the Senate's wish list was to prove crucial to the NEA's and NEH's survival. Despite the astounding success the two agencies had achieved in encouraging and supporting cultural and scholarly programs, the agencies continued to be defined by a few grants involving "dirty pictures and dirty words." Since the inception of the NEA, congressional critics eagerly scrutinized grant awards that could be ridiculed and weaponized to abolish the agency. These included a $5,000 grant to Erica Jong in 1973 that assisted her writing *Fear of Flying*, whose pages brought the phrase "zipless fuck" to the eyes of the U.S. people; a $6,025 grant to LeAnne Wilchusky in 1977 to throw crepe paper streamers out of an airplane as a "sculpture in space" that "called attention to the higher spirit of mankind"; and a grant to Aram Saroyan for a poem whose title and full text were "Lighght." Yates and his allies, however, were able to nullify most of the controversies. During the "Lighght" debate, for example, a congressional hearing was headed off by a joke from a Yates committee ally, Representative Clarence "Doc" Long: "Mr. Chairman, I don't pretend to know too much about poems, but this is the first one I've been able to memorize."[18]

Two events, however, brought the NEA to the edge of extinction.

The first came as a result of the 1980 election of Ronald Reagan, whose coattails gave the Republicans a Senate majority for the first time since the Eisenhower administration. The Reagan Revolution proclaimed the end of big government, and among the agencies targeted were NEA and NEH. According to the plan of Office of Management and Budget (OMB) Director David Stockman, the endowments were to have their budgets reduced by 50 percent during the first year of the Reagan administration and would be eliminated during the second. A sister agency, the Institute of Museum Services, was to be closed immediately. Yates did not hide his contempt for Stockman, noting that "As a Member [of the House] . . . his influence was limited. Now in his new position as Reagan's director of OMB, he is like the new kid on the block with the tough big brother, wielding an axe against almost every agency in government except his own."[19] He later described Stockman as someone who "uses numbers the way a card sharp deals his cards," and added, "Mark Twain once said: 'Figures don't lie, but liars figure.'"[20]

In order to save the nation's cultural programs from the Stockman-Reagan assault, Yates first had to secure his own subcommittee, which was composed of six Democrats and three Republicans. Unlike other committees, which were rife with partisan rancor, Yates held his members together. Ralph Regula, who succeeded Yates as chairman upon the Republican takeover in 1995, recalled, "Sid was always a gentleman. . . . He respected everyone's opinion. When I was Ranking Member and later when I was Chairman and he was Ranking Member, we were like the Odd Couple. It was like a marriage . . . and we always worked together."[21]

Yates was always willing to exchange favors with his subcommittee members for support for the arts. Sometimes, however, it wasn't necessary. During the "markup" for the fiscal 1982 Interior bill, Jack Murtha strode into the Interior Subcommittee's meeting room in B-308 Rayburn, on the first basement level of the marble-clad building. As always, it seemed as if the doorframe would not be wide enough to admit Murtha's six-foot-six bulky figure. Yates, sitting with subcommittee clerk Fred Mohrman, looked up. Markup was the session where the subcommittee, based on Yates's and Regula's recommendations, would edit the part of the president's budget that was under the subcommittee's jurisdiction and determine their own priorities for spending. This was the first of Yates's appropriation bills challenging the Reagan-Stockman budget. Yates expected some questions and reactions to his spending decisions, but for the most part he had taken care of his subcommittee's individual earmark requests, particularly Murtha's, and did not anticipate any major headaches from his committee. The fight, if any, would be on the House floor, where the Reagan true believers would get involved, and then in the Senate, now controlled by Republicans. But to get there, he needed to make sure his subcommittee held firm, in particular on the arts. Now that he was a chairman, he appreciated Clarence Cannon's dislike of dissension.

Looking every bit the former marine, Murtha took his seat with the other sub-committee members. He had won a special election in 1974 and was the chamber's first Vietnam War veteran. Murtha's constituency was centered in his hometown of Johnstown, Pennsylvania, about sixty miles east of Pittsburgh, in the valley of the Laurel Mountains. Johnstown was solidly blue-collar, and Murtha himself called it "redneck."[22] Coal, iron, and steel were the main industries, but they had been declining for years, and unemployment was high. Murtha knew that if his district was to survive, he needed to find another source of economic development.

Murtha requested Appropriations because that's where the money was, and over the years he would become known as the "king of earmarks," directing, in the aggregate, an estimated $2 billion of projects into Pennsylvania's 12th Congressional District.[23] His first two subcommittee assignments were Military Construction, where he quickly learned how to open those massive sluiceways that had millions to spend on projects, and Yates's Interior Subcommittee, which oversaw the fossil-fuel programs of the Department of Energy, essential to keeping what was left of Johnstown's coal industry afloat. Ultimately, Murtha would join the Defense Subcommittee, rising eventually to chairman, where not only would he have billions to spend but also would receive hundreds of thousands of dollars in political contributions from potential beneficiaries.

The gruff, stocky Murtha and the urbane, slender Yates found common ground on Interior. Yates supported Murtha's earmark requests for the most part, and in turn, Murtha always backed Yates on the arts, though he couldn't see the point of the NEA and the other agencies dear to the chairman.

On July 19, 1977, the third of the great Johnstown floods occurred. It was called the once-in-a-thousand-years flood, sending more than a foot of rainfall in ten hours. The Flood Prevention System put into place after the 1936 flood could not hold the water, which reached as high as eight feet in places. While fatalities did not come near to the 2,200 people who died in the original Great Flood of 1889, more than 50,000 people were rendered homeless. Compounded by aging facilities and regulatory difficulties, the flood hastened Bethlehem Steel's withdrawal from Johnstown, and unemployment rose to 24 percent.[24]

Murtha immediately began securing government grants and loans for rebuilding. He found, however, that, as the months went on, people were not applying for the assistance, and instead were abandoning the city. He was advised that something was needed to reinstill a sense of community to the people of Johnstown. Among the suggestions made to Murtha was that the arts could help provide that morale booster.

Murtha called Yates and requested assistance. Although one of the NEA's most cherished tenets was that all awards were made solely on merit, by peer panels of artists removed from political pressure, there was a small category of discretionary funding called chairman's grants. These were grants of modest amounts that could be written directly by the NEA chairman, without going through peer review or the National Council on the Arts. Yates got Liv Biddle, the NEA chairman, on the telephone.

Livingston Ludlow Biddle Jr.'s ancestors traced back to the Biddles of Philadelphia, who had fought in the American Revolution, as well as the Drexels of Philadephia, the banking family that founded Drexel, Morgan and Company—which would become J. P. Morgan and Company—and Drexel University. Poor eyesight kept him out of active service in World War II, but he had nevertheless served as an ambulance driver in Africa for the American Field Service.[25] An author and journalist, Biddle joined the staff of his St. George's prep school and Princeton University friend Claiborne Pell when his schoolmate was elected U.S. senator for Rhode Island. With Pell, Biddle helped draft the original legislation creating the NEA. Upon Jimmy Carter's election, Biddle was nominated to head the NEA.

Liv Biddle's political sense was acute. He did not need to be told that when the congressman in charge of his agency's budget called for a favor, the only responses were "how much?" and "how soon?" Working with Murtha's staff, Biddle made a chairman's grant to the Johnstown Symphony Orchestra for a series of free public concerts. Indeed, the concerts seemed to work, bringing people together, reminding them of their common values, and encouraging them to apply for the federal monies that Murtha had secured to rebuild their city.

As he began the hearing, Yates gently rapped his knuckles on the conference table to bring the session to order. Murtha stood up. "Mr. Chairman," he stated, "before we get started, I just wanted to say something." Murtha told the story of the Johnstown Symphony Orchestra and what the NEA grant had accomplished in bringing the citizens of Johnstown together after the flood. "Mr. Chairman, I have not been a great believer in the NEA," Murtha continued, "but I have supported it because you believed in it and you have always been a fair chairman to me and to the needs of my constituents. But I have now seen what the arts can do, and I want you to know that you will not have to trade me for my support for the NEA ever again." As Murtha sat down, Fred Mohrman whispered to Yates, "Do you think it's too late to cut Murtha's earmarks?" Yates just shook his head and smiled. He would be ready for Reagan.

Yates also had the tacit, and sometimes not so tacit, support of the NEA itself. Although President Reagan's appointee Frank Hodsoll, who replaced Biddle as NEA chairman, never publicly rebuked the Stockman budget proposals, Hodsoll fought an ongoing battle behind the scenes with OMB. As Hodsoll recalled, "I didn't know what the appropriate amount for the arts endowment should be, but I didn't think it ought to be cut."[26] In addition, the directors of the various discipline programs of the NEA, music, dance, theater, and so on frequently, and clandestinely, communicated with Yates's staff to provide statistics and anecdotal materials to bolster the endowment's case. Finally, many members of the National Council on the Arts, who had been appointed under prior presidents, publicly opposed Reagan's budget proposals. Carter appointee Theodore Bikel, the renowned actor and singer, and president of Actors' Equity Association, was adamant: "We must pray that we not be thrown right back into the dark ages, where it's dog eat dog—we deserve better." [27]

Yates was the first chairman to recognize the support that could be generated by harnessing the star power of the arts community. With the assistance of arts service organizations such as the American Symphony Orchestra League, the American Association of Museums, Theatre Communications Group, and Opera America, coordinated by the American Arts Alliance and its executive director, Ann Murphy, Yates held two days of public hearings in support of the endowments' appropriations that featured such celebrity witnesses as James Earl Jones, Stockard Channing, E. L. Doctorow, Geraldine Page, and *Star Wars* composer John Williams. Members of the committee leapt to be photographed with these luminaries, some of them star-struck, but the more savvy realized that the connections could also be of value in later fund-raising and reelection campaigns. [28]

Without dissent, the House Interior Appropriations Subcommittee issued a report stating, "Suddenly, this year OMB has decided that these excellent programs should be dismantled by proposing a 50-percent cut in appropriations upon the representation that the private sector would be willing and able to increase their contribution to more than make up for the reduction in government funding. The Committee cannot accept either OMB's arbitrary action nor its premise for its action." [29] Yates's bill passed the House and moved to the Senate.

The Republican leadership in the Senate urged all its new Republican committee chairmen to support the president. And, indeed, other Reagan economic programs, such as the Gramm-Latta Budget bill and the Kemp-Roth tax-cut bill, passed overwhelmingly. Nevertheless, as the statistics for fiscal year 1982 indicate, although the Senate originally cut $68.5 million from the House markup of the endowments' budget, the final conference figures show that $52 million was restored.

Similar results followed over the next several years. Then came Serrano and Mapplethorpe, and the "dirty pictures."

Compromise was not really an option. Not only was the American Family Association of Tupelo, Mississippi, using the "immoral, anti-Christian" NEA grants as a fund-raising tool, but right-wing politicians were having a field day and saw no reason to let up. Senator Alphonse D'Amato (R-NY) tore up a copy of a Serrano catalog on the Senate floor, calling it "a deplorable, despicable display of vulgarity." Columnist and presidential candidate Pat Buchanan vowed to "close, padlock, and fumigate" the NEA.

The Department of the Interior and Related Agencies Appropriations bill for fiscal year 1990, including the NEA budget, was scheduled for floor action on July

12, 1989. Yates, as subcommittee chairman, would act as floor manager for the bill. Neal Sigmon, who had taken over as subcommittee staff director when Morhman was promoted to director of the full Appropriations Committee, confirmed that two amendments would be introduced to cut the NEA appropriations. The first, by Republican congressman Dana Rohrabacher of Orange County, California, would remove the NEA's entire $171 million budget. The action was not censorship, Rohrabacher asserted. "I believe censorship is not the solution. The answer is getting government out of the arts."[30] But Rohrabacher was only a freshman, a former Reagan speechwriter whose election was backed by billionaire Charles Koch and by Iran-Contra figure Oliver North. Yates knew that Rohrabacher's amendment was too draconian for most of the House, and that the freshman did not have the time or experience to organize a winning coalition.

The second amendment was more problematic, both because of its substance and because of its sponsor. This amendment would cripple the NEA, cutting $14 million, or approximately 10 percent, of the endowment's program budget. Its sponsor was Texas Republican Dick Armey. Armey had been chairman of the Economics Department at North Texas State University and had a good grasp of budget issues. In addition, unlike many of the radical right-wing Republicans, he was cheerful and collegial and had been in the House long enough to have made friends on both sides of the aisle. He could sell a 10 percent cut and make it appear reasonable, even though it would devastate the work of the endowment.

Armey was slick. And he was devious. A few weeks earlier, Jack Murtha let Yates know that Armey was meeting with members of Yates's subcommittee, including Murtha, to get them to sign a letter to Hugh Southern, acting chairman of the NEA, demanding to know what Southern was doing to stop the funding of "morally reprehensible trash."[31]

Yates was furious at this attempt to drive a wedge into his subcommittee. He confronted Armey and warned him to stay away from his panel. If Armey had a problem, he should come to Yates himself. Armey, not at all abashed, took Yates up on the purported invitation. The two of them, along with Murtha, summoned Southern to a private meeting in Yates's office. There, Yates did everything he could to head off a confrontation. Acting every bit the professor, Yates displayed for Armey's examination a copy of Picasso's *Crucifixion*, showing an abstraction of Christ on a Tao Cross, and asked the Texan whether he was offended. Armey, clearly recognizing the obvious trap being laid, said he was not. Yates then launched into a history lesson, lecturing on how much antagonism the work had engendered in the 1930s. This was the same situation.

Armey was not impressed. He told Yates that even his constituents, backward though Yates might think them, could tell the difference between an interpretive work and Jesus sitting in a pitcher of piss. Armey let Yates and Murtha know that not only was he going to introduce an amendment to cut the NEA appropriation, but that he would place a copy of the Mapplethorpe catalog on the tables where members entered their electronic voting cards so that they could review the evidence before they voted. "I'll blow your budget out of the water," he warned.[32]

On July 12, 1989, as was their custom when Congress was in session, Bain drove from her house on leafy Woodley Road in McLean, Virginia, to the tall apartment building on Cathedral Hill and waited for Yates to come down for their ride to the Rayburn Building. She knew he hated the air conditioning, but even on an overcast day like today, the windshield was already fogging up from the humidity of a traditional July in Washington. It couldn't be helped, she thought, and turned the defroster in the champagne-colored Lincoln Continental to high.

Bain could tell that "the Boss" was preoccupied. Bringing the bill to the floor was always a taxing affair, the culmination of six months of hearings, markups, and cajoling, listening politely to other members, less cordially to lobbyists, both from interest groups and from the agencies themselves. Some requests were granted, favors given, but for the most part Yates had to decline the majority of requests for earmarks, report language, and agency directives. But he knew it was a fair bill, and one on which Ralph Regula and the other subcommittee Republicans had been extensively consulted and which they had bought into. But the NEA debate added an extra layer of aggravation. It was a self-inflicted wound by the NEA that Yates would have to suture. He was irritated that $45,000, the amount awarded by the NEA to the Southeastern Center for Contemporary Art and the Institute of Contemporary Art, which had been used for the Serrano and Mapplethorpe exhibits, could blow up the entire $11 billion Interior bill. The car ride was unusually quiet, as Yates highlighted the text of a *Wall Street Journal* article on offshore drilling that he intended to refer to in his remarks.

Yates knew he had to neutralize Armey. Armey recognized, as did Yates, that the House wanted, indeed needed, to take some punitive measure. Members, even those from constituencies that supported the arts and would normally reject any form of censorship, were getting hundreds of angry letters demanding action. Yates acknowledged that, if not given an alternative, the House would agree to Armey's plan. He needed to turn the pressure valve just enough to bleed some steam, giving his colleagues cover so that they could report to their constituents that they had done something.

Despite his misgivings, and in the face of objections of arts advocacy organizations and anticensorship purists, Yates decided that only a reduction in the endowment's appropriation would satisfy the House. But it couldn't be a vote for either Rohrabacher's bomb throwing, or Armey's more subtle amputation. He decided that a symbolic cut could be defended as sufficient and discussed with Regula the possibility of reducing the NEA appropriations by $45,000, the exact amount of the grants that had been given for the two controversial exhibits. Regula told Yates that such a small reduction would never satisfy the conservatives on either the Democratic or Republican side. "Not if we can get the right conservative to offer the amendment," Yates replied. Regula was skeptical. But Yates already had someone in mind, and he began to outline his strategy.

At approximately 11 AM, the House resolved itself into the Committee of the Whole House on the State of the Union, known informally as the Committee of the Whole, to consider the Interior Appropriations bill.[33] This was a parliamentary mechanism under which the entire House membership acted as a single committee and could consider Yates's bill under committee rules governing amendments and debates, a more flexible procedure than the general House rules permitted. Yates took his place at the leadership table as floor manager. Regula set up at the minority leader's table.

The first hour of debate was given to general discussion of the bill, divided equally between the majority and minority, time allocated by Yates and Regula. The most heated arguments during this portion of the bill's consideration had nothing to do with the arts. Instead, they involved the subcommittee's decision to impose moratoria on oil exploration, drilling, and production in large swaths of the Outer Continental Shelf, including areas in Alaska, Florida, and California, and also halting land sales and leases in the Mid-Atlantic states. The Bush Administration opposed the extent of the moratoria, and congressmen from oil- and gas- producing states expressed their unhappiness. But the recent Exxon oil spill in Prince William Sound in Alaska, with its accompanying pictures of miles of despoiled coastlines and dying oil-coated waterfowl and marine mammals, made approval of the moratoria a foregone conclusion and the debate, while contentious, was perfunctory.

After the general discussion, Congressman Rick Boucher sitting as chairman of the Committee of the Whole, opened the bill for debate and amendment by title. The consideration of Title I, appropriations for the agencies within the Department of the Interior, went smoothly, with minor technical amendments approved without objection. Members held scheduled "colloquies" with Yates, a staged dialogue of previously prepared questions and answers read into the record about the bill that clarified certain appropriation decisions and could be used, if necessary, as legislative history.

Debate on Title I concluded, and Boucher opened Title II, Related Agencies, for amendment. Regula immediately sought recognition to introduce an amendment forbidding recipients of NEA grants to make subgrants without the agency's approval. This provision, if previously in the law, would have forbidden the Southeastern Center for Contemporary Art from giving Serrano a subgrant for *Piss Christ*. Although it was a long shot, Yates and Regula still hoped that a nonmonetary amendment, especially one offered by a Republican, might be sufficient to head off a more severe penalty. It was quickly shot down. Rohrabacher raised a point of order objecting to the inclusion of authorizing, or nonmonetary, language, in an appropriations bill, and his objection was sustained by the chair. Although Yates could have called for a vote to overturn the chair's ruling, he decided not to risk it.

Then it was Rohrabacher's turn. The freshman rose to offer an amendment to strike the pages of the bill that appropriated all the NEA dollars, in effect eliminating the agency. Walter Leslie "Les" AuCoin and Norman DeValois Dicks immediately jumped up, seeking recognition in opposition to the amendment. After letting his junior members have their say, Yates rose, comparing the proposal to "the justice of the Ayatollah Khomeni to the claimed blasphemy in Salman Rushdie's book. 'Off with His Head,' cried the Red Queen in Alice in Wonderland." Warming to his argument, Yates continued, "When it was brought out that the Department of Defense was spending $600,000 for toilet seats, there was not any motion to stop the purchase of toilet seats by the Department of Defense. Are we going to close down HUD because of what has happened . . . because of favoritism or because of fraud or abuse? No, we are going to let [HUD Secretary] Jack Kemp clean it up."

Debate continued, but before a vote could be taken on the Rohrabacher amendment, Dick Armey rose. "Mr. Chairman, I offer a perfecting amendment to the bill," which, instead of eliminating the NEA, simply "perfected" the existing appropriation by reducing the amount of the appropriations by 10 percent.[34] Under the rules of the Committee of the Whole, Armey's amendment now took precedence over Rohrabacher's.

Unlike the angry Rohrabacher, Armey was charming and collegial in his remarks. He referred to the meeting he and Yates had with the NEA, emphasizing that he had tried to work with the agency, but to no avail. He was not supporting Rohrabacher's drastic solution but merely wanted to send a message: "If you do not want to be sensitive, responsive, respectful, and tolerant of the taste of the vast majority of the American people, if you insist instead to be clearly, blatantly, obtrusively and obnoxiously in violation of the tastes of the clear and vast majority of the American people, you will have your funding reduced. [Let's] send a message that we represent the American people in this matter."

It was now 2 o'clock. They had been debating the arts for almost two hours, and Yates could tell that members were tired of the issue and wanted to move on. He saw them nodding their heads in agreement with Armey. It was time to take action. He subtly signaled, and Charlie Stenholm of Texas slowly stood up, seeking recognition. Members looked up in surprise, no one more so than Dick Armey. "Mr. Chairman," Stenholm called, in his clear voice, and offered an amendment to the perfecting amendment. "In lieu of $129,825,000 in the amendment, insert $144,205,000," changing the fourteen million dollar cut to the $45,000 that Yates and Regula originally planned.

Stenholm was about as conservative a Democrat as there was in the House. He was a cotton farmer from Stamford, about forty-one miles north of Abilene in West Central Texas. Elected to Congress in 1978, he helped found the House Conservative Democratic Forum and joined the "Boll Weevils," southern conservative Democrats who supported the Reagan budget and tax cuts in the '80s.[35] But Stenholm got along fine with Yates. They were currently both deputy whips, helping to count and secure Democratic votes for Speaker Tom Foley, and had worked on and off together for years. Besides, Stenholm detested fellow Texan Armey. Armey, along with radical conservative activist Grover Norquist, was trying to defeat conservative Democrats, particularly in the South, so that the only option for conservative voters would be the Republican Party. "I'd rather beat Charlie Stenholm than beat Barney Frank," Norquist had said, referring to the ultraliberal, openly gay, congressman from Brookline, Massachusetts.[36] Messing with Armey's plans was always a good move for Stenholm.

As an amendment to Armey's perfecting amendment, Stenholm's proposal took precedence over both the other amendments. Stenholm gave other conservatives, who were not inclined to oppose either the chairman or the ranking Republican of an appropriations subcommittee, the cover they needed. They could tell their constituents that they had followed the recommendation of a member whose conservative credentials could not be challenged. Armey desperately tried to keep the debate going, seeking additional time, but Yates got agreement to close off all debate after a final twenty-five minutes on all current and future amendments. At approximately 3:15 PM, a vote was called on Stenholm's proposal. It passed 361 to 65.

Armey tried one final ploy. Under the rules, he was not permitted to offer an amendment to his own amendment, so he got Cliff Stearns, a freshman Republican from Georgia, with a 93 percent rating from the American Conservative Union and a 0 percent rating from the AFL-CIO's Committee on Political Education, to offer a 5 percent cut to the NEA budget. But since Yates had been able to close all debate, the amendment went straight to a vote. By this time the House had had enough and Stearns's amendment failed 95 to 328.

The committee immediately moved to the vote on Armey's amendment, now as amended by Stenholm. It passed without debate 332–94, and with that vote, both Armey and Rohrabacher went down in defeat.[37]

Finally done with the arts, the Committee of the Whole turned to the remaining sections of the Interior Appropriations bill, resolving a few remaining technical amendments. Yates then moved that the Committee of the Whole rise, and reconstitute itself as the House of Representatives for a vote on final passage of the bill. At 5:55 PM, almost seven hours after commencing debate, Yates's bill passed, 374–49.

Members crowded around Yates and Regula, offering congratulations. Rohrabacher, furious, stayed at his seat. Armey, however, walked over from the Republican side to where Yates was gathering up his papers, reached out his hand and, with a grin, said "You got us."[38] Later, Armey would tell others, "Yates whipped me fair and square."[39]

Yates accepted the praise with thanks, but he knew that this was only one battle. The next part of the culture wars would be with the Senate. But that was for tomorrow. Right now he was exhausted. He left the chambers to head back to his office, ready to go home but knowing that Bain had a pile of reporters' calls for him to return. And she had the car.

As Yates rode home that evening, House clerks walked the Interior Appropriations bill to the Senate side of the Capitol, where it was referred to the Senate Interior Appropriations Subcommittee, again controlled by the Democrats. That subcommittee marked up the House version on July 24. The next day the full Appropriations Committee met. The Senate committee agreed to the $45,000 cut but also imposed a five-year ban on grants to the Southeastern Center for Contemporary Art and the Institute of Contemporary Art, the recipients of the grants that had caused all the trouble.

On July 26, two weeks after the House debate, Senator Robert Byrd of West Virginia, chairman of the Senate Appropriations Committee as well as chairman of the Interior subcommittee, brought the Interior Appropriations bill up for consideration by the Senate. In contrast with the House proceedings, senators briefly exchanged perfunctory remarks and speeches and then opened up the bill for amendment. Recorded votes required a quorum, but unless a senator "suggested the absence of a quorum," most business could be conducted by voice vote of the handful of senators who were managing the bill, and senators would watch out for their absent colleagues' interests. While the amendment process droned on, and the afternoon receded into evening and then night, Senator Jesse Helms of North Carolina introduced two amendments.[40] The first amendment, cosponsored by John Chafee of Rhode Island, provided additional funds for construction and acquisition of facilities relating to sport fishery and wildlife resources. It was passed by a desultory voice vote of the few senators in attendance. Helms then proposed a second amendment, which appeared to be similarly noncontroversial. That was far from true.

The Helms amendment, as the media labeled it, provided that

> None of the funds authorized to be appropriated pursuant to this Act may be used to promote, disseminate, or produce—
>
> (1) obscene or indecent materials, including but not limited to depictions of sadomasochism, homo-eroticism, the exploitation of children, or individuals engaged in sex acts; or
>
> (2) material which denigrates the objects or beliefs of the adherents of a particular religion or non-religion; or
>
> (3) material which denigrates, debases, or reviles a person, group, or class of citizens on the basis of race, creed, sex, handicap, age, or national origin.[41]

"Mr. President," Helms drawled, "if Senators want the Federal Government funding pornography, sadomasochism, or art for pedophiles, they should vote against my amendment. However, if they think most voters and taxpayers are offended by Federal support for such art, they should vote for my amendment."[42]

Chairman Byrd announced that Helms had previously discussed the amendment with him and he was ready to accept it. James McClure of Idaho, the ranking Republican on Interior Appropriations, similarly agreed. Brief remarks followed from liberal Howard Metzenbaum from Ohio, who expressed concerns over "Congress telling the art world what is art" but also said that "I am not going to oppose it because it is hard to oppose an amendment of this kind. It sounds so right."[43]

Senator Chafee, still on the floor, noted that the wording of the amendment would prevent funding of "material that debases or reviles Hitler," and expressed his opposition. Nevertheless, without further debate, the amendment was passed by voice vote.[44]

Later that night, the Senate passed its version of the Interior Appropriations bill, again by voice vote. The Senate was directed to request a conference with the House. Senate conferees were appointed to meet with their House counterparts and come to agreement on a final bill.

"Bobby" Byrd was a lover of the arts, if not necessarily the NEA. He had played the violin since he was seven and had been in the orchestra at Mark Twain High School in Statesbury, West Virginia.[45] He continued to play his "fiddle," as he called it, for the enjoyment of his colleagues, often singing along to such tunes as "Old Joe Clark" and "Cumberland Gap." Just as Yates had played his guitar as a way to break the ice at campaign stops in his first race for Congress in 1948, Byrd used his fiddle to get elected to the West Virginia House of Delegates in 1946.[46] On the merits, Byrd probably did not want the Helms amendment to go into law. But Byrd, a wily trader who had negotiated with Yates over many years, was delighted to bring to conference something he knew Yates would hate. Byrd was confident he could exact concessions from the House in exchange for striking the Helms amendment, for Yates would never allow that language to remain in the version of the bill to be sent to the president for signature.

The House adjourned on August 5 for its summer recess and wouldn't return until after Labor Day. Although the work schedule was more relaxed, Yates, Regula, and the staff kept busy preparing for conference with the Senate. The Senate had passed 168 changes to the House version, and each amendment would have to be agreed to, rejected, or negotiated to a compromise by the House and Senate conferees, in order that both branches of Congress ultimately pass the same bill. Congressmen whose earmarks had been removed by the Senate, in favor of earmarks wanted by senators, were pressing members of the subcommittee to reject the amendments.

In the midst of this preparation, support on the House side for the Helms amendment was picking up steam. Armey, his fun finished, had no appetite for another battle. Rohrabacher, however, was basking in the publicity and accolades he received from the morality crowd. Few freshmen had been accorded such attention and he was ready to run with it. He would not be trapped by the arcane parliamentary procedures of the House again and spent the summer studying the House rules, while gathering support for Helms. Rohrabacher asked William Dannemeyer, his fellow Orange County Republican congressman, for help.

Dannemeyer was conservative even by Orange County standards, and he was obsessed with AIDS and homosexuality, alleging that AIDS victims "emit spores" that can spread the disease.[47] He was roundly disliked, even by Republicans, but was an expert on what he called "legislative guerrilla warfare." He was just what Rohrabacher needed to prepare a parliamentary battle.[48]

Yates was equally ready, however. He had a close rapport with the House parliamentary staff, frequently going over to their office just to chat. He never brought a bill to the floor without a thorough consultation.[49] When his old friend and fellow Illinoisan Paul Simon came to him for advice after his election to Congress in 1974, Yates suggested, just as Judge Sabath had suggested to him twenty-five years earlier, that Simon spend some time in the chamber when the House was in session and get a feel for the currents of the proceedings, the ebb and flow of the debates. "Watch how the rules operate in practice," he advised. Now, of course, Yates's days were increasingly consumed by committee matters, not only Interior, but the other subcommittees he sat on. Nevertheless, when there was a free hour or so, Yates would tell Bain he was going over to the floor just to watch whatever bill happened to be up for consideration, to see what motions were being made, what points of order were sustained or rejected. You never knew when you could learn something new, he thought.

Back from recess, Yates walked to the chamber. He saw members gathered around easels near the Speaker's Lobby. Helms had thoughtfully sent over copies of the Mapplethorpe photographs, which Dannemeyer and Rohrabacher were displaying. Yates went over to the parliamentarian to find out the propriety of this display. The parliamentarian told him that there was no bar to keeping them where they were, but a point of order could be made if there was any attempt to bring them on the floor.

House rules established a choreography for the House-Senate conference. The Senate had passed a motion to request a conference. It was now up to the House to agree or reject the request. On September 13, 1989, Yates addressed the Speaker and requested unanimous consent that "the House disagree to the Senate Amendments and agree to the conference asked by the Senate."[50] There was no objection to this request.

Under the rules, one motion was permitted to instruct the House conferees about their negotiations at conference. Under the rule granted by the Rules Committee, the motion to instruct had to be made by a member of the minority party.[51] Rohrabacher sought recognition to instruct the conferees to accede to the Helms amendment. But, following the plan devised by Yates and Regula, Regula stood up at the same time, seeking recognition for his own instruction. The Speaker, according to tradition, gave priority to Regula, the ranking minority member of the committee.

Regula's motion instructed the conferees to accede to another of the 168 amendments, one offered by Senator Byrd that forbade use of appropriated funds for lobbying. It was clearly a good government amendment, preventing organizations from using money received from Congress to pay lobbyists to ask Congress for more money. Almost as an afterthought, the instruction also told the conferees to "address the concerns" raised by the Helms amendment.

Under House precedents, a motion to instruct has no binding power, and the conferees were free to disregard it. This was a recognition of the latitude that members of the House needed in order to hammer out a final bill with the Senate. The concern, however, was that Rohrabacher's instruction would require members to cast a recorded vote on whether, as Helms put it, members "want the Federal Government funding pornography, sadomasochism, or art for pedophiles." As in July with the $45,000 cut, Yates figured that approval of the far weaker and more ambiguous language of the Regula alternative would, at least for now, give sufficient cover to the other representatives by showing concern for the matters raised in the Helms language without having to cast an up or down vote.

The rules provided that one hour's debate was permitted for the motion to instruct, after which Regula could "move the previous question," a parliamentary device that prevents any amendments to the motion to instruct and triggers an immediate vote. Rohrabacher would try to defeat the motion on the previous question and, if successful, then move to amend the instruction to substitute his own instruction.

Regula, sponsor of the motion to instruct, opened the debate, explaining the importance to good government and sunshine in acceding to the Byrd amendment. He briefly turned to the language in the Helms amendment, noting in particular that the language applied not only to the NEA, but to all the agencies within the subcommittee's jurisdiction. "Are we going to name a czar for the United States that is going to decide whether an Indian chief speaking to his tribe is violating the Helms amendment?"[52]

Yates added that under the Helms language, the Holocaust Memorial Council, an agency funded by the bill, could not say anything that would denigrate the Nazis. "Mr. Speaker, this is the start of George Orwell's Big Brother. This is the Communist approach to art. . . . I ask the House: Is that the kind of censorship that we want to create?"[53]

At times, the debate turned personal. Henry Hyde, a Republican from the Chicago suburbs, rose to speak. Hyde and Yates, miles apart philosophically, had a close and cordial relationship. Hyde turned to Yates and asked whether he could make a comment "in all candor to my dear friend. . . . [V]iewing a crucifix submerged in urine may well be somebody's idea of first-amendment expression or art. I understand that. But I would suggest the emotive response would be quite different if it was a Star of David submerged in urine." Yates's face froze for a moment, but he quickly responded: "I am just as opposed to the crucifix in the jar of urine as I would be to a Star of David."[54]

Dannemeyer accused Yates of censorship on the grounds that he was keeping Rohrabacher from submitting his motion. "The toleration of pornography and homosexuality . . . is the symptom of a moral decay in a society that has lost the ability to say that there are standards in this world."[55]

Robert Walker, a Republican from Lancaster County, Pennsylvania, and another student of the House rules, asked the Speaker what his ruling would be if the Mapplethorpe photographs were brought inside the chambers. George Brown of California, acting as Speaker pro tempore, on the advice of the parliamentarian, and primed by Yates's private inquiry earlier, stated that he would rule the action to be a disruption of the proper decorum of the chamber and would prohibit their display.

Finally, time expired. Rohrabacher warned, "if there are some in this hall who have trouble understanding this clear and direct language, I am certain that there are voters around this country who are willing to explain it to them in the next election." Yates won the vote on the motion to order the previous question, ending all debate and amendments. Immediately, the House voted on Regula's instruction. This vote was overwhelmingly in favor, 410 to 3. The House conferees were appointed and directed to schedule the conference. As members began filing out of the chamber, Yates made a parliamentary inquiry. "Mr. Speaker, is it in order for this Member to thank the Chair for the excellent way in which he conducted the hearing?" George Brown, still in the Speaker's chair, responded with a chuckle, "If he does it by letter."[56]

Conference would take place in about two weeks. By tradition, the House conferees consisted of the members of the subcommittee along with Jamie Whitten of Mississippi and Silvio Conte of Massachusetts, the chairman and ranking minority member, respectively, of the full Appropriations Committee. Yates again would chair the conferees. He was comfortable with most of the bargaining positions he and his subcommittee had set and already could predict which Senate amendments he would eliminate and which ones he would have to accept. The Helms amendment, however, would be more of a problem. Feeling the tenor of the debate over the motion to instruct, Yates now realized that the $45,000 cut wasn't going to be sufficient. He would have to bring back to the House something proactive as well. He decided on a two-part solution.

First, in order to get rid of the despicable, and probably unconstitutional, Helms language, he would propose to add a provision to the appropriations bill that essentially tracked the U.S. Supreme Court's 1973 obscenity ruling in *Miller v. California*. This language, applicable to both the NEA and the NEH, prohibited projects that "may be considered obscene, including but not limited to, depictions of sadomasochism, homoeroticism, sexual exploitation of children, or individuals engaged in sex acts which, when taken as a whole, do not have serious literary, artistic, political, or scientific value."

Although harsh sounding, the language was meaningless. The Supreme Court in *Miller* had stated that if a challenged work had artistic value, it did not fit into the definition of obscenity. The very fact the NEA awarded a grant meant that a government agency, through a rigorous process, determined that the work had artistic value. Logically, therefore, no work funded by the NEA could be obscene.

Next, Yates drew upon his Chicago political background to find a way to release the rest of the pent-up steam. The page came from the late Mayor Richard J. Daley's playbook. Whenever a scandal erupted in city government, and there were plenty during the Daley years, the mayor would quickly appoint a blue-ribbon commission to investigate. The commission, studded with high-profile names, would be announced with great fanfare, go off for six months or a year to "investigate," and by the time the panel's report was issued, the scandal was long forgotten. Meanwhile, Daley looked as if he had taken decisive action.

Yates proposed that the conferees create a bipartisan independent commission to review the NEA grant-making system and "to consider whether the standard for publicly funded art should be different from the standard for privately funded art."[57] It would consist of twelve members, four each appointed by the House, the Senate, and the president. Congressmen could report to constituents that they had taken decisive action.

Conference lasted three days. Of the 168 amendments proposed by the Senate, Yates agreed to 21 without change. Byrd agreed to "recede" from 36 of the Senate's amendments, leaving the House language untouched. The remaining 111 amendments were negotiated and a compromise reached.[58] Yates proposed two changes to the Helms language that pervaded the discussions and were raised in each of the three days of conference, both in formal sessions and in many informal conversations among both staff and conferees. Senator McClure, the senior Republican conferee, agreed to represent Helms's position, but he had no taste for a fight that had nothing to do with bringing money to Idaho. He was ready to compromise. McClure needed just one final push, and Yates provided it by attacking the "western" front.

The House appropriation for the Bureau of Land Management was $121 million less than the Senate's appropriation for the agency. Almost every one of those dollars was going to western states, including Idaho, represented by Senate conferees. Yates presented an ultimatum. He would give most of the BLM money back, but only if the Senate removed the Helms amendment, deleted the five-year ban on the two grantees, removed the additional cuts, and restored the cuts that the Senate had made to the NEA appropriation. Byrd had no problem with this proposal; it was the reason he accepted the Helms amendment in the first place. McClure reluctantly agreed as well.

The conference report was filed in the House on October 2, 1989, and easily passed the next day. The Senate took up the conference report in a rare Saturday session on October 7. Helms made one final effort to reinstate his amendment and to attack his adversary on the other side of the Capitol. "Here is the point, Mr. President: Congressman Yates—who, by the way, received a standing ovation down at a black-tie dinner with the arts crowd the other night—is a hero because he defeated Helms, do you not see? Big deal. He did not defeat Helms. He defeated the vast majority of the American people who are disgusted with the idea of giving the taxpayers' money to artists who promote homosexuality insidiously and deliberately, who desecrate crucifixes by immersing them in urine. . . . Mr. President, I have a message for the Congressman. Old Helms has been beat before. But old Helms does not quit."[59] Senators politely listened and then voted down his motion 62–35. On October 23, 1989, President George H. W. Bush signed the legislation into law.[60]

Bain showed Yates the *Congressional Record* containing Helms's remarks. Yates laughed, particularly at the part about the standing ovation. It had been a good fight. He had found the pressure valve he needed for his House colleagues and shown the young Turks in Congress that, even at eighty, he could still manage a bill with a mastery about which they could only dream. Moreover, as Helms had bitterly noted, he was even more of a national hero to the arts community than before. Many members of Congress had championed the arts: Clayborne Pell and John Brademas, who helped write the legislation creating the NEA; Ted Kennedy, who always made eloquent speeches; New York senators like Jacob Javits and Pat Moynihan, for whose state the arts were a major economic engine. But they all took a back seat now to Yates. Though he would never tell anyone except Addie Yates and Bain, Yates felt pretty good about that.

As to his own constituents, Yates realized he need not make excuses for the NEA. Instead, he turned to the principles and ideals that he hoped might some-day replace the realpolitik with which he had been so successful. Recapping the prior fight and preparing for the next one, he wrote this to his constituents in June of the following year:

> We are going to face another constitutional question on freedom of expres-sion in connection with the bill to continue federal funding for the arts which is scheduled to reach the floor of the House shortly. Almost since the dawn of time when they carved representations of animals on the walls of caves, artists have found themselves in difficulty with governmental authority. Even while the ancient Greeks were creating the Parthenon, their beautiful vases, and magnifi-cent sculptures—the great philosopher, Plato, was exiling artists from his ideal Republic. They were troublemakers, he said. They endangered the stability of the state; they experimented, they reacted to emotion rather than reason, they questioned, they called for change.
>
> If an enlightened person like Plato regarded artists with such suspicion, one can understand why many members of Congress are not likely to be friendly to the artistic expressions of a few artists. . . . The members of Congress, . . . [i]n concerted attacks using Mapplethorpe and Serrano as typical of NEA grants, . . . have sought to impress the public—and the Congress—that NEA is the government's Sodom and Gomorrah.
>
> The great artists of our time, or of any time, have been rebels and risk-takers who were derided for their efforts.
>
> It will be a difficult fight. No member wants to be branded a supporter of ob-scenity. In my opinion, the issue has been overblown and distorted like the fable of Chicken Little. . . . Certainly, the people of the 9th Congressional District do not believe the sky is falling.[61]

The 101st Congress moved into its second session on January 23, 1990. Bush sent his proposed budget for fiscal year 1991 to the Hill on January 29, and the appropriations process began anew. As promised, Helms kept up the fight, as did Rohrabacher. Their initial target this time was not the NEA appropriation, but instead the NEA authorization bill. In the division of legislative responsibilities, an authorization bill creates an agency or a program, and the appropriations bill then determines how much money it will receive for the fiscal year. The legislation authorizing the NEA had expired, and the House Committee on Education and Labor, which had jurisdiction over its continued existence, began its deliberations, even as Yates and his appropriators commenced their hearings on the fiscal year 1991 Interior funding bill.

Meanwhile, the Yates-created Independent Commission met and held its own hearings throughout the hot summer of 1990 and completed its "Report to Congress on the National Endowment for the Arts" on September 11.[62] To the surprise of many cynics, the panel came up with a substantial report on the future of the NEA.[63] Its most far-reaching recommendation arose from its determination whether the NEA was meant to serve the artistic community or the U.S. people in general. If the former, the direction taken by Roger Stevens to "do more daring things" would continue. If the latter, the agency would need to take into account, not only artistic excellence, but also "considerations that go beyond artistic excellence. Publicly funded art must take into account the conditions that traditionally govern the use of public money."[64] The Independent Commission chose the latter answer, in effect stating that just because something had artistic merit and was therefore not obscene by *Miller* standards, it was not necessarily entitled to NEA funding.

Relying on the Independent Commission Report, the Education and Labor Committee revised the NEA's authorizing language to require it to take into consideration "general standards of decency and respect for the diverse beliefs and values of the American public."[65] After a lengthy and rancorous debate, the House passed the Arts, Humanities, and Museums Amendments of 1990 Act on October 11, 1990.[66]

The following day, Yates prepared to take the fiscal year 1991 Interior Appropriations bill to the floor. He thought that, for a change, the arts would not be the centerpiece of the discussions. The House had used up all its energy on the authorizing bill debate the prior afternoon and would not want to rehash "dirty pictures" all over again. Instead, Yates believed, the fights in this year's appropriations bill would revolve around more traditional issues. The Outer Continental Shelf moratorium was again in play. In addition, the committee was recommending limitations on chopping down trees in the National Forests in order to protect the spotted owl, which had just been placed on the endangered species list by the

Fish and Wildlife Service. This evoked a classic battle between the conservation policies of the Department of the Interior and the commercial harvesting policies of the Department of Agriculture, home to the Forest Service, aided by their respective environmentalist and logging industry constituencies. Moreover, the subcommittee had placed a moratorium on issuing mining patents by the Bureau of Land Management, to the outrage of the Nevada delegation. And finally, buried in the General Provisions section of the bill was the annual prohibition against using any funds "to finance changing the name of the mountain located 63 degrees, 04 minutes, 15 seconds west, presently named and referred to as Mount McKinley." The Ohio delegation, and especially Regula, whose district included Canton, President McKinley's hometown, was going to make sure that their favorite son's name would not be removed from the nation's highest peak and be replaced by the indigenously correct "Denali," despite continued requests from the Alaska delegation.[67] Yates would support the subcommittee's recommendations on those matters but felt less personal pressure to succeed. If necessary, other members of the subcommittee, particularly Dicks and AuCoin from Washington and Oregon, respectively, would carry the water on these provisions. As Yates had anticipated, with the exception of the grazing fees amendment, there was only perfunctory debate. It was an election year, and with all 435 members up for reelection, most were eager to go home for the final weeks of the campaign.

But the arts would not go away. Regula, usually in lockstep with Yates on the arts, told his chairman that he was going to offer an amendment forbidding the NEA to make any grant that would be considered either "obscene or indecent" under Supreme Court standards. Yates didn't care about the first part. His reasoning that the NEA could not award an obscene grant still held. Indecency was another matter. There was no precise definition for indecency the way there was for obscenity. By itself, indecent speech was protected by the First Amendment, and an absolute prohibition on such grants was clearly content restriction forbidden under his reading of the Constitution. He urged Regula not to offer the amendment, but Regula refused.

Late on the evening of October 11, after the House had recessed for the day, and on the eve of the Appropriations bill debate, Pat Williams of Montana, chairman of the Education and Labor Postsecondary Education Subcommittee, which was responsible for the authorization bill, sought out Joe Moakley, Rules Committee chairman, for an emergency hearing. Williams wanted the Rules Committee to permit his NEA reauthorization bill to be attached to Yates's appropriations bill as an amendment to and a replacement for the Regula amendment. Williams worried that, with Congress adjourning within a few days, his bill would never get through the Senate. Yates's appropriations bill, however, had to be enacted into law, or the Department of the Interior would shut down. Williams's maneuver was extraordinary. The Rules Committee, however, agreed to the request, even though under normal procedures, authorizing language, let alone a full authorizing bill, was not permitted on an appropriations bill.

Jamie Whitten was incensed. In his deep Mississippi mumble, he declared, "So let me tell you, and I am not going to call any names, but if you think you can put a legislative bill in an appropriations bill and run the risk of tying up the Congress in view of the Senate and the Senate amendments and the Senate rules or lack thereof, you are just fixing to tie the country into a knot. It will be the first time I remember seeing such a thing done on the floor in my lengthy experience in Congress."[68]

Yates, like most appropriators, had no qualms about appropriating money for an agency even without an authorization for it, as he believed that the mere fact of passing an appropriations inherently authorized the program that was receiving the funds. His subcommittee had added plenty of its own legislative language to bills in the past. But although he was opposed to the use of decency as one of the criteria for grantmaking, Williams's language was better than Regula's absolute prohibition. Annoyed with Regula, Yates voted to replace the Ohioan's amendment. It easily passed by a vote of 342–58. On the next vote, to attach Williams's bill to the Interior Appropriations bill, Yates, along with Whitten, voted no. Nevertheless, the amendment overwhelming passed.

The remainder of the debate on the bill moved quickly. Late in the evening on October 15, an exhausted House passed the fiscal year 1991 Interior Appropriations 327–80.

The Senate didn't begin deliberations until October 22. The clock to Election Day was ticking. Only one-third of the Senate would be up for election. Byrd was still in the middle of his term, and McClure was retiring and in no rush to complete what would be his final actions after twenty-four years in the House and Senate. But other subcommittee members, including Ted Stevens of Alaska, Bennett Johnston of Louisiana, Thad Cochran of Mississippi, and Pete Domenici of New Mexico, were up this year and, like their House counterparts, were eager to leave Washington and get back to their constituencies.

The spotted owl, grazing fees, and mining patents took up most of the Senate's time. Despite Jamie Whitten's fears, the Senate followed the House's lead on the arts, attaching a version of its own NEA authorization bill that had passed the Senate Labor and Human Resources Committee but had not reached the floor. Even Helms, facing a strong reelection challenge from Harvey Gantt, the first African-American mayor of Charlotte, North Carolina, wanted to leave Washington to get back on the stump. His opposition was perfunctory, but he warned, "Assuming that I am still in the Senate next year . . . I say to those in the arts community, and all of the homosexuals and all the rest, . . . You ain't seen nothing yet."[69] The Senate passed the Interior Appropriations bill on October 24, 1990, by a vote of 92–6.

The pressure to adjourn was forefront when the conferees met the next day. The Senate readily receded to the House position on the language of the Williams amendment. At 9:56 PM on Saturday night, October 27, the House agreed to the conference report. It was rushed over to the Senate, which approved it by a unanimous voice vote. Congress adjourned the next day. President Bush signed the bill into law a week later, just one day prior to Election Day.

Yates's general election prospects would be unlike his bitter Illinois primary race earlier that year against Edwin Eisendrath, and his victory wasn't in doubt. He was running against a perennial Republican opponent, urologist Herb Sohn. Sohn was soft-spoken, polite, and respectful. Yates had beaten him in 1984 by 75,000 votes, in 1986 by 56,000 votes, and in 1988 by 68,000 votes.[70] Somehow, and perhaps because no one else wanted to take on Yates in the general election, Sohn was again the party's nominee in 1990. Yates flew home to Chicago for a week of not-very-strenuous campaigning. He recorded a few radio spots, met with township and ward committeemen, attended some rallies, and spoke to uniformly friendly audiences. On election night, Yates received 71 percent of the vote, beating Sohn by a margin of 57,526 votes.

The next Congress, convening in January 1991, was not markedly different from its predecessor. As frequently happens in midterm elections, the party affiliated with the president suffered a few losses. The Democrats picked up 1 seat in the Senate, raising their number to 56. In the House, the Democrats increased their majority from 251 to 270. On Appropriations, the makeup of Yates's subcommittee remained the same on both the Democratic and Republican sides. The president's budget was submitted to the House on February 4, 1991, and the process began its annual dance.

As the ritual of hearings and markups proceeded, Yates hoped for a peaceful fiscal year 1992 appropriations bill, at least with respect to the arts. But the culture wars continued to rage at both ends of the political spectrum. Four performance artists, Karen Finley, John Fleck, Holly Hughes, and Tim Miller, filed a federal lawsuit against the NEA for denial of grants that had been approved by NEA's peer panels. NEA chairman John Frohnmayer, fearing Congress's wrath, had personally intervened in the decisions, asking the panel to reconsider and determine whether the grants met the new decency standards. At issue before the court was the right of the NEA to revoke a grant after it had been recommended, as well as the constitutionality of the "decency clause" inserted into Yates's bill by the Williams amendment.[71]

Karen Finley, in particular, inflamed the passions of the right. A prior NEA grantee, she had, in 1989, created a performance piece entitled "We Keep Our

Victims Ready." Inspired by the 1987 Tawana Brawley false rape hoax, Finley smeared her naked body with chocolate, representing the feces with which Brawley had claimed her alleged rapists had covered her. Her candy-coated breasts bouncing on stage in the center of the spotlights, Finley then threw tinsel onto the sticky confectionery, stating "no matter how bad a woman is treated, she still knows how to get dressed for dinner."[72]

And there were others. Ellen Steinberg, a.k.a. "Annie Sprinkle," a former prostitute and pornographic movie star, had turned to performance art in the late 1970s. She published the *Sprinkle Report*, a newsletter devoted to "piss art." In 1989, as the congressional debates were raging, she performed one of her most controversial pieces, "Public Cervix Announcement," during which Sprinkle was featured onstage with her legs spread, inviting the audience to view her cervix with the aid of speculum and flashlight. As described on Sprinkle's website, "She shamelessly presented her vagina in all its glory, personalized and not as an object of pleasure, but as an area of empowering beauty and mystery. Sprinkle's show climaxed with a 'sex magic masturbation ritual,' where she invoked the legend of the ancient sacred prostitute."[73]

"Tongues Untied," a documentary funded by both NEA and NEH, explored black gay culture in America. Directed by and starring the Emmy award–winning Marlon Riggs, it was first shown in 1989 and later aired by PBS. Its tag line, "Black men loving Black men is the revolutionary act," and its brief glimpses of nudity and sex inflamed both sides of the debate.

To the Rohrabachers and Helmses of the world, these examples demonstrated the decline of the United States into depravity and immorality. In graphic and clinical detail, they described the performances. Rev. Donald Wildman and his American Family Association, originally the National Federation for Decency, begged for funds to prevent federal support of such immoral trash. Pat Buchanan, considering a challenge to President George H. W. Bush for the Republican nomination in 1992, accused Bush of funding pornography. All this would spill over into the Interior Appropriations bill.

But so would grazing rights.

An adult cow with a calf eats about 900 pounds of forage every month. That's the same amount that five adult sheep will eat in the same period. Of the 540 million acres of the United States owned by the federal government, nearly 300 million acres in federal rangelands in sixteen western states are licensed by the Bureau of Land Management and the Forest Service to livestock operators for the grazing of their cattle and sheep. Permit fees are based on the animal unit month, calculated on that 900 pounds of grass eaten by those five sheep or the cow and calf. In 1991, the federal government charged $1.97 per animal unit month.[74] For example, if a rancher with a herd of two hundred cattle grazed on federal rangelands for three months, that rancher would pay a fee of 200 x 3 x $1.97, or $1,182.00.

Ranchers operating in states without the availability of public lands, however, had a harder time. In 1991, a livestock operator grazing on private lands paid an average of $9.66 per animal unit month, almost five times as much as their counterparts grazing on public land. For years, members of Congress representing ranchers not lucky enough to partake of the federal subsidy had demanded that federal fees be raised, if not to parity with the private market, at least to a number that could level the playing field somewhat. On the other side, the ranchers whose animals grazed on the federal land claimed that public lands were in far worse shape than privately held rangelands, with far fewer water sources available and a poorer forage quality. These ranchers claimed that they were required to bring in water tanks and salt licks, construct ponds, erect fencing, and provide road maintenance, reducing their net profits. Whatever the merits, the western state overbalance of representation on the Senate Interior Appropriations Subcommittee ensured that grazing fees would never be raised. Yates, recognizing these parochial necessities in the other body, had not bothered much with the issue and had not inserted grazing language in his bill. He had other budget items in the BLM appropriations to trade with the Senate if necessary.

Opponents of these indirectly subsidized grazing fees found an unexpected, but not necessarily welcome, ally in the environmental movement, which charged that grazing did serious damage to the native plants of the West. One of the more radical groups, Earth First!, demanded a complete end to the grazing program. With battle cries of "Cow free by '93," and "No more moo by '92," and aided by books such as *Sacred Cows at the Public Trough*, by Denzel and Nancy Ferguson, Earth First! confronted congressmen and ranchers.[75] Even those congressmen and senators opposed to the grazing fee giveaway didn't want the entire program scrapped. They just wanted it to cost a little more.

On June 24, 1991, Yates brought his bill up for initial consideration by the Committee of the Whole House. General debate concluded that evening. Under the rule granted by the Rules Committee, Mike Synar, a liberal Democrat from Oklahoma and a rancher, would be permitted to offer an amendment the next day that would establish a structured step up in grazing fees, starting at $4.35 per animal unit month in fiscal year 1992 and increasing to $8.70, or fair market value, by fiscal year 1995.

Debate resumed just after noon on June 25. As Title I of the bill, containing the Department of the Interior's appropriations, was opened for amendment, Yates allowed himself a brief moment of self-pity. He was tired. He was tired of having to fight the same battle year after year about the NEA, he was tired of listening to the self-serving, self-righteous yahoos on the right, and he was tired of the carping by backbenchers on individual details of a bill that was as delicately crafted and balanced as any piece of legislation involving money could be. The moment passed. He had fought his harshest election battle in years the previous March against Eisendrath to keep this seat and this chairmanship. He was doing so because he wanted to. He was ready for whatever skirmishes would come. And, as Sigmon, sitting next to him at the manager's table, reminded him, the first attacks were aimed at him personally, as two pieces of Chicago pork that Yates had inserted among the many earmarks suddenly were brought into the light.

Yates had never been reluctant to use his prerogatives as chairman to include money for Chicago when possible. The Interior bill was larded with earmarks for urban parks in Chicago, urban forestry projects in Cook County, Department of Energy grants for Argonne National Laboratory, and other worthies that could be justified under the missions of the various agencies within the subcommittee's jurisdiction. Although the grand total came nowhere close to the amounts that Murtha or Byrd were able to extract, these line items helped to return some of the federal tax dollars that Illinois, and the well-to-do residents on the 9th District's lakefront, sent to Washington. They also helped to counteract the complaints frequently raised by local political opponents that Yates was far more interested in national issues than he was in bringing home the bacon.

To some extent, those complaints were true. While someone like Senator Al D'Amato of New York reveled in being labeled "Senator Pothole," interested only in parochial concerns, Yates thought of himself as a national legislator, a philosopher statesman even. He enjoyed the intellectual give-and-take with witnesses who came before the subcommittee, presiding over decisions affecting the whole country. He accepted, as any longtime incumbent did, the necessity of handling local chores, carrying water for the mayor of Chicago or the Cook County Board president, but he didn't want those tasks to tarnish the independent image he had so carefully nurtured.

Buried in the National Park Service appropriation were two earmarks requested by Mayor Daley. The first was a $2 million grant for the restoration of the Chicago Public Library's former main branch. Completed in 1897, it was a grand neoclassical building between Randolph and Washington Streets along Michigan Avenue in downtown Chicago, with three-foot-thick walls of fine-grade Bedford limestone on a granite base. It had not been used as a library for years, and the City proposed turning it into a cultural center and the headquarters of the Department of Cultural Affairs. The building was already on the National Register of Historic Places, and Yates had included language in the bill permitting the grant to the Cultural Center "as if authorized by the Historic Sites Act of 1935."

The second grant, also requested by City Hall, was for $3,650,000 for construction of "Gateway Park" at the Chicago end of the Illinois and Michigan Canal National Heritage Corridor, the ninety-eight-mile canal that, from 1848 through 1900, was a freight-and-passenger connection between the Illinois River and Lake Michigan.

President George H. W. Bush had not included either of these items in his fiscal 1992 budget, and the Interior Appropriations Subcommittee held no hearings on their merits. If ranked against the hundreds of projects requested by members and denied by the subcommittee, neither might have made the cut. Nevertheless, it was understood that these were personal marks of the chairman, and no one on the subcommittee or the full committee would think of objecting. Indeed, most members of the House, even assuming they were aware the projects existed in the bill, would not dare to challenge Yates, knowing full well that such a challenge would be remembered if ever they were in need of a favor.

Dan Burton, however, didn't care about long-term consequences. He was a conservative Republican from Indiana who had made the budget deficit his holy cause. Since he expected never to request an earmark from any of the Appropriations subcommittees, he was unconcerned about offending anyone. He offered amendments to delete both Chicago projects. Yates listened as Burton explained that he understood the value of helping a public library, but he could not support a project that had neither been recommended by the president nor considered by the Appropriations Committee.

But, as Yates knew, the grant would not be helping a library. It was renovating a cultural center and bureaucratic offices. If Yates corrected Burton, it was quite possible that the project would be seen as traditional pork. Members who would give the benefit of the doubt to a library might be less willing to support paying for some deputy commissioner's comfort. Yates hated the thought of his image being tainted. He could still win the vote, if only on the basis of his being a chairman whose favors would be sought, but then he would owe his supporters, and he hated the idea of ever being beholden. If he let Burton's comments go uncorrected, he could later argue that any members who voted for the renovation did so only because of the merits. He merely responded that the building was a historic structure, described by the National Register as one of the most beautiful buildings in the country. Yates concealed his annoyance as he spoke, but he was privately outraged, both at Burton as well as at Daley for placing him in what he felt was a justifiable, but ethically ambiguous position.

As expected, Burton's amendments were defeated. Even conservative Henry Hyde voted with Yates.

The rest of Title I passed quickly and it was on to Title II and the arts. Yates's impatience was increasingly evident as Phil Crane, from the conservative enclaves of the northwest suburbs of Chicago, offered the annual amendment to strike all funds from the NEA. First elected in 1969 in a special election to replace Don Rumsfeld, who had become President Nixon's head of the Office of Economic Opportunity, Crane had challenged Ronald Reagan in the 1980 Republican presidential primaries, claiming to be a purer libertarian. Consistently reelected to the House, he had accomplished little except as an arch-conservative voice for free markets and national defense and against the transfer of the Panama Canal to Panama.

Yates listened restlessly as he heard the same recycled arguments. Finally, Crane was done. "Mr. Chairman," Yates began, "this is the annual attempt by Members who do not agree with the purposes of the NEA to kill the NEA. Last year it was the gentleman from California. This year it is the gentleman from Illinois." The rest of the members were similarly unimpressed. Crane's amendment was easily rejected.

Immediately following was the annual move to cut the NEA budget by a percentage. This time it was Clifford Stearns, a restaurant and motel owner from Ocala, Florida, whose major crusade up to this point was an unsuccessful attempt to lower the salaries of congressional staff. The second-term Republican proposed a 5 percent reduction. With little debate, the House flicked away the amendment like an Ocala earwig, and the NEA had once again survived the first round.

Title III was opened and Mike Synar introduced his grazing amendment. Yates took no part in the hour-long debate. Regula, however, was particularly peeved at the legislation, as he had tried to get permission to submit his own amendment that would increase the grazing fees by one-half of what Synar wanted, but the Rules Committee had turned him down without explanation. Synar's motion passed 232–192, Yates voting for the amendment, Regula voting against it. The Committee of the House as a Whole rose to adjourn soon thereafter and the whole House then voted on final passage 345–76. The arts were untouched but the House was now on record for the most massive increase in grazing fees in the program's history. It was an open challenge to the Senate subcommittee and its western constituency. Yates knew that he would soon be dealing with the issue again.

In contrast with the compressed timetable of the fiscal 1991 bill, the Senate did not take up the fiscal 1992 Interior Appropriations bill for almost two months after the House completed its work. In his opening remarks on September 12, Byrd assured his colleagues that the Synar amendment had been removed from the Senate version of the bill. As the bill was opened for amendment on September 16, 1991, however, Jim Jeffords, a liberal Republican from Vermont, introduced an amendment to increase the grazing fees. Not as extensive as Synar's, Jeffords's plan, cosponsored by Ohioan Howard Metzenbaum, would increase the fees by one-half of the House's increases, the same formula Regula had proposed.

As expected, senators from the western states rose in opposition. Kent Conrad of North Dakota, Conrad Burns of Montana, Larry Craig of Idaho, and Malcolm Wallop of Wyoming all joined in, describing how the higher fees would drive small family ranches out of business. They all, in more or less direct terms, accused the northeasterner Jeffords of not having "the faintest notion of how this system works, or how it affects people."[76] Harry Reid of Nevada read a lengthy bit of cowboy doggerel bemoaning the economic tightrope that ranchers walked. In the poem, a rancher is asked by a town dweller whether it's better to start out ranching with just a few cows or with a large herd. The rancher responds,

> So here is the answer to this little test,
> "The man with the fewest is doin' the best.
> Only he's not makin' more, like you might guess,
> The fact is, my friend, he's just losin' less."[77]

More persuasive was the practical negotiating advice given by Pete Domenici of New Mexico. "Please understand, . . . we have to go to conference with an appropriations bill from the House that has the Synar amendment in it. It is already higher than $8 in the fifth year. We think we ought to go to conference with nothing from the Senate."[78] If the Senate accepted the Jeffords amendment, it would be negotiating against itself before having to make a deal with Yates, making the margin for bargaining, or even splitting the difference, much smaller. The Senate agreed and on the next morning voted to table the amendment 60–38, sending it into parliamentary oblivion.

Debate on the bill, with occasional interruptions for other legislation, continued for several days. On September 19, 1991, it was the NEA's turn. Nancy Kassenbaum of Kansas offered the by-now ritual amendment to cut the NEA by 10 percent. It was rejected 27–67. Helms left the on-deck circle and took his place in the batter's box. He had a few amendments ready. Each year, after consultation with conservative interest groups, he had fine-tuned the language on the content of the grants. This year's version would ban the NEA from funding works that "depict or describe, in a patently offensive way, sexual or excretory activities or organs."

"Think about Annie Sprinkle, Holly Hughes, Karen Finley, the Kitchen Theater. Think of the live sex acts on stage—all of this financed by the taxpayers' money," Helms declared.[79] He inserted in the record a resolution adopted by the Southern Baptist Convention stating that "God has ordained government to do good works" and calling on the Congress to prevent funding of "highly offensive, morally repugnant, and sacrilegious 'Art,'" or otherwise to cease funding the NEA.[80] With minimal debate, Helms's amendment passed 68–28.

Pressing his advantage, Helms then offered an amendment to shift 75 percent of the NEA's program budget to the states, up from 25 percent, on the grounds that state arts councils were more responsible than the NEA and less likely to make obscene and blasphemous grants. The formula Helms would use, however, guaranteed each state, however small the population, and without regard to the number of resident arts organizations or potential grantees, a sizable minimum grant. This meant that those states with large concentrations of artists and arts organizations whose residents had been successful in securing multiple grants would have their total share reduced. California, New York, and Illinois, as well as middle markets in Minnesota and Massachusetts, would all lose money. When even Al D'Amato, whose distaste for the NEA was exceeded only by his desire to bring as much federal money to New York as possible, opposed the amendment, Helms agreed to withdraw the measure. A few remaining amendments were quickly dealt with, and the Interior Appropriations bill passed the Senate with only three dissenters. The final shape of the bill again would be up to the conference committee.

Yates moved for the appointment of conferees on September 24, 1991. As Rohrabacher had unsuccessfully tried two years earlier, Dannemeyer moved to instruct the conferees to accept the Helms amendment. But it never came to a vote, being finessed by a senior motion by Bill Green of New York to instruct on a noncontroversial item on low-income weatherization. Green's motion was coupled with a motion for the previous question, thereby forbidding Dannemeyer from offering an amendment to add his own instruction. Some of the members were surprised that Green was playing the role that normally would be assumed by Regula. But when Regula, who had not spoken during the debate on Green's motion, voted with Dannemeyer, they knew something must have happened. Nevertheless, the previous question passed, and Green's motion to instruct was included as part of the conferees' appointment.

Yates, Regula, and the subcommittee staff spent several weeks preparing the House's position. Neal Sigmon informally communicated with his Senate counterparts to see how many of the 226 points of disagreement could be resolved before the conferees met. It soon became clear, however, that much of the negotiating would have to be among the principals when they met across the conference table.

The conferees met on October 15. It was the House's year to host the conference, which took place in room H-137 in the Capitol, next to the full Appropriation Committee's offices. The conference was open to the press, but seating was limited. No stenographer was present to record the conversations. Yates and Byrd exchanged cordial remarks. Like professional tennis players who had faced one another over the years, each knew the other's style of play. They could recognize the difference between a feint and a charge. Methodically, they plowed through the amendments. As they had in previous matches, each of them had deliberately removed personal earmarks of the other from their respective versions of the bill. Yates, in fact, had a standing order to the subcommittee staff not to put any West Virginia earmarks in the House version of the bill.[81] He assumed that Byrd did the same, as there were never any earmarks for Chicago in the Senate version. So Yates insisted on the appropriations for the Chicago Cultural Center and Gateway Park, and the Senate gave in. Yates, in turn, conceded to the Senate's additional money for Harpers Ferry National Historic Park in West Virginia, dear to Senator Byrd. Budget line by budget line, the conferees reconciled their differences.

There was an informal hierarchy for the review of earmarks in dispute. If at all possible, conferees tried to accommodate requests made by members of the conference committee, the other Appropriations Subcommittee cardinals, and the congressional leadership of each of the two houses. Since the bill was under a budget cap, accepting an earmark triggered a zero-sum game, and someone else's request would have to be eliminated.

There were also many conflicting policy directions to agencies included in the two versions. A direction to the government of American Samoa, a territory under the jurisdiction of the Department of the Interior, to get its books in order needed to be resolved, as did a direction to the Forest Service to create a timber salvage program in California, Oregon, and Washington. These policy directives also followed the earmark hierarchy, but they included more discussion on the merits. Both the Synar amendment on grazing fees and the Helms amendment on the NEA fell within this latter category. The conferees tentatively addressed each of them several times but, recognizing the intensity of feelings, quickly pulled back and returned to the less controversial amendments in disagreement. The word was out that Yates would not allow the Helms amendment to become law.

Conference continued on the next day. Suddenly, in the midst of the negotiations, Yates rose and adjourned the deliberations to hurry over to the House floor, a few steps away from the conference room. Dannemeyer was presenting a privileged motion to instruct the House conferees to accept the Helms amendment. Because of the length of time that had elapsed since the conferees were appointed in September without finalizing their negotiations, Dannemeyer was permitted to reoffer his motion to instruct, and this time, under the rules, he could not be preempted. Yates's only chance to keep it from being discussed was a nondebatable motion to table, which would immediately kill the instruction. The House summarily rejected Yates's motion.

Yates was not entirely surprised. Even the more liberal members of the House did not like motions that prevented debate. But he wanted to know how loyal his subcommittee had been. Of the Democrats, Jack Murtha, Norm Dicks, Les AuCoin, and Chester Atkins had all supported him. All the Democrats, in fact, except Tom Bevill. Yates couldn't do anything about Bevill. The Alabaman was a cardinal in his own right, chairman of the Energy and Water Development Appropriations subcommittee, and wasn't worried about any potential antagonism from Yates.

On the Republican side, Joe McDade had supported Yates. But Regula and William Lowery of California had sided with Dannemeyer. Yates didn't much care about Lowery's defection. As the most junior member of the subcommittee on the minority side, Lowery's voice was the least regarded. He was irritated, however, that Regula had not stood with him. Yates had included Regula in almost every aspect of the subcommittee's work since Regula had become ranking minority member.

Dannemeyer finally had the chance to bring his instruction up for full debate and a vote. He went through the litany: 'Tongues Untied,' Annie Sprinkle, Holly Hughes. Yates reminded the House that Senator Reed Smoot of Utah, most famous for the Smoot-Hawley tariff bill of the 1920s, once added an antipornography amendment to the tariff act, which was used to ban James Joyce's *Ulysses* from entering the United States until the amendment was declared unconstitutional. Now, seventy years later, Dannemeyer was trying to advance the same agenda. But Yates saw that his arguments, supported by speeches from Pat Williams and Dick Durbin, were not persuasive. In frustration, he said, "There is no use talking to a closed mind."[82] Dannemeyer's instruction carried 286–135. Regula again voted with Dannemeyer. Dicks voted with Yates until he saw the vote margin. Realizing that, as a result of the margin, his nay vote would not matter, he changed his vote and went over to Regula's side.

Yates took the House vote as a personal affront, as well as a sign of potential weakness that he was sure Byrd would try to exploit. As conference resumed, he startled both his own and the Senate's conferees by stating that, not only would he not accept the Helms amendment, but that he would insist that the Synar grazing fee increase remain in the bill unless the Helms amendment was removed. He would accept language reaffirming the current law instead. It was now Byrd's turn to consider consequences. Accept Yates's offer and be subjected to castigation from Helms, or reject it and face an uprising from both Democratic and Republican western senators. Byrd accepted Yates's deal. The conferees swiftly moved through the remaining items in dispute.

Word quickly spread to the House chambers, where Dannemeyer was still accepting congratulations. He demanded recognition. "This is arrogance of the worst order!" he cried.[83] He stated that as soon as the House met the next day, he would introduce a second motion to instruct. And he hoped that Mike Synar would join him. "So there were people in the conference committee who wanted to get rid of that increase on grazing fees and also in this instance on the use of taxpayer' money to fund pornographic material, and so I guess there was a swap here of some accommodation of corn for porn. I am not sure of the relationship, but that seems to be the relation between those two interesting coexisting ideas."[84]

The headline "Corn for Porn" was too good to pass up and became the national characterization of the trade to eliminate both the Helms and Synar amendments. On October 17, Dannemeyer offered the same instruction one more time. He conceded that, under the precedents of the House, instructions were not binding. Instead, he accused Yates of showing contempt for the body by rejecting the instruction so quickly after it was sent.

Yates was tired of Dannemeyer. Staring directly at the Californian, he shouted, "I reject this cry of arrogance, particularly when it comes from him. . . . I want to get back to the conference, and I will resume that as soon as we have disposed of this motion."[85] Then, as quickly as he had raised his voice, Yates resumed his professorial mode. There was no contempt for the House. There were 226 issues to be compromised. This was part of a larger package, and it was his responsibility as chairman of the House conferees to do what was best to uphold the whole of the House's positions. One or two issues would inevitably have to be lost, but in the end, the will of the House on the entire bill would prevail. Members would have a chance to review the whole package when the Conference Report was brought back to the House for approval. That was the appropriate time to see whether Yates had abused his discretion in ignoring the Dannemeyer instruction. The House rejected his arguments, voting a second time for the Dannemeyer instruction. Regula, still angry over the rejection of his prior amendment, and Dicks again sided with Dannemeyer. Despite Dannemeyer's attempt to corral the grazing fee proponents as allies, Mike Synar voted with Yates.

In truth, Yates was arrogant, and he knew it. He walked back to the conference, where the senators were still waiting. Once again, he had specifically been directed to accept the Helms amendment. Byrd looked at him quizzically as he entered H-137. "No change," Yates said. "The deal stands." "Fine," responded Byrd. "Let's finish up." Within an hour, all remaining issues had been resolved. Yates adjourned the conference. Neal Sigmon met with his Senate counterpart to prepare the Conference Report that would be taken back to their respective chambers for passage.

Dannemeyer was not done. Before the report could be filed, he again sought recognition from the Speaker, and offered a motion to discharge the House conferees and appoint new ones, who presumably would listen to instructions. This was the nuclear option. For Yates, this would be the equivalent of a vote of no confidence. It was a personal attack. It was also a challenge to the authority of the Appropriations Committee and the Democratic leadership itself. Others now stepped in. Butler Derrick moved to table the motion. Derrick was a Democratic representative from Strom Thurmond's home town of Edgefield, South Carolina, respected on both sides, and a favorite of the leadership, which had placed him on the Rules Committee. Derrick was next in line to become chairman of Rules. His presence was a signal that the leadership was behind Yates, if not personally, then to prevent a dangerous precedent.

No debate was permitted, and the motion to table passed 286–126. This time Bevill voted with Yates, in part to make sure that this type of action didn't come around to bite him when his own appropriations bill was up. So did most of the rest of the Democrats who had been willing to cross over to support the Helms language. Regula persisted in voting with Dannemeyer. Yates never forgave that vote. He didn't really care that, just as the Democratic leadership had made this a required vote, so probably had the Republicans, and that Regula would be discharged as a conferee along with Yates.

The vote was a personal attack against Yates and his chairmanship, and Regula had joined in. For a moment, he flashed back to his decision so many years earlier to support his chairman, Albert Thomas, over Clarence Cannon. Yates and Regula would continue to maintain a cordial relationship over the years, including the later years of Republican majority when Regula would become chairman. To intimates, however, Yates confided that he "couldn't stand Regula," and would distrust him for the rest of his career.[86]

Yates filed the Conference Report on the evening of October 17, 1991. It was signed by all the conferees. Regula filed an exception to Amendment 212, which had removed the Helms language from the bill.

The Conference Report came up for approval on October 24. Lowery moved to recommit the bill back to conference with yet a third instruction to accept the Helms amendment. But the House was ready to move on, particularly after Yates warned the members that, should the bill go back to conference under a recommittal, "every single issue that is in the conference report, including all those that we have agreed upon in connection with land acquisitions and every other kind of agreement would be up for discussion."[87]

While his words were neutral, his meaning was clear. He had had enough. There would be consequences if he lost this vote. Representatives knew Yates could be vindictive. Back in 1982, he had been redistricted so that part of the 9th District was in the suburbs for the first time. Seeing an opportunity, the Republican Congressional Campaign Committee, under the chairmanship of Congressman Guy Vander Jagt of Cadillac, Michigan, had sent money and support to Yates's opponent, Republican Cathy Bertini. When Yates had reviewed the members' requests for the upcoming Interior Appropriations bill, he saw that committee staff had recommended a $9 million appropriations for Sleeping Bear Dunes National Lakeshore, a National Park Service facility in Vander Jagt's district. Yates had taken his pen and struck the earmark, throwing the page back to the staff.

Those members who had received earmarks or favorable policy language in this year's bill could expect no support if Yates had to go back to the Senate. Enough members depended on those earmarks to tip the balance. The motion to recommit failed narrowly, 205–214, Regula again siding with the Helms supporters. But that ended the controversy. The Conference Report was accepted immediately thereafter. It was now up to the Senate to ratify the compromises.

Helms, as expected, roared his disapproval at the corn-for-porn trade, demanding that the Senate reject the compromise and recommit his amendment back to conference. Breaking with Senate protocol, Helms fingered Yates as the culprit. "Several of my best friends—and I am reluctant to say this—made a deal with Congressman Yates that if the conference would support [removal of my amendment], he, Congressman Yates, would go along with the Senate's grazing fee provision which is, of course, important to a lot of my friends. . . . I suppose it can be fairly said that this is the first time an amendment, certainly one that I have offered, has been defeated by a bunch of bull."[88] As before, he pointed the finger at Yates. "I do not like the process in the House of Representatives, particularly by one man, who said publicly that he did not care how the House voted with respect to this; he was not going to yield [to] the will of the body."[89]

But Harry Reid, whose Nevada ranchers needed the grazing fee compromise, reiterated Yates's warning that a rejection of the Conference Report would open up the entire bill. "They will find a way, if this is sent back, to put other matters that are contentious back into this bill and will cause many of us to lose things that are important to this country and to our respective States."[90] With understatement, Don Nickles, the ranking Republican, correctly observed that "I will tell you, the Congressman from Illinois, Congressman Yates, is very steadfast in his position." If the Senate sends back the Helms amendment, "they are going to be vindictive."[91]

Byrd moved to table the Helms amendment. The motion passed 73–25, and President Bush signed it into law on November 13, 1991.

The NEA appropriation would continue to be debated over the next years, but never to the extent of the three-year culture wars of 1989–91. Trades continued between NEA and BLM appropriations, with pundits calling the later trade the "grass for ass" compromise.[92] As a practical matter, the controversy subsided because NEA, under President Bill Clinton, agreed to eliminate grants to individual artists, the source of so much of the turmoil. In doing so, the agency ensured its continued existence but lost its soul. The adjective *daring* would never again be ascribed to the NEA.

To his constituents, Yates wrote that "The glory of the endowments was that you didn't have the Government judging applicants; they were judged by their fellow artists."[93] He believed in the aspirations of John Adams for the place of the arts and humanities as a statement about our civilization. But he also understood, as no one had before, that to protect the arts, they had to be treated as a special interest, subject to the same logrolling and trading as any other interest. With the culture wars, he had redefined the role of government in the arts. In the process, he had not only ignored, but had spurned, the will of both the House and the Senate. After all the years of waiting to become a chairman, he had shown how to exercise a cardinal's power.

10

"THE LAST SANHEDRIN
MET IN 70 CE"

January 25, 1984.

"Let's talk black talk." Sitting over breakfast with *Washington Post* reporter Milton Coleman at the coffee shop adjacent to Butler Aviation Terminal at Washington National Airport, Rev. Jesse Jackson thought he was signaling to a "brother" that his subsequent comments would be off the record. The New Hampshire Democratic primary was only a month away, and Jackson was waging the first serious presidential run by any African American in history. Coleman, however, had a different take. Having covered Jackson for years, he knew those words established that the conversation would be "on background," printable, but without attribution. Coleman nodded his agreement and Jackson began to talk.

A few weeks later, buried in the thirty-seventh and thirty-eighth paragraphs of a fifty-two-paragraph story by *Washington Post* reporter Rick Atkinson, with Coleman listed as a contributing reporter, the following lines appeared:

> In private conversations with reporters, Jackson has referred to Jews as "Hymie" and to New York as "Hymietown."
>
> "I'm not familiar with that," Mr. Jackson said Thursday. "That's not accurate."

Jackson was already distrusted by many in the Jewish community. They pointed to his bear hug of a grinning Yasir Arafat, the Palestinian Liberation Organization leader, in 1979 as clear evidence of his anti-Israel sympathies. Jackson's endorsement by the virulently anti-Semitic Louis Farrakhan, head of the Nation of Islam, had raised further concerns. "Hymietown" was confirmation.

Spurred on by many, including his wife Jacqueline, not to apologize, Jackson continued to deny the quote, charging that he was "being hounded by certain members of the Jewish community" and even accusing Jews of making him the target of a Jewish conspiracy to ruin him.[1] Hymietown was consuming all the oxygen of the Jackson campaign.

With just days to go before the primary, Rev. Jackson appeared before four hundred Jewish leaders, politicians, and congregants of Temple Adath Yeshurun in Manchester, New Hampshire, to apologize. But it was too late. Jackson came in a distant third, behind Senator Gary Hart of Colorado and former vice president Walter Mondale. Although Jackson continued his campaign, winning primaries in South Carolina, Louisiana, and the District of Columbia, he never recovered. Jackson's most ardent supporters blamed the Jews for his poor showing. Jews, for their part, responded in kind. Why hadn't Jackson denounced Farrakhan?

Farrakhan condemned Milton Coleman as a "traitor to your people. . . . One day we will punish you with death," and Jackson continued to defend his supporter. Then, in a sermon broadcast over radio station WBEE in Harvey, Illinois, a Chicago suburb, Farrakhan called Judaism a "dirty religion."[2]

Leaders in both the African American and Jewish communities realized that the situation could cause irreparable damage to relations between the two groups. National Democratic officials told Jackson that, despite having the third-most delegates, he would not be allowed to address the Democratic National Convention unless he distanced himself from Farrakhan. In addition, congressional leaders foresaw a disaster in the November elections if the schism continued.

California congressman Julian C. Dixon, chairman of the twenty-one-member Congressional Black Caucus, was particularly disturbed. He was marked for stardom as soon as he came to Congress in 1979, being put on Appropriations as a freshman, and getting a subcommittee chairmanship, District of Columbia appropriations, after only one term. His African-American colleagues in the House, recognizing his talents and access to the leadership, easily named him their spokesman. At the same time, Dixon's Los Angeles district contained a large Jewish population, and he had worked diligently to keep their support, requesting and receiving membership on Appropriations' Foreign Operations Subcommittee, where he became a stalwart supporter of foreign aid to Israel.

The Democratic National Committee had named Dixon chairman of the Rules Committee for the convention. He dreaded being caught in the middle of a Jackson-Jewish skirmish over floor rights and nominating speeches.

At the conclusion of an appropriations hearing in May, Dixon saw Yates packing up his hearing notes. He pushed back the adjacent chair and sat down. "Sid, it's up to you and me to do something." Yates immediately knew what Dixon wanted. Dixon was head of the Congressional Black Caucus. Yates was the senior Jew in Congress, the dean of the informal Jewish caucus. "Let's get lunch," Yates said. Yates didn't usually have lunch outside his office, preferring to eat at his desk, but today he and Dixon walked over to the Members' Dining Room in the Capitol and sat in a spot where all the other patrons could see them together. Over bean soup and sandwiches, Yates pulled out a legal pad and they began to write a joint statement. It was vital to ensure that, whatever tensions might be roiling African Americans and Jews outside, their historic coalition in the Congress must not dissolve.[3]

There had been Jews in Congress since 1845, when Lewis Levin was elected to represent Pennsylvania's 1st District under the banner of the anti-Catholic Know Nothing Party. But it wasn't until the rise of Hitler that Jewish representatives began to think of themselves as a bloc. Even then there were divisions. When Manny Celler and Samuel Dickstein, both of New York, publicly criticized FDR's reluctance to assist Jewish refugee immigration in the 1930s, they were opposed by the House's senior Jewish member, Adolph Sabath, a fierce Roosevelt supporter who did not want to see the president attacked and embarrassed by members of his own party. Leading Jewish organizations such as the American Jewish Committee and the American Jewish Congress also supported FDR, to avoid being seen as arguing for a special interest that could provoke a new wave of domestic anti-Semitism.[4] Celler, however, was undeterred. By the end of World War II, he had become the main Jewish spokesman in Congress and, despite Sabath's seniority, had eclipsed his older colleague as leader of the Jewish members.[5] Soon after FDR's death, Celler led a delegation of all nine Jewish congressmen to meet with Harry Truman to argue for the rights of Jewish Americans. He received a stern rebuke. Truman said that everyone was coming to see him on behalf of Poles, Italians, Greeks, and every other special interest. "Doesn't anyone want something for the Americans?" the exasperated president complained.[6]

Over the next twenty-five years, Celler continued to organize the Jewish members, Republicans as well as Democrats, particularly in support of Israel. Chairman of the Judiciary Committee and a powerful insider, his summons was not lightly ignored. When Celler demanded that Representative Charles S. Joelson join him and other caucus members in a secret meeting at the White House to pressure LBJ to support Israel, Joelson hesitated but reluctantly agreed. "I felt like a goddam conspirator," Joelson said, "but I went along because I didn't want to feel like an Uncle Irving."[7]

When Yates arrived in 1949, he was one of eleven Jewish members of Congress, the most since the 70th Congress in 1927, which included twelve. There were no Jewish senators when the 81st Congress commenced, but Herbert Lehman, the former governor of New York, would be elected to fill a vacancy at the end of 1949 as New York's junior senator in November 1949. It was still a period when hotels and clubs were "restricted" and real estate deeds contained covenants prohibiting the sale of houses to Jews. Only two years earlier, *Gentleman's Agreement*, the film based on the novel by Laura Z. Hobson, won the Academy Award for best picture for its portrayal of anti-Semitism in middle-class America.

As a young and handsome war veteran, Yates's arrival was celebrated by the national Jewish organizations. After being in Congress for only one month, he was an invited speaker, along with Sabath and Abe Ribicoff, at the convention of the American Association of English Jewish Newspapers.[8] Later that year, he made the first of many congressional trips to Israel, meeting with Prime Minister David Ben-Gurion in his Tel Aviv office soon after the signing of the 1949 Armistice Agreements temporarily settling the first Arab-Israeli war.[9]

Yates's efforts on behalf of Kennedy in 1952 and the Rickover fight in 1953 cemented Yates's reputation as a champion of Jewish causes. He received scores of requests for assistance from fellow Jews who believed they had been discriminated against by the government. In 1954, for example, Yates received a letter from a Navy veteran who, in 1947, "being of Jewish faith," volunteered to serve as an officer on a ship bringing almost one thousand Jewish refugees from Europe to Palestine. While en route, the Palestine partition and the creation of the State of Israel occurred. At a port along the way, the ship onloaded a shipment of arms for use by the Israelis against the attacking Arabs. More than six years later, the veteran, now an electrical engineer, was suspended from his job. He had been designated by the Armed Services Security Board as a security risk for having participated in that mission. Yates vowed to "fight vigorously" on behalf of the young man.[10]

Yates was convinced that the Eisenhower State Department, headed by Secretary of State John Foster Dulles, was no friend of Israel, or of Jews in general. He wrote to Dulles in the spring of 1954 suggesting that Arab nations and Iraq be required to make peace with Israel as a condition of getting arms, and he was furious at Dulles's patronizing reply, communicated by Assistant Secretary Thruston B. Morton, that Arabs "do not possess the intention or the capability of adopting a policy of aggression against Israel."[11] In a floor speech on April 28, 1955, he criticized the administration for providing free arms and military assistance to Arab countries while requiring Israel to pay for arms. "The policy of our State Department in the Middle East is moving more toward promoting hostility rather than peace."[12] In 1956, he again wrote Dulles, demanding that the State Department protest as strongly as possible human-rights violations by Egypt against its Jewish citizens. He contrasted the administration's condemnation of Soviet atrocities against Hungarians with the State Department's silence on Egypt's similar cruelties against the Jews.[13] In a speech before the Illinois Conference of Jewish Organizations meeting at the Sherman House in Chicago, he criticized the State Department and called for a United Nations investigation of the continuing oppression of Egyptian Jews.[14]

Dulles did not try to disguise his contempt for Israel and its congressional allies. Speaking at a press conference during the Suez crisis, he declared, "I am aware how almost impossible it is in this country to carry out a foreign policy not approved by the Jews. . . . I am very much concerned over the fact that the Jewish influence here is completely dominating the scene and making it almost impossible to get Congress to do anything they don't approve of. . . . The Israeli Embassy is practically dictating to the Congress through influential Jewish people in this country."[15]

Dulles had crafted a Middle East foreign policy for President Eisenhower, whose foremost purpose was to compete with and prevent Soviet influence and dominance of Arab governments. In its search for allies, Israel accepted aid from the Soviet Union. Just three days after the swearing in of the new Congress on January 3, 1957, Eisenhower, breaking precedent, made a dramatic appearance before a joint session of Congress to set forth what became known as the "Eisenhower Doctrine" and to request $200 million to support Arab nations "dedicated to the maintenance of national independence."[16] Yates, along with many members, were skeptical, particularly at the lack of details concerning the distribution of the money, and feared that Arab countries would be given weapons and American advisers without any guarantees that the arms would not be used against Israel.[17] Dulles did nothing to appease those fears when, appearing before the Senate Appropriations Committee, he refused to "telegraph his punches" to the Soviets and would not specify how he would spend the money.[18]

Yates opposed the Eisenhower Doctrine, calling it a blank check for an administration that would not guarantee Israel's safety.[19] "Members of Congress ought not to be mere 'yes-men' for the President," he wrote. "They, too, have a constitutional duty to perform; and if the President asks them to share his responsibility in the field of foreign policy, he must share with them at least the minimum amount of information which underlies his recommendations."[20]

One aspect of the Eisenhower Doctrine was particularly offensive. The United States had, from 1946, constructed and maintained a strategic air base at Dhahran, in the Eastern Province of Saudi Arabia, under a series of short-term leases.[21] The original airstrip had been built by Aramco, an oil company then owned jointly by Standard Oil of California, Standard Oil of New Jersey, Texaco, and Mobil, which controlled the largest oil reserves in the world and maintained its headquarters in Dhahran. It paid 50 percent of its net profits to the Saudi king.[22] In 1956, the lease was up for renewal. In a meeting held with Eisenhower in Washington, King Saud demanded improvements for the civil aviation facilities at the base, and military training for his own forces, all to be paid for by the United States.[23] In addition, he insisted that no Jewish military personnel be permitted to serve at Dhahran Air Base. Eisenhower, determined to appease the Saudis and to protect Aramco's oil interests, agreed to the terms.[24] The lease was signed in April 1957.

Yates was outraged at this official sanction of anti-Semitic discrimination, particularly as it was aimed at Jewish American GIs and airmen. Throughout 1956 and 1957, he made a series of floor speeches denouncing the lease. Coordinating with Senators Lehman and Javits, he introduced resolutions condemning Saudi Arabia.[25] Dulles blamed the Truman administration, alleging at a congressional hearing that the prior Dhahran lease, signed in 1951, had a similar ban. President Truman, who had taken heat for desegregating the U.S. military in 1948, would not allow this charge of religious discrimination on his watch to stand. He immediately issued a statement from his home in Independence, Missouri, denying Dulles's testimony, declaring that there had never been a religious condition in the lease.[26]

Then Dulles turned on New York mayor Robert Wagner, who he said offended King Saud during a visit to New York earlier in the year by calling him anti-Jewish, anti-Catholic, and a supporter of slavery.[27] The New York Times ridiculed Dulles's allegation as "a pretty sorry excuse,"[28] as did Wagner and several Jewish organizations.[29] In fact, King Saud—given a military escort by a Navy destroyer squadron and six B-47 Air Force bombers as he arrived in New York Harbor, and a reception by a sixty-five-piece Navy band and a Marine Corps guard when he disembarked—was unlikely to be offended by anything Wagner might have said. More likely, King Saud was annoyed at Wagner's direction to the police that the king's motorcade "observe all traffic regulations re speed and traffic lights, thus denying him the experience of a sirens blazing ride through Manhattan."[30]

Yates, joined by fellow Appropriations Committee members John Rooney of New York and James Roosevelt of California, made a final attack on the lease during debate on the Department of Defense appropriations bill for fiscal 1958. He knew that speaking against an appropriations bill would once again incur Clarence Cannon's wrath, but "I could not in good conscience permit this bill to leave the house without making my protest against the flagrant discrimination toward military personnel of Jewish faith—American citizens mind you— which exists today in the Middle East." In a barb clearly directed at Dulles, Yates reminded the House that under "the leadership of Secretary of State [John W.] Foster, grandfather of our present Secretary of State John Foster Dulles, a treaty of friendship was abrogated in 1911 because of Russia's discrimination against American citizens of Jewish faith."[31] Nevertheless, the bill passed overwhelmingly.

As the appropriations measure worked its way through the Senate and House-Senate conference committee, Yates and Henry Reuss introduced resolutions calling upon Eisenhower to terminate any existing agreements with countries that discriminated against U.S. citizens on religious grounds. The resolutions were referred to the House Foreign Affairs Committee, and it died there.[32]

The State and Defense Departments' complicity with Saudi Arabia and other Arab countries' anti-Semitism, which transcended administrations, would be a constant target of Yates's anger. As late as 1975, well after the United States had closed the Dhahran base, Yates railed against the Army Corps of Engineers submission to the Saudis' demand, even after President Gerald Ford had denounced the discrimination, that Jewish servicemen be prohibited from working on projects within its borders. In a letter to Ford's attorney general, Edward Levi, prepared in consultation with Congresswoman Elizabeth Holtzman, Yates denounced the "official lawlessness" practiced by State and Defense in "honoring Arab-inspired discrimination against Jews," a practice which was "legally, and certainly morally, intolerable."[33] Levi, a former president of the University of Chicago and the first Jewish attorney general, was an old friend. Two years younger than Yates, Levi's undergraduate and law school studies at the University of Chicago had overlapped with Yates's own, and they had frequently worked together over the years. The attorney general promised a quick response, adding that any U.S. companies that honored Arab demands to boycott companies who did business with Israel would raise serious antitrust questions.[34]

Yates's status as a Jewish leader after the Dhahran fight continued to grow. He was a sought-after keynote speaker at Jewish functions and in 1961 was named Man of the Year by the Jewish National Fund, which dedicated a forest in his name in the Judean Hills near Jerusalem, planting one hundred thousand trees in his honor.[35]

Mayor Daley's decision to slate Yates for the U.S. Senate in 1962 had many reasons, but included in Daley's calculations were his own reelection plans in 1963 and the need to keep Jewish voters from straying. Not only did Daley slate Yates, but he also put up prominent Jewish politicians Seymour Simon and Marshall Korshak for president of the Cook County Board and sanitary district trustee, respectively. As ward committeeman Joe Gill said, "The Jews likely won't forget that Daley this year 'recognized them as never before.'"[36]

Yates used his time as ambassador to plan his return to Congress and to solidify his position as a predominant Jewish leader. He was keynote speaker at the installation of the president of the Synagogue Council of America, held at the Carnegie International Center in New York[37] and then returned home to speak at the fundraising dinner for the Combined Jewish Appeal held at the predominantly Jewish Bryn Mawr Country Club in Lincolnwood, Illinois, which bordered the 9th District at the time.[38]

Returning to the House in January 1965, Yates quickly reestablished himself as a voice in Middle East Affairs and a maverick on the Appropriations Committee.

In an early vote in the 89th Congress, he broke with President Johnson, Speaker John McCormack, and Appropriations Chairman George Mahon to support an amendment preventing the Commodity Credit Corporation from purchasing agricultural products for the United Arab Republic. The ban was aimed at UAR president Gamal Abdel Nasser, who, Yates asserted, "has intervened in the internal affairs of almost every troubled country in Africa and the Middle East. . . . He has sent arms into Cyprus, into the Congo, into Yemen, into Algeria. He has made quite plain his disapproval of our policies by incidents which continue to mount up, such as permitting the sacking and burning of the John F. Kennedy Library in Cairo, by shooting down an unarmed American commercial plane, by telling our Ambassador in Cairo 'to jump in the lake' if he didn't like his actions."[39] The amendment passed with seventy-six Democrats deserting the administration.[40]

Johnson claimed that the vote handcuffed his ability to conduct foreign affairs. Yates disagreed, believing not only that Congress had the right to use the power of the purse in foreign policy, but that Nasser was an anti-Semitic dictator obsessed with Israel's destruction. Moreover, Yates felt no reason to be loyal to Johnson, who had clearly sided with Dirksen in the Senate race. Any misgivings Yates had over his vote were erased when Johnson, after Senate action watered down the House restrictions, praised "the very fine speech made by the Minority Leader, Senator Dirksen."[41]

As Yates worked to restore his seniority on Appropriations and consider his next career moves, he continued to speak up on issues involving Israel and the Jewish community. During the weeks surrounding the Six-Day War between Israel and the bordering Arab states of Egypt, Jordan, and Syria during June 1967, Yates spoke at numerous rallies, including an open-air rally for Israel held at the Grant Park band shell in Chicago, which was attended by more than twenty thousand people. To the cheers of the crowd, Yates called for Israeli control of Jerusalem: "The Arabs have had their turn. In the holy city of peace and good will they showed hate and discrimination. There can be no return to this kind of intolerable and degrading situation."[42]

The Six-Day War ended with an unquestioned military victory by Israel, effectively eliminating the air forces of all three opposing states.[43] But the calls by Arab activists for a "second round" against Israel along with the rearming of the UAR by the Soviet Union, which, within a few months of the war, was delivering six to nine shiploads a month of MIG jet fighter-bombers, tanks, and other equipment, convinced Yates that the administrations of Lyndon Johnson, and later, Richard Nixon, needed to do more to ensure Israel's survival.[44] When he learned that the United States was about to resume arms sales to Jordan in February 1968, he demanded that a nonmilitary solution be pursued instead.[45] In 1970, he traveled to Israel for discussions with military and government officials about the security situation. General Aharon Yariv, chief of Israeli Military Intelligence, told him that the continuing Soviet buildup gave Egypt and Syria a superiority in airplanes of 6 to 1 over Israel. After a briefing by Walworth Barbour, U.S. ambassador to Israel, Yates met for dinner with Prime Minister Golda Meir at the Knesset's restaurant. He assured Meir that he "had urged the President [Nixon] to approve Israel's offer to buy additional Phantom and Skyhawk supersonic planes from us and that I thought he would do so."[46]

Another result of the Six-Day War was the growth of the Soviet Jewry movement, as U.S. Jews became aware of the plight of "refuseniks," Soviet Jews who were denied permission to emigrate to Israel. As Natan Sharanksy, a leading refusenik, described it, Israel's victory "penetrated the Iron Curtain, forging an almost mystic link with Soviet Jews. Like a cry from a distant past, it told us that we were no longer powerless, and no longer alone. We now had a country that wanted us, and a people who stood behind us. But it was not just pride that Israel's victory evoked among the Soviet Jews. It was also a near unheard-of willingness to take on the Kremlin."

Yates became a leading voice for the refuseniks. Speaking at a conference of world Jewish leadership in Brussels, Belgium, in February 1971, he accused the Soviet Union of becoming "a mass detention camp" for Jews.[47] The next month, he spoke at a rally in Chicago along with Leonid Rigerman, a refusenik he helped escape the Soviet Union.[48]

Later that fall, he escorted Enoch and Marjorie Silverstein, a married couple from Evanston, Illinois, and Judah Graubart from the Chicago office of the American Jewish Committee, to see the Russian ambassador at the Russian Embassy in Washington. They brought petitions holding the signatures of one hundred thousand Chicago residents demanding the end of the "inhuman persecution of Jews in the Soviet Union." Appearing in front of the Beaux-Arts mansion on Sixteenth Street with fifty-four steel-bound cartons, they were met by Yuri M. Yushakov, second secretary in the embassy, and Grigory Rapota, a press officer, who refused to accept the petitions. Yushakov bluntly told Yates, "We're letting people go all the time. We will not change our procedures. We run the country the way we want. The fact that you don't like it doesn't impress us."[49]

Taking the petitions back, Yates and his group traveled to New York and joined by Philip E. Hoffman, president of the American Jewish Committee, presented the petitions to George H. W. Bush, United States Ambassador to the United Nations. Bush, a former congressman from Texas who had served two terms with Yates, cordially accepted the petitions.[50]

Yates flew again to Israel in the spring of 1972, where he met with Soviet emigrants lucky enough to have received exit visas. "All of them had experienced the fury and reprisals which the Soviet officials bring down upon their citizens who indicate they want to leave the Soviet Union: the loss of jobs, the dismissals from teaching positions, the suspension of their children from colleges and universities. . . . In some cases they had been jailed and some had been placed in mental institutions."[51] On his return to the House, he cosponsored another resolution urging President Nixon to demand that the Soviet Union permit emigration.[52]

Manny Celler's loss to Elizabeth Holtzman in the 1972 New York Democratic primary meant that Yates would become the senior Jewish member of the House.[53] His new status was quickly recognized by the national Democratic Party, as Democrats prepared to nominate a candidate to face President Nixon in November. Although not a delegate to the convention, Yates flew to Miami on July 13, 1972, at the request of the Democratic National Committee to address the Jewish delegates. The convention had been brutal and divisive, with bitter fights over the platform and credentials battles in two of the most important Democratic states. The convention awarded all 271 California seats to Senator George McGovern, although he had won the California primary by only 5 percent and the convention rules forbade winner-take-all. The convention also denied credentials to Mayor Daley and his 58 Illinois Democratic organization regulars, instead seating an unelected slate led by Jesse Jackson and Chicago reform alderman William Singer. The vice presidential nomination process descended into chaos, with seven candidates nominated in addition to McGovern's choice, Senator Thomas Eagleton, and votes cast for more than 60 people not nominated, including Archie Bunker and Mao Zedong. McGovern gave his acceptance speech in the middle of the night to a television audience who had long since gone to sleep, and there were already reports that many of the traditional Democratic constituencies were planning to sit the election out.

Among the groups worrying the DNC were the Jews. There was concern throughout the primary season that McGovern was not sympathetic to Israel, a concern that the McGovern campaign blamed on rumors allegedly spread during the California primary by Hubert Humphrey, the 1968 nominee whose attempt at a comeback had faltered early in the spring. Yates, along with Senator Abraham Ribicoff, who had given one of the nomination speeches for McGovern, were summoned to the Deauville Beach Resort. For two hours, they attempted to soothe the Jewish delegates and prevent them from encouraging Jewish voters to vote for Nixon, who was actively courting the Jewish vote.[54] Yates promised he would tell McGovern "what bothers you" about the nominee, while Ribicoff denounced "self-righteous" and self-aggrandizing Jews who had already raised $5 million for Nixon. The delegates were not assuaged, as the speakers were frequently shouted down.[55] Neither Yates nor the delegates were satisfied as the meeting ended. The convention now over, the delegates returned, dispirited, to their respective states.[56]

Illinois, including Cook County, went solidly for Nixon in a 1972 landslide, but Yates comfortably won reelection. As the new Congress organized, he kept his seat on the Interior and Transportation Subcommittees of Appropriations, where he was now the second-ranking Democrat on each, and added a third subcommittee, Foreign Operations. Foreign Ops had jurisdiction over all U.S. foreign aid, including both economic aid and military assistance. It was also the primary source of U.S. aid to Israel. Although Israel had been only a modest recipient of foreign aid in the 1950s and 1960s, the Six-Day War had increased public sympathy as well as congressional pressure to enlarge Israel's share.

Yates, now the senior Jewish member of Congress, was also the only Jew on the Appropriations Committee. The other Jewish congressmen, along with representatives of national Jewish organizations, urged him to go onto Foreign Ops as a way to protect Israel, since, even as a junior member, he could not only work to direct funds to Israel but also keep appropriations away from its enemies. Bain and others on his staff argued that the move would be popular in the 9th District and would cement his status in the Jewish community.

For fiscal year 1974, the first year in which Yates participated in drafting the subcommittee recommendations, military loans to Israel jumped from $307.5 million to $982.7 million. In addition, and for the first time, in part prompted by the October 1973 Yom Kippur War, Congress appropriated a military aid grant of $1.5 billion, which, along with economic aid and other grants, made Israel the largest recipient of U.S. aid in 1974.[57] Yates's constituents, in Chicago and around the country, were delighted. It was widely assumed that Yates would stay on Foreign Ops and eventually become chairman. When David Obcy, a liberal Democrat from Wausau, Wisconsin, and a member of the full committee, was deciding which subcommittees to bid for, he was advised by San Francisco congressman Phil Burton not to seek Foreign Ops, but to go on Interior instead: "Yates is the senior Jew on Appropriations and will probably take [Foreign Ops] because of his interest in Israel, rather than taking Interior."[58]

But Yates did not want to be perceived solely as the Jewish congressman, his reputation associated only with Israel and Jewish causes, important as those were. He was offended when a high-ranking army officer, meeting with him to discuss the Department of Defense budget, began by reciting the amount of military aid sent to Israel. "I am an American and a Congressman first and a Jew second," he retorted. He particularly did not want to feel "owned" by the Jewish constituencies as their man in Congress and have his independence on the subcommittee questioned whenever he took a position. He confided to Obey that if he became chairman of Foreign Operations, "the Jewish community would come after [me] for every goddam issue."[59] In addition, the practical politician in him also understood that there was not a lot he could do for Chicago from Foreign Operations.

Moreover, while Foreign Operations sent its money outside the country, Interior handled domestic appropriations and could be bartered with the other cardinals who oversaw agencies more closely associated with the needs of Chicago. An earmark from Interior granted to California's John McFall, chairman of the Transportation Subcommittee, could be exchanged for needed public transit money in Illinois, keeping Mayor Daley happy and allowing Yates to maintain his comfortably removed, if not warm, relationship with the Cook County Democratic machine.

Finally, and, perhaps most important to his decision making, Yates had served on Appropriations for a combined twenty-six years without his own subcommittee. He was not prepared to wait however many more years it might take to get Foreign Ops. To the dismay of many, in the Jewish community as well as his staff, when the chairmanship of the Interior Subcommittee opened up in 1975, he exercised his seniority and took it, going off Foreign Ops entirely, which allowed Clarence Long of Maryland to head the latter subcommittee. Yates would rejoin Foreign Ops in the following Congress and would remain a senior member there for the remainder of his career, but he ensured that his legacy would not be limited to his religion.

His new status as dean of Jewish congressmen created a new relationship with congressional leadership, the White House, and the Israeli government. When Ovadia Yosef, chief Sephardic rabbi of Israel, came to Washington on behalf of four thousand Jews seeking to emigrate from Syria, he went directly to Yates's office. Dressed in his ceremonial deep purple robe decorated with gold braid and oriental embroidery and wearing a blue turban, he pled his case to the Jewish members assembled by Yates, who subsequently sent a cable to Secretary of State Henry Kissinger urging him to intercede with the Syrian government.[60]

When three Arab terrorists took eighty-five Israeli students hostage in the northern Israeli town of Maalot in May 1974, killing sixteen high school students, Yates authored a resolution, cosponsored by 321 members, condemning the "brutal act of violence" by the terrorists.[61]

In March 1975, after the failure of Secretary of State Henry Kissinger's "shuttle diplomacy" to broker a peace between Israel and Egypt, a frustrated President Ford announced a "reassessment" of U.S. policy toward Israel. Kissinger, who blamed Israeli Prime Minister Yitzhak Rabin for the lack of progress, froze arms deliveries to Israel, in particular the previously promised Lance surface-to-surface missiles and F-15 fighter jets. The Israeli government quickly responded by appealing to its friends in Congress and in the national Jewish organizations.[62] The chief target of the lobbying campaign was the Senate, particularly the Committee on Foreign Relations, but Yates was not neglected. Among his most frequent visitors was Zvi Rafiah, the congressional liaison of the Israeli Embassy. Rafiah had been present with Rabbi Yosef at Yates's inaugural meeting as Jewish dean, and he became a well-known face in Yates's office.[63] Yates's staff believed Rafiah was an agent of Mossad, the Israeli spy agency, and Congressman Charlie Wilson of Texas, a major supporter of Israel and a close friend of Rafiah, believed it as well, but Rafiah, when asked directly, consistently denied the connection. Rafiah had in-and-out privileges and would stop by Yates's office without an appointment. If Addie Yates happened to be in when Rafiah came by, he would pull up a chair and share gossip while waiting for Yates to return from the floor or a committee meeting.[64] Rafiah also did personal favors for the Yates family. When Charlie Holleb, one of Addie Yates's relatives, was visiting Israel in 1974 and wanted tickets to the Knesset, Vickie Winpisinger, Yates's office manager, called Rafiah for help. Rafiah sent a cable the same day and not only got the tickets but made reservations for Holleb at the King David Hotel in Jerusalem.[65] This was not an unusual occurrence.

As pro-Israel pressure mounted over the spring against the Ford reassessment, the president called Yates to the White House on May 13, 1975, for a fifteen-minute private meeting. Ford wanted to explain his plans for a Middle East settlement and to get Yates's support for his proposal. Yates and the president were both freshmen in the 81st Congress and had a long and friendly relationship, including serving together on Appropriations. Yates welcomed Ford's succession after Nixon's resignation and had joined in the standing ovation when President Ford returned to the House soon after his swearing-in to address his old colleagues.[66] Ford made sure that Yates and Addie were guests at his state dinner on September 12, 1974, in honor of Rabin.[67]

Sitting around Ford's desk in the Oval Office, the president smoking his pipe in his leather-upholstered reclining chair with Yates to his left in a wicker-backed wooden armchair, the conversation was relaxed. As Ford recounted the next day to Kissinger and Lt. Gen. Brent Scowcroft, Kissinger's deputy on the National Security Council, "I told Sid Yates that we would probably have to go to Geneva, and we have warned both of them [Egypt and Israel] about making military moves," prompting Kissinger to remark that he would need to notify the Russians if Ford went to Geneva.[68] Yates wanted to know what Jordan, which was also part of the Geneva Conference, would be getting. Ford simply set out all the concessions given to Israel. "We have no apologies," he said. Yates was noncommittal, but he made clear that any reassessment that punished Israel would not be acceptable to Congress. Yates and Kissinger later met in June at a private dinner hosted by the Israeli Embassy in honor of Rabin, who had come to Washington to meet with Ford and try to settle their differences.[69]

Soviet Jewry issues returned to the forefront during the August 1975 congressional recess. Yates flew to the Soviet Union as part of a congressional delegation led by Speaker Carl Albert. Albert appointed Yates and Congresswoman Millicent Fenwick, the pipe-smoking Republican of New Jersey, as cochairs of a delegation subcommittee charged with looking into Jewish emigration and human-rights issues. After three days in Leningrad, Yates and the subcommittee traveled to Moscow, meeting a group of Soviet Jews in the second-floor lobby of the Sovetskaya Hotel. At the meeting, Natan Sharansky gave Yates a list of several hundred Jews and Ukrainians refused permission to emigrate and requested that the list be presented to Soviet Communist Party leader Leonid I. Brezhnev, whom the delegation would be seeing later that week. Yates promised he would.[70]

A few days later, meeting in Yalta near Brezhnev's Crimean retreat, Yates challenged the party chairman on emigration. Standing up in the conference room of a two-story glass pavilion in a pine grove overlooking the resort city, he held up the list as he spoke. Brezhnev, clearly irritated, repeatedly sighed while listening to Yates. "Again!" Brezhnev cried. "That's all I hear, always immigration. Anyone can leave the Soviet Union if he has no criminal record or if he doesn't know any state secrets. The reason I sighed is that this is the 155th time that I have had to speak to that question. In fact, it is true that the number of applications from Jews who want to leave the Soviet Union is dropping. What am I to do? If you have a list of people who want to leave, give it to Secretary Ponomarev. He will take good care of it." Yates gave the list to Boris Ponomarev, a member of the Communist Party Central Committee and chief of its International Department. As Yates said later, "He took good care of it. I never heard from him again."[71] Sharansky would later be charged by the Soviet authorities with treason against the Soviet Union.

Israel again commanded Yates's attention upon his return to Washington. The United Nations' Social, Humanitarian and Cultural Committee, known as the Third Committee, had just passed a resolution, backed by the Soviet Union and Arab states, that equated Zionism with racial discrimination. The resolution would go to the General Assembly for a vote in a few weeks. UN Ambassador Daniel P. Moynihan branded the resolution an "obscene act," and an official endorsement by the United Nations of anti-Semitism. In a show of support, Moynihan embraced Israel's UN representative, Chaim Herzog, immediately after the vote.[72]

Yates swiftly moved to prepare a response by the House. In what was described as "an amazing personal achievement," Yates personally canvassed members to sign onto a resolution, formally sponsored by Majority Leader Tip O'Neill, condemning the Third Committee's action and urging the General Assembly to vote down the measure. Yates was able to get 433 of the House's 435 members to cosponsor his resolution. "He literally did it alone," an observer told the Jewish Telegraph Agency. When Yates called Moynihan with the numbers, the ambassador was amazed and delighted. The Senate soon followed, passing a similar resolution. Despite their efforts, the General Assembly approved Resolution 3379 on November 10, 1975, by a vote of 72 to 35, with 32 countries abstaining.[73]

Jews and many others around the world condemned the resolution. One of many consequences, however, to equating racism with Zionism was the additional tension it generated between blacks and Jews in the United States. The great black-Jewish coalitions that had reached their pinnacle during the civil rights battles of the 1950s and 1960s had begun to fray, and wedge issues such as affirmative action, busing, and low-income housing had already caused former allies to turn against each other. Yates was determined to keep the alliance intact. When Ed Koch, representative from New York's "silk stocking" district on the Upper East Side, tried to get Yates's help to overturn a Small Business Administration loan program, he knew he had to step carefully. Although the legislation appeared simply to prohibit the SBA from discriminating in the making of loans based on race, national origin, or sex, Yates saw that the practical effect was to close down the SBA's affirmative-action policies assisting minority businesses. Koch had already lost a fight in the Banking and Currency Committee for his idea and wanted Yates to support a floor fight.

Yates was aware that if Koch, poster child for the stereotypical brash New York Jew, persisted, and most certainly if he did so with Yates's help, it would be seen as an attack on minorities by the Jews. Yates had no intention of getting into that morass, but he didn't want to offend Koch. Without committing, Yates suggested, "Before we do anything, why don't we talk to Joe Rauh?" Joseph L. Rauh Jr. was a founder of Americans for Democratic Action and a member of the NAACP Executive Board. He was respected by both the Jewish and the black communities and was one of the most prominent liberals in the country. As Koch described it,

> So, we are at a party at Governor Harriman's house in Georgetown—this huge estate, one block square—and there is Joe Rauh. I know Joe: Mr. Liberal. So Sid and I went over to him. "Joe," Yates said. "Ed here has a question and I think he ought to get your point of view. Ed, tell him what your story is." I then proceeded to explain. . . . Rauh simply became enraged. "We will fight you in the streets!" he cried. "We will fight you in the cities!" It was like a speech by Churchill! If I dared to do as I proposed, they, the liberal Establishment, would crush me."[74]

Koch dropped the plan and Yates avoided a major headache.

In addition to tamping down plans that would divide blacks and Jews, Yates worked to promote more positive ones. In January 1976, he joined with Congressman Charles Rangel of New York, then chair of the Congressional Black Caucus, as honorary cochairs of a committee establishing the Dr. Martin Luther King Jr. Memorial Forest in Israel.[75] The committee's statement that the forest would honor King's "dream of justice, dignity and peace for all mankind" was juxtaposed with

King's own statement that "Israel is one of the greatest outposts of democracy in the world. . . . an oasis of brotherhood and democracy."[76]

As the 1976 presidential and congressional races got under way, diplomatic progress in the Middle East slowed as parties on both sides of the world waited to see who would be leading the United States. Yates remained active. He joined a federal lawsuit brought by House members against the secretaries of Commerce and Interior, alleging violation by their departments of antiboycott laws by cooperating with Arab boycott demands.[77] He once again flew to Brussels, Belgium, as part of the congressional delegation to the Second World Conference on Soviet Jewry.[78] He joined a four-month vigil of floor speeches in the House to bring attention to the plight of Soviet Jews separated from their families, making an appeal that Felix Aronovich, a Leningrad engineer, be permitted to join his mother and brother in Chicago.[79]

Occasionally, his role as the dean required him to arbitrate disputes among the other Jewish members. In the summer of 1976, Bella Abzug accosted Yates on the floor. "Ed Koch is trying to destroy me!" she said. Abzug, whose Greenwich Village–Lower East Side congressional district abutted Koch's, was leaving the House to run for the Senate. Koch disliked his flamboyant, hat-wearing neighbor intensely and enjoyed the idea of scuttling her campaign.[80] He discovered that Abzug's name was on the letterhead of a letter criticizing seventy-six U.S. senators who, in response to Ford's reassessment, had demanded that Ford continue to sell fighter jets to Israel. Koch published the letter in the *Congressional Record* and, under his congressional franking privileges, sent it to hundreds of Jewish organizations and hundreds of thousands of his constituents, all of whom were potential voters in the statewide election. Now rabbis were calling Abzug in the middle of the night, screaming at her, and national Jewish money was drying up. "Sid," Abzug said, "You've got to call a meeting of the Jewish delegation and get Ed to stop. And you've got to get his mailing list so I can respond." "Bella," Yates said, "The last Sanhedrin met in the year 70 CE."

Yates said he wouldn't call a meeting of the caucus, but he agreed to see Koch. "What's going on?" he asked. Koch had no apologies, and, in any event, it was too late for Yates to do anything even if he had been willing.

Abzug lost the Democratic primary to Ambassador Moynihan by less than 1 percent.[81] Yates won an easy reelection in 1976, winning with 72.2 percent of the vote over token Republican opposition. Jimmy Carter lost Illinois but narrowly won the presidential election. The number of Jews elected to the House rose to a record 22.

The true feelings held by the born-again Georgia Baptist Jimmy Carter toward the U.S. Jewish community and toward Israel continues to be disputed to the present day. His administration is rightfully celebrated, however, for the 1978

Camp David Accords between Egyptian President Anwar El Sadat and Israeli Prime Minister Menachem Begin, which led to the signing of the Egypt-Israel peace treaty in 1979. During the many months leading up to the accords and the treaty, Carter maintained frequent communication with Yates, bringing him to the White House for regular consultations and seeking both his counsel and his assistance in maintaining an often-strained relationship between the president and the Jews.

A sore spot for Jews in the 1976 campaign was Carter's disavowal of the Democratic Party platform provision calling for recognition of Jerusalem as the capital of Israel and the relocation of the U.S. Embassy there from Tel Aviv.[82] Yates and Congressman Abner Mikva invited Carter to speak at Niles Township Jewish Congregation, a synagogue in Skokie, to show his support for Jewish issues in general, if not this specific one. Yates had not known Carter prior to the campaign, but they had a common connection from an unlikely source. Carter, as a young naval lieutenant in 1951, had been personally selected by Captain Hyman Rickover to work on the nuclear submarine program. Carter later said that, next to his parents, Rickover was the most important influence in his life. The title of Carter's presidential campaign biography, *Why Not the Best?*, in fact, had come from Carter's grueling employment interview with Rickover:

> Finally he asked me a question and I thought I could redeem myself. He said, "How did you stand in your class at the Naval Academy?" . . . I swelled my chest with pride and answered, "Sir, I stood 59th in a class of 820!" I sat back to wait for the congratulations—which never came. Instead the question: "Did you do your best?" I started to say, "Yes, sir," but I remembered who this was . . . I finally gulped and said, "No sir, I didn't always do my best." He looked at me for a long time, and then turned his chair around to end the interview. He asked one final question, which I have never been able to forget—or to answer. He said, "Why not?"[83]

Carter was under Rickover's command when the captain was passed over for promotion and Yates's long battle to get him the admiral's star began. Their shared reminiscences broke the ice. Despite Yates's and Mikva's assurances, the Carter campaign worried about the reception the Georgia governor might get at the synagogue. On the day before the Skokie appearance, therefore, Press Secretary Jody Powell released the text of a telegram Carter had sent to a leader of the refuseniks, Vladimir Stepak, expressing his solidarity with the dissident movement. It helped. More than two thousand congregants cheered the candidate as he entered with the two congressmen.[84]

Carter's election brought the Democrats back to power after eight years of Nixon and Ford. The "Georgia Mafia," Carter's core of advisers from Atlanta, streamed to Washington to set up the new administration. High among them was Carter's chief domestic policy adviser, thirty-two-year-old Stuart Eizen-stat. Chicago-born but raised in a Jewish neighborhood in Atlanta, Eizenstat belonged to the conservative Ahavath Achim Synagogue, where his grandfa-ther had helped hire the congregation's legendary rabbi, Harry Epstein, and his father was known as the Torah "pinch hitter" because his knowledge of Torah and Haftorah were so proficient that he could fill in if a reader was needed. Ei-zenstat had worked as a speechwriter for President Johnson and as Humphrey's research director in his 1968 presidential campaign. He was issues director for Carter's successful gubernatorial run but did not join the governor's adminis-tration, deciding instead to practice law. Eizenstat appreciated the drawbacks of growing up Jewish in the South. Despite a Harvard Law School degree, and unmatched governmental experience, the only major Atlanta law firm that made him an offer was Powell, Goldstein, Frazer and Murphy, one of whose founding partners was Jewish.

Carter was term-limited as governor to one term. Eizenstat urged him to run for president, a plan that Carter and his executive secretary, Hamilton Jordan, had been implementing since his swearing-in. Carter invited Eizenstat to join the campaign and, along with Jordan, Charlie Kirbo, Jody Powell, and Peter Bourne, became part of the inner circle that guided Carter's unlikely rise to president, and they now oversaw the new administration.

Yates was introduced to Eizenstat early in the transition and formed a quick affinity with the intense young man who rushed home every Friday evening to celebrate Shabbat dinner with his wife Fran and their two young sons. Eizenstat called Yates his surrogate father. The Yates and Eizenstat families became regu-lar dinner companions and Addie and Fran grew to be close friends. Yates was a source of fatherly advice on navigating Congress and helping Eizenstat get Carter's agenda through Appropriations. One time Eizenstat found himself on the front page of the *Washington Post* after a confidential memo to Carter was leaked. Carter was hugely unpopular at the time because of skyrocketing energy costs and historically high inflation rates. Eizenstat suggested in the memo that the president "shift the cause for inflation and energy to OPEC, to gain cred-ibility with the American people . . . to regain our political losses."[85] Yates called Eizenstat to warn him that the House Republicans were planning to raise hell over the memo, and Yates provided advice and reassurance, and defended him as well when the expected attacks came.[86]

Eizenstat became Yates's main conduit to President Carter. Although Eizenstat's portfolio was domestic policy (Zbigniew Brzezinski being Eizenstat's foreign-policy counterpart), Yates would tell Bain to "get me Stuey" when Yates needed to reach Carter about Israel. Similarly, when Carter appeared to be taking a harder line toward Israel, and particularly Begin, than Hamilton Jordan, who would become chief of staff, and Vice President Mondale thought prudent, Eizenstat ensured that Yates was brought into the conversation.

In late June 1977, for example, the State Department, just weeks prior to Begin's first official meeting with Carter, appeared to put preconditions on Middle East settlement talks, including a possible requirement that Israel return territory won during the various Arab wars in exchange for "normalization" and minimal Arab concessions. The Israeli government, and even the opposition parties, were furious with Carter. Yates called the White House for an appointment and was soon meeting with the president and Brzezinski in Carter's private office off the Oval Office. Yates told Carter that the State Department's position was in opposition to Carter's own prior statements and asked whether it reflected a new policy. Carter assured Yates that his position had not changed. The president nodded as Yates recounted the State Department's antagonism to Israel since the Truman administration and added that State should be following, not leading, the president. Carter responded that he had ordered both the State Department and his own aides to stop commenting on the Middle East until Begin arrived in Washington. He promised that Begin would be given "a most cordial and friendly reception." Yates left the meeting reassured.[87]

Yates continued to have regular meetings with Carter as the president attempted to broker peace in the Middle East. Like Ford, Carter suggested reconvening the Geneva Conference. Unlike Ford, who avoided raising the issue of Palestinian participation and recognition, Carter issued a joint statement with the Soviet Union requiring the acceptance of the "legitimate rights" of the Palestinians and the attendance of the Palestinians at Geneva. Jewish-American groups were outraged and Jewish members of Congress interpreted the statement as U.S. recognition of the PLO and the creation of a Palestinian state, even though the PLO publicly refused to recognize the Jewish state's right to exist. As tensions mounted, Yates organized an impromptu meeting with Carter and the Jewish caucus in the Cabinet Room of the White House on October 6, 1977. Surrounded by the congressmen around the oval mahogany table donated by Richard Nixon six years earlier, and flanked by portraits of Washington and Lincoln on one end, and Harry Truman at the other, Carter expressed his surprise at the hostile reaction to the U.S.-Soviet statement. The president thought that the phrase "legitimate rights" meant only that the Palestinians were entitled to a separate land, not a permanent Palestinian state in Israeli-occupied territory. He protested that "I would rather commit political suicide than hurt Israel." Yates, as the prime spokesperson, complimented Carter on his candor but told him that he would be sending him a formal letter, signed by 137 members, denouncing the statement.[88]

As Carter continued the slow process leading to the Camp David Accords, Yates was a frequent confidante. Despite Carter's promise to be "cordial," Begin frustrated the president greatly, a feeling that the prime minister heartily returned. Eizenstat said that Yates was the "calming voice," helping to temper Carter's irritation with Begin. Carter confided to Eizenstat that he trusted Yates. Unlike some members of Congress, who showed their fervor for Israel by criticizing the president, Carter said that he knew that Yates was not "grandstanding" to the Jewish community.[89] As they continued to work together, Carter would later write in his diary that Yates was the "leading member of the House on the Mideast, and I think everyone trusts him and he can be a very valuable ally."[90]

Yates flew to Israel in November 1977 as part of a congressional delegation to meet with Begin and Sadat during Sadat's surprise visit to Jerusalem.[91] Sadat came to the United States in February 1978 and was a guest of Carter at Camp David. Helicoptering from Camp David directly to the South Grounds of the White House in the fading sunlight of the late afternoon on Sunday, February 5, 1978, Carter summoned Yates, along with Senators Javits, Ribicoff, and Richard Stone, to the White House for an evening meeting. It was understood that the meeting was confidential. Carter knew that Sadat would be making a harsh speech at the National Press Club on Monday. For more than an hour and a half that night, Carter, along with Vice President Mondale, tried to reassure the legislators that he was not endorsing Sadat's charge that Israel was destroying the peace process.[92] At the conclusion, Carter asked Yates and Ribicoff to take a personal message to Begin on the negotiations. Yates asked for a day or two to think it over. Carter agreed, and the visitors left the White House shortly after 9 PM. Yates discussed Carter's request with Bain on Monday and prepared to call Carter to agree. On Tuesday morning, however, Yates woke to find a front-page story in the *New York Times* covering the Sadat speech. In the story jump on page 4, the content of the White House meeting, along with a list of participants, was disclosed. Yates was stunned and angry. His first thought was that the president would think he was the source of the leak. Yates called the White House to assure the president that he would never betray a confidence. Carter told Yates not to be concerned. "I should have known better than to trust Ribicoff," he said. But the mission to Begin was scrapped.[93]

Two weeks later, Carter asked Yates to return alone to the Oval Office. Secretary of State Cyrus R. Vance was scheduled to testify before the Foreign Operations Appropriations Subcommittee to defend linking the sale to Israel of seventy-five F-16 and fifteen F-15 fighter jets, the latter being the Air Force's most advanced jet, with the subcommittee's approval of sales of warplanes to Saudi Arabia and Egypt. Carter's staff thought the subcommittee, under Clarence Long, had fallen into disarray and wanted Yates to exert his own leadership. The meeting was sufficiently significant that Frank Moore, Carter's assistant for congressional affairs, had prepared talking points, reminding the president that the "highly respected Yates consults regularly with all portions of the American Jewish community and is in regular contact with Israeli government officials." Moore wanted the president to reassure Yates he would not use arms for Israel as a means of pressuring the Jewish state during the peace negotiations. He suggested that Carter consult with Yates how best to ensure that Jewish members be kept up to date, even suggesting that Carter ask Yates "to function as 'your eyes and ears' within the Jewish community as you asked Rep. Mo Udall to do with western Members."[94]

But when Vance subsequently appeared, Yates was not sympathetic, particularly when Vance said the United States would withdraw the sale to Israel if the committee tried to block the Egyptian and Saudi Arabia purchases. Vance joined the long list of secretaries of state interrogated by Yates about their department's perceived antagonism to Israel.

Moreover, Yates did not want to appear to be carrying the president's water. He was in conference committee one afternoon when Vickie Winpisinger, his office manager, ran down with a message that the president had called and needed to speak with him. Yates knew that Carter wanted him to push for certain language regarding OPEC sanctions, and he didn't want to commit. He took the pink message slip from Winpisinger without comment. At Bain's request, Winpisinger returned several times to see if he'd called back. Finally, conference finished, Yates returned the call and told the president that he would be pleased with the result.

The House leadership also took notice of Yates's influence with the administration. Tip O'Neill was elected Speaker a few weeks before Carter's inauguration, and the two got off to a very rocky start even before the president was sworn in. According to several published reports, O'Neill was disturbed that the tickets he'd purchased for the Kennedy Center inaugural gala were in the last two rows in Orchestra Hall. He called Hamilton Jordan: "I said to Jordan," the Speaker recalled, "'When a guy is Speaker of the House and gets tickets like this, he figures there's a reason behind it.' Jordan replied, 'If you don't like it, I'll send back the dollars.'" And the speaker exploded, "I'll ream you out, you son of a bitch!" After that, Jordan was "Hannibal Jerkin."[95]

Carter had run as an outsider and distrusted Congress. While governor, he had frequently gone over the heads of the Georgia legislature to appeal directly to the people, and he told O'Neill he thought he could do likewise in Washington. O'Neill was not impressed. On an even more personal level, O'Neill, who enjoyed his food and drink, was incensed at Carter's frugal hospitality. The Baptist president had banned hard liquor from the White House. O'Neill appreciated the value of sharing a glass as a way to lubricate political discussion. As a young congressman, he had been permitted, through the intervention of John McCormack,

O'Neill's mentor, to attend a few of Speaker Sam Rayburn's after-hours "board of education" gatherings. He could never get comfortable with the abstemious Carter.

Equally irritating, Carter had stopped the practice of serving a full meal at congressional leadership breakfasts, providing a platter of sugar cookies instead. "Mr. President," O'Neill said at one of these unfulfilling breakfasts, "You know, we won the election." O'Neill would later arrange that Carter's appropriation for hospitality funds be cut, as punishment for not using those funds to pay for breakfast.

O'Neill first came to the House in the 1952 elections, taking over the seat vacated by John F. Kennedy. The Kennedy family did not back O'Neill in the Democratic primary, preferring instead to support an Italian, state senator Michael LoPresti, whose demographics Joe Kennedy thought would be more helpful to JFK in his Senate race than another Irishman: "[O'Neill] doesn't help us. We need LoPresti on the ballot."[96] O'Neill never forgot the slight.

Notwithstanding their mutual treatment by the Kennedys, O'Neill and Yates were not particularly intimate as they each found their paths through the House, but they were urban liberals and both were close to Edward Boland, a Democratic representative from western Massachusetts elected at the same time as Tip, and who, like Yates, was now a cardinal, chairman of the Subcommittee on HUD and Independent Agencies. Millie O'Neill, Tip's wife, had not wanted to move to Washington, and so Boland, a bachelor until he was sixty-one, and O'Neill shared an apartment in Washington, staying there during session and returning home whenever possible. The arrangement remained until Tip became Speaker and Millie joined her husband in Washington, buying a home in the Chevy Chase neighborhood in the northwest quadrant of the city.

O'Neill said that there was "nobody more trustworthy than Eddie." He was "dedicated to the country and dedicated to keeping his mouth shut."[97] Yates felt the same way about him. Unlike the large, boisterous, disheveled O'Neill, Eddie Boland was quiet, slender, and intellectual, a personality match for Yates. Boland's endorsement of O'Neill was an important factor when Yates supported O'Neill in the Democratic caucus in his races for whip, majority leader, and Speaker. O'Neill, in turn, appointed Yates deputy whip and came to rely on him as the Middle East gained increasing prominence in congressional debates. "Here's how it works," he told a reporter. "So and so will come to me and say, 'Don't you think we ought to do something about the C-135s that the President wants to sell to Egypt?' I'll say to him, 'Clear it with Sid. Find out whether he wants us to fight on this one, and let me know.'"[98]

"Clear it with Sid" soon became a response whenever issues involving Israel or Jews came up. It had a familiar ring. Franklin Roosevelt had used it in reference to

Sidney Hillman, the founder and president of the Amalgamated Clothing Workers of America, when he decided to name Harry Truman as his running mate in 1944. Publicly, Yates downplayed his influence: "Tip gets requests and inquiries from Jewish groups from time to time with respect to the status of legislation or with respect to his attitude on matters relating to Israel or matters that affect the Jewish community throughout the country, and he's kind enough to ask them to ask for my opinion."[99]

Yates's influence with the Speaker had its limits, however. One time, Yates requested that he be included in a congressional delegation led by O'Neill to Moscow to continue his efforts on behalf of Soviet Jewry. But the Speaker was angry with Yates for refusing to put an earmark in the Interior Appropriations bill that would help Jerry Colbert, O'Neill's former media adviser, to stage a Memorial Day concert at the Capitol for public television. "If I take a Jew, I'll take one I like," the Speaker responded.[100]

Yates had balked at the earmark, running in the National Park Service budget, which didn't seem to have any merit except rewarding a pal of the Speaker and of Joe McDade, the Scranton Republican whose district included PBS station WVIA, Colbert's home studio. That by itself would not have been a reason for Yates to refuse a request from the Speaker, particularly since McDade was also the ranking minority on Interior Appropriations. But Yates felt the Speaker should have come to him, which would have given Yates the opportunity to grant a favor that could be redeemed later. He did not appreciate McDade making a deal with the Speaker behind his back.

Yates later found a reason on the merits to agree to the earmark. The National Symphony Orchestra (NSO), the Kennedy Center's resident symphony, was in terrible financial straits. Jack Golodner, director of the AFL-CIO Department for Professional Employees, which included the American Federation of Musicians, and a great friend of the Yates office, pleaded that the Capitol concerts would provide essential income for the NSO's musicians. After several meetings with Golodner, Austin Kiplinger, and Leonard Silverstein from the NSO board, and Oleg Lobanov, the NSO's executive director, Yates agreed to an appropriation that would provide for four seasonal concerts, linked to Memorial Day, July 4, Labor Day, and a fourth floating concert. An important stipulation was that each performance would include three rehearsals, so that in labor union terms, the musicians got paid for a total of sixteen services, enough to keep the NSO afloat. O'Neill would later tell the *Washington Post* that Yates was "the father of the idea for the concert,"[101] In private, however, the speaker held a grudge over the fact that Yates hadn't simply agreed to his request.

O'Neill had a second reason for not wanting Yates on the Moscow trip. On long overseas delegation flights, O'Neill liked to play cards with the other members, swap stories, and share a drink. On such trips, Yates would instead sit by himself with a book to pass the time or nap. He seldom requested anything more potent than a Sanka from the flight steward. He was not the type of traveling companion O'Neill enjoyed.

The Camp David Accords would be the highlight of Carter's efforts in the Mideast. But he continued to be distrusted by much of the Jewish community. A singular low point came in August 1979, when it was disclosed that UN ambassador and former Georgia congressman Andrew Young, the highest-ranking black in the State Department, had held an unauthorized meeting with a representative of the PLO. Government policy forbade such meetings until the PLO finally accepted Israel's right to exist. Compounding the problem, Young originally told Secretary Vance that the meeting was only a casual exchange of greetings rather than the substantive discussion it was later revealed to be. After a formal protest from the Israeli government, who some believed had tipped off the newspapers, and an expression of "displeasure" from Vance, Young submitted his resignation to Carter, and the president accepted it.

Carter was in a no-win situation. Jews were incensed, as all their suspicions of Carter's sympathies toward the PLO were reinforced. Blacks were equally outraged. As Congressman Parren Mitchell of Maryland, a former chairman of the Congressional Black Caucus, put it, "out on the streets, the feeling is that the Israeli Government went out of its way to embarrass and humiliate a black man."[102]

Eizenstat was particularly pained. Both he and his wife Fran had been early supporters of Young in his races for Congress and had helped run his successful campaigns. He knew that Young had not acted out of any animus toward Israel. As tensions between the black and Jewish communities mounted, Eizenstat said that Yates, who had worked with Young in the House, tried to be a peacemaker among the Jewish groups to tamp down any rising hostility.

Eizenstat would be responsible for what arguably was Carter's greatest contribution to the Jewish community, and for which Yates played a vital role, the creation of the United States Holocaust Memorial Council and the United States Holocaust Memorial Museum. Mark A. Siegel, Carter's liaison with the Jewish community, had asked Ellen Goldstein, one of Eizenstat's assistants, to research Holocaust memorials in other countries. On March 28, 1978, as U.S.–Israeli relations were at one of their low periods, Goldstein presented a memo to Eizenstat suggesting that Carter promote a Holocaust memorial in the United States. She recognized that, in the current political situation, the idea "might appear . . . to be glib public relations." Nevertheless, Eizenstat was intrigued. "I myself lost a number of relatives in the Holocaust," he said. "I thought it was terribly important that documentation be made so clear that no one could ever seriously question" the reality and scope of the Holocaust.

On April 25, 1978, Eizenstat prepared a memo for the president. He noted that the recent NBC miniseries *Holocaust* had been seen by more than 100 million viewers. While some criticized the production for trivializing the Holocaust and denounced the frequently jarring commercial breaks—a scene in which Adolf Eichmann complained about the stench of burning bodies from the concentration camp ovens was followed by a commercial extolling the odor-fighting power of Lysol cleaner—Eizenstat argued that the telecast had raised American consciousness about the Holocaust and that there was "stronger support than ever among many Americans—not just Jewish Americans—for an official memorial."[103] Carter agreed and, on May 1, 1978, at a White House ceremony honoring Israel's thirtieth anniversary, announced plans for a memorial to be overseen by a commission. Elie Wiesel, the Holocaust survivor and scholar, would head the commission. Eizenstat called Yates and Javits for advice. Many prominent Jews, including Henry Kissinger, were against the idea of a Holocaust museum, but Yates would spearhead the drive to get congressional approval for the commission and for securing the land on which the museum would be built.

Yates assigned his foreign operations staffer, Don Fisher, to call the General Services Administration to see what government-owned buildings might be available. Fisher, along with Mark Talisman, the vice chairman of the commission, helped draft the legislation creating the commission, using as a model the legislation establishing the Franklin Delano Roosevelt Commission in the 1950s. Fisher accompanied Hyman Bookbinder, Washington representative of the American Jewish Committee, and Talisman to tour some of the buildings. They approached a two-story red brick building between Fourteenth and Fifteenth Streets SW near the Mall. It was in terrible condition, with broken windows and a barracks-like appearance. "Oh my God," said Bookbinder, "This looks like Auschwitz." Fisher told them that the building used to be part of the Department of Agriculture, and GSA said it was available as surplus. Fisher subsequently asked GSA if legislation was needed to transfer the building to the commission. No, the GSA representative said, the agency would just turn it over to the group.[104]

Yates made sure that appropriations for the federal side of the Holocaust museum ran through his Interior subcommittee. He arranged that the government would donate the land and the building and provide specified operational funding. The construction of the museum would be raised with private funds. The museum formally opened in 1993. According to the museum's website, more than 17.5 million visitors representing 240 countries and territories visited the museum's website in 2016.

One of the most striking permanent exhibits in the museum is the Children's Tile Wall, in the lower level. The wall was the inspiration of Addie Yates, who with the help of Bain and a group of congressional wives and other women formed the

Committee to Remember the Children, commemorating the estimated 1.5 million children killed during the Holocaust. Schoolchildren around the country sent in painted tiles that were incorporated into the wall.[105] Upon Yates's retirement in 1999, the Auditor's Building Complex, situated next door to the Holocaust Museum on Fourteenth Street SW, and housing the United States Forest Service, was renamed the Sidney R. Yates Federal Building. The buildings stand side by side, commemorating the unthinkable event and the congressman who made sure it would never be forgotten.

Meanwhile, Yates's influence with the White House on Jewish affairs diminished during the Republican administrations of Ronald Reagan and George Herbert Walker Bush. Yates would speak with Reagan mostly at ceremonial events, such as the annual Holocaust Days of Remembrance, which Reagan agreed to hold at the White House in 1981, and at such events as the laying of the cornerstone at the Holocaust Museum. Yates and Reagan sat together at these occasions, at which Yates conducted the candle-lighting ceremony. They had little direct substantive interaction, and Yates spent most of the Reagan years fighting battles in the Appropriations Committee against Reagan's proposed massive cuts to domestic spending.

Yates's influence also diminished when Jim Wright of Fort Worth succeeded O'Neill as Speaker in 1987. Yates and the wild-browed Texan had little in common. Wright had voted against the Civil Rights Act of 1964, and yet his opponents had called him too liberal for his district. He was a little too obvious in his power seeking for Yates, who appreciated subtlety. Yates kept his distance from Wright, who always seemed to be on the edge of scandal. His instincts were justified with the publication of *Reflections of a Public Man*, a slender volume that Wright wrote and that friends and lobbyists bought in bulk, Wright receiving a royalty of 55 percent on the sales. The arrangement prompted an ethics investigation that finally forced his resignation as Speaker.

In 1983, Wright, then majority leader, asked Yates to include the newly formed National Endowment for Democracy within the jurisdiction of his Interior Appropriations subcommittee. The NED was created by Congress in response to disclosures that the CIA had secretly been funding newspapers and political parties around the world to influence elections in foreign countries. The NED, a nongovernmental entity, but almost completely dependent on appropriations, had the purpose of encouraging democratic development and electoral processes openly. Critics, however, charged that it would simply be taking over the CIA's programs of overthrowing unfriendly governments, but with the patina of teaching democracy. Wright wanted to hide the NED appropriations among existing endowments, the National Endowment for the Arts and the National Endowment for the Humanities, where it would not stand out. Unlike his eagerness to assume jurisdiction over the Holocaust Commission, Yates refused to let the NED into his subcommittee. He distrusted the NED and suspected that, despite its impressive board of directors, it would end up as a tool of the CIA, or worse, of hawkish congressional leaders. Like the O'Neill turndown on Colbert, Wright was annoyed that Yates had refused to accept his direction. Wright felt no need to "Clear it with Sid."

Yates continued to challenge the State Department, opposing the sale by the Reagan administration to Saudi Arabia of five Boeing E-3 Sentry aircraft, commonly known as AWACs, for airborne early warning and control. With look-down radar and a 360-degree view of the horizon, AWACs could detect and track air and sea targets simultaneously. The Air Force boasted that AWACs could provide direct information needed for interdiction, reconnaissance, airlift, and close air support for friendly ground forces, providing information for commanders of air operations to gain and maintain control of the air battle.[106] Combined with the F-15 fighters and the Sidewinder missiles that the United States had already sold to the Saudis, Yates believed that the sale would put Israel in jeopardy. Yates's Israeli connections told him that "nowhere in Israel could we escape the eye in the sky." Questioning Reagan's Secretary of State Alexander Haig during a Foreign Ops Appropriations Subcommittee hearing, he accused the secretary of going back on his "oft-repeated declarations of the Administration's support of Israel, particularly in light of Saudi Arabia's assertion that its number one enemy was Israel."[107]

Haig's successor, George Shultz, fared no better in the subcommittee. Yates attacked Shultz's attempt to equate military aid to the strongmen ruling El Salvador with that of assistance to Israel.[108] At a subsequent hearing, Yates, along with fellow subcommittee member David Obey, lectured Shultz on the administration's failures in Lebanon and El Salvador. The normally professorial Shultz exploded. "I really don't understand you people," he shouted.[109]

Yates fought with Shultz over arms sales in the Mideast throughout the secretary's term, but their relationship was actually quite close. Prior to joining the administration, Shultz had been on the faculty and was later dean of the School of Business at the University of Chicago, one of Yates's favorite recipients for federal earmarks. In addition, Shultz had been head of the Office of Management and Budget, as well as secretary of labor and secretary of the treasury. In all those positions, he had been a frequent witness before the Appropriations Committee.

Shultz met with the Jewish caucus on several occasions, including a meeting on arms sales to Jordan held at what was supposed to be an off-the-record dinner at the four-level, seven-bedroom Georgian mansion owned by Congressman James Scheuer in Washington's ritzy Kalorama neighborhood. Scheuer couldn't help telling the *New York Times* that while most of the meetings were held in

Yates's office, dinner meetings were always held at Scheuer's house.[110] Yates didn't mind. His apartment on Cathedral Avenue NW could never have accommodated twenty-two Jewish congressmen and the secretary of state at a sit-down dinner.

The plight of Soviet Jews continued to occupy Yates during this period. In 1986, as part of a general loosening of restrictions under Mikhail Gorbachev, Natan Sharansky was released after nine years in various Soviet prisons and allowed to emigrate. O'Neill invited Sharansky to speak to the House and appointed Yates to conduct the ceremony. Meeting with Sharansky in the Speaker's officer prior to the event, Yates reminded the refusenik of their prior meeting when Sharansky had given him the list of dissidents to present to Brezhnev. "Not only do I remember you," said Sharansky. "You should know that the KGB named Congressman Yates as one of my coconspirators at my trial in Moscow."[111]

Yates's standing with congressional leadership would improve when his old friend, Tom Foley of Washington state became Speaker after Wright's resignation. The strength of their connection was demonstrated when Foley broke with tradition in 1989 to come to Chicago and endorse Yates in a contested Democratic primary election against Alderman Edwin Eisendrath. "I have never seen Sidney Yates do anything, take any action, support any legislation, advance any position in the Congress, that wasn't done out of a sense of conviction and principle and with great effectiveness," said the Speaker to the reporters assembled at the press conference. "Of the members of Congress that I know, no one has a greater respect among the membership."[112]

The Jewish caucus grew to a high-water mark of thirty-five congressmen elected in 1990 during the George H. W. Bush midterm elections. A major split within the caucus occurred over Bush's decision to go to war against Iraq in order to remove Iraqi troops from Kuwait. Yates opposed the Gulf War and was bitterly attacked by the American Israeli Public Affairs Committee, AIPAC. Even some of Yates's most ardent Jewish contributors in Chicago were upset. Prior to the vote on the war, one of them called Don Fisher and asked him to report back "if he strays." Fisher refused. Yates voted against giving Bush authorization. "It was not enough [for the president to say] that our vital national interests were being threatened by Saddam, a general statement which did not specify which national interests were threatened," Yates wrote. "When the President proposes to take our nation to war, I want better reasons than those given by President Bush before I give him my vote."[113] The Gulf War Resolution passed by a majority of 67 votes. The 17 Jewish members who voted against it used Yates's no vote as cover for their own action.

The rise of Bill Clinton briefly brought Yates's counsel back to the White House. Eizenstat, though no longer situated next to the Oval Office, remained an important connection and friend as he achieved increasingly high appointments in the Clinton administration, becoming U.S. ambassador to the European Union, undersecretary in the Departments of Commerce and State, and deputy secretary of the Department of the Treasury. But the takeover of the House by the Republicans in the 1994 midterm elections sapped much of Yates's influence, and the White House's priorities were scrambled as it diverted its energies to defending the president against impeachment and domestic scandal. In addition, Yates detested Clinton's strategy of triangulation and pursuit of a more conservative agenda through the center-right Democratic Leadership Council and let him know it.[114]

In a White House meeting called by Clinton with the now-deposed Democratic cardinals, Yates, sitting next to the president, upbraided Clinton for his actions: "Mr. President, I ran as a liberal Democrat in my district supporting liberal issues. I won by 67 percent of the vote. I campaigned for you, Mr. President, as a liberal and you carried my district. Now it appears that you're moving away from your liberal philosophy and becoming more conservative. I hope you don't move too far, because I want to continue to support your positions." Clinton just stared at Yates without responding. David Obey, on Clinton's other side, sought to break the tension. "67 percent of the vote? I only won by 52 percent. Can't I get some of your voters?" "Sure, David," Yates replied. "All you have to do is be more liberal."[115] The president joined in the laughter that followed from around the table.

Clinton, however, did not enjoy being called out in front of the congressmen and quietly sounded out the Democratic congressional leadership about the possibility of removing Yates as ranking member from his subcommittee.[116] Clinton was unsuccessful, but by that time it didn't really matter. Yates's advancing age— he was eighty-five when he lost his chairmanship to his Republican counterpart Ralph Regula in 1995—and his decreasing energy allowed others to take the first chair in Israeli-American relations. By the time Clinton, in the last months of his administration, tried to move away from his domestic problems to find an eventually unsuccessful route to peace in the Middle East with Yasir Arafat and Ehud Barak, Yates was long retired and played no part in the plan.

Like Fight Club, the first rule of the congressional Jewish caucus was that its members did not talk about the congressional Jewish caucus. Unlike the Congressional Black Caucus, which was a formal organization recognized by the House of Representatives and eligible to receive funding and administrative support, Jewish members were sensitive to charges of undue Jewish influence in national affairs.[117] Institutionalizing a caucus would just be putting another target on their backs and feeding the anti-Semitism that, either openly or incidentally, in what today are referred to as "microaggressions," bubbled in the Congress.

Yates never officially acknowledged that there was a "caucus." "It's a group," he told a reporter, "to provide the Jewish members with information I think is important for them to have. It's not a formal summoning like the blowing of the shofar. We just try to keep abreast of all developments."[118]

Yates saw raw anti-Semitism from his first moments in Congress. The chairman of the House Veterans Affairs Committee, John Rankin of Mississippi, who was in his final term as Yates began his freshman year, had once called the columnist Walter Winchell "the little kike" on the House floor. He similarly had referred to Julius and Ethel Rosenberg as a "pair of Communist kikes." Manny Celler re-counted to Yates his own experiences with Rankin reaching back into the 1920s. "[T]he loneliest moments I experienced in the House were in the running battle with my former colleague, Mr. John Rankin of Mississippi . . . [who] became bolder as the years went by and to his theme of white supremacy he added that of anti-Semitism. To listen to his harangues on the floor became, for me, an agony." Celler told Yates that he would wait, usually in vain, for another member of the House to challenge Rankin, until finally Celler was forced to rise in response.[119]

Despite his public statements, Yates believed that anti-Semitism played a major role in the Rickover matter, and in his own treatment by Clarence Cannon on Appropriations. Moreover, he had no doubt that the Dirksen campaign's anti-Semitic "Yackevitch" and German-American attacks played a large role in his 1962 defeat.

Yates thought his relations with Julia Butler Hansen, Yates's chairman on Inte-rior Appropriations prior to 1975, were friendly and cordial. He was disappointed, therefore, if not particularly surprised, to learn that, within earshot of several members of Congress on the floor of the House during consideration of Israel's foreign aid appropriations request, she had casually remarked, "You know, I was once cheated by a Jew. He was a storekeeper, and what he did was to sell inferior merchandise." According to Ed Koch, one of the nearby observers, she told Clar-ence Long that from that time on, she didn't like Jews, including, apparently, the congressman from Illinois who sat to her right at subcommittee and whose warm greeting was always smilingly returned.[120]

But while always a strong voice against anti-Semitism abroad, occasionally Yates looked the other way closer to home. After his victory over the Daley del-egation at the 1972 Democratic convention, Alderman Bill Singer challenged Daley in the mayoral election in 1975. Singer was Jewish, his ward was in Yates's district, and many of Yates's liberal constituency thought the congressman might endorse the young politician. Other influential Jewish supporters, however, such as Jack Guthman, a well-known lawyer and philanthropist with close ties to both Yates and the mayor, urged Yates to back Daley. Yates's ultimate endorsement of Daley was a major blow to Singer and infuriated many independent voters and organizations, who had hoped that, at a minimum, Yates would stay neutral. But

Yates had no interest in antagonizing Daley and, in any event, he knew Singer had no hope of winning.[121]

The Daley machine took no chances, however. Supporters of Daley in the segregated white neighborhoods on the southwest side of the city were distributing leaflets warning "if Mayor Daley is not elected, then Chicago will belong to the Jews and Negroes. . . . We the Catholics and Christians must unite to defeat the Jewish candidate, William Singer." Yates was repeatedly beseeched to denounce the anti-Semitic attacks on Singer. Neither he nor his office ever responded to those requests. Singer never forgave Yates. After his expected drubbing by Daley, although he did narrowly win in the 9th District, Singer publicly considered, and abandoned, a challenge to Yates in the 1976 primary election. Fifteen years later, Singer would chair the unsuccessful campaign of Edwin Eisendrath to unseat Yates in 1990.

Episodes of casual anti-Semitism continued even during Yates's most powerful years. As he prepared for conference committee on the Interior Appropriations bill during a period when the Republicans controlled the Senate, he set up a meeting with Idaho senator Jim McClure, his counterpart on the Senate Interior Appropriations subcommittee. This was a traditional preconference meeting to go over the earmarks that each side had inserted into the respective House and Senate versions of the bill.

A staunch western conservative, McClure had served in the House with Yates, and, like most of the pragmatists on Appropriations, they had gotten along relatively well despite their vast philosophical differences. They efficiently went through the list of members' requests, agreeing to keep or reject some and putting off others until conference. Yates looked at the next request and raised an objection to the amount asked for in a senator's earmark. It wasn't an important project for McClure. "Don't worry, Sid," McClure agreed, "We're going to Jew him down." McClure suddenly stopped himself, abashed, and began to apologize. Yates just moved on to the next earmark on the list. He told Bain the story when he returned to his office and she was incensed. Yates told her not to worry about it.[122] He was reconciled that he would always be the "Jewish congressman." He would fight the battles he could—Israel, Soviet Jewry, black-Jewish relations—and ignore the rest.

11

THE FINAL YEARS

The 1994 midterm elections were a brutal repudiation of the Clinton administration and the Democratic Party. The unpopularity of Clinton's signature universal health-care plan, combined with the Republicans' "Contract with America," a policy statement signed by all but two of the GOP incumbents and candidates, resulted in a 54-seat swing from Democrats to Republicans, and the return of Republican control of the House for the first time since 1955. Thirty-four incumbent Democrats were defeated, including Yates's fellow Chicagoan Dan Rostenkowski, chairman of Ways and Means; Jack Brooks, chairman of Judiciary; and Speaker Tom Foley, the first Speaker of the House to be defeated for reelection since 1862. The Senate also switched from Democratic to Republican. As David Wilhelm, chairman of the Democratic National Committee, put it, "Well, we made history last night. Call it what you want: an earthquake, a tidal wave, a blowout. We got our butts kicked."[1]

The conservative tide rolled over Yates without effect, as he easily received 66.1 percent of the vote. Seeing the national results, however, he called Ralph Regula, the ranking minority member of Interior Appropriations, at his Canton, Ohio, headquarters, to congratulate him on his new majority status. "Congratulations, Mr. Chairman," Yates began. Regula interrupted. "No. No. It's Mr. Co-Chairman. Sid, you've always treated me as the co-chair of the committee. Nothing is going to change. We'll continue as co-chairs." Yates thanked Regula, but he knew that, whatever Regula's sincerity and good intentions, Newt Gingrich, the first Republican Speaker in two generations, was not going to permit that type of comity.

Yates attended his twenty-third swearing in on January 3, 1995. He was the only member on either side of the aisle who had been in the House the last time there was a Republican Speaker. He had lost his chairmanship and his influence.

He was eighty-five years old. He responded to the many congratulatory notes sent by other Democratic congressmen, both the survivors and the defeated. To each, he recounted his days in the minority in 1953 and reminded them that the Democrats had regained control two years later. He encouraged them to keep the faith. But he wondered if he could still do the same.

He had begun to husband his energy for the times when he needed it the most. In a postelection meeting with President Clinton and Democratic appropriators, he vigorously challenged Clinton not to desert liberal Democratic values. He sparred with Bob Livingston of Louisiana, chairman of the full Appropriations Committee, over rescissions of previously appropriated funding. When an attempt was made to expand logging in Alaska's Tongass National Forest, Yates battled the Republicans and killed the plan.[2] He continued to press against reductions in funding for the National Endowments for the Arts and Humanities. But illness caused his voting record to drop to 82 percent, the lowest in his career, and, significantly, he was missing important votes, including a pro-environmental vote that, in his absence, failed on a tie. When asked about his failure to vote, Yates told the press that he had felt "queasy." He also stopped writing newsletters, instead sending out only two questionnaires in 1995 and one questionnaire in 1996.

Yates debated whether to run again in 1996. The Illinois Election Code required that he file nominating petitions in December 1995 for the March 19, 1996, Democratic primary. He wavered back and forth, even advising Howard Carroll, a prominent state senator in the Ninth District, that he was not going to file. Other potential successors were already organizing. Both State Representative Jan Schakowsky, a liberal consumer activist, and J. B. Pritzker, an investment banker and an heir to the Hyatt Hotel fortune, had formed exploratory committees and raised about $150,000 each. They also had begun to circulate petitions. Schakowsky and Pritzker said they would not run if Yates filed, but Pritzker's campaign manager, Mark N. Poole, sent letters demanding that Yates retire. Schakowsky excoriated Pritzker for the letter. "J. B. should have the integrity to honor his pledge or have the guts to run against him," she said.[3] Bain tried to quash any rumors of indecision, telling the press that he would run. At the same time, she called longtime allies and former staff members to write to Yates and urge him to stay in Congress.

Yates confided to Bain that he had two fears about running again. He did not want to end up like Manny Celler, who served for fifty years in Congress only to be defeated in the Democratic primary, at the age of eighty-four, by thirty-one-year-old liberal attorney Elizabeth Holtzman. Nor did he want to finish his career like Mel Price, who died in office at eighty-three. The Democratic caucus removed Price as chairman of the House Armed Services Committee because of his age and feebleness. Even worse, to Yates's thinking, Price became an object of pity as members watched his staff physically prop him up in order to speak or cast his vote.

Nevertheless, encouraged by much well-wishing and many letters of support, and annoyed by what he felt were premature predictions of his demise, he filed his nominating papers in Springfield. "I can serve my district much better than any newcomer can," he said.[4] He also enjoyed irritating the *Tribune*, which had run an editorial gleefully bannered "Time to Hang It Up, Sid."[5] Schakowsky and Pritzker withdrew from the race. Saying that this would probably be his final term, he breezed through his primary, defeating two third-tier candidates and, despite an aggressive campaign waged by a young Republican opponent who tried to use Yates's age and infrequent visits to Chicago as issues, won his twenty-fourth term with 63.4 percent of the vote.

Bill Clinton also won another term, but the House remained in Republican control and Yates was still in the minority. As he suspected, the working relationship with Regula had changed and had become decidedly partisan. The Republican leadership denied Regula the chairmanship of the Appropriations Committee, to which he was entitled under traditional seniority rules, and even warned him against bipartisan cooperation on Interior Appropriations lest he lose that chairmanship as well. Regula and Yates no longer worked together as before.

His attention to details was also slipping, as both Yates and Bain increasingly relied on their staff, occasionally to painful effect. Language was slipped into the Interior Appropriations report directing the National Park Service to install a dog run at Meridian Hill Park, a Washington, DC, facility used by a Yates staffer to walk his dog. An angry National Park Service employee leaked the information to nationally syndicated columnist Jack Anderson, who devoted a full column to the matter. Soon it was on the front page of the *Washington Post* and picked up by the Chicago papers, including an editorial by a *Tribune* editorial board delighted for the rare opportunity to legitimately ridicule the congressman. Bain called the dog run a "dumb idea" and told *Roll Call*, the widely read Capitol Hill newspaper, that the aide had acted without Yates's knowledge, a point disputed by the staff member. Yates immediately wrote Roger Kennedy, Director of the National Park Service, requesting that all activity cease on the Meridian Hill project.[6] The entire matter was a huge embarrassment for Yates and reinforced his feeling that it was time to retire. Yates let Carroll and Schakowsky know that he would not seek another term in 1998. He cast his final votes on Saturday, December 19, 1998, in opposition to the Articles of Impeachment filed against President Clinton. The eighty-nine-year-old congressman retired at the conclusion of the 105th Congress on January 3, 1999, fifty years from his first swearing in.

Over several days in July 1998, Yates brought his final Interior Appropriations bill to the floor, although not as manager, but as ranking minority member.

Congressmen, Republicans and Democrats, rose to pay tribute to the veteran legislator. They praised his leadership, his dignity, his mastery of the legislative process. A common theme was his ability to work respectfully and productively with those whose positions he opposed. Phil Crane, whose 100 percent American Conservative Union ratings mirrored Yates's 100 percent ratings from Americans for Democratic Action, was typical in his remarks: "Mr. Chairman, this is a little repetitious. We have been through this so many times. But I want to take advantage of an opportunity to pay tribute to a very distinguished colleague who was first elected to Congress when I graduated from high school. That is the gentleman from Illinois. The gentleman is a dear friend. He has been a devoted and committed Member of this body. We sometimes have our disagreements on all kinds of issues, but I respect him profoundly and I wish him all the best." Dick Armey, with whom he had fought bitter annual battles over the National Endowment for the Arts, stated, "Every summer of my life since 1985, I have found myself in a contest with the gentleman from Illinois. We have never been in anything other than rigorous disagreement . . . but in all those summers and in all those contests, while I cannot recall Mr. Yates ever did a kind thing to me, he was never unkind in the manner in which we dealt with one another. He was a gentleman. He was considerate. . . . I will miss you."

The Democrats were equally lauding. David Obey noted that "In so many fields, he has set the highest example of what public service is supposed to be all about. He has been fighting for justice. He has been fighting for humanity and decency in the actions that our government takes both at home and abroad. . . . He has graced this institution and honored this country with his service here. He has enriched the lives of each and every one of us who have served with him."

Nancy Pelosi summed it up: "He is not only a great leader, teacher, mentor, legislator, gentleman, but a great patriot. I am reminded of what was said about Pericles when I think of the great Sid Yates . . . , 'He was a lover of the beautiful and he cultivated the spirit without a loss of manliness.' I cannot think of anyone that applies to more than the very distinguished gentleman from Illinois."[7]

EPILOGUE

Yates died on October 5, 2000, at age 91.

In today's Congress, bipartisanship, collegiality, and political compromise have become foreign concepts, and personal acrimony and partisan discord are the norm. As Steve Chapman of the *Chicago Tribune* wrote, the current state of U.S. politics is "a bicycle with a rusty chain, flat tires and no brakes. It's broken, and it's not taking any of us where we want to go."[1] Sidney Yates's forty-eight-year career in the House of Representatives serves as a prime example of how politics ought to be practiced. It also provides a formula for reform.

Former republican representative and secretary of transportation Ray LaHood, whose career in national politics itself spanned nearly forty years, remembers a time when members of Congress of all stripes of party, temperament, and ideology fought over difficult issues but together reached compromise and passed legislation. "Partisanship is here to stay, of course," LaHood observed after retiring from President Obama's cabinet. "Republicans and Democrats have legitimate ideological and policy differences over issues large and small. We can't and shouldn't paper over these differences. There is no point or virtue in what we called the mushy middle. But disagreements between Republicans and Democrats should not be poisonous."[2] Yates would have seconded LaHood's conclusion.

Elected in 1948, as a Jewish, urban, New Deal liberal, Yates learned early on to tackle tough problems like segregation in the Washington, DC, schools, McCarthy-era demagoguery, and discrimination in the U.S. Navy over promotions. He accepted defeat and betrayal by political allies with grace and dexterity. He was uncompromising on the First Amendment, due process, and threats to our liberties posed by demagogues like Senator Joseph McCarthy and his allies. Perhaps because he straddled the worlds of old school Democrats such as Adolph Sabath and Jake Arvey, and the new era reformers, Yates understood the need to bargain hard for his position, forge compromises, and then pass legislation. Even though he had his setbacks and disappointments as he gradually moved up the House seniority ladder, Yates adjusted but didn't despair. He didn't expect to win every issue every time but, no matter how challenging, he never demonized his legislative opponent.

David Obey admiringly recalled Yates as an "elegant, classy, committed liberal of immense decency, he was also the smartest man in any room he entered."[3]

As Yates became a more skillful legislator, the one characteristic that consistently stood out was his collegiality. He was an aggressive leader but remained dignified, never offensive, regardless of the intensity of the debate. During the SST, ABM, and Indiana Dunes debates, Yates remained civil and respectful of his opponents and, in each case, won the admiration of the membership and forged bipartisan coalitions to his position. His was a time when members of Congress debated issues, and when a willingness to reach across the aisle to work with others of different ideology or partisanship was valued.

Later, as chairman of the Appropriations Subcommittee on the Interior, Yates worked closely with Republican colleagues to pass an annual bill, despite intense debate over the future of the National Endowment for the Arts and other controversies. There were at least four commonly accepted rules that governed the legislative process. A return to these basic rules of engagement would help resurrect a meaningful legislative process that has been abandoned for the sake of ideological purity and temporary political advantage.

FIND COMMON INTERESTS WITHIN DELEGATIONS

Regular state delegation meetings would be a good start. The Illinois congressional delegation met regularly throughout Yates's career. In 1953, for example, Brach's, a candy company headquartered in Chicago, came to see the Illinois delegation to request their support for a provision in the farm bill that lowered peanut prices. Tommy O'Brien, the senior member of the delegation, spoke for the others and agreed to back the bill. But as the Brach's official, beaming with success, left the room, O'Brien turned to Yates and said "Sid, you don't look too happy about this." Yates responded, "Well, Tommy, I'll do anything you want, but I'm kind of upset because those people contributed a lot to my opponent, Bob Siegrist, this past election." "For Christ's sake, Sid, why didn't you say so?" O'Brien erupted, and told his clerk to find and bring back the confectioner. He entered, still smiling. O'Brien asked, "Is it true you tried to defeat Yates?" Smile now gone, the Brach's representative replied, "Well, yeah. We did give some money to the other guy." And O'Brien said, "Well, you can just kiss my ass. Get out of here!" And the entire delegation, Republican and Democrat alike, voted against the peanut bill.

During the 1970s and 1980s, the Illinois congressional delegation met once each month in the spacious office of Republican minority leader Bob Michel. Democratic senator Alan Dixon acted as secretary and prepared the agendas. Comments were off the record and staff was excluded except for a single aide charged with preparing a list of action items. Guests were invited to meet with the delegation to discuss the needs of Illinois, Chicago, or projects important to the members personally. It was expected that members would keep the deliberations private and that Dixon, representing the delegation, would make all the announcements, unless otherwise explicitly agreed upon.

The members enjoyed the monthly get-togethers. It was an opportunity to swap stories and tell an exaggerated heroic tale or two. They enjoyed each other's company, away from news media, constituent demands, and their staff. Not every member universally admired every other, but they were professional, had a lot in common, and got along well.[4]

At the meetings, new members met their senior colleagues and learned how the system functioned and how to get things done. Practical bipartisanship was the governing principle. One important example stands out. Nicholas Melas, president of the Metropolitan Water Reclamation District of Greater Chicago (which serves the greater part of Cook County), was once invited to make a presentation to the delegation on the Deep Tunnel project, a multibillion dollar public works project, the aim of which was to purify water and to reduce flooding that had plagued the Chicago metropolitan area for decades. After some discussion and study, the delegation decided to support the water district's efforts. At one of the delegation meetings, Republican congressman Henry Hyde, a conservative hero, turned to Yates. "Sid, you'll need to be point man on Appropriations on this one." "I'll do it but I need an assurance that President Reagan won't veto it labeling us 'taxers and spenders,'" Yates replied. Hyde easily responded that he'd talk with the president. A few days later Hyde called Yates, letting him know that Reagan would not push the appropriations but would sign the bill.

Yates inserted the Tunnel and Reservoir Plan line item in the Appropriations bill. The Deep Tunnel became a reality through a combination of federal and local funding and the cooperation of the Illinois delegation. Millions of homes have been saved from regular flooding and billions of gallons of runoff water has been purified to serve the public because of that cooperation.

Delegations have occasional rifts but familiarity can often overcome even the biggest of them. Governor Jim Thompson, for example, met with the Illinois congressional delegation at least twice each year. During those visits, he'd meet individually with members in their offices as a follow-up on specific projects. Most years, the governor would supply Yates with a letter listing the state's appropriations needs, particularly requesting federal assistance for the Regional Transportation Authority, which governed the mass transit for the Chicago Transportation Authority; Metra, the region's rail system; and Pace, the suburban bus system.

On one occasion, as Yates later told the story, Thompson ran into a serious problem with funding for the RTA in the Senate Appropriations Subcommittee on Transportation. In an unusual move, he called Yates at home to ask him to intercede with the Senate chairman. Yates was reluctant because House cardinals did not usually call Senate cardinals unless they chaired counterpart subcommittees. When Yates suggested that it would be more appropriate for Senator Percy to make the call, Thompson replied that Percy was the problem. Apparently Percy had offended the chairman, who now was taking out his anger in committee. Yates agreed to call but only on the condition that the conversation would remain private. Thompson agreed and Yates called the senator at home. After a lengthy conversation, the chairman agreed to restore the funding in the bill but made clear that he was doing it for Yates and Thompson only, not for Percy.

COURTESY AND RESPECT

Members need to respect and attribute the best of motives—political or personal—to colleagues in the heat of debate and in contentious negotiations. Yesterday's opponent may well be tomorrow's ally. Sometimes the simplest of human courtesies can go a long way in revealing personal character and forming a member's reputation.

Yates's ability to create and nurture relationships with other members had several practical advantages. In 1982, Yates had a bitter primary challenge from John McCauley, backed by a young Democratic ward committeeman angry because Yates had refused a favor. During the campaign, Yates was cautioned by his staff about a rumor circulating that two Jewish committeemen were campaigning behind the scenes for his opponent. Yates ignored the warning until Congressman Daniel Rostenkowski, a ward committeeman and the ultimate political insider, called to say that he'd just left a meeting of the Cook County Democratic Organization. He warned Yates, "Watch your back, my friend. Watch your back." With that alert, Yates concentrated on those wards with an increase in personal campaigning and direct mail. Yates won the primary handily in all the wards.

In the general election of 1982, after the decennial census and reapportionment, Yates's newly drawn district contained nearly 40 percent fresh territory, most of which was suburban. He was understandably nervous about the election. His Republican opponent, Catherine Bertini, was a bright, articulate, and attractive moderate. Portions of the new area had been reliably Republican and, even in some Democratic areas, Yates wasn't a favored household name. When the local weekly newspaper chain in the new area invited him to its endorsement session, Yates initially balked. "Why go? It's a waste of time. They're Republican and won't endorse a liberal Democrat." It wasn't until Bain insisted that Yates reluctantly agreed to attend the interview.

Yates hardly talked with his campaign staffer on the trip from his residence on North Lake Shore Drive up to Wilmette, Illinois. Uncharacteristically, Yates fidgeted while waiting in the lobby for the interview. Through the glass wall, Yates could see the figure of a burly white-haired man in a dark suit with his back to the door regaling the laughing editors with stories. Then the figure stood, turned, came out the door, and exclaimed, "Sid, what are you doing here?" Henry Hyde, beloved by the conservative editors, put his arm on Yates's shoulder and escorted him to the doorway, exhorting them, "Listen up. This is the guy who brings the money back to Illinois. You need to support him."

The Yates staffer, astounded at what he'd just witnessed, looked at Hyde's equally shocked aide. They quickly agreed never to make known in their districts what they had just witnessed. Yates's interview with the editors went well and he received the newspaper chain's endorsement.

In 1990, during Yates's bitter primary against Edwin Eisendrath, Representative Nancy Pelosi offered her assistance, arranging a series of fundraisers for Yates with wealthy donors in San Francisco. Pelosi had appreciated the warmth and support offered to her by Yates and Bain when she had first come to the House in 1987. "I got the facts of life" from Yates, she recalled. Pelosi was delighted and honored when they assured her that she would become the first woman Speaker of the House, a prediction Pelosi fulfilled when she was sworn in to that position in 2007.[5] In turn, Yates provided significant support in the Interior Appropriations Subcommittee to Pelosi in her efforts to turn the Presidio, a historic U.S. Army military fort in San Francisco overlooking the Golden Gate Bridge, into a National Park.[6]

END THE TUESDAY–THURSDAY CLUB

Members need to spend more time in Washington, DC, on the weekends. It's counterintuitive, but members today spend too much time in their districts chasing campaign funds and keeping up their local political contacts. They hardly get to know each other as human beings, stripped of their partisan selves. Yates was satirized and criticized regularly for not returning to his district enough. Even Yates's staff urged him to return more often. The congressman persisted, however, in remaining in Washington on most weekends, coming back to Chicago once a month and during recess breaks. While in the capital, Yates and Addie socialized with colleagues at dinners, golf, or concerts. As a result, lasting relationships formed. Opponents on issues were adversaries, not enemies, people first and congressmen second.

Cultivating those relationships can even pay off in the national interest. One of President Bill Clinton's first legislative proposals was a tax increase on the upper income brackets. The atmosphere on the floor of the House the day of final passage was tense. The only certainty was that the vote would be close. As he entered the chambers, a fellow Democratic deputy whip asked Yates to talk to Jamie Whitten, the former Appropriations chairman, who was refusing to support the president's legislation. Whitten and Yates had served on the Appropriations Committee together for decades but were as different as their home states, Mississippi and Illinois. Nevertheless, they had struck up a friendly relationship over the years. Yates sat down next to his colleague and asked how he intended to vote. Whitten responded as expected. The Mississippi delegation was intent on voting against the bill and Whitten didn't feel he could desert them.

Yates appealed to Whitten's sense of patriotism: "Jamie, we're not going to be here much longer. This young president needs us. It's his first legislative initiative. If he fails here he might not recover. We need to do what's best for the country." They then reminisced about past battles on the floor. Yates and Whitten both voted for the Clinton bill, which passed by only a two-vote margin.

The problem of members' absence from Washington even affects the operations of the White House. According to Denis McDonough, former chief of staff to President Obama: "These guys get here on Monday night or Tuesday night and they leave on Thursday night. Right? So that leaves you Tuesday nights and Wednesday nights for when the president presumably can schmooze with these guys. Why doesn't the president go golfing with these guys on the weekend? Well, because they're not here."[7]

RESTORE EARMARKS

Earmarks grease the legislative process and provide incentives to maintain party discipline. Essentially, members of Congress want to ensure that their districts and states receive benefit for their tax dollars. There is no more visible way of showing local communities that their federal tax dollars are at work for them than water-filtration plants, road resurfacing, airport improvements, and enhanced security by supporting public safety officials.

Without question there have been abuses of earmarks. The public good, however, far outweighs the bad. Going through the federal bureaucracy to obtain funding for a worthy project is a daunting task challenging the most talented staff and the best of intentions. No one knows the needs of their districts and states better than members of Congress. For the system to function, earmarks need to be divided up in a fair, bipartisan way.

Yates, as chairman of the Interior Appropriations Subcommittee, had no objection to what he called "responsible pork," and he regularly met with the ranking Republicans, Joe McDade and later Ralph Regula, to discuss the "members' requests."[8] Each would bring a stack of members' request letters from their colleagues. In one memorable instance, Regula brought up the need for a fish hatchery in North Dakota. Yates pointed out that the district was on the Democratic Congressional Campaign Committee's list of targeted Republican seats in the upcoming elections. Nevertheless, Yates asked whether the project was supported by the Fish and Wildlife Service. It was, and Regula produced Fish and Wildlife's report. Yates agreed to include the project in their appropriations bill and told Regula that he expected the chairman of the DCCC to be "steamed" at him for the earmark. Shortly afterward, the DCCC chairman, Tony Coelho, spotted Yates on the floor of the House and read him the riot act about the earmark. The day after the election, a staffer picked up Yates to drive him to the airport. The first question Yates asked was how the race in North Dakota had gone. When told that the Republican had won handily, Yates said simply, "It was that fish hatchery, wasn't it?"

NOTES

ABBREVIATIONS

CST   *Chicago Sun-Times*
CT   *Chicago Tribune*
EMD   Everett M. Dirksen Papers, Dirksen Congressional Center
HRP   Henry Reuss Papers, University of Wisconsin–Milwaukee
JTA   Jewish Telegraphic Agency
MC   Miller Center, University of Virginia (online)
NL   Newsletters of Sidney R. Yates
NYT   *New York Times*
PHD   Paul. H. Douglas Papers, Chicago History Museum
SRY   Sidney R. Yates Papers, Chicago History Museum
WP   *Washington Post*
WS   *Washington Star*
WSJ   *Wall Street Journal*

CHAPTER 1. THE ROAD TO CAPITOL HILL

1. William Hines, "Clear It with Sid," *CST* magazine, Dec. 3, 1976.

2. FBI Background Report (Yates UN appointment), Jan. 17, 1963, received by authors through Freedom of Information Act request.

3. Stone, *Congressional Minyan*, 548; Fourteenth Census of the United States: 1920—Population; Fifteenth Census of the United States: 1930—Population Schedule.

4. Petition for Naturalization, U.S. Dept. of Labor, Nov. 7, 1914; Certificate of Naturalization, Oct. 5, 2015.

5. University of Chicago *Cap and Gown* (1928–31), University of Chicago Alumni Office. Transcripts of Yates's academic records at University of Chicago were made available to the authors by the Registrar's Office.

6. Arvey's role in the creation of the Chicago Democratic "machine" has been well chronicled: Royko, *Boss*; O'Connor, *Mayor Daley*; Rakove, *We Don't Want Nobody*; Cohen and Taylor, *American Pharaoh*.

7. Good sources on Jake Arvey, Moe Rosenberg, and other prominent Chicago Jewish politicians include Cutler, *Jews of Chicago*; Cutler, *Jewish Chicago*; and Hartley, *Battleground 1948*.

8. Gottfried, *Boss Cermak*, provides lengthy discussions of Kerner, Arvey, and Chicago politics.

9. James Doherty, "To Win Office Scorn Politics but Get Votes. Here's Easy Lesson of 46th Ward," CST, Mar. 17, 1946; Leon M. Despres, "A Candid Assessment of Jews in Chicago Politics since 1920," Chicago Jewish History (Winter 2008), 14–15.

10. Sidney R. Yates, "Design for Chicago Transit: London Style," *Journal of Land and Public Utility Economics* 17, no. 3 (August 1941): 320–32.

11. Interview with Dr. Doris Holleb, July 11, 2011. Dr. Holleb was Yates's sister-in-law.

12. Cutler, *Jews of Chicago*, 224–25; Hartley, *Battleground*, 22.

13. Quote from Douglas, *In the Fullness of Time*, 91; Hartley, *Battleground* 1948, 19–20.

14. George Tagge, CT, Aug. 18, 1962.

15. Quoted in Grant, *Mr. Speaker*, 63–64.

CHAPTER 2. THE CLASS OF '49

1. "Welcome Fete Will Be Given for Newcomers"; "125 New Legislators Will Dine Tuesday with Board of Trade"; Mrs. Karl Mundt, "Pity the Congressman's Wife," all WS, 1/2/1949. At the time, the District was governed by the U.S. House of Representatives.

2. C. P. Trussell, "80th Congress Dies in Brief Session; 81st Picks Leaders," NYT, Jan. 1, 1949.

3. Robert Howard, "Congressmen Finding Homes in Washington," CT, Dec. 27, 1948.

4. Steve Neal, "West Side Ties Kept Atomic Subs Afloat," CST Dec. 27, 1989.

5. "Humphrey's Tax Appeal Denied; $74,617 due U.S.," CT, Jan. 29, 1942.

6. "For Mayor: Green vs. Kelly," CT, Mar. 1, 1939.

7. NL 32, Jan. 15, 1950.

8. Yates speech to Americans for Democratic Action, July 1951, SRY, box 54, folder 20.

9. Kevin Mereda, "Sen. Trent Lott and a Troublesome Tie," WP, Mar. 29, 1999; Perryman, *Whites, Blacks* (Book Publishers Network, Bothell, WA, 2010); Colbert I. King, "Who's Sorry Now," WP, Dec. 14, 2002.

10. Remarks of John McCormack, Cong. Rec., 38 (1953).

11. Nelson, *John William McCormack*.

12. Many of the events of this meeting are described in a handwritten draft speech of Yates to ADA. See n. 6.

13. Vernon Jarrett, "William L. Dawson: A Look at 'the Man,'" CT, Nov. 15, 1970; Dawson, William Levi, US House of Representatives, *History, Art and Archives*, http://history.house.gov/People/Detail/12028.

14. Nelson, *John William McCormack*; Yates speech to ADA, July 1951.

15. J. A. O'Leary, "House Democrats Vote, 176–48, to Cut Rules Committee Powers; Battle Due on Floor Tomorrow," WS, Jan. 2, 1949; Charles Hurd, "House Democrats Act to Free Bills from Rules Block," NYT, Jan. 2, 1949.

16. C. P. Trussell, "Truman Aides Win House Rules Curb," NYT, Jan. 4, 1949.

17. CR, Jan. 3, 1949, 7.

18. Ibid.; Truman, *Congressional Party*, 18; "House Vote Lost by GOP," NYT, Jan. 4, 1949; "House Seats Davies as Fuller Protests," NYT, Jan. 4, 1949.

19. NL 14, June 24, 1949; "Sabath, Cox Mix It during Housing Row," Owosso (MI) *Argus-Press*, June 22, 1949; C. P. Trussell, "Sabath and Cox Trade Blows in Bitter Feud over Housing," NYT, June 23, 1949; John Fisher, "Rep. Sabath Punched in House Fight," CT, June 23, 1949.

20. Fenno, "Interview Notes," National Archives, https://www.archives.gov/legislative/research/special-collections/oral-history/fenno/interview-notes.html.

21. NL 23, Aug. 26, 1949.

22. Harold Smith, "Nash Boys Tell Kocialkowski It's Good-By," CT, Feb. 22, 1942; John D. Morris, "New Congress Chairmen in Foreign-Affairs Posts," NYT, Nov. 11, 1956.

23. Memorial services held in the House of Representatives of the United States, together with remarks presented in eulogy of Martin Gorski (late a representative from Illinois) prepared under the direction of the joint committee on printing (Washington, DC: GPO, 1950).

24. Official Congressional Directory, 81st cong., 1st sess. (1949); Godfried, *WCFL*, 177.

25. CR, Jan. 18, 1949, 72.

26. Fenno, "Interview Notes," National Archives.

27. Clarence Cannon interview, April 1964, National Archives. http://www.archives.gov/legislative/research/special-collections/oral-history/fenno/cannon-1964.

28. "A Concise History of the House of Representatives Committee on Appropriations," House Committee Print, 111th cong. 2d sess., Dec. 2010.

29. In 1971, the District of Columbia was granted a nonvoting delegate to the House of Representatives.

30. Harold B. Rogers, "D.C. Measures Pledged Speedy Action in House," WS, Jan. 2, 1949.

31. "Six in House Indorse Home Rule for D.C. at AVC Press Conference," WS, Jan. 16, 1949.

32. Hearings before the Subcommittee on Appropriations House of Representatives on the District of Columbia Appropriation Bill for 1950 (GPO, 1949), 20.

33. Rep. Marcy Kaptur, "A Tribute to Sidney Yates," Cong. Rec., E 2078, Nov. 3, 2000.

34. Speech to the Austin Lodge of B'nai B'rith, September 1949, SRY, box 54, folder 5.

35. NL 98-8, Sept. 30, 1983.

36. Harold Smith, "Jonas Calls for Brake on Rising Taxes," CT, Oct. 29, 1950.

37. Jack Barbash, "Unions and Rights in the Space Age" United States Department of Labor, https://www.dol.gov/general/aboutdol/history/chapter6.

38. NL 17, July 15, 1949.

39. Faith, *Bob Hope*, 255; Hope, *Have Tux*, 76–77.

40. NL 51, June 3, 1950; "Celebrities Let Down Hair in Meet—Get Wet!" CT, June 4, 1950; "Hogan Shows Way in Golf at Capital," NYT, June 4, 1950. Among Yates's caddies during this time was the young Chicago lawyer Newt Minow, then a law clerk to Chief Justice Fred M. Vinson, who would later, as the head of the Federal Communications Commission, become famous for his description of television as "a vast wasteland" (Newt Minow interview.)

41. Genevieve Reynolds, "Sidney and Addie Yates Relax to Music," WP, Apr. 10, 1949.

42. Cong. Rec., 1257 (1949).

43. Cong. Rec., 1684 (1949).

44. Cong. Rec., 3065 (1949).

45. Cong. Rec., 2739, 5624 (1949).

46. NL 22, Aug. 19, 1949; Wolanin, *Constantino Brumidi, Artist of the Capitol*, S. Doc. 103–27, 1998 at 69.

47. NL 54, June 23, 1950.

48. NL 57, July 22, 1950.

49. NL 25, Sept. 9, 1949.

50. "Congressional Perquisites," 1089n206, citing 57 Cong. Rec. (App.) 334 (1919); Cover, "Contacting Congressional Constituents," 131n11, citing Tacheron and Udall, *Job of the Congressman*, 115.

51. NL 1, Mar. 17, 1949.

52. Two newsletters were numbered 31.

53. Russell Baker, "My Dear Constituent . . .," NYT, May 1, 1955.

54. Alan L. Otten, "Letter Writing" WSJ, Apr. 12, 1973.

55. NL 25, Sept. 9, 1949.

56. "Congressional Perquisites," 1078.

57. *Broadcasting: The Newsweekly of Radio and Television*, Oct. 25, 1948.

58. Yvonne Shinhoster Lamb, "Vernon Jarrett, 84; Journalist, Crusader," WP, May 25, 2004.

59. "WJJD Alone Airs Wallace Chi Talk," *Billboard*, May 24, 1947.

60. SRY, box 54, folder 6; "Radio-Television Highlights" CT, May 7, 1949.

61. George Tagge, "Twyman's 'No' Fans Congress Desires in 9th," CT, Nov. 3, 1949.

62. A third candidate, Pat Clary, had no organized party support and was not considered to be a factor.

63. Harold Smith, "New Aspirants Mentioned for Church's Seat," CT, Mar. 26, 1950; Harold Smith, "Tide to Rename Late Church to Congress Rises," CT, Apr. 2, 1950.

64. "Conference Report on the Internal Security Act of 1950," H.R. Rep. No. 3112, at 15265–66.

65. Cong. Rec., 15294 (1950).

66. Cong. Rec., 15293–98 (1950).

67. Cong. Rec., 15629–33 (1950); "Influential Representative Richard Bolling Dies at 74," WP 4/23/1991; Mary Bain interview, Dec. 2, 2005.

68. NL 65, Sept. 22, 1950.

69. "Commendations," campaign handout, SRY, box 54, folder 7.

70. Harold Smith, "Jonas Hits U.S. Lack of Modern War Weapons," CT, Aug. 6, 1950.

71. Harold Smith, "Goodwin Lashes 'Commiecrats' in Federal Pay," CT, Sept. 24, 1950.

72. Harold Smith, "Odds Narrowed in 9th and 12th Congress Races," CT, Oct. 15, 1950.

73. Harold Smith, "Goodwin Assails Red Trend," CT, Oct. 29, 1950.

74. "Congressmen from City and Suburbs," CT, Nov. 6, 1950.

75. "Jonas Calls for Brake on Rising Taxes," CT, Oct. 29, 1950.

76. WCRW Speech, Nov. 27, 1950, SRY, box 54, folder 7.

77. Harold Smith, "Political Pot on Low Heat in North Area," CT, Mar. 16, 1952.

78. O'Hara would be reelected in 1952 and serve until 1969.

79. George Tagge, "Congress Race in 9th Opened by Merryman," CT, Sept. 11, 1951.

CHAPTER 3. "HERE COMES THIS NICE, GOOD-LOOKING GUY"

1. Reeves, *Infamy*, 1–31, is especially informative in describing the early days after Pearl Harbor. See also Cahan and Williams, *Un-American*, 20.

2. Cahan and Williams, *Un-American*, 20.

3. Reeves, *Infamy*, 20.

4. Reeves, *Infamy*, 33.

5. Reeves, *Infamy*, 37.

6. Reeves, *Infamy*, 51–53.

7. Reeves, *Infamy*, xvi–xvii; DeWitt quoted in Cahan and Williams, *Un-American*, 21.

8. Cahan and Williams, *Un-American*, 30.

9. See dissenting opinion, *Korematsu v. United States,* 323 US 214 (Dec. 18, 1944).

10. *Asian American Compass*, http://www.advancingjustice-chicago.org/wp-content/uploads/2015/08/aai_compass_2-27-2011.pdf; "Curious City," WBEZ 91.5 FM, Aug. 18, 1917; Matsunaga, "Japanese Americans," Part 3, http://www.discovernikkei.org/enljournal/2015/12/3/oakland-kenwood-3/.

11. Regenerations Oral History Project, *Rebuilding Japanese American Families, Communities, and Civil Rights in the Resettlement Era, Chicago Region*: vol. 1, ed. Japanese American National Museum, http://texts.cdlib.org/view?docId=ft7n39p0cn;NAAN=13030&doc.view=frames&chunk.id=d0e26005&toc.id=d0e997&brand=calisphere.

12. Jean Mishimi interview and speech at Skokie Public Library, 7/20/2017, author's collection; Ross Harano interview (via e-mail), Aug. 21, 2017, and the Ross Harano personal archives.

13. "The Immigration Act of 1924," Office of the Historian, Dept. of State, https://history.state.gov/milestones/1921–1936/immigration-act.

14. Cong. Rec., 1675–84 (1949); "Vote to end 'Insulting' on Asiatic Immigrants," CT, Mar. 2, 1949.

15. Mike Masaoka obituary, NYT, June 29, 1991.

16. *Densho Encyclopedia*, s.v. "Mike Masaoka," accessed Aug. 24, 2018, http://encyclopedia.densho.org/Mike_Masaoka/.

17. Masaoka to Yates, Mar. 3, 1949, SRY, box 104, folder 4; and "Yates," July 16, 1949, SRY, box 44, folder 18; *Chicago Shimpo,* July 20, 1949; SRY Scrapbook 18; CST, Oct. 5, 1952,

SRY Scrapbook 19; *Chicago Shimpo*, Apr. 4, 1953, and *Pacific Citizen*, Mar. 27, 1952, SRY Scrapbook 19.

18. Wakamatsu interview, Regenerations Oral History, cited above; "Repeal of Title II of the Internal Security Act of 1950 ('Emergency Detention Act')," http://encyclopedia .densho.org/Repeal_of_Title_II_of_the_Internal_Security_Act_of_1950_%28%22 Emergency_Detention_Act%22%29/; Izumi, "Prohibiting American Concentration Camps"; "The Japanese Internment, after 40 Years US Is Finally Clearing the Air," CST, Sept. 13, 1981; Ross Harano Papers, Japanese American Service Committee Legacy Collection, Chicago, box 2, folder 9; Okamura, "Background and History."

19. NL 118, June 16,1952.

20. Wakamatsu interview.

21. Johnson, *How We Drafted Adlai Stevenson*, 22, 32–33, 48, 101, and 110; untitled speech, Sept. 8, 1952, City Club of Chicago, SRY, box 55, folder 7; Halberstam, *The Fifties*, 219–23, 234–45; Biles, *Crusading Liberal*, 91–94.

22. Harold Smith, "Douglas Gives Yates a Hand in 9th District," CT Oct. 19, 1952.

23. "Your Congressman," CT, Oct. 26, 1952.

24. Harold Smith, "Battle Rages for Congress Seat in 9th.: Siegrist Drives to Unseat Yates," CT, Oct. 12, /1952; Lincoln Belmont *Booster*, Nov. 5, 1952; and untitled speech, Oct. 16, 1952, SRY, box 55, folder 1.

25. See SRY, box 3, folder 1, for HR 7258 (May 6, 1957), HR 2849 (Jan. 14, 1957), 4913; Cong. Rec., June 26, 1958; Resolution of Chicago City Council, April 24, 1959; Rep. John Fogarty to Yates May 3, 1957; Valerie Long to Yates (undated) and Yates to Long, June 11, 1956. See also http://stiletto-italiano.com/eng/banswitchblade.htm; Clark, "Youth Gang"; Hearing before the H. Committee on Interstate and Foreign Commerce, 85th Cong., 2nd Sess., Apr. 17, 1958 and July 23, 1958; and "The History of the Federal Switchblade Act of USA," http://www.knife-expert.com/swbl-leg.txt.

26. On Yates's amendment regarding the SACG, see memorandum, Peter Manikas to Yates, May 12, 1972, and NL 316, May 31, 1972, both in SRY, box 21, folder 4.

27. Lawrence E. Davies, "Speeches of Major Parties Tell Negro Why He Should Aid Them," NYT, June 30, 1956; and Richard F. Weingroff, "A Day in History: June 29, 1956," https://www.fhwa.dot.gov/interstate/thisday.cfm. For repeal of Title II, see Ross Harano to Yates, 10/7/1971; Mike Masaoka and David E. Ushio, JACL, to Yates, Sept. 21, 1971, and Rep. Spark Matsunaga to SRY, Sept. 17, 1971, all in SRY, box 184, folder 7.

28. William Hohri, National Council for Japanese Americans, to Yates, Sept. 20, 1974, Japanese American Service Committee Legacy Collection, Chicago, box 2, folder 7. Also Hohri, *Repairing America*, 54 and 94.

29. Mishimi interview; Statement of Honorable Sidney R. Yates, Public Hearings at Northeastern Illinois University, Sept. 22, 1981, 20–24 (reel 5); Report of the Commission on Wartime Relocation and Internment of Civilians, *Personal Justice Denied, Report and Part 2 (Recommendations)* (Seattle: University of Washington Press, 1997); Smith, "Wartime Internment"; news release, Commission on Wartime Relocation and Internment of Civilians, Feb. 24, 1983, Japanese American Service Committee Legacy Collection, Chicago; Maki, Kitano, and Berthold, *Achieving the Impossible Dream*, 92, 159, 176, 203,

212, 255n26, 267n87; and Maga, "Ronald Reagan," http://www.mansell.com/e09066/Maga .html; and Michael Briggs, "Reagan Oks Japanese Internee Bill," CST, Aug. 11, 1988.

CHAPTER 4. "THE JUDGMENT OF ADMIRALS"

1. Nasaw, *Patriarch*, 667; John A. Blatnik, recorded interview by Joseph E. O'Connor, Feb. 4, 1966, at 1, John F. Kennedy Library Oral History Program.

2. Remarks of Rep. Machrowicz, Cong. Rec., 33 (1953).

3. NL 120, July 3, 1952.

4. NL 99, Oct. 22, 1951.

5. NL 99-13, July 8, 1986.

6. Polmar and Allen, *Rickover*, 30.

7. Ibid., 37.

8. Allen and Polmar, *Rickover*, xiii.

9. Polmar and Allen, *Rickover*, 51. To send someone to Coventry is an English idiom meaning to deliberately ostracize someone.

10. Allen and Polmar, *Rickover*, 21.

11. Duncan, *Rickover*, 117.

12. Duncan, *Rickover*, 117.

13. Polmar and Allen, *Rickover*, 187.

14. Duncan, *Rickover*, 119.

15. Ibid., 120.

16. NL 122, Jan. 23, 1953.

17. Duncan, *Rickover*, 121.

18. NL 247, Apr. 24, 1961.

19. Doris Holleb interview, July 11, 2011.

20. Duncan, *Rickover*, 123.

21. NL 99-13, July 8, 1986.

22. Ibid.

23. Yates to Aaron Soble, Feb. 27, 1953, SRY, box 45, folder 8.

24. Polmar and Allen, *Rickover*.

25. "Klein Stripped of His Troops in State Guard," CT, July 28, 1951; Harold Smith, "Feeling Runs High in House Battle in 9th," CT, Oct. 26, 1952; John M. Thompson, "Controversial Order Retires Brig. Gen. Klein," CT, Feb. 17, 1953; " Summary of Activities of Brig. Gen. Julius Klein Re Case of Capt. Hyman Rickover, " confidential memo prepared for Jewish War Veterans committee, SRY, box 45, folder 8.

26. Duncan, *Rickover*, 123.

27. NL 99-13, July 8, 1986; Rockwell, *Rickover Effect*, 147–49.

28. NL 99-13, July 8, 1986.

29. Ibid.

30. Remarks of Yates, Cong. Rec., 499 (1953); NL 122, Jan. 23, 1953.

31. Yates's staff memo (unattributed), Jan. 26, 1953, SRY, box 45, folder 1.

32. Berman to Yates, and Yates to Berman Feb. 9–10, 1953, SRY, box 45, folder 8.

33. News release (undated) SRY, box 46, folder 4.

34. "Navy Rules Scored in High Promotions," NYT, Feb. 13, 1953.

35. Duncan, *Rickover*, 126.

36. Klein to Yates, Feb. 17, 1953; SRY, box 45, folder 8; Graff to Yates, Feb. 18, 1953, SRY, box 45, folder 8.

37. Blair, *Atomic Submarine*; NL 99-13, July 8, 1986.

38. Cong. Rec., 1220–21 (1953); Duncan, *Rickover*, 125. Julius Klein stated that it was his efforts that convinced Saltonstall to make this decision.

39. Polmar and Allen, *Rickover*, 203.

40. Yates HR staff memo (undated), SRY, box 45, folder 1.

41. Cong. Rec., 1553–62 (1953); press release (embargoed for delivery), SRY, box 45, folder 1; NL 126, Mar. 7, 1953; Harold B. Hinton, "Senators Rebuff Navy on Rickover," NYT, Feb. 26, 1953; Duncan, *Rickover*, 124–27.

42. NL 126, Mar. 7, 1953; NL 127, Mar. 14, 1953.

43. Duncan, *Rickover*, 127–28.

44. Sec. Anderson to Sen. Saltonstall, Mar. 6, 1953, SRY, box 45, folder 1.

45. Yates HR staff memo (undated), SRY, box 45, folder 1.

46. Sen. Stennis to Yates, Mar. 13, 1953, SRY, box 45, folder 1.

47. Kevin Hennessey, "How Ike Saved the U.S. from Another 'Dreyfus Case,'" *Confidential* magazine, November 1954, SRY, box 46, folder 9.

48. Rockwell, *Rickover Effect*, 154.

49. Memo (undated), SRY, box 45, folder 1.

50. "Discrimination in the Navy," *Cleveland Plain Dealer*, Mar. 16, 1953.

51. Yates to Maslow, SRY, box 46, folder 3.

52. Cong. Rec., 11104 (1953).

53. NL 180, Apr. 23, 1956.

54. Ibid.

55. Polmar and Allen, *Rickover*, 220–21.

56. NL 247, Apr. 24, 1961.

57. NL 175, Feb. 1, 1956.

58. NL 215, Aug. 19, 1958.

59. Rickover to Yates, Jan. 24, 1955, SRY, box 45, folder 1.

60. Blair quoted in Steve Neal, "West Side Ties Kept Atomic Subs Afloat," CST, Dec. 27, 1989.

61. SRY, box 46, folder 7.

62. Exchange of letters between DeWoskin (Apr. 2, 1953) and Yates (Apr. 6, 1953), SRY, box 46, folder 3.

CHAPTER 5. YATES FOR SENATE

1. "Witwer, Douglas Debate," CT, Sept. 18, 1960.

2. "Mary Teresa Norton," U.S. House of Representatives History, Art and Archives, *Women in Congress* featured Artifacts, http://history.house.gov/Exhibitions-and-Publications/WIC/Artifacts/.

3. Preston had won the popular vote but had received insufficient "county units," which was similar to electoral votes.

4. "Democrats Vote to Bolt Party in Georgia Primary," CT, Sept. 15, 1960.

5. Rep. Sidney R. Yates interview with Richard F. Fenno Jr., June 24, 1959, U.S. National Archives Special Collections, http://archives.gov/legislative/research/special-collections/oral-history/fenno/yates-june-1959.pdf.

6. Ibid.

7. Ibid.

8. Ibid.; Rep. Clarence Cannon interview with Richard F. Fenno Jr., June 10, 1959, U.S. National Archives Special Collections, http://www.archives.gov/legislative/research/special-collections/oral-history/fenno/cannon-1959.html.

9. Guthrie, *Statistics*.

10. Quoted from Nordlander, "Madalyn Murray O'Hair."

11. A poll was taken by Paddock Publications: "Poll Indicates Rep. Paul Simon Top Contender to Oppose Dirksen," UPI, in campaign brochure, in Simon Papers, "1962 Campaign" folder, Morris Library, Southern Illinois University.

12. George Tagge, "Political Outlook," CT, May 13, 1961.

13. "*Paul Powell Shoebox Scandal*," Sangamon County Historical Society Newsletter, July 15, 2015. When his executor went to Powell's residential suite at the St. Nicholas Hotel, he found more than $800,000 in cash stuffed in shoeboxes, briefcases, and strongboxes. Continuing to search, the executor discovered that Powell, who as a public servant never earned more than $30,000 a year, also had stashed $1 million in racetrack stock, forty-nine cases of whiskey, fourteen transistor radios, and two cases of creamed corn.

14. Paul Douglas, *In the Fullness of Time*, 572–73.

15. For the Harris poll, see "Louis Harris and Associates, Inc.," in papers of Mayor Richard J. Daley, University of Illinois at Chicago, box S11 SS1 B50, folder 50-1, "Campaign—Studies—1962 Election." Harris compared Stevenson's viability only with Paul Powell and Irving Dillard.

16. Ibid., 573; Max Frankel, "Stevenson Says He May Run in '62 for Dirksen Seat," NYT, Dec. 3, 1961; McKeever, *Adlai Stevenson*, 503–5.

17. See Simon, *P.S.*, 75–76, for important background information. Also see campaign brochure, "We want to tell you why we believe Paul Simon is a winner in the race for U.S. Senator, which explains the case for Simon as the Democratic nominee," Paul Simon Papers; Hartley, *Fullness of Time*, 105–7; John Manion to Paul Simon, Mar. 13, 1961, Simon Papers, Abraham Lincoln Presidential Library (hereafter, ALPL), box 62, folder 26; Chuck Hayes to Simon, May 1961, ALPL, box 82, folder 26; Simon to James McCulla, July 19, 1961, ALPL, box 82, folder 26; Irving Dilliard, former editor of *St. Louis Post Dispatch*, to Dale G. Gonemeier, July 1, 1961, ALPL, box 15, folder 9; "Simon Boosted for U.S. Senate," *Carterville Herald*, Aug. 31, 1961.

18. John Dreiske, "Mack May Be Choice to Face Sen. Dirksen," CST, June 6, 1961; Charles Finston, "Rep. Mack Tops Dems. to Oppose Dirksen," *Chicago American*, July 27, 1961.

19. Royko, *Boss*, 83–84, and Everett M. Dirksen Congressional Center, Pekin, Illinois (hereafter, EMD), folder 4334.

20. Douglas, *Fullness of Time*, 573; Hartley, *Paul Simon*, 107–8; Simon, *P.S.*, 75–76.

21. For a good summary of the Gilbert affair, see Ron Grossman, "Who Was Dan Gilbert: 'The World's Richest Cop,'" CT, Feb. 25, 2016.

22. For information on Senator Dirksen, see especially Schapsmeier and Schapsmeier, *Dirksen*, 53–64, 127–46, 172; MacNeil, *Dirksen*, 31–32, 52, 55; Neal, *Rolling*, 76–78.

23. Schapsmeier and Schapsmeier, *Dirksen*, 53.

24. For a good description of Dirksen's change of heart about President Eisenhower, see Schapsmeier and Schapsmeier, "Everett M. Dirksen," 9–10.

25. George Tagge, "Dirksen Gets Ready to Bid for New Term," CT, May 27, 1961.

26. Eisenhower's speech and testimonial information are stored in EMD, folder 4430, "Speeches" and "Politics: 1961."

27. See Steve Neal, *Rolling on the River*, 76–78; The phrase "Ev and Charlie Show" was coined by Tom Wicker of the *New York Times*. Schapsmeier and Schapsmeier, *Journal of the Illinois State Historical Society*, 76 (Spring 1983), 10.

28. Quoted in Robert Davis, "Where Are the Vito Marzullos? Review Essay," Apr. 7, 2011, 3, https://www.lib.niu.edu/2000/ii001120.html.

29. Yates emphasized his support for President Kennedy throughout the campaign. See "2 in Illinois Push Drive for Senate," NYT, Feb. 18, 1962; also: Robert Howard, "Yates Sticks to One Speech in Campaign," CT Sept. 21, 1962; Michael Pakenhaw, "Yates Boosts Democrats to Win in Illinois," CT Oct. 20, 1962; SRY Speech (untitled), Sept. 10, 1962, before Illinois Democratic State Convention, SRY, box 247, folder 5.

30. "Health Bill Alternative to Socialism: Yates," CT, May 21, 1962; "Medicare Rally. Johnson Predicts Victory for Bill," NYT, May 21, 1962.

31. Pat Munroe, "Yates Pursuing TV Debates with Dirksen," *Chicago American*, Mar. 19, 1962; the Yates news release (undated) in EMD, folder 4443; Harold Rainville to Republican committeemen, (undated) 1962, in EMD folder 4362.

32. The Lou Harris poll can be found at "Harris 1962 Illinois Election Survey," No. 1195, Odum Archive Database, https://dataverse.unc.edu/dataset.xhtml?persistentId=hdl:1902.29/H-1195.

33. Dallek, *Unfinished Life*, 175, and Yates to Kennedy, July 11, 1952, John Fitzgerald Kennedy Presidential Library, Personal Papers (PPD), box 104. Kennedy narrowly defeated Lodge, with 51.5% of the vote, by 70,737 votes out of a total of 2,353,231.

34. For the personal and political relationship between President Kennedy and Senator Dirksen, see Schapsmeier and Schapsmeier, *Dirksen*, ch. 7; Hulsey, *Everett Dirksen*, 160–71.

35. Douglas, *Fullness of Time*, 573.

36. Quote in Schapsmeier and Schapsmeier, *Dirksen*, 136; Sorensen, *Kennedy*, 349–50.

37. Everett M. Dirksen to Senator Mike Mansfield, Oct. 4, 1961, Mansfield folder: 1961, EMD.

38. Douglas, *Fullness of Time*, 573.

39. Ibid., 573–74; Biles, *Crusading Liberal*, 168.

40. Transcript, Everett McKinley Dirksen Oral History Interview May 8, 68, by William S. White, Internet Copy, LBJ Library. For descriptions of the LBJ-EMD relationship, see

the Unger and Unger, *LBJ*, 310; Caro, *Lyndon Johnson*, 362–63; Caro, *Passage of Power*, 186; Dallek, *Flawed Giant*, 195.

41. LBJ telephone call with Dirksen, Apr. 25, 1966, recording Identification: lbj_wh6604_04_10048, Miller Center, University of Virginia, Charlottesville.

42. Stevenson to Daley, May 17, 1962, Johnson, ed., *Papers of Adlai Stevenson*, 8:246–47. There also is extensive correspondence on Stevenson's participation in the Yates campaign: Stevenson to Douglas, May 23, 1962; Stevenson to Walter J. Cummings Jr., Mar. 12, 1962; Stevenson to Yates, Mar. 22, 1962; Stevenson to Yates, Mar. 23, 1962; Yates to Stevenson, Mar. 28, 1962; Stevenson to Yates, Mar. 30, 1962, Seeley G. Mudd Manuscript Library, Princeton University, box 90, folder 11, "Sidney Yates."

43. Rakove, "Sen. Adlai Stevenson III"; Nancy Stevenson interview, Mar. 23, 2017.

44. Mary Bain interview, Dec. 2, 2005.

45. Rainville (undated) EMD-Papers. As noted earlier, Yates's father had changed the family name from "Yatzofsky."

46. David S. Broder, "Germans for Dirksen Hit Democrats on War," WS, Oct. 16, 1962; "Dirksen Not Consulted on Racist Election Appeal, Campaigner States," JTA, Oct. 23, 1962.

47. Cong. Rec. V. 108, No. 149, Aug. 22, 1962, in EMD, "Remarks, Releases, Interview," folder "August 1962"; series 18, box 12, folder 3, Maureen and Mike Mansfield Library, University of Montana, Missoula; Douglas, *Fullness of Time*, 574.

48. David S. Broder, "Illinois' Yates Labors to Make Self Known," WS, Oct. 15, 1962; Charles Cleveland, "Yates Offers Deal on Redistricting," Chicago Daily News, July 14, 1961; "Yates Denies He is a Party to a Reapportionment Deal," (no byline) CST, July 19, 1961; and James McCartney, "Yates Denies Deal on Remap," Chicago Daily News, July 18, 1961, all in SRY Scrapbook, 21.

49. "The Leader," *Time*, Sept. 14, 1962, 27–31; Ben H. Bagdikian, "Golden Voice of the Senate," *Saturday Evening Post*, Oct. 6, 1962, 28–29.

50. "Expect 2 Crowds of 5,000 for Kennedy Visit Friday," CT, Oct. 17, 1962, "Here Is Text of Kennedy's Fund Speech. Urges Election of Yates to Senate," CT, Oct. 20, 1962; Hulsey, *Everett Dirksen*, 168–70. Ben H. Bagdikian, "Golden Voice of the Senate," *Saturday Evening Post* 235, no. 35 (Oct. 6, 1962), 28–29; "The Leader," *Time*, 80, no. 11 (Sept. 14, 1962), 27–31.

51. Salinger, *With Kennedy*, 251–52.

52. White, *Missiles in Cuba*, 112; text of President Kennedy's Oct. 22, 1962 speech can be found at https://www.jfklibrary.org/Asset-Viewer/sUVmCh-sBomoLfrBcaHaSg.aspx.

53. On April 17, 1961, a small force of Cuban exiles and U.S. military personnel invaded Cuba with the intention of overthrowing Fidel Castro's regime there. The invasion failed dramatically. Beschloss, *Crisis Years*, 480–81.

54. Beschloss, *Crisis Years*, 480–81; Reeves, *President*, 392–93; Hulsey, *Everett Dirksen*, 170–71; "Both Parties Give Support to President," CT, Oct. 23, 1962.

55. Hulsey, *Everett Dirksen*, 169.

56. Hulsey, *Everett Dirksen*, 170–71; Beschloss, *Crisis*, 480; Reeves, *President Kennedy*, 392–93; "'You've Got It in Bag,' Dirksen Claims JFK Said on Reelection," Peoria *State Journal*, Oct. 27, 1962; George Tagge, "Yates Hurls 'Lie' at Story He Can't Win," CT, Oct. 27, 1962; Douglas, *Fullness of Time*, 574.

57. Douglas, *Fullness of Time*, 574; Sorensen, *Kennedy*, 688; Allison, *Essence*, 194–95.

58. Grant Pick, "Three of a Kind," *Chicago Reader*, Jan. 29, 1998.

59. Bain interview; Pick, "Three of a Kind."

60. Douglas, *Fullness of Time*, 574.

61. William P. Roberts to Douglas, Apr. 30, 1962, and Douglas to Roberts, May 28, 1962, both in box 72, "Political File 1962," PHD; Robert Wiedrich, "Yates Admits Defeat after Tense Hours," CT, Nov. 9, 1962; Pensoneau, *Powerhouse*, 166.

62. William Singer interview, Mar. 2, 2017.

63. Shapiro, *Last Great Senate*, 12–13.

64. Paul Douglas to president John F. Kennedy (with enclosed memorandum), Nov. 9, 1962, "Personal Files," folder K, PHD; "Expect Decker Nomination to U.S. Bench. Held Up by Kennedy Until after Election," CT, Nov. 9, 1962; Biles, *Crusading Liberal*, 168.

65. George Tagge, "Yates Given Ambassador's Post in U.N.," CT, Jan. 12, 1963; "Yates Named Formally to U.N. Council," CT, Feb. 19, 1963; "Yates Is OK'd by U.S. Senate for U.N. Post," CT, Mar. 9, 1963; "Yates Begins New Duties," CT, Mar. 21, 1963; Johnson, ed., *Stevenson,* 413; Stevenson to Harlan Cleveland, June 7, 1963, Stevenson to Yates, Jan. 2, 1963, and Yates to Stevenson, Jan. 3, 1963, all in Stevenson Papers, Mudd Library, box 90, folder 11 ("Sidney Yates").

66. Transcript, Clarence Mitchell Oral History Interview I, Apr. 30, 69, by Thomas H. Baker, Internet copy, LBJ Library.

67. Bergan interview, Sept. 22, 2016.

CHAPTER 6. TO THE UNITED NATIONS AND BACK

1. FBI investigation. Report of Jan. 23, 63, received via Freedom of Information Act request by authors.

2. U.S. Senate Committee on Foreign Relations, *Report of Proceedings on Nomination of Sidney R. Yates*, Mar. 5, 63.

3. George Tagge, "Political Outlook," CT, May 30, 63; George Tagge, "Political Outlook," CT, Apr. 27, 63.

4. Yates quoted in William Fulton, "U.N. Law Put above U.S. by Afro-Asians," CT, Nov. 15, 1963.

5. Dr. Dan Beard, former Yates staffer and commissioner of Bureau of Reclamation, Department of the Interior, interview, May 22, 2017.

6. Congressman Robert Michel, a Republican from Pekin, Illinois, was the other member of the Illinois delegation to serve on the Appropriations Committee.

7. R. Eric Petersen and Sarah J. Eckman, "Casework in a Congressional Office," Congressional Research Service Report, Jan. 3, 2017, fn1.

8. Sen. McCarthy to Herbert H. Lehman, Aug. 29, 1962, Herbert H. Lehman Collection (Columbia University Libraries), Special Collection at McCarthy, Eugene, letter, 1962 August 29, ldpd_leh_0603_0013, Herbert H. Lehman Papers, Special Correspondence Files, Rare Book and Manuscript Library, Columbia University Library, http://lehman.cul.columbia.edu/ldpd_leh_0603_0013.

9. Philip Warden, "Yates Gets Backing for Igoe Court Seat," CT, July 30, 1965.

10. *Pekin Times*, Dec. 9, 1965. The *Chicago Tribune* (Aug. 22, 1965) speculated: "If Sen. Douglas does not announce soon that he will seek reelection, Rep. Sidney R. Yates (D, Ill.) is the first choice of his House colleagues from Illinois to make a bid for the Senate seat."

11. Michael Kilian, "Yates, Pucinski Maneuver to Keep Congressional Seats," CT, Oct. 20, 1968; William Kling, "Clark-Daley Break Broadens with National Campaign Move," CT, Oct. 3, 1968; James Yuenger, "Lyndon Makes Much of Ev's Photograph," CT, Sept. 14, 1968.

CHAPTER 7. "THIS PRECIOUS RESOURCE"

1. There are three excellent secondary sources especially helpful in understanding the background of the SST: Conway, *High-Speed Dreams*; Horwitch, *Clipped Wings*; and Levy, *People Lobby*.

2. A transcript of President Kennedy's remarks can be found at MC, https://millercenter.org/the-presidency/presidential-speeches/june-5–1963-remarks-us-air-force-academy.

3. NL 234, Feb. 29, 1960.

4. NL 271, Sept. 13, 1966; NL 276, July 13, 1967.

5. Additional Views of Robert N. Giamo, Jeffrey Cohelan, Sidney R. Yates, "Military Construction Appropriations Bill, H.R. Rept. No. 90-1754 (1968).

6. NL 287, Jan. 21, 1969; NL 288, Mar. 6, 1969; NL 289, Apr. 23, 1969; and NL 290, June 4, 1969.

7. For an understanding of President Nixon's views, see Nixon, *RN*, 415–18, 524.

8. "Yates Disputes Teller on ABM," *Chicago Daily News*, June 2, 1969 in SRY, Scrapbook 4 (1969).

9. Cong. Rec., 28134–35 (1969).

10. Nixon, *RN*, 417, notes the effect of Senator Jackson in leading the fight to approve the ABM.

11. Aldo Beckman, "Rep. Yates Not About to Give Up Fight over ABM," CT, Mar. 2, 1969; Pat Pastin, "Laird Silent on Nike Sites," Lerner (Booster) Newspapers, Sept. 14, 1969; Sheldon Hoffenberg, "Yates Rips Nixon Speech," Lerner Home Newspapers, Sept. 8, 1969; "Credit Yates, too," Lerner Newspapers, Aug. 17, 1969, all in SRY, Scrapbook 4 (1969).

12. Flippen, *Nixon*, is a good secondary source on the politics and policy of the Nixon administration on the SST and other environmental matters.

13. Quoted in Levy, *People Lobby*, 13. A good source of primary materials on Congressman Reuss's activities in opposition to the SST can be found in HRP, box 45, folder 16 (1963–65); box 45, folder 17 (1963–65); and box 54, folders 12 and 13 (1970).

14. Cong. Rec., 32599–613 (1969). See "Final Report of the Ad Hoc Supersonic Transport Review Committee," in SRY, box 34, folder 4.

15. Alan L. Otten, "How Not to Study," WSJ, Nov. 12, 1969, in SRY Scrapbook 4 (1969).

16. NL 295, Nov. 25, 1969; Cong. Rec., 34674 (1969).

17. Shirley Elder, "Battle Lines Forming on Supersonic Transport," *Evening Post*, 11/12/1969, in SRY Scrapbook 4 (1969).

18. Levy, *People Lobby*, 13–14.

19. George W. Liebman, "Memorandum of Meeting on the SST, March 24, 1970," MIT Institute Archives and Special Collections, MIT Libraries, Cambridge, MA, box 6, "Citizens against the Sonic Boom" (MC00012).

20. Interview with Hal Bergan, Sept. 22, 2016.

21. NL 301, May 25, 1970; Jim Kershner, "NEPA, the National Environmental Policy Act," (Aug. 2, 2011), 8, http://www.historylink.org/File/9903; "Boeing 2707 SST Problems," https://www.globalsecurity.org/military/systems/aircraft/b2707-problem.htm; Levy, *People Lobby*, 32–43. Garwin was no stranger to controversy. He had expressed very serious doubts about Nixon's ABM proposal. Hal Bergan stayed in touch with Garwin: Bergan to Yates, Jan. 20, 1971, and Garwin to Bergan, Feb. 1, 1976, SRY, box 37, folder 8, and box 265, folder 3, respectively.

22. Cong. Rec., 17298–320 (1970); "Dear Colleague," Dec. 4, 1970, SRY, box 39, folder 7.

23. "SST Is a Boondoggle," CST, May 27, 1970. Chicago *Daily News*, "SST Gains Another Foe," June 10, 1970.

24. Levy, *People Lobby*, 36–37; Horwitch, *Clipped Wings*, 305–6; "Predict Senate Defeat of SST Appropriations," *Chicago Today*, July 14, 1970. The administration expressed its concern that such a reduction in spending would "increase program costs on a 2-for-1 ratio," NYT, Dec. 2, 1970, SRY, box 40, folder 10; "Statement by the President," Dec. 5, 1970, SRY, box 39, folder 8; see also Coalition against the SST, "SST Action Next Week," May 15, 1971, in SRY, box 265, folder 7.

25. Hal Bergan interview, Sept. 22, 2016.

26. Yates to Lindbergh, Jan. 20, 1971, and Lindbergh to Yates, Feb. 3, 1971, SRY, box 37, folder 8. Reich, "From the Spirit of St. Louis to the SST."

27. See Hearings before a Subcommittee of the Committee on Appropriations, Appropriations Subcommittee on Transportation, House of Representatives, "Continuing Appropriations 1971," Civil Supersonic Aircraft Development (SST), March 1971, 92nd Cong., 1st Sess.

28. "Separate Views of Representative Sidney R. Yates against the SST," in Report 92-41, "Certain Further Continuing Appropriations, 1971," 92nd Cong., 1st Sess.

29. The debate is recorded in 117 Cong. Rec., 6812–47 and 6999–7023 (1971).

30. 117 Cong. Rec., Mar. 17, 1971, 6812–47, and Mar. 18, 1971, 6999–7023. The vote appears on 7023–24 (1971).

31. NL 305, Mar. 19, 1971.

32. John Madigan commentary, WBBM radio (Chicago); David S. Broder, "The New Rule Works in House," WP (undated), in SRY, Scrapbook 6 (1971–72). See also Obey, *Raising Hell for Justice*, 135–36; *Chicago Daily News*, Mar. 18, 1971; Irv Kupcinet, "Kup's Column," CST, Mar. 21, 1971; Dave Anderson, "Defeat of SST Analyzed," Lerner Home Newspapers, Mar. 21, 1971; and William Hines, "Rep. Yates' 4-Year War on SST," CST, Mar. 21, 1971—all in SRY, Scrapbook 6 (1971–72). See further Friends of the Earth, Nov. 26, 1972, for plans to combat any effort to resurrect the SST, SRY, box 36, folder 5; J. H. Shaffer, Administrator, FAA, to Yates, Jan. 31, 1972, SRY, box 36, folder 5; for expressions of support and congratulations, see Yates, "District Letters of Congratulations on SST Defeat," SRY, box 36, folder 8.

33. Robert Benjamin, "Yates Endorsed by Sierra Club," CT, Feb. 16, 1982.

34. *Chicago Daily News*, Aug. 31, 1970, SRY, Scrapbook 5 (1970).

CHAPTER 8. AMERICA'S COMMITTEE

1. David Obey interview, Oct. 6, 2017.

2. Remini, *The House*, 442–43, 446.

3. William V. Shannon, "The Kennedy Problem," NYT, Aug. 18, 1974.

4. Obey, *Raising Hell*, 168.

5. NL 94-1, Jan. 28, 1975. See also Obey, *Raising Hell*, 166–69; Farrell, *Tip O'Neill*, 383–415; Remini, *The House*, 446–47. For Yates's support of Udall, see William V. Shannon, "Rep. Yates Not About to Give Up Fight on ABM," CT, Mar. 2, 1969.

6. NL 94-1, Jan. 28, 1975.

7. Dan Beard interview, May 22, 2017.

8. "National Parks and Recreation Act of 1978 Statement on Signing S 791 into Law," November 10, 1978, at the American Presidency Project, http://www.presidency.ucsb.edu/ws/?pid=30143; National Park Service, "What Is Urban Parks and Recreation Recovery (UPARR)?" at https://www.nps.gov/uparr/ (URL removed by Trump administration, available from archived sites).

9. For the hearing record, see Department of Interior and Related Agencies Supplemental Appropriations 1979, held at 5917 North Broadway, Chicago, Illinois, Saturday, Feb. 10, 1979, 95th Cong., 1st Sess.

10. 16 U.S.C. §460u; Dale Engquist, e-mail to author, Jan. 23, 2017; Mr. Engquist was a superintendent of the Indiana Dunes National Lakeshore. "Douglas Dunes Name Bill Passes," CT, July 13, 1978.

11. Paul Merrion, "NU Wins Federal Funds for Rust Belt Research," *Crain's Chicago Business*, Oct. 15, 1984; Robert Enstad, "Industry Lifesaver Forming in Evanston," CT, Oct. 28, 1984; Ali Sewers, "Evanston Plan to Build 2nd Downtown," CST, Oct. 5, 1984; Tom Lassier, "Fed $$$ Okayed for Research Lab," Evanston *Review*, Oct. 18, 1984; Yates Speech and Gov. Thompson's speech in SRY, box 255, folder 8. See also David Mintzer to Yates, June 27, 1984; "An Economic Development Proposal for the Basic Industrial Institute and the Evanston University Research Park at Northwestern University" (March 1984), in "Basic Industry Research Laboratory Correspondence, Clippings, Economic Development Plan, Northwestern University Archives, Deering Library, Evanston, IL; "Background of Creation of Research Park. Tax Controversy," May 6, 1992, in file "Basic Industry Research Laboratory: Final Analysis, Proposed Charter, Staffing, and Budget," in Northwestern University Archives; memo from William Ihlanfeldt, Vice President for Institutional Relations, to Lester Crown, Newton Minow, John Perkins, Arnold Weber (pres.), Mar. 1, 1985, in Records of the Evanston/University Research Park, 1984–1996, Series 8/2/2014, box 1. For legislative history, see H. Rep. No. 98-886, Department of Interior and Related Agencies Appropriations Bill, 1985 (June 29, 1984), at 96–96, and PL 98–473.

12. NL 97-14, July 23, 1982.

13. "Department of Housing and Urban Development—Independent Agencies Appropriations Act, 1983," 97th Cong., 2nd Sess., H. Rep. No. 97-720, 15–16.

14. Cong. Rec., Aug. 11, 1982, 20514–28.

15. Irwin Molotsky, "EPA Plans to Curb Use of Toxaphene, a Pesticide," NYT, Oct. 17, 1982; Ward Sinclair, "House Passes Tough Pesticide Bill," WP, Aug. 12, 1982; E. G. Vallianatos, "Revoke EPA's Licenses to Pollute," *Common Dreams*, Aug. 5, 2008, at http://www.commondreams.org/views/2008/08/05/revoke-epas-licenses-pollute.

CHAPTER 9. THREE YEARS OF THE CULTURE WARS

1. Straight, *Twigs*, 15.

2. Biddle, *Our Government*, 123.

3. National Foundation on the Arts and the Humanities Act of 1965 (Pub. L. 89-209).

4. Abigail and John Adams, *Book of Abigail and John*, 260.

5. Netzer, *Subsidized Muse*, 205.

6. Ibid., 57.

7. Biddle, *Our Government*, 17.

8. Straight, *Nancy Hanks*, 94.

9. Berman, *Culture and Politics*, 1.

10. Interview with Jack Golodner, former president, Department of Professional Employees, AFL-CIO, May 2007.

11. Netzer, *Subsidized Muse*, 58.

12. NL 94-7, July 30, 1975.

13. NL 94-14, Mar. 22, 1976.

14. NL 95-4, Apr. 29, 1977.

15. NL 100-5, June 19, 1987.

16. NL 100-11, Apr. 7, 1988.

17. Dorf, "Western Senators," 150.

18. Dorf, " Artifactions," 34.

19. NL 97-5, July 3, 1981.

20. NL 98-5, June 30, 1983.

21. Interview with Congressman Ralph Regula, Mar. 14, 2005.

22. Zengerle, "Murthaville."

23. Ibid.

24. Johnstown Area Heritage Association, "History of Steel in Johnstown," https://www.jaha.org/attractions/heritage-discovery-center/johnstown-history/history-steel-johnstown/.

25. Biddle, *Our Government*, 5.

26. Judith Michaelson, "Frank Hodsoll Leaves Endowment as Advocate for Arts," *Los Angeles Times*, Feb. 18, 1989.

27. "Cut in U.S. Aid to Arts Opposed," NYT, Feb. 14, 1981.

28. Interview with Anne Murphy, former executive director of American Arts Alliance, May 6, 2003.

29. H. Rep. 97-163.

30. Lori Silver, "House Chastises Arts Endowment with $45,000 Cut," *Los Angeles Times*, July 13, 1989.

31. William H. Homan, "Congressional Anger Threatens Arts Endowment's Budget," NYT, June 20, 1989.

32. Ibid.

33. HR 2788. CR July 12, 1989, H3588.

34. From $144,250,000 to $129,825,000.

35. Barone and Ujifusa, *Almanac of American Politics 1992*, 1218.

36. Drew, *Whatever*, 156.

37. Under the rules of the Committee of the Whole, by passing Armey's perfecting amendment, as amended, Rohrabacher's original amendment to strike was no longer in order and it was rejected without a vote.

38. Neal Sigmon, interview, Mar. 1, 2016.

39. Basil Talbot, "Arts Funds Survive Attack in Congress," CST, July 13, 1989.

40. Amendments No. 419 and 420.

41. Cong. Rec., July 26, 1989, S8807.

42. Ibid.

43. Ibid., S8808.

44. After the amendment's passage, remarks were inserted by Senators Coats, Kennedy, Jeffords, Pell, Moynihan, and Heinz on the Helms Amendment. Ibid., S8809–S8815.

45. Biddle, *Our Government*, 91.

46. Byrd 2004 interview with National Public Radio, published after his death at http://www.npr.org/templates/story/story.php?storyId=128172325.

47. Barone and Ujifusa, *Almanac of American Politics 1992*, 177.

48. William H. Honan, "Helms Amendment Is Facing a Major Test in Congress," NYT, Sept. 13, 1989.

49. Sigmon interview.

50. Cong. Rec., Sept. 13, 1989, H5630.

51. Elizabeth Rybicki, Cong. Research Serv. 98-381, Instructing House Conferees (2015).

52. Cong. Rec., Sept. 13, 1989, H5639.

53. Ibid., H5632.

54. Ibid.

55. Ibid., H5635.

56. Ibid., H5641.

57. A Report to Congress on the National Endowment for the Arts, submitted by the Independent Commission, September 1990, 1.

58. Conference Report, H.R. Rep. No. 101–264.

59. Cong. Rec., Oct. 7, 1989, S12968.

60. Pub. L. No. 101-121, 103 Stat. 701.

61. Unnumbered NL, June 22, 1990.

62. The Independent Commission's legislation required it to complete its report by April 23, 1990. Its members were not sworn in, however, until June 6, 1990, the date of its first meeting.

63. The authors wish to note that coauthor Michael Dorf was retained as "legal affairs consultant" to the Independent Commission.

64. Independent Commission Report to Congress, 57.

65. Enacted as 20 U.S.C. §954(d)(1).

66. HR 4825.

67. On August 28, 2015, the Department of the Interior officially changed the name of Mount McKinley to Denali. The Alaska Board of Geographic Names and the State of Alaska had changed the name to Denali in 1975 but had been unable to get federal approval.

68. Cong. Rec., Oct. 15, 1990, H9677.

69. Cong. Rec., Oct. 24, 1990, S17980.

70. Yates's margin surpassed that of both Democratic nominees for president during these elections.

71. The litigation went all the way to the U.S. Supreme Court, which ruled that the decency clause, in a grant-making context, did not violate the First Amendment. "We recognize, as a practical matter, that artists may conform their speech to what they believe to be the decision making criteria in order to acquire funding. . . . But when the Government is acting as patron rather than as sovereign, the consequences of imprecision are not constitutionally severe." NEA v. Finley, 524 U.S. 568, 589 (1998). With respect to the four denied grants, the NEA agreed to pay the plaintiffs the amount of the vetoed awards, as well as attorney's fees and damages. 524 U.S. 568 at 578.

72. Beth Potier, "Karen Finley Provokes, Reveals in Lecture," *Harvard Gazette*, 2/14/2002. See also http://www.nytimes.com/2013/06/03/booming/revisiting-the-tawana-brawley-rape-scandal.html?_r=0 for a good recap of the Tawana Brawley claims and the determination that it was a hoax.

73. Tom Garretson, "The Sprinkle Story: The First 25 Years," Annie Sprinkle website, http://anniesprinkle.org/the-sprinkle-story/. Two venues in which Sprinkle performed did receive government grants. The Maryland Art Place in Baltimore received $10,000 from the NEA, and New York's Kitchen Theater received $60,000 from the New York Arts Council. Neither of the grants was used to support the performance. Annie Sprinkle had never received an NEA grant.

74. Speech by Sen. James Jeffords, Cong. Rec., Sept. 16, 1991, S13011.

75. Joseph Bauman, "'No More Moo by '92' on West Ranges May Be a Simplistic Approach," *Deseret News* [Salt Lake City], Aug. 2, 1990.

76. Remarks of Malcolm Wallop, Cong. Rec., Sept. 16, 1991, S13024.

77. Nyle Henderson, "How Many Cows?" Cong. Rec., Sept. 16, 1991, S13033.

78. Cong. Rec., Sept. 16, 1991, S13019.

79. Cong. Rec., Sept. 19, 1991, S13267. As noted above, Annie Sprinkle received no government money.

80. Ibid., S13268.

81. Mary Bain interview, Dec. 2, 2005.

82. Cong. Rec., Oct. 16, 1991, H7879.

83. Ibid., H7972.

84. Ibid.

85. Cong. Rec., Oct. 17, 1991, H7989.

86. Neal Sigmon interview, Mar. 1, 2016.

87. Cong. Rec., Oct. 24, 1991, H8502.

88. Cong. Rec., Oct. 31, 1991, S15646–7.

89. Ibid., S15667.

90. Ibid., S15657.

91. Ibid., S15663.

92. Alexander, *Command Performance*, 117.

93. Dorf, "Artifactions," 35.

CHAPTER 10. "THE LAST SANHEDRIN MET IN 70 CE."

1. *Los Angeles Times*, 10/19/1986, quoting from Faw and Skelton, *Thunder in America*.

2. There continues to be debate about whether the phrase used by Farrakhan was "gutter religion" or "dirty religion." The consensus, however, is the latter.

3. Steven V. Roberts, "Fighting the Fires of Black-Jewish Hostility," NYT, June 20, 1974.

4. Medoff, *Jewish Americans*, 284–90.

5. Ibid.

6. Celler, *You Never Leave Brooklyn*, 118.

7. William Hines, "Clear It With Sid," *CST* magazine, Oct. 3, 1976.

8. JTA, 2/20/1949.

9. NL 98-8, Sept. 30, 1983.

10. NL 152, May 14, 1954.

11. JTA, May 18, 1954.

12. "*U.S. Middle East Policy Termed Unfair to Israel in Congress,*" JTA, Apr. 29, 1955.

13. JTA, Dec. 19, 1956.

14. CT, Dec. 16, 1956.

15. Kinzer, *Brothers*, 244.

16. Ibid., 225; NL 186, Jan. 16, 1957.

17. NL 187, Feb. 4, 1957.

18. Kinzer, *Brothers*, 225.

19. NL 186, Jan. 16, 1957.

20. NL 187, Feb. 4, 1957.

21. Nate Herring, "A Lasting Legacy: The Dhahran Airfield and Civil Air Terminal," Army Corps of Engineers, May 23, 2014. https://www.tam.usace.army.mil/Media/News-Stories/Article/485031/a-lasting-legacy-the-dhahran-airfield-and-civil-air-terminal/.

22. After the United States backed Israel in the 1973 war, Saudi Arabia took a 25% interest in Aramco and took full control in 1980.

23. Herring, "Lasting Legacy."

24. NL 194, May 28, 1957.

25. Medoff, *Jewish Americans*, 307.

26. "Truman Disputes Bias in Arab Pact," NYT, Mar. 4, 1956.

27. "Dulles Calls Wagner's Snubbing of Saud Factor in Jewish G.I. Ban," NYT, Apr. 24, 1957.

28. "Americans in Arabia," NYT editorial, Apr. 25, 1957.

29. "City Hall Disputes Dulles on Saud Ban; Leaders of Jewish Groups Also Protest," NYT, Apr. 25, 1957.

30. Charles G. Bennett, "Mayor Bars Fete for Saud, Here Today on State Visit," NYT, Jan. 29, 1957.

31. Cong. Rec., May 29, 1957, 8095–96.

32. "Congress Gets Resolution Banning Pacts with Lands Barring U.S. Jews," JTA, July 3, 1957.

33. NL 94-2, Feb. 28, 1975; "120 Lawmakers Ask Levi to Probe Arab-Inspired Bias against Jews by Some Federal, Private Firms," JTA, Mar. 10, 1975.

34. "Antitrust Aspect Is Sought in Deals Tied to Arabs' Demands," NYT, Mar. 29, 1975.

35. "Jewish Group Honors Yates at Fund Event," CT, Sept. 18, 1961; "Forest in Israel Is Named after Yates," CT, Oct. 18, 1961.

36. George Tagge, "Political Lookout," CT, June 18, 1962.

37. "Rabbi Miller Installed as President of Synagogue Council of America," JTA, Oct. 17, 1963.

38. "Jewish Drive at 2.3 Million," CT, June 18, 1964.

39. NL 256, Feb. 15, 1965.

40. "House Acts to Bar U.S. Food Aid to U.A.R.," NYT, Jan. 27, 1965.

41. "Johnson Asks the House for a Free Hand on Food for Cairo," NYT, Feb. 5, 1965.

42. "Israel Deserves Support of U.S.: Percy: Criticizes Policy on Middle East at Park Rally," CT, June 19, 1967.

43. "Fast and Furious—Nine Amazing Facts about the Six Day War," *Military History Now*, May 28, 2015, http://militaryhistorynow.com/2015/05/28/fast-and-furious-nine-amazing-facts-about-the-six-day-war/.

44. "Arabs: Suspension of Disbelief," NYT, June 18, 1967; "Moscow Steps Up Arms Diplomacy," NYT, Sept. 5, 1967.

45. "U.S. Again to Send Arms Aid to Jordan," NYT, Feb. 15, 1968; NL 281, Feb. 21, 1968.

46. NL 298, Feb. 28, 1970.

47. "Jewry Talks End in Plea to Soviets," CT, Feb. 26, 1971.

48. "Publicity about Jews Called Soviets' Fear," CT, Mar.15, 1971.

49. "Russ Envoy Rejects Jewish Petitions," CT, Oct. 21, 1971; "100,000 Petitions Spurned," JTA, Oct. 21, 1971.

50. "Russ Urged to Let Jews Go," CT, Oct. 22, 1971.

51. NL 315, Apr. 28, 1972.

52. Ibid.

53. "Celler Looking to a Recount," NYT, June 22, 1972.

54. "Ribicoff Nominated 'Old and Good Friend,'" JTA, July 14, 1972; "Convention Reverberations—Jewish Political 'Seminar' Was No 'Caucus,'" JTA, July 18, 1972.

55. "Convention Reverberations—Jewish Political 'Seminar' Was No 'Caucus,'" JTA, July 18, 1972.

56. Nixon's efforts to court the Jewish vote had some effect. Although McGovern ended up winning the Jewish vote by a 65–35% margin in 1972, Hubert Humphrey had won the

Jewish vote against Nixon by a margin of 81–17%. *Jewish Virtual Library*, "U.S. Presidential Elections: Jewish Voting Record (1916–Present)," http://www.jewishvirtuallibrary.org/jewish-voting-record-in-u-s-presidential-elections.

57. Jeremy M. Sharp, "U.S. Foreign Aid to Israel," *Congressional Research Service*, Dec. 22, 2016.

58. Obey, *Raising Hell*, 129. Obey became chairman of Foreign Ops in 1985; David Obey interview, Oct. 6, 2017.

59. Obey interview; Mary Bain interview, Dec. 2, 2005.

60. "Rabbi Yosef Meets with Lawmakers to Discuss Plight of Syrian Jews," JTA, May 1, 1974. The article refers to Rabbi Yosef's ceremonial robes, which are more fully described in Koran, *Rabbis*, 167; and "Obituary: Rabbi Ovidia Yosef," *Telegraph*, Oct. 7, 2013, http://www.telegraph.co.uk/news/obituaries/10361625/Rabbi-Ovadia-Yosef.html.

61. "House Urges Nixon to Act on Terrorism," JTA, May 17, 1974; "Israel Toll Is 24 as 4 Students Die," NYT, May 17, 1974.

62. For a concise overview of the "reassessment," See Walter, *Limits of Influence*.

63. Photograph, SRY, box 75, folder 1.

64. Donald Fisher interview, Feb. 21, 2017.

65. Staff memo (undated) SRY, box 2, folder 6.

66. NL 93-17, Aug. 20, 1974.

67. *The Daily Diary of President Gerald R. Ford*, Sept. 12, 1974, the President's Daily Diary Collection, Gerald Ford Presidential Library and Museum, box 72.

68. Memorandum of Conversation, *Foreign Relations of the United States, 1969–1976*, 16:558 (May 14, 1975); *The Daily Diary of President Gerald R. Ford*, May 13, 1975, the President's Daily Diary Collection, Gerald Ford Presidential Library and Museum, box 75. Geneva referred to the continuation of the Geneva Conference of 1973, which attempted to create a final settlement of Arab-Israeli tensions after the Yom Kippur War ceasefire.

69. "Leading Personalities to Attend Embassy Dinner for Rabin," JTA, June 13, 1975; "Kissinger's Assurances Buoy Israelis," NYT, June 14, 1975.

70. "House Delegation Sees Soviet Jews," NYT, Aug. 11, 1975; Sharansky, *Fear No Evil*, 109.

71. "Brezhnev Hints Delay on Rights," NYT, Aug. 16, 1975; NL 99-9, May 21, 1986.

72. "U.N. Unit Endorses Draft Linking Zionism to Racism," NYT, Oct. 18, 1975; NL 94-10, Oct. 30, 1975.

73. "401 House Members Sign Resolution Urging General Assembly to Repudiate Third Committee," JTA, Oct. 24, 1975; NL 94-10, Oct. 30, 1975; "U.N. Votes, 72–35, to Term Zionism Form of Racism," NYT, Oct. 18, 1975. The United Nations officially revoked Resolution 3379 in 1991 at the insistence of the George H. W. Bush administration. Resolution 46/86, Dec. 16, 1991.

74. Koch, *Mayor*, 18–19.

75. "Martin Luther King Forest," JTA, Jan. 15, 1976.

76. Martin Luther King Jr. speech before the Annual Convention of the Rabbinical Assembly, Mar. 25, 1968, quoted in https://www.jewishvirtuallibrary.org/martin-luther-king-on-israel-s-security.

77. JTA, Nov. 18, 1975.

78. "20 Here to Attend Conference on Soviet Jewry," CT, Feb. 5, 1976.

79. "Congressional Vigil on Soviet Jewry," JTA, Mar. 18, 1976.

80. Koch, *Politics*, 212.

81. Koch, *Mayor*, 31–32. Abzug tried to return the favor by endorsing Mario Cuomo over Koch when the two ran against each other for mayor in 1977. Koch nevertheless won.

82. "U.S. Embassy in Israel as an Issue in Campaign," NYT, Apr. 2, 1984; "Behind the Headlines Carter, Jerusalem and Propaganda," JTA, Nov. 17, 1976.

83. Carter, *Why Not the Best?* 59.

84. "2 Campaign Trails to Cross Here," CT, Oct. 26, 1976; "Carter," CT, Oct. 27, 1976.

85. Martin Schram, "Carter Urged to Blame OPEC, Save Himself," WP, July 7, 1979.

86. Eizenstat interview, Mar. 28, 2017.

87. *The Daily Diary of President Jimmy Carter*, the Jimmy Carter Presidential Library and Museum, July 1, 1977, https://www.jimmycarterlibrary.gov/assets/documents/diary/1977/d070177t.pdf; NL 95-6, July 5, 1977.

88. *The Daily Diary of President Jimmy Carter*, the Jimmy Carter Presidential Library and Museum, Oct. 6, 1977, https://www.jimmycarterlibrary.gov/assets/documents/diary/1977/d100677t.pdf; "Congressional Jewish Leaders Get Carter's Reassurance on Mideast," CT, Oct. 7, 1977; "Carter Assures Representatives on Israel," NYT, Oct. 7, 1977.

89. Eizenstat interview, Mar. 28, 2017.

90. Carter, *White House Diary*, 173.

91. NL 95-9, Nov. 23, 1977.

92. Jimmy Carter Daily Diary, Feb. 5, 1978; "Sadat Asserts Begin Hardens His Stance," NYT, Feb. 7, 1978.

93. Mary Bain interview; Jimmy Carter Daily Diary, Feb. 7, 1978; "Sadat Asserts," NYT, Feb. 7, 1978.

94. Frank Moore memo to President Carter, "Meeting with Rep. Sid Yates," Feb. 21, 1978.

95. Martin Tolchin, "An Old Pol Takes On the New President," NYT, July 24, 1977; Mary Russell, "Jordan Meets with Rep. O'Neill, Gets Taken Down a Peg or Two," WP, July 19, 1979. Jordan has denied the story about the gala tickets. Hamilton Jordan Oral History, Nov. 6, 1981, Miller Center, University of Virginia, https://millercenter.org/the-presidency/presidential-oral-histories/hamilton-jordan-oral-history-advisor-white-house-chief.

96. Farrell, *Tip O'Neill*, 126.

97. Adam Bernstein, "Mass. Representative Edward Boland, 90, Dies," WP, Nov. 6, 2001.

98. William Hines, "Clear It with Sid," *CST* magazine, Oct. 3, 1976; Amy Stone and David Szonyi, "Jews in Congress," *Moment*, May–June, 1976, 31–32.

99. William Hines, "Clear It with Sid," William Hines, *CST* magazine, Oct. 3, 1976.

100. Farrell, *Tip O'Neill*, 18.

101. WP, Feb. 7, 1979.

102. "Who Did Andrew Young In, and Why?" NYT, Aug. 26, 1979.

103. Phil McCombs, "The Politics of Creating the Holocaust Memorial," WP, Apr. 13, 1983; Linenthal, *Preserving Memory*, 12–51; Stuart Eizenstat interview; Donald Fisher interview.

104. Donald Fisher interview.

105. Barbara Gamarekian, "Tiny Memorial Tiles of the Holocaust," NYT, May 3, 1988; FAQ No. 10, "What Is the Story behind the Children's Tile Wall?" *Holocaust Museum* website, https://www.ushmm.org/collections/ask-a-research-question/frequently-asked -questions#10.

106. United States Air Force Fact Sheet, "E-3 Sentry (AWACS)," 9/22/2015, http://www .af.mil/About-Us/Fact-Sheets/Display/Article/104504/e-3-sentry-awacs/.

107. NL 97-3, Apr. 30, 1981.

108. "Shultz Suggests Israel-Salvador Analogy," NYT, May 20, 1983.

109. "Shultz, House Critics Exchange Volleys on Lebanon, El Salvador," WP, Mar. 7, 1984; "Shultz Says House Panel Wants to 'Walk Away' from Salvador," NYT, Mar. 7, 1984.

110. "Shultz Promotes Arms to Jordan," NYT, Sept. 13, 1985; Steve Neal, "Yates Helped Forge U.S.-Israeli Alliance," CST, Nov. 6, 1989.

111. NL 99-11, May 21, 1986.

112. R. Bruce Dold, "Yates Campaign Gets Some Capitol Assistance," CT, Dec. 13, 1989.

113. NL 102-1, Jan. 29, 1991.

114. Mary Bain interview, Dec. 2, 2005.

115. Undated handwritten notes by Yates.

116. Debra Yates interview, Aug. 15, 2017.

117. Ori Nir, "Congressman Pushes to Abolish Racial Caucuses," *The Forward*, Oct. 17, 2003.

118. Stone and Szonyi, "Jews in Congress," 30–31.

119. Celler, *You Never Leave*, 176.

120. Koch, *Politics*, 184.

121. Michael Coakley, "Yates, Kingpin in Singer Land, Backing Daley," CT, Feb. 7, 1975; "Michael Coakley, Singer Camp Eyes Rep. Yates Post," CT, Mar. 6, 1975; Michael Coakley, "Vicious Leaflet Blasted," CT, Feb. 25, 1975; Neil Mehler and Michael Coakley, "Never Been Prejudiced, Says Daley; Pledges Jobs," CT, Feb. 10, 1975.

122. Larry Chernikoff interview, Jan. 27, 2017; Bain interview.

CHAPTER 11. THE FINAL YEARS

1. Adam Clymer, "The 1994 Elections: Congress the Overview," NYT, Nov. 10, 1994.

2. Mike Robinson, "Sid's Last Run," Associated Press, Oct. 31, 1996.

3. Lynn Sweet, "Pritzker Camp Says Yates Should Retire," CST, Nov. 24, 1995.

4. Stephen Lee, "Yates May Not Run—Next Time," CT, Jan. 26, 1996.

5. CT, Sept. 29, 1995.

6. Jack Anderson and Jan Moller, "A Dogged Run for Your Money," WP, Dec. 26, 1996; Linda Wheeler, "Mutts Ado about Nothing," WP, Jan. 30, 1997; "Please Keep Your Aide on a Leash," CT, Jan. 17, 1997.

7. Remarks of Phil Crane, Cong. Rec., H6001; Remarks of Nancy Pelosi, Cong. Rec., H6147; Remarks of David Obey, Cong. Rec., H6217; Remarks of Dick Armey, Cong. Rec., H6218.

EPILOGUE

1. Stephen Chapman, "How to Bring Moderation Back to American Politics," CT, July 5, 2017.

2. LaHood, *Seeking Bipartisanship*.

3. Obey, *Raising Hell*, 235.

4. Dixon, *Gentleman*, 241–45.

5. Pelosi interview, Mar. 20, 2018.

6. Chernikoff interview, Jan. 27, 2017; Pelosi interview, Mar. 20, 2018.

7. Whipple, *Gatekeepers*.

8. David Obey interview, Oct. 6, 2017.

REFERENCES

RESEARCH SOURCES

ARCHIVES AND LIBRARIES

George H.W. Bush Presidential Library Center, Texas A&M University, College Station
Jimmy Carter Presidential Library, Atlanta, GA
Richard J. Daley Papers, University of Illinois, Chicago
Everett M. Dirksen Congressional Center, Pekin, IL
Paul H. Douglas, Chicago History Museum, Chicago
Dwight D. Eisenhower Presidential Library and Museum, Abilene, KS
John M. Flaxman Library of the School of the Art Institute of Chicago, Chicago
Gerald Ford Presidential Library and Museum, University of Michigan, Ann Arbor
Ross Harano Archives, Chicago, Illinois
Japanese American Citizens League Archives, San Francisco
Lyndon B. Johnson Presidential Library and Museum, University of Texas, Austin
LBJ Library Oral History Collection, the Lyndon Baines Johnson Presidential Library, Austin, TX
Hamilton Jordan Oral History, Miller Center, University of Virginia, Charlottesville
John Fitzgerald Kennedy Presidential Library and Museum, Boston
Abraham Lincoln Presidential Library and Museum, Springfield, IL
Maureen and Mike Mansfield Library, University of Montana, Missoula
Richard Nixon Presidential Library and Museum, Yorba Linda, CA
Northwestern University Archives, Deering Library, Evanston, IL
Office of the Historian, US House of Representatives, Washington, DC
Ronald Reagan Presidential Library, Simi Valley, CA
Congressman Henry Reuss Papers, Wisconsin Historical Society Archives, University of Wisconsin, Madison

Paul Simon Papers, Norris Library, Southern Illinois University, Carbondale
Adlai Stevenson Papers, Seeley G. Mudd Manuscript Library, Princeton University, Princeton, NJ
Syracuse University, Special Collections Research Center, Syracuse, NY
Harry S. Truman Presidential Library and Museum, Independence, MO
University of Chicago, Special Collections Research Center, University of Chicago Library, Chicago
Sidney R. Yates Papers, Chicago History Museum, Chicago

INTERVIEWS

Andrus, Governor Cecil (ID), interview by the authors, Boise, ID, Oct. 26, 2012
Bain, Mary Anderson, interview by the authors, Washington, DC, Dec. 2, 2005
Beard, Dan, phone interview by Michael C. Dorf, May 22, 2017
Bergan, Harold, interview by the authors, Chicago, IL, Sept. 22, 2016
Broder, David, interview by the authors, Washington, DC, Jan. 4, 2005
Burke, Alderman Edward (Chicago), interview by Michael C. Dorf, Chicago, IL, Mar. 13, 2017
Carroll, Howard, interview by Michael C. Dorf, Lincolnwood, IL, Oct. 28, 2016
Chernikoff, Larry, phone interview by Michael C. Dorf, Jan. 27, 2017
Durbin, Senator Richard (IL), interview by Michael C. Dorf, Chicago, IL, June 9, 2017
Duvall, Fran, multiple phone interviews by Michael C. Dorf
Eisendrath, Edwin, phone interview by George Van Dusen, May 24, 2018
Eizenstat, Ambassador Stuart, phone interview by Michael C. Dorf, Mar. 28, 2017
Fisher, Donald and Judith, phone interview by Michael C. Dorf, Feb. 21, 2017
Golodner, Jack, phone interview by Michael C. Dorf, Jan. 4, 2009
Guthman, Jack, interview by Michael C. Dorf, Chicago, IL, Mar. 1, 2017
Harano, Ross, interviews by George Van Dusen, Skokie, IL, Aug. 8, 2014 and Nov. 13, 2017
Holleb, Doris, interview by the authors, Chicago, IL, June 11, 2011
Kovler, Peter, multiple phone and in person interview by Michael C. Dorf, Washington, DC
Lanyon, Richard, interview by George Van Dusen, Evanston, IL, June 15, 2017
Marchese, Steve, phone interview by Michael C. Dorf, Mr. 23, 2018
Marovitz, William, interview by George Van Dusen, Chicago, IL, Dec. 21, 2017
Massey, Walter, interview by Michael C. Dorf, Chicago, IL, Oct. 6, 2011
Minow, Newton, interview by the authors, Chicago, IL, Apr. 6, 2017
Mishima, Jean, interview by George Van Dusen, Wilmette, IL, Aug. 24, 1917
Moss, Adrianne, phone interview by Michael C. Dorf, Nov. 16, 2016
Murphy, Anne (former executive director of American Arts Alliance), interview by Michael C. Dorf, Washington, DC, May 6, 2003
Obey, Representative David (WI), interview by the authors, Alexandria, VA, Oct. 6, 2017
Pelosi, Representative Nancy (CA), interview by the authors, Washington, DC, Mar. 20, 2018
Reger, Larry, phone interview by Michael C. Dorf, Mar. 3, 2017
Regula, Representative Ralph (OH), interview by Michael C. Dorf, Washington, DC, Mar. 14, 2005

Schakowsky, Representative Janice D. (IL), interview by the authors, Chicago, IL, June 19, 2017

Sigmon, Neal, phone interview by Michael C. Dorf, Mar. 2, 2016

Simon, Scott, phone interview by Michael C. Dorf, May 3, 2018

Simpson, Dick, interview by George Van Dusen, Chicago, IL, Jan. 27, 2016

Singer, William, interview by Michael C. Dorf, Chicago, IL, Mar. 2, 2017

Sloan, Cliff, phone interview by Michael C. Dorf, Feb. 10, 2017

Stevenson, Nancy, interview by Michael C. Dorf, Chicago, IL, Mar. 23, 2017

Suffredin, Lawrence, interview by George Van Dusen, Evanston, IL, Nov. 9, 2017

Wainwright, Barbara, interviews by Michael C. Dorf, Washington, DC, Mar. 14, 2005, Mar. 13, 2017

Winpisinger, Vickie, phone interview by Michael C. Dorf, July 20, 2017

Yates, Debra, interview by the authors, Chicago, IL, Aug. 15, 2017

Yates, Jonathan, interview by the authors, Chicago, IL, Aug. 15, 2017

Yoshino, Bill, interview by George Van Dusen, Chicago, IL, Sept. 11, 2017

BIBLIOGRAPHY

Adams, Abigail and John. *The Book of Abigail and John: Selected Letters of the Adams Family, 1762–1784.* Edited and with an Introduction by L. H. Butterfield, Marc Friedlaender, and Mary-Jo Kline. Cambridge, MA: Harvard University Press, 1975.

Alexander, Jane. *Command Performance: An Actress in the Theatre of Politics.* Boston: Da Capo, 2000.

Allen, Thomas B., and Norman Polmar. *Rickover: Father of the Nuclear Navy.* Washington, DC: Potomac, 2007.

Allison, Graham. *Essence of Decision.* Boston: Little, Brown, 1971.

Barone, Michael, and Grant Ujifusa. *The Almanac of American Politics 1992.* Washington, DC: National Journal Group, 1991.

Berman, Ronald. *Culture and Politics.* Lanham, MD: University Press of America, 1984.

Besschloss, Michael R. *The Crisis Years: Kennedy and Khrushchev, 1960–1968.* New York: Edward Burlingame, 1991.

Biddle, Livingston. *Our Government and the Arts: A Perspective from the Inside.* New York: ACA, 1988.

Biles, Roger. *Crusading Liberal: Paul H. Douglas of Illinois.* DeKalb: Northern Illinois University Press, 2002.

Blair, Clay Jr. *The Atomic Submarine and Admiral Rickover.* New York: Holt, 1954.

Caro, Robert A. *Lyndon Johnson: Master of the Senate.* New York: Alfred A. Knopf, 2002.

———. *The Passage of Power.* New York: Alfred A. Knopf, 2012.

Carter, Jimmy. *Why Not the Best?* Nashville, TN: Broadman, 1975.

———. *White House Diary.* New York: Farrar, Straus and Giroux, 2010.

Celler, Emanuel. *You Never Leave Brooklyn: The Autobiography of Emanuel Celler.* New York: John Day, 1953.

Clark, Charles S. "Youth Gangs: Worsening Violence Prompts Crackdowns and Community Mobilization." *CQ Researcher,* 1, 753–76.

Cohen, Adam, and Elizabeth Taylor. *American Pharoah: Mayor Richard J. Daley—His Battle for Chicago and the Nation*. Boston: Little, Brown, 2000.

"Congressional Perquisites and Fair Elections: The Case of the Franking Privilege." *Yale Law Journal* 83, no. 5 (April 1974), 1055–99.

Conway, Eric M. *High-Speed Dreams: NASA and the Technopolitics of Supersonic Transportation, 1945–1999*. Baltimore: Johns Hopkins University Press, 2005.

Cover, Albert D. "Contacting Congressional Constituents: Some Patterns of Perquisite Use." 24 *American Journal of Political Science*, 24, no. 1 (February 1980): 125–35.

Cutler, Irving. *The Jews of Chicago: From Shtetl to Suburb*. Urbana: University of Illinois Press, 1966.

———. *Jewish Chicago: A Pictoral History*. Chicago: Arcadia, 2000.

Dallek, Robert. *Flawed Giant: Lyndon Johnson and His Times, 1961–1973*. New York: Oxford University Press, 1998.

———. *An Unfinished Life: John F. Kennedy, 1917–1963*. New York: Little, Brown, 2003.

Dixon, Alan. *The Gentleman from Illinois*. Carbondale: Southern Illinois University Press, 2013.

Dorf, Michael C. "Artifactions: The Battle over the National Endowment for the Arts." *Brookings Review* 11, no. 1 (Winter 1993): 32–35. doi:10.2307/20080362.

———. "Culture Wars in the Nation's Attic." *Social Identities* 13, no. 2 (2007): 201–15.

———. "Western Senators against the Arts: Passion or Politics?" *Culturelink* 11, no. 32 (November 2000): 150–54.

Douglas, Paul H. *In the Fullness of Time: The Memoirs of Paul H. Douglas*. New York: Harcourt Brace Janovich, 1971.

Drew, Elizabeth. *Whatever It Takes*. New York: Viking Penguin, 1997.

Duncan, Francis. *Rickover: The Struggle for Excellence*. Annapolis, MD: Naval Institute Press, 2001.

Engel, J. Ronald. *Sacred Sands: The Struggle for Community in the Indiana Dunes*. Middleton, CT: Wesleyan University Press, 1983.

Faith, William R. *Bob Hope: A Life in Comedy*. Boston: Da Capo, 2003.

Farrell, John A. *Tip O'Neill and the Democratic Century*. Boston: Little, Brown, 2001.

Faw, Bob, and Nancy Skelton. *Thunder in America*. Austin: Texas Monthly Press, 1986.

Fenno, Richard F. "Fenno Interview Notes." Washington, DC: US National Archives, Center for Legislative Archives. https://www.archives.gov/legislative/research/special-collections/oral-history/fenno/interview-notes.html.

Flippen, J. Brooks. *Nixon and the Environment*. Albuquerque: University of New Mexico Press, 2000.

Godfried, Nathan. *WCFL, Chicago's Voice of Labor, 1926–78*. Urbana: University of Illinois Press, 1997.

Gottfried, Alex. *Boss Cermack of Chicago: A Study of Political Leadership*. Pullman: University of Washington Press, 1962.

Grant, James. *Mr. Speaker! The Life and Times of Thomas B. Reed, the Man Who Broke the Filibuster*. New York: Simon and Schuster, 2011.

Guthrie, Benjamin J. *Statistics of the Presidential and Congressional Election of November 8, 1960.* Washington, DC: US GPO, 1961.

Halberstam, David. *The Fifties.* New York: Random House, 1993.

Hartley, Robert E. *Battleground 1948: Truman, Stevenson, Douglas and the Most Surprising Election in Illinois History.* Carbondale: Southern Illinois University Press, 2013.

———. *Paul Simon: The Political Journey of Illinois Original.* Carbondale: Southern Illinois University Press, 2009.

Hines, William. "Clear It with Sid!" *CST Magazine,* October 3, 1976.

Hohri, William. *Repairing America: An Account of the Movement for Japanese-American Redress.* Pullman: Washington State University Press, 1988.

Hope, Bob. *Have Tux, Will Travel: Bob Hope's Own Story.* With Peter Martin. New York: Simon and Schuster, 1954.

Horwitch, Mel. *Clipped Wings: The American SST Conflict.* Boston, MA: MIT Press, 1982.

Hulsey, Byron C. *Everett Dirksen and His Presidents.* Lawrence: University Press of Kansas, 2000.

Izumi, Masumi. "Prohibiting American Concentration Camps, 1941–1971." *Asian American Law Journal* 13, no. 1 (January 2006): 1–30.

Kinzer, Steven. *The Brothers.* New York: TimesBooks, 2013.

Koch, Edward I. *Mayor.* New York: Warner, 1985.

———. *Politics.* With William Rauch. New York: Simon and Schuster, 1985.

Koran, Roman. *Rabbis of Our Time: Authorities in the Religious and Political Ferment in Modern Times.* London: Taylor and Francis, 2016.

LaHood, Ray. *Seeking Bipartisanship: My Life in Politics.* With Frank H. Mackaman. Amherst, NY: Cambria, 2015.

Levy, Elizabeth. *The People Lobby: The SST Story.* New York: Delacourte, 1973.

Linenthal, Edward T. *Preserving Memory: The Struggle to Create America's Holocaust Museum.* New York: Columbia University Press, 2001.

MacNeil, Neil. *Dirksen: Portrait of a Public Man.* Cleveland, OH: World, 1970.

Maga, Timothy P. "Ronald Reagan and Redress for Japanese-American Internment, 1983–88," *Presidential Studies Quarterly* 28 (Summer 1998): http://mansell.com/e09066/Maga.html.

Maki, Mitchell, H. L.Kitano, and S. Megan Berthold. *Achieving the Impossible Dream: How Japanese Americans Obtained Redress.* Urbana: University of Illinois Press, 1999.

Matsunaga, Erik. "Japanese Americans in Chicago's South Side—Oakland/Kenwood, 1040s-1950s, Part 3." December 3, 2015. http://www.discovernikkei.org/en/journal/2015/12/3/oakland-kenwood-3/.

McKeever, Porter. *Adlai Stevenson: His Life and Legacy.* New York: William Morrow, 1989.

Medoff, Rafael. *Jewish Americans and Political Participation.* Santa Barbara, CA: ABC-CIO, 2002 at http://www.abc-clio/ABC-CLIOCorporate/product.dspx?pc=A1264c.

Nasaw, David. *The Patriarch: The Remarkable Life and Turbulent Times of Joseph P. Kennedy.* New York: Penguin, 2012.

Neal, Steve. *Rolling on the River: The Best of Steve Neal.* Carbondale: Southern Illinous University Press, 1999.

Nelson, Garrison. *John William McCormick: A Political Biography.* New York: Bloomsbury, 2017.

Netzer, Dick. *The Subsidized Muse: Public Support for the Arts in the United States.* Cambridge: Cambridge University Press, 1978.

Nixon, Richard. *RN: The Memoirs of Richard Nixon.* New York: Grosset and Dunlap, 1978.

Nordlander, Robert E. "Madalyn Murray O'Hair: The Making of a Modern Myth." *Freethought Today*, November 1988, https://ffrf.org/legacy/fttoday/back/myth.html.

Obey, David. *Raising Hell for Justice: The Washington Battles of a Heartland Progressive.* Madison: University of Wisconsin Press, 2007.

O'Connor, Len. *Mayor Daley and His City.* Chicago: Henry Regnery, 1979.

Okamura, Raymond. "Background and History of the Repeal Campaign." *Amerasia Journal* 2, no. 2 (Fall 1974): 73–94.

Pensoneau, Taylor. *Powerhouse: Arrington of Illinois.* Baltimore, MD: American Literary Press, 2006.

Perryman, Wayne. *Whites, Blacks, and Racist Democrats: The Untold Story of Race and Politics.* Pennsauken, NJ: BookBaby, 2012.

Polmar, Norman, and Thomas B. Allen. *Rickover.* New York: Simon and Schuster, 1981.

Rakove, Milton. "Sen. Adlai Stevenson III." *Illinois Issues*, November 1977, 21–23.

———. *We Don't Want Nobody Nobody Sent.* Bloomington: Indiana University Press, 1979.

Reeves, Richard. *Infamy: The Shocking News of the Japanese American Internment in World War II.* New York: Henry Holt, 2015.

———. *President Kennedy: Profile in Power.* New York: Simon and Schuster, 1993.

Reich, Leonard S. "From the Spirit of St. Louis to the SST: Charles Lindbergh, Technology and Environment." *Technology and Culture* 36, no. 2 (1995): 351–93. DOI: 10.2307/3106376.

Remini, Robert. *The House: The History of the House of Representatives.* New York: Smithsonian Books/HarperCollins, 2006.

Rockwell, Theodore. *The Rickover Effect.* Annapolis, MD: United States Naval Institute Press, 1992.

Royko, Mike. *Boss: Richard J. Daley of Chicago.* New York: Plume, 1988.

Salinger, Pierre. *With Kennedy.* New York: Doubleday, 1966.

Schapsmeier, Edward, and Frederick Schapsmeier. *Dirksen of Illinois: Senatorial Statesman.* Urbana: University of Illinois Press, 1985.

———. "Everett M. Dirksen of Pekin: Politician par Excellence." *Journal of the Illinois State Historical Society* 76 (Spring 1983): 3–16.

Shapiro, Ira. *The Last Great Senate: Courage and Statesmanship in Times of Crisis.* New York: Public Affairs, 2012.

Sharansky, Natan. *Fear No Evil.* New York: Public Affairs, 1998.

Simon, Paul. *P.S.: The Autobiography of Paul Simon.* Chicago: Bonus, 1999.

Smith, Cindy K. "Wartimes Internment of Japanese-Americans: An Examination of Current Reparation Proposals." *University of Puget Sound Law Review* 6, no. 1 (Fall 1982): 97–121.

Sorenson, Theodore C. *Kennedy.* New York: Harper and Row, 1965.

Stone, Rabbi Kurt. *The Congressional Minyan*. KTAV, Hoboken, NJ, 2000.

Straight, Michael Whitney. *Nancy Hanks: An Intimate Portrait; The Creation of a National Commitment to the Arts*. Durham, NC: Duke University Press, 1988.

———. *Twigs for an Eagle's Nest: Government and the Arts, 1965–1978*. New York: Devon, 1979.

Tacheron, Donald G., and Morris K. Udall. *The Job of the Congressman*. Indianapolis, IN: Bobbs-Merrill, 1970.

Truman, David B. *The Congressional Party*. New York: Wiley, 1959.

Unger, Irwin and Diebie. *LBJ: A Life*. New York: Wiley, 1999.

Walter, Aaron T. *The Limits of Influence: Gerald Ford, Yitzhak Rabin, and the 1975 Reassessment of US-Israeli Relations*. n.p., JoySpring, 2014.

White, Mark J. *Missiles in Cuba: Kennedy, Khrushchev, Castro and the 1962 Crisis*. Chicago: Ivan R. Dee, 1997.

Whipple, Chris. *The Gatekeepers: How the White House Chiefs of Staff Define Every Presidency*. New York: Crown, 2017.

Wolanin, Barbara A. *Constantino Brumidi, Artist of the Capitol*. Sen. Doc. No. 103–27 (1998).

Yates, Sidney R. "Design for Chicago Transit: London Style." *Journal of Land and Public Utility Economics* 17, no. 3 (August 1941): 320–32.

Zengerle, Jason. "Murthaville," *New Republic*, August 31, 2009, https://newrepublic.com/article/68877/murthaville.

INDEX

Page numbers in *italics* refer to photographs.

ABM (antiballistic missile system), 119–21
Abzug, Bella S. (rep., D-NY), 198, 248n81
acidified paper, 147
Adams, Ansel, 44
Adams, John, 144–45, 182
Adams, John Quincy, 111, 145
Advisory Council on the Arts, 146
AFL-CIO, 145; Actors' Equity, 146; American Federation of Musicians, 145; Committee on Political Education, 114, 157; Department of Professional Employees, 205; International Alliance of Theatrical Stage Employees, 146; Screen Actors Guild, 146
Akagi, Dick, 41
Albert, Carl B. (Speaker, D-OK), 111, 196
Allen, Leo E. (rep., R-IL), 24
Allen, Thomas B., 58
American Arts Alliance, 152
American Association of English Jewish Newspapers, 186
American Conservative Union, 157, 218
American Family Association, 143, 152, 170
American Federation of Musicians, 205
American Israel Public Affairs Committee (AIPAC), 210
American Jewish Committee, 185, 191
American Jewish Congress, 185
American Labor Party, 38
Americans for Constitutional Action (ACA), 114

Americans for Democratic Action (ADA), 12, 35, 114, 197, 218
American Veterans' Committee, 28
Anderson, Jack, 217
Anderson, Robert B., 67
Andrews, George W. (rep., D-AL), 89–90
Andrus, Cecil, xi
Angolan independence movement, 110
antiballistic missile system (ABM), 119–20; Nike Hercules, 121; Safeguard, 120; Sentinel, 119–20
Anti-Defamation League, 68
anti-Semitism: at Annapolis, 58; in Chicago, 213; in Congress, 185–86, 212; at Dhahran Air Base, Saudi Arabia, 187–89; in Dirksen campaign, 101; and Egyptian Jews, 186–87; in Germany, 29; in Jackson campaign, 183–84; in U.S. Navy, 58, 60, 61–62, 68
Appropriations Committee. *See under* House committees
Arafat, Yasir, 183, 211
Aramco (Arabian American Oil Company), 187–88, 245n22
Arends, Leslie C. (rep., R-IL), 2
Armey, Richard K. "Dick" (rep., R-TX), 153, 154, 156–57, 158, 218, 243n37
Aronovich, Felix, 198
Arts and Humanities, 146, 147
Arts, Humanities, and Museums Act Amendments of 1990, 166
Arvey, Jacob "Jake," 7–8, 10, 34, 49, 90, 220
Atkins, Chester G. (rep., D-MA), 178

Atkinson, Rick, 183
Atomic Energy Commission, 26, 59
AuCoin, W. Leslie "Les" (rep., D-OR), 136, 167, 178

Babb, John E., 34, 39
Bailey, Cleveland M. (rep., D-WV), 66
Bain, Mary Anderson, x–xii; 71, 75, 84; as campaign manager, 50, 90; and Carter, 200, 202; on Committee to Remember the Children, 208–9; on constituent mail, 112; on House campaigns: (1982) 223; (1996) 216; on Jewish community, 193, 213; and NEA, 143–44, 154, 158; on retirement, 217; on Rickover, 60, 64; on Senate campaign (1962), 2, 100, 104, 105
Baker, Robert Gene "Bobby," 102
Baker, Russell, 32
Barak, Ehud, 211
Barbour, Walworth, 191
Barkley, Alben W., 49
Barrett, George Francis, 9
Basic Industry Research Laboratory (Evanston, IL), 141
Bates, Joseph B. "Joe" (rep., D-KY), 28, 37, 56
Battisstella, Annabelle, 134
Bauler, Mathias "Paddy," 12
Bayh, Birch E. (sen., D-IN), 106
Bay of Pigs invasion, 103, 104
Beard, Daniel P. "Dan," 137–38
Begin, Menachem, 199, 201–2
Belmont Harbor ABMs, 121
Ben-Gurion, David, 29, 186
Bentsen, Lloyd M. (sen., D-TX), 16
Bergan, Harold "Hal," 107, 124, 126
Berman, Arthur (IL state sen.), 139
Berman, Irving, 57–58, 61, 64
Bertini, Catherine "Cathy," 181, 222
Bevill, Tom D. F. (rep., D-AL), 178, 180
Biddle, Francis B., 43
Biddle, Livingston L. "Liv," Jr., 150–51
Bikel, Theodore, 152
Bilandic, Michael A., 139
Bingham, Jonathan, 109
Blaine, James G. (Speaker, R-ME), 14
Blair, Clay, Jr., 65, 69
Boeing Co., 118, 121, 127–28, 129
Bohemian Lawyers Association of Chicago, 8
Boland, Edward P. (rep., D-MA), 115, 125, 142, 204
Bolling, Richard W. (rep., D-MO), 37
"Boll Weevils," 157
Bookbinder, Hyman H., 207
Booster (Lerner Home Newspapers), 51, 69

Boucher, Frederick C. "Rick" (rep., D-VA), 155
Bourne, Peter G., 200
Brademas, S. John, Jr. (rep., D-IN), 165
Brezhnev, Leonid I., 196, 210
Broadway Armory, Chicago, 62, 138, 141
Broder, David S., 101, 129
Brooks, Charles Wayland "Curly" (sen., R-IL), 9, 13
Brooks, Jack B. (rep., D-TX), 215
Brooks, T. Overton (rep. D-LA), 66
Bourne, Peter, 200
Brower, David, 119
Brown, George E., Jr. (rep., D-CA), 142, 162, 163
Brown, Oscar, Jr., 33
Brzezinski, Zbigniew, 200
Buchanan, James, 145
Buchanan, Pat, 152, 170
Buckley, James V. (rep., D-IL), 26, 39
Bureau of Land Management. See under Department of the Interior
Bureau of Ships (BuShips), 57, 59, 71
Burleson, Omar T. (rep., D-TX), 111
Burns, Conrad R. (sen., R-MT), 175
Burton, Dan (rep., R-IN), 173, 193
Burton, Phillip (rep., D-CA), 16, 135, 138
Bush, George H. W., 164, 170, 173, 181, 191, 208, 210, 247n73
Byrd, Robert C. (sen., D-WV), 158–60, 161, 168, 177, 178, 179, 181

Camp David Accords (1978), 199, 201, 206
Cannon, Clarence A. (rep., D-MO), 27–28, 31, 88–89, 109, 111, 180
Cannon, Joseph G. (Speaker, R-IL), 17, 55, 56
Capone, Al, 19
"Cardinals," 25, 134, 141, 142, 182, 222
Carroll, Howard, 216, 217
Carson, Rachel, 115–16; Silent Spring, 115
Carter, James E. "Jimmy," Jr., 81, 138, 151, 152, 198–204, 206
Case, Clifford P. (sen., R-NJ), 123
Castro, Fidel, 104
Catholic Interracial Council, 92
Celler, Emanuel "Manny" (rep., D-NY), 47, 55, 185, 192, 212, 216
Central Intelligence Agency (CIA), 208–9
Cermak, Anton J., 7, 8–9
Cermak, Helena, 9
Chaffee, John L. H. (sen., R-RI), 158, 159
Chambers, Whittaker, 23
Chapman, Steve, 219
Chatelain, Mrs. Leon, Jr., 17
Chesney, Chester Anton (rep., D-IL), 26, 39

Chicago Bar Association, 29
Chicago City Council, 7, 9, 18, 22, 52
Chicago Cultural Center, 172, 173, 177
Chicago Public Library. *See* Chicago Cultural
  Center
Chinese Exclusion Act of 1882, 42
Church, Marguerite Stitt (rep., R-IL), 87
Citizens' League Against the Sonic Boom, 119
City Club of Chicago, 52
Civil Liberties Act of 1987, 53–54
Civil Rights Act of 1957, 21, 52
Civil Rights Act of 1964, 107, 208
Clark, William G., 114
Clary, Pat, 230n62
"Clear it with Sid," 204
Clinton, William J., 181, 210–11, 215, 216, 217, 224
Coalition Against the SST, 124
Cochran, W. Thad (sen., R-MS), 168
Coelho, Anthony L. "Tony" (rep., D-CA), 225
Colbert, Jerry, 205
Cole, William S. (rep., R-NY), 65
Coleman, Milton, 183, 184
Colmer, William M. (rep., D-MS), 21, 22
Combined Jewish Appeal, 189
Commission on Wartime Relocation and In-
  ternment of Civilians, 53; *Personal Justice
  Denied,* 53
committees. *See under* House committees
Commodity Credit Corporation, 190
communism, 35–39, 48, 50–51, 97, 145
communist accusations, 23, 37, 38, 93, 162, 212
Concorde SST, 117, 124, 125, 126
Conference Committee (House/Senate), 31–32,
  176–77, 179; report, 36–37, 179, 180, 181
Conference of Jewish Women's Organizations,
  87
Congress: 80th (1947), 15, 20, 35; 81st (1949), 15,
  23, 30–31, 185; 83rd (1953), 55; 87th (1961), 90;
  89th (1965), 112, 190; 92nd (1971), 133; 101st
  (1989), 166; 102nd (1991), 169; 104th (1995),
  215; 105th (1997), 217
Congressional Black Caucus, 184, 197, 211
Congressional Record, 47, 107, 122, 165, 198
Congressional Research Service, 137
Conrad, Kent (sen., D-ND), 175
Considine, Bob, 65
Consumer Federation of America, 123
Conte, Silvio O. (rep., R-MA), 122, 125, 127, 129,
  142, 163
Cook County Democratic Central Commit-
  tee, 18
Cook County Democratic machine, 11, 19, 105,
  194

Cook County Democratic Party, 10, 99
Coolidge, Calvin, 46
"Corn for Porn," 179, 181
Council on Environmental Quality (CEQ), 124
Courtney, Thomas J., 9, 19
Cox, Edward E. "Goober" (rep., D-GA), 21,
  24–25, 56
Craig, Larry E. (sen., R-ID), 175
Crane, Philip M. "Phil" (rep., R-IL), 173–74, 218
Crown, Lester, 140
Cuban missile crisis, 1–2, 102–5, 106

Daley, Richard J., *80*; on Chicago Cultural Center, 172; on Clark Senate campaign (1968), 114;
  on dealing with scandals, 163; at Democratic
  National Convention, (1968) 16; (1972) 192,
  212; on Gateway Park, 173; on 9th District
  House seat, 100; Singer mayoral challenge
  (1975), 212–13; on switchblade legislation, 52;
  on Yates Senate campaign (1962), 90, 91, 92,
  100, 105, 189; on Yates on Appropriations, 111
D'Amato, Alphonse M. (sen., R-NY), 152
Dannemeyer, William E. (rep., R-CA), 160, 161,
  162, 177, 178, 179, 180
Davies, John C., II (rep., D-NY), 24
Dawson, William Levi (rep., D-IL), 21–22, 37
DDT. *See under* environmental issues
Dean, Gordon E., 59
Decker, Bernard, 99, 106
de Gaulle, Charles, 116
De La Cour, Joseph L. (rep. and sen., D-IL), 90
Delaney, James J. (rep., D-NY), 25
Dellums, Ronald V. "Ron" (rep., D-CA), 135
Democratic Leadership Council, 211
Democratic National Committee (DNC), 184,
  192
Democratic National Conventions: (1952) 50;
  (1972) 192; (1984) 184
Department of Agriculture, 115, 116, 146; Na-
  tional Forests, 166; U.S. Forest Service, 133,
  136, 167, 170, 177, 208
Department of Commerce, 88
Department of Energy, 133, 136, 140, 141, 146
Department of Professional Employees of the
  AFL-CIO, 145–46
Department of State, 110
Department of the Interior and Related Agencies, 9, 133, 139, 146, 152; American Samoa,
  177; Bureau of Land Management (BLM), 133,
  136, 148, 164, 170; Fish and Wildlife Service,
  136, 139, 142, 167, 225; grazing fees, 170–71,
  174, 17, 177, 178, 179, 181; National Park Service, 133, 136, 139, 205, 217

Department of Transportation (DOT), 115, 119, 122, 123, 125
Derrick, Butler C. (rep., D-SC), 180
Dewey, Thomas E., 12, 14
DeWitt, John L., 43, 44
DeWoskin, Morris R., 69
Dhahran Air Base, Saudi Arabia, 187–88, 189
Dichlorodiphenyltrichloroethane (DDT). See under environmental issues
Dicks, Norman D. (rep., D-WA), 136, 167, 178, 179
Dickstein, Samuel (rep., D-NY), 185
Dillard, Irving, 91–92
Dillon, C. Douglas, 105
Dirksen, Everett McKinley (rep. and sen., R-IL), 76, 96, 193; anti-Semitism in 1962 campaign, 100–101; and Civil Rights Act of 1963, 107; Cuban missile crisis, 1–2, 102–6; Democratic support in 1962 campaign, 98–102; on federal judicial nominations, 106, 113; as Minority Leader, 90, 94, 190; and 1963 Nuclear Test Ban Treaty, 106; Senate campaigns: (1950) 55; (1956) 94; (1962) 91, 95, 96, 97; (1968) 114; on UAR, 190; on Yates at UN, 109
District of Columbia, 27–28
Dixiecrats, 12, 14, 20, 21, 24, 51, 56, 134
Dixon, Alan J. (sen., D-IL), 221
Dixon, Julian C. (rep., D-CA), 184–85
Domenici, Pete, (sen., R-NM), 168, 175
"do-nothing Congress," 14, 15, 35
Doughton, Robert L. (rep., D-NC), 24
Douglas, Emily Taft, 10, 93
Douglas, Paul H. (sen., D-IL), 75, 76; as Chicago alderman, 9, 11; endorsement of Yates for Senate (1962), 93; on federal judicial nominations, 57, 99, 106; on Indiana Dunes National Lakeshore, 118, 137, 140; on 1962 Senate race, 91, 92; Senate campaigns: (1948) 13, 14; (1966) 113; on Stevenson nomination (1952), 49; World War II service, 13; and Yates House campaigns: (1950) 37; (1952) 50; (1962) 105, 107
Dreiske, John, 101
Dulles, John Foster, 186–87, 188
Duncan, Robert B. (rep., D-OR), 136, 139
Durbin, Richard J. "Dick" (sen., D-IL), 178

Eagleton, Thomas F. (sen., D-MO), 192
earmarks, 150, 172–73, 224–25
Earth Day, First Annual (1970), 124
Earth First!, 171

Eberharter, Herman P. (rep., D-PA), 77
Economic Cooperation Administration, 27; Economic Recovery Tax Act of 1981 (Kemp-Roth tax cut), 152
Edwards, W. Jackson "Jack" (rep., R-AL), 129
Egypt, 190, 194–95; arms sales to, 202, 203, 204; Camp David Accords, 199; Jews, 186–87
Eisendrath, Edwin, 169, 210, 213, 223
Eisenhower, Dwight D., 12, 51, 52, 94, 116, 118; Cultural Presentations Abroad, 145; and Dirksen, 94, 95–96; Eisenhower Doctrine, 187; on Rickover promotion, 63, 66, 67, 68
Eizenstat, Fran, 200
Eizenstat, Stuart E., 200, 202, 206–7, 210–11
Emanuelson, Chester, 89
Emergency Detention Act of 1950. See under Internal Security Act of 1950
Engel v. Vitale (1962), 90
environmental issues, 115, 130; conservation groups, 118; conservation movement, 115; DDT (Dichlorodiphenyltrichloroethane), 115; energy conservation, 141; Environmental Defense Fund, 116; Environmental Protection Agency (EPA), 116, 126, 141–42; Everglades National Park airport, 123; Federal Water Pollution Control Act of 1960, 118; First Annual Earth Day (1970), 124; Indiana Dunes National Lakeshore, 118; pesticides, 115, 116, 141–42; President's Science Advisory Committee (PSAC), 116, 122; supersonic transport (SST), 116–18, 119, 121, 122–30
Environmental Protection Agency (EPA), 116, 126, 141–42
Evanston Research Park. See Northwestern University/Evanston Research Park
Everglades National Park airport, 123
Executive Order 9066, 44, 53
Exxon Valdez oil spill, 155

Fair Deal, 21, 24, 51
Farrakhan, Louis, 183, 184, 245n2
Federal Aviation Agency / Federal Aviation Administration (FAA), 117
Federal Insecticide, Fungicide, and Rodenticide Act Amendments of 1982, 142
federally owned lands, 136; grazing fees, 170–71, 174, 175, 177, 178, 179, 181
Federal Water Pollution Control Act of 1960, 118
Fenwick, Millicent (rep., R-NJ), 196
Ferguson, Denzel and Nancy, 171
Field, Marshall, III, 33

Finley, Karen, 169–70, 175
Finnegan, Edward R. (rep., D-IL), 110
Fish and Wildlife Service. *See under* Department of the Interior
Fisher, Don, 207, 210
Fitchie, Robert, C., 19
Foley, Thomas S. "Tom" (Speaker, D-WA), 157, 210, 215
Ford, Gerald R., 16, 24, *81*, 113, 189, 194
Forest Service. *See under* Department of the Interior
Foster, John W., 188
442nd Regimental Combat Team, 44–45, 46, 48
four rules for better legislative process: bipartisanship, 220–22; courtesy, 222–23; ending Tuesday-Thursday club, 223–24; earmarks, 224–25
Frank, Barney (rep., D-MA), 157
Frankel, Max, 91
franking privilege, 33
Freedman, Milt, 68
Friedman, Milton, 127, 128
Friends of the Earth, 123
Frohnmayer, John E., 169
Fulbright, J. William (sen., D-AR), 104, 109
Fuller, Hadwen C. (rep., R-NY), 24
Furcolo, J. Foster (rep., D-MA), 28, 31

Galbraith, John Kenneth, 127
Gallup poll, 14, 103
Galvão, Henrique, 110
Gantt, Harvey B., 168
Garfield, James A., 5
Garwin, Richard L., 122, 124, 240n21
Gary, J. Vaughan (rep., D-VA), 28, 31
Gateway Park, Chicago, 173, 177
General Electric, 118, 121
Geneva Conference (1973), 195, 201, 247n68
German-American Committee for Senator Dirksen, 101
Gilbert, Daniel A. "Tubbo," 39, 93
Gill, Joseph L., 9, 12, 34, 35, 39
Gillette, Wilson D. (rep., R-PA), 36
Gingrich, Newt (Speaker, R-GA), 215
Godfrey, Arthur, 30, 72
Goldstein, Ellen, 206
Goldwater, Barry M. (sen., R-AZ), 95, 106
Golodner, Jack, 145, 205
Goodwin, Maxwell, 34, 38
Gorbachev, Mikhail, 210
Gordon, Thomas S. (rep., D-IL), 22, 25

Gorski, Martin (rep., D-IL), 22, 26
Graham-Latta Budget bill (1981), 152
Graubart, Judah, 191
Great Society antipoverty programs, 135
Green, Dwight H., 9, 13
Green, S. William (rep., R-NY), 176
Greif, Ken, 119
Gulf of Tonkin Resolution, 114
Gulf War (1990), 210
Guthman, Jack, 212

Haderlein, John, 12
Hague, Frank, 12
Haig, Alexander M., Jr., 209
Halberstam, David, 49
Halleck, Charles A. (rep., R-IN), 96, 104, 118
Hansen, Julia Butler (rep., D-WA), 133, 136, 212
Harano, Ross, 45–46, 53
Harpers Ferry National Historic Park, WV, 177
Harris, John, 67
Harris, Louis "Lou," polls, 91, 97–98, 100, 104
Hart, Gary W., 184
Hartigan, Neil, 139
Hartke, R. Vance (sen., D-IN), 140
Hays, Wayne L. (rep., D-OH), 16, 113
Hébert, F. Edward (rep., D-LA), 135
Heller, Louis B. (rep., D-NY), 66
Helms, Jesse A., Jr. (sen., R-NC): amendment on NEA, 158–81, 243n44
Herzog, Chaim, 196
Hickenlooper, Bourke B. (sen., R-IA), 98, 99
Hillman, Sidney, 205
Hiss, Alger, 23
Hobson, Laura Z., 185
Hodsoll, Francis S. M. "Frank," 151
Hoffman, Philip E., 191
Hohri, William, 54
Holleb, Adeline. *See* Yates, Adeline
Holleb, A. Paul, 7, 8, 12
Holleb, Charlie, 195
Holleb, Marshall, 8, 9, 10, 12, 49–50
Holloway, James L., Jr., 61
Holocaust Days of Remembrance, 208
Holocaust Memorial Council, United States, 162, 206
Holocaust Memorial Museum, United States, 206–8; Committee to Remember the Children, 208
Holtzman, Elizabeth (rep., D-NY), 189, 192, 216
Honda, Noby, 41
Hoover, J. Edgar, 43

Hope, Bob, 30, *73*
Horner, Henry, 7
House Appropriations subcommittees, 129; Commerce, 88, 89; Commerce and General Government Affairs, 90; Defense, 150; District of Columbia, 27–28; Economy in Government, 124; Education and Labor Postsecondary Education, 167; Foreign Aid, 27, 28, 31; Foreign Operations, 133, 193–94, 202; General Government Matters, 89; Housing and Urban Development (HUD), 142; Independent Offices, 88–89; Interior and Related Agencies, 6, 133, 137, 139, 146, 150, 152 193, 208; Military Construction, 150; Permanent Appropriations, 90; Transportation, 115, 119, 124–25, 193; Treasury, Post Office, and Executive Offices, 111, 115
House committees: Administration, 110–11; Agriculture, 142; Appropriations, 6, 25–26, 27, 88, 111, 126, 128, 137, 150, 193; Banking and Currency, 197; Commerce, 121; Education and Labor, 166; Expenditures, 25; Foreign Affairs, 26, 87, 112, 189; Foreign Relations, 194; Freedom of Information, 122; Interior and Insular Affairs, 121; Interstate and Foreign Commerce, 52; Judiciary, 26, 47; Oversight and Government Reform, 21–22; Rules, 18, 20, 167–68; Un-American Activities (HUAC), 23; Veterans Affairs, 212; Ways and Means, 18; of the Whole House, 57, 155, 158, 171, 174, 243n37
House Conservative Democratic Forum, 157
House Office buildings, 17
House of Representatives: African American members, 22; cardinals, 25; diversity, 5; Jewish members, 10, 185, 193, 198, 209, 210, 211; ranking members, 6; seniority system, 6
Humphrey, Hubert H. (sen., D-MN), 37, 102, 114, 145, 192, 246–47n56
Humphreys, Murray "the Camel," 19
Hyde, Henry J. (rep., R-IL), 162, 173, 221, 223

Igoe, Michael L., 113
Illinois and Michigan Canal National Heritage Corridor, 173
Illinois Commerce Commission, 9, 27
Illinois Conference of Jewish Organizations, 186
Illinois Democratic Party, 90
Illinois Federation of Republican Women, 95
Illinois National Guard, 62, 138

Illinois's 9th Congressional District. *See* 9th Congressional District, Illinois
Immigration Act of 1924 (Johnson-Reed Act), 42, 46, 48
Immigration and Nationality Act of 1952 (McCarran-Walter Act), 48
Independent Voters of Illinois, 49
Indiana Dunes National Lakeshore, 118, 136–37, 140
Inouye, Daniel (sen., D-HI), 106
Institute of Contemporary Art, Univ. of PA, 143–44, 154, 158
Institute of Museum Services, 149
Internal Security Act of 1950 (McCarran Act), 35, 36; Title II: Emergency Detention Act, 36, 48, 53
International Association of Machinists and Aerospace Workers (IAM), 121, 127
internment camps. *See* Japanese-American internment
Israel, 29, 185, 190, 192, 194, 200; aid to, 193; arms sales to, 191, 202, 203; Camp David Accords (1978), 199, 201, 206; first Arab-Israeli war (1948), 29, 186; Jerusalem, 199; Six-Day War (1967), 190, 191, 193; statehood, 11, 186; U.S. Embassy in, 199; Yom Kippur War (1973), 193, 245n22, 247n68
Issei, 42, 46, 48
Izaak Walton League of America, 52, 118

Jackson, Henry M. "Scoop" (rep. and sen., D-WA), 63, 67, 121
Jackson, Jesse, 183–84, 192
Jackson, Robert H., 44
Japanese American Citizens League (JACL), 41, 45, 46
Japanese-American internment, 41, 42, 43–44, 53
Japanese Americans for Sid Yates Campaign Committee, 46
Japanese redress, 53
Jarrett, Vernon, 33
Javits, Jacob K. (rep. and sen., R-NY), 145, 165, 188, 202
Jeffords, James M. "Jim" (sen., R-VT), 174–75
Jewish: and black communities, 206; citizens in Egypt, 186–87; citizens in Soviet Union, 191–92, 196, 198; community in Chicago, 7, 8, 10, 17, 18; members of the House, 10, 185, 193, 198, 209, 210, 211; military personnel, 188, 189; refugee immigration, 185; voters, 192, 245n22

Jewish War Veterans (JWV), 62; National Defense Committee, 62
Joelson, Charles S. (rep., D-NJ), 185
John F. Kennedy Center for the Performing Arts, Washington, DC, 144, 205
Johnson, Lyndon B., 76, 80; and ban on UAR, 190; on NEA and NEH, 144, 146; on 1968 decision not to run, 16; and SST, 119; and support of Dirksen, 99–100, 114; and Vietnam War, 16, 114
Johnson, Walter, 49
Johnson-Reed Act. See Immigration Act of 1924
Johnston, J. Bennett (sen., D-LA), 168
Johnstown, PA, flood (1977), 150; Johnstown Symphony Orchestra concerts, 151
Joint Congressional Committee on Atomic Energy, 26, 63, 65
Jonas, Edgar A. (rep., R-IL), 62
Jong, Erica, 148
Jordan, Hamilton, 200, 203, 248n95
Judd, Walter H. (rep., R-MN), 46–47

Kaplan, Leonard, 58
Kassenbaum, Nancy L. (sen., R-KS), 175
Kay, Danny, 72
Keane, Tom, 105
Kefauver, Estes (sen., D-TN), 49, 50, 93
Kelly, Edward J., 9, 10, 11, 19
Kemp, Jack, 156
Kemp-Roth tax cut bill, 152
Kennedy, Edward M. (sen., D-MA), 106, 165
Kennedy, Eunice, 92
Kennedy, Jacqueline, 146
Kennedy, John F., 77; on arts and humanities, 146; and Bentsen, 16; Cuban missile crisis, 102–4, 106; and Dirksen, 1–2, 98–100; and Jewish vote, 55–56, 87; on National Cultural Center, 144; nominated Yates to UN, 109; Nuclear Test Ban Treaty (1963), 106; presidential campaign (1960), 88; Senate election (1952), 204; on SST, 116–17; and Stevenson, 91
Kennedy, Joseph P., 55, 92, 204
Kennedy, Robert F., 99, 102–3, 107
Kennedy, Roger, 217
Kennelly, Martin, 11
Kerner, Otto, Jr., 9
Kerner, Otto, Sr. (Illinois AG and gov.), 8–9, 92, 113
Kimball, Dan A., 59
King, Cecil R. (rep., D-CA), 23

King, Martin Luther, Jr., 197–98
Kiplinger, Austin H., 205
Kirbo, Charles H., 200
Kissinger, Henry, 194, 207
Klein, Julius, 62, 65, 234n38
Know Nothing Party, 185
Koch, Charles, 153
Koch, Edward I. "Ed" (rep., D-NY), 197, 198, 212, 248n81
Korean War, 35, 49
Korematsu, Fred, 44
Korshak, Morris J. "Marshall," 189

LaHood, Ray (rep., R-IL), 219
Laird, Melvin, 120
Lange, Dorothea, 44
Laws, Bolitha J., 17
Legislative Reform Act. See Legislative Reorganization Act of 1970
Legislative Reorganization Act of 1970, 129
Lehman, Herbert H. (sen., D-NY), 112, 185, 188
Lerner, Leo, 49, 51
Levi, Edward H., 189
Levin, Lewis Charles, 185
Lewis, John L., 29
Libby, Ruthven E., 62
Library of Congress, 147
Liebmann, George, 119
Lifschulz, David, 8
Lindbergh, Charles, 126
Linehan, Neil J. (rep., D-IL), 26, 39
Livingston, Robert L. "Bob," Jr. (rep. R-LA), 216
Lobanov, Oleg, 205
Lodge, Henry Cabot, Jr. (sen., R-MA), 55
Long, Clarence D. "Doc" (rep., D-MD), 148, 202
Long, Russell B. (sen., D-LA), 104
Long, Valerie, 51
Longworth, Nicholas (Speaker, R-OH), 17
LoPresti, Michael, Jr., 204
Lowery, William D. "Bill" (rep., R-CA), 178
Lucas, Scott W. (sen., D-IL), 55, 93–94
Lytle, Jay, 141

MacArthur, Douglas, 62
Mack, Peter F., Jr. (rep., D-IL), 26, 52, 92
Madigan, John, 129
Magnuson, Warren G. (sen., D-WA), 121
Magruder, William M., 127, 129
Mahon, George H. (rep., D-TX), 111, 126–27, 128, 136, 137, 138, 190

Mandil, Harry, 62, 65, 66, 67
Mansfield, Mike (sen., D-MT), 76, 99, 101–2, 105
Maplethorpe, Robert, 143–44, 152, 154, 161, 162
Marcantonio, Vito (rep., Lab-NY), 38
Maremont, Arnold, 92
margarine tax, 20–21
Marshall Plan, 13, 27, 88
Martin, John T., 140
Martin, Joseph W., Jr. (Speaker, R-MA), 17, 56
Masaoka, Mike, 46, 48, 53
Maslow, Will, 68
Masuda, Tom, 41
Matsumoto, Kimiye "Doris," 53
Matsunaga, Spark M. (rep. and sen., D-HI), 53
Mayerson, Goldie. See Meir, Golda
McCarran, Patrick A. "Pat" (sen., D-NV), 35
McCarran Act. See Internal Security Act of 1950
McCarran-Walter Act. See Immigration and Nationality Act of 1952
McCarthy, Eugene J. (rep. and sen., D-MN), 16, 112
McCarthy, Joseph R. (sen., R-WI), 93, 94, 219; McCarthyism, 49
McCauley, John, 222
McCloy, John J., 29
McClure, James A. (sen., R-ID), 136, 168, 213
McCormack, John W. (rep., D-MA), 21, 22, 23, 37, 111, 135, 190
McDade, Joseph M. (rep, R-PA), 178, 205
McDonough, Denis, 224
McFall, John J. (rep., D-CA), 127, 129, 194
McGovern, George S. (sen., D-SD), 106, 192, 246n56
McKay, K. Gunn (rep., D-UT), 136
McKeever, Porter, 91
McNamara, Robert S., 117, 118
Medicare, 97, 101
Meir, Golda, 29, 191
Melas, Nicholas, 221
Metzenbaum, Howard M. (sen., D-OH), 175
Michel, Robert H. (rep., R-IL), 221
Mikva, Abner J. (rep., D-IL), 199
Miller v. California (1973), 163, 166
Mills, Wilbur D. (rep., D-AR), 134
Miner, Julius, 110
Minow, Newton, 140, 230n40
Mintzer, David, 141
Mishimi, Jean, 45–46, 53
Mitchell, Billy, 68
Mitchell, Clarence M., Jr., 107

Mitchell, Parren J. (rep. D-MD), 206
Moakley, J. Joseph (rep. D-MA), 167
Mohrman, Frederick G., 138, 149
Mondale, Walter F., 184, 201, 202
Montgomery, James Shera, 23
Moore, Frank, 202–3
Morton, Thruston B., 186
Moss, Lawrence, 119, 123
Mount McKinley/Denali, 167, 244n67
Moynihan, Daniel Patrick "Pat," 165, 196, 198
Mudge, Verne D., 66
Muller, Paul Herman, 115
Mundt, Karl E. (rep. and sen., R-SD), 16
Mundt, Mary, 16
Murphy, Ann, 152
Murrow, Edward R., 43
Murtha, John P. "Jack" (rep., D-PA), 149–50, 153, 178
Muskie, Edmund (sen., D-ME), 122

Nash, Patrick A. "Paddy," 19
Nasser, Gamal Abdel, 190
National Advisory Committee on Aviation, 116
National Aeronautics and Space Administration (NASA), 117
National Art Commission (1859), 145
National Association for the Advancement of Colored People (NAACP), 52, 197
National Cancer Institute, 141
National Council for Japanese American Redress, 54
National Council on the Arts, 150
National Cultural Center. See John F. Kennedy Center for the Performing Arts, Washington, DC
National Defense Education Act of 1958, 69
National Endowment for Democracy (NED), 208–9
National Endowment for the Arts (NEA), 134, 163, 165, 182, 208; authorization bill, 166, 167, 168; funding, 148, 154–55, 174, 175–76, 181, 216, 218; grants, 152, 155, 164, 167; Independent Commission, 164, 166, 243nn62–63; Mapplethorpe and Serrano, 143–44, 152, 154, 155, 161, 162, 165
National Endowment for the Humanities (NEH), 134, 182, 208, 216
National Foundation on the Arts and the Humanities Act of 1965, 144
National Park Service. See under Department of the Interior
National Rifle Association (NRA), 52

National Science Foundation, 145
National Symphony Orchestra (NSO), 205
National Wildlife Federation, 123
Native American programs, 146; Bureau of Indian Affairs, 133, 146; Indian Health Service, 146
Naval Selection Board, 57, 59, 60, 63, 64–65, 66–67
NEA. *See* National Endowment for the Arts
"Negro Newsfront" (WJJD radio), 33
Nelson, Gaylord A. (sen., D-WI), 106, 122
New Deal: federal arts projects, 145; opponents, 13, 21, 29, 34, 51; supporters, xi, 8, 27, 96, 97
New Frontier, 91, 96, 98, 102
Nickles, Donald L. "Don" (sen., R-OK), 181
Nike-Hercules (ABM), 121
9th Congressional District, Illinois, 38, 51, 136; candidates for, 11, 12, 14, 50; district office, 112; Japanese-American population, 45–46; Native American population, 146; Nike-Hercules site, 121; redistricting, 141, 180, 222
Nisei (children of Issei), 43
Nixon, Richard M.: on ABM, 120–21; "Compact of Fifth Avenue," 95; election to Senate (1960), 94; Environmental Protection Agency, 116; planes to Israel, 191; presidential elections: (1968) 114; (1972) 246–47n56; resignation, 16, 134; on Soviet Jews emigration, 192; on SST, 121, 123, 126; TV debates, 97; Watergate, 134
Norman, Lloyd, 63
Norquist, Grover, 157
North, Oliver, 153
Northwestern University/Evanston Research Park, 140–41
nuclear-powered-ship program, 57
Nuclear Test Ban Treaty (1963), 106

Obey, David R. (rep., D-WI), 133, 193, 209, 211, 218, 220
O'Brien, Lawrence F., 99, 102, 105
O'Brien, Thomas J. (rep., D-IL), 18–19, 23, 76, 220–21
O'Connell, Daniel, 37, 38, 60
O'Donnell, Kenneth, 99, 105
O'Dwyer, William, 12
Office of Management and Budget (OMB), 148–49, 151
Ogilvie, Richard B., 106
O'Hara, Barratt (rep., D-IL), 26–27, 33, 34, 37, 39, 55, 112

Okimoto, Mrs. S., 41
Olson, Cuthbert L., 42, 43
OMB. *See* Office of Management and Budget
O'Neill, Millie, 204
O'Neill, Thomas P. "Tip" (Speaker, D-MA), 6, 134, 196, 203–4, 205–6, 210
OPEC, 200, 203
Otten, Allen L., 33, 123
Outer Continental Shelf moratorium, 155, 166
Overton, George, 50

Page, Raymond H., 106
Palestine Liberation Organization (PLO), 206
Palestinians, 201
Panoff, Robert, 62, 65, 66, 67
Paul H. Douglas Center for Environmental Education, Indiana Dunes, 140
Pell, Claiborne (sen., D-RI), 151
Pelly, Thomas M. (rep., R-WA), 123
Pelosi, Nancy (Speaker, D-CA), 218, 223
Percy, Charles H. (sen., R-IL), 95, 113–14, 125, 222
pesticides, 115, 116
Pinchot, Gifford, 115
Polmar, Norman, 58
Ponomarev, Boris, 196
Poole, Mark N., 216
Portugal, 110
postal franking privilege, 33
Powell, Joseph L. "Jody," 199, 200
Powell, Paul T., 90, 235n13
Presidential Citizens Medal, *84*
President's Science Advisory Committee (PSAC), 116, 122
Presidio National Park, 223
Preston, Prince H., Jr. (rep., D-GA), 88, 235n3
Price, Charles Melvin "Mel" (rep., D-IL), 22, 26, 34, 65, 66, 91–92, 216–17
Pritzker, Jay R. "J. B.," 216, 217
Program for Cultural Presentations Abroad, 145
Progressive Citizens of America, 33
Progressive Party, 13, 14
Proxmire, E. William (sen., D-WI), 118, 122, 124

Quayle, J. Danforth "Dan," 16

Rabin, Yitzhak, 194, 195
Rafiah, Zvi, 194–95
Rainville, Howard, 100, 101
Rangel, Charles B. (rep., D-NY), 197

Rankin, John E. (rep., D-MS), 24, 212
Rapota, Grigory, 191
Rauh, Joseph L., Jr., 197
Rayburn, Samuel T. "Sam" (Speaker, D-TX), 17, 19, 21, 23, 24, 57, 88, 204
Reagan, Ronald, 54, 148, 149, 208, 221
Reed, Thomas Brackett "Czar," 56
Reese, Robert, 38
refuseniks, 191
Regional Transportation Authority (RTA), 222
Regula, Ralph S. (rep., R-OH): on Conference Report, 181; on conference with the Senate, 160, 163; on grazing fees, 174, 179; on Helms amendment, 161–62, 178; and Interior Appropriations bill, 158; as Interior Appropriations chair, 149, 211, 215, 217; on NEA, 154–55, 157; NEA amendment on "obscene," 167, 168
Reid, Harry M. (sen., D-NV), 175
Republican Party: Compact of Fifth Avenue, 95; Congressional Campaign Committee, 180; National Committee, 2, 62; National Convention (1960), 95; Special Committee on Program and Process, 95
Resa, Alexander J. "Alex" (rep., D-IL), 12
Reuss, Henry S. (rep., D-WI), 122, 123, 124, 135, 188
Ribicoff, Abraham A. (rep. and sen., D-CT), 16, 55, 106, 112, 192, 202
Rickover, H. G., 57–69, 199
Rickover, Ruth Masters, 61
Riggs, Marlon, 170
Roberts, William P., 105
Rockefeller, Nelson A., 95
Rockwell, Theodore, 62–63, 65, 66, 67
Rodino, Peter W., Jr. (rep., D-NJ), 16, 113
Rohrabacher, Dana T. (rep., R-CA): amendment to defund NEA, 153, 154, 156, 157, 243n37; on Helm amendment, 161–62; and Interior Appropriations bill, 158; and "morality" crowd, 160; on NEA authorization bill, 166
Roncolio, Teno (rep., D-WY), 128
Rooney, John J. (rep., D-NY), 88, 188
Roosevelt, Eleanor, 43
Roosevelt, Franklin D., 8, 15, 42, 43, 185, 204–5
Roosevelt, James (rep., D-CA), 188
Roosevelt, Theodore, 115
Root, Russell W., 11
Roper poll, 12
Rosenberg, Moe, 7, 8
Rostenkowski, Dan (rep., D-IL), 92, 111, 222
Ruckelshaus, William, 126

Rules Committee. See under House committees
Rumsfeld, Donald H., 106, 174
Russell, Richard, Jr. (sen., D-GA), 67

Sabath, Adolph J. "Judge" (rep., D-IL), 17–18, 72, 220; advice to Yates, 30; dean of Jewish House members, 10, 185; death, 56, 60; and Dixiecrats, 21; and Edward Cox, 24–25; on McCarran bill, 37; and Rickover, 58; as Rules Committee chair, 47
Sadat, Anwar El, 199, 202
Safeguard (ABM), 120
Saltonstall, Leverett A. (sen., R-MA), 61, 65, 66, 67, 234n38
Samuelson, Paul A., 127, 128
Saroyan, Aram, 148
Saud, King, 188
Saudi Arabia, 147, 189, 245n22; arms sales, 187, 202, 203, 209; Dhahran Air Base, 187–88
Schakowsky, Janice D. "Jan," 216, 217
Scheuer, James H., 209–10
Schlafly, Phyllis, 95
Schnitz, Janet, 124
Schroeder, Patricia Nell Scott "Pat" (rep., D-CO), 135
Schurcliff, William, 119
Scott, Hugh D. (rep., R-PA), 52
Scott, William J., 106
Scowcroft, Brent, 195
Second World Conference on Soviet Jewry (1976), 198
segregation, 28, 219; desegregation, 28, 92; segregationists, 12, 20, 21, 90, 135
Senate committees: Appropriations, 158; Armed Services, 60, 63, 66; Foreign Relations, 109; Labor and Human Resources Committee, 168; Public Works, 76
Senate subcommittees: Interior Appropriations, 136, 158, 171, 213; Transportation Appropriations, 222
Sentinel (ABM), 119–20
Serrano, Andres, 143, 152, 154, 155
Shannon, William, 135
Sharanksy, Natan, 191, 196, 210
Shawnee National Forest, 137
Shriver, Sargent, 92
Shultz, George P., 209
Sidney R. Yates Federal Building, 208
Siegel, Mark A., 206
Siegrist, Robert R., 50–51, 55, 62, 220
Sierra Club, 118, 119, 123, 130
Sigmon, Neal, 153, 179

Silent Spring, 115
Silverstein, Enoch and Marjorie, 191
Silverstein, Leonard L., 205
Simon, Paul M. (rep. and sen., D-IL), 91–92, 93, 94, 160
Simon, Scott, 112
Simon, Seymour, 189
Singer, William S., 105, 192, 212–13
Sleeping Bear Dunes National Lakeshore, 181
Small Business Administration (SBA), 89, 197
Smith, Floyd E., 127
Smith, Howard W. (rep., D-VA), 23
Smithson, James, 145
Smithsonian Institution, 145, 146–47
Smoot, Reed, 178
Social Security, 38, 96–97, 112
Sohn, Herbert, 169
Sorensen, Theodore C. "Ted," 98, 105
Soucie, Gary, 123
Southeastern Center for Contemporary Art, 143, 154, 155, 158
Southern, Hugh, 153
Southern Baptist Convention, 175
Soviet Jewry, 191–92, 195–96, 198, 205, 210
Soviet Union, 125, 187, 190, 195, 201; communism, 145, 196; Cuban missile crisis, 1–2, 102–5, 106; Sputnik, 69, 103, 116; SST, 116, 117
Sparkman, John J. (sen., D-AL), 51, 109
"Sprinkle, Annie." *See* Steinberg, Ellen
Sputnik, 69, 103, 116
SST (supersonic transport), 116–18, 119, 121, 122–30, 240n24
Stearns, Clifford B. "Cliff" (rep., R-FL), 157, 174
Stein, Julius, 138
Steinberg, Ellen, 170, 244n73
Stengel, Richard, 94
Stenholm, Charles W. (rep., D-TX), 156–57
Stennis, John C. (sen., D-MS), 67
Stepak, Vladimir, 199
Stevens, Roger L., 144
Stevens, Theodore F. "Ted" (sen., R-AK), 136, 168
Stevenson, Adlai E., II (IL gov.), 73, 75; gubernatorial campaign (1948), 13, 14; on Naval Selection Board, 68; presidential campaigns: (1952), 49, 50; (1956) 52, 94; on senate campaign (1962), 91, 100, 107; at UN, 91, 109
Stevenson, Adlai E., III (sen., D-IL), 100, 114
Stimson, Henry L., 43, 44
Stockman, David, 148–49, 151
Stone, Richard B. (sen., D-FL), 202
Stratton, William G., 10
Subversive Activities Control Board, 35, 53

supersonic transport (SST), 116–18, 119, 121, 122–30; SST Ad Hoc Review Committee, 122, 123
switchblades, 51–52, *74*
Synagogue Council of America, 189
Synar, Michael L. "Mike" (rep., D-OK), 179; amendment, 171, 174, 177, 178 179
Syria, 194

Taft, Robert A., Sr. (sen., R-OH), 29–30, 94
Taft-Hartley Act, 29
Tagge, George, 95, 110
Talisman, Mark, 207
Teller, Edward, 120
"tellers," 129
Tennessee Valley Authority (TVA), 31
Texas Lost Battalion, 45
Thomas, Albert R. (rep., D-TX), 88–89, 180
Thompson, James R., 141, 221–22
Thurmond, J. Strom (sen., D, R-SC), 12, 14
Tongass National Forest, 216
toxaphene, 141–42
Train, Russell, 124–25
Truman, Harry S., 33, 34, 62; on civil rights, 20, 135; on Dhahran Air base, 188; election (1944), 205; election (1948), 14, 15; and Fair Deal program, 24; on Jewish-American rights, 185; labeled "Commiecrat," 38; recognized State of Israel, 11; on Rickover, 58; veto of McCarran Act, 37
Twyman, Robert J. (rep., R-IL), 10, 11, 34

Udall, Morris K. "Mo" (rep., D-AZ), 135, 203
United Arab Republic, 190
United Nations (UN), 247n1/3; Social, Humanitarian and Cultural Committee, "Third Committee," 196; Trusteeship Council, 109, 110
United States Conference of Mayors, 139
Urban Park and Recreation Recovery Act of 1978 (UPARR), 138, 139
U.S. Army Corps of Engineers, 28, 189
U.S. Navy: Naval Academy at Annapolis, 58; Naval Selection Board, 7, 59, 60, 63, 64–65, 66–67; Nuclear Power Branch of the Bureau of Ships, 57, 59; system of promotion, 60, 63, 65, 66
USS *Nautilus*, 57, 59, 68, 69, *74*

Vance, Cyrus R., 202, 203, 206
Vander Jagt, Guy (rep., R-MI), 180–81
Vietnam War, 113, 114, 135, 149; Gulf of Tonkin Resolution, 114
Vinson, Carl (rep., D-GA), 61

Volpe, John A., 127

Wagner, Robert F., Jr., 188
Wagner-Ellender-Taft Housing bill, 20
Wakamatsu, Shig, 41, 45, 48
Walker, Irwin, 12
Walker, Robert S. (rep., R-PA), 162
Wallace, Henry A., 13, 14, 33
Wallop, Malcolm (sen., R-WY), 175
Walter, Francis E. (rep., D-PA), 23, 25
Ward, Harold G., 9
Warden, Philip, 113
Warren, Earl, 42, 43
Washington, Harold, 82
Watergate, 16, 134
"Watergate babies," 134, 135
WCFL, 27, 33
WCRW, 38
Webber, Charlie, 12
Wegman, Richard, 123
WGN, 50
white supremacy, 211
Whitten, Jamie L. (rep., D-MS), 163, 168, 224
Wiesel, Elie, 206
Wilchusky, LeAnne, 148
Wilderness Society, 118
Wildman, Donald, 170
Wiley, Alexander (sen., R-WI), 2
Wilhelm, David, 215
Will, Hubert, 49
Williams, J. Patrick "Pat" (rep., D-MT), 167,
    178; amendment ("decency clause"), 168,
    169, 244n71
Wilson, Charles N. (rep., D-TX), 195
Wilson, Dave, 137–38
Winpisinger, Vickie, 195, 203
WJJD, 33, 97
Wolf, Robert E., 137
Wood, John Stephens (rep., D-GA), 36
Wright, James C. "Jim," Jr. (Speaker, D-TX),
    208–9

Yamada, Dick, 41
Yariv, Aharon, 191
Yates, Adeline Holleb "Addie," 8, 9, 75, 80, 93,
    142, 195, 200, 207–8, 224
Yates, Charles, 13, 30
Yates, Louis and Ida, 6–7, 18
Yates, Richard (IL gov.), 100
Yates, Sidney Richard, 71, 83; on ABMs, 119–21,
    220; accused of communist sympathies, 36,
    38–39, 50, 97; on African-American and

Jewish schism, 184–85; alderman candidate, 9, 70; and anti-Semitism, 29, 62, 68,
101, 186–89, 212–13; on arts and humanities,
147; on Asians, naturalization restrictions
of, 31, 47; basketball star, 7, 70; on Belmont
Harbor ABM, 121; birth, 7; on Broadway Armory, Chicago, 138; at Bryn Mawr Golf Club,
Lincolnwood, IL, 29, 87, 189; on Chicago
Cultural Center, 172, 173, 177; on civil rights,
48, 51, 52, 98, 208; death, 219; on Deep Tunnel project, 221; district office, 112; editor of
Bulletin of the Decalogue Society of Lawyers,
10; on Eisenhower Doctrine, 187; on Evanston Research Park, 140–41; on Everglades
National Park airport, 123; on environment,
6, 118, 123, 130, 216; and federal judgeship, 57,
101, 110, 113; on Foreign Operations Subcommittee, 193–94; four legislative rules, 220–25
(*see also* four rules for better legislative process); on Gateway Park, Chicago, 173, 177; on
Great Society, 135; as golfer, 29–30, 72, 87; at
Hebrew school, 7; and Holocaust Memorial
Museum, 206–7; on House Appropriations
Committee, 25, 27; on House Appropriations subcommittees, 27, 28, 111, 115, 119, 124,
125–26, 133, 193 (*see also* Yates, Sidney Richard, on House Appropriations subcommittees); House campaign (1948) 13–14; House
campaign (1950) 32; House campaign (1952)
50–51; House campaign (1966) 114; House
campaign (1990) 169, 210, 244n70; House
campaign (1994) 215; House campaign (1996)
75, 82, 216–17; on House procedures, 24, 111,
129; in Illinois AG's office, 8, 9, 27; on Indiana Dunes National Lakeshore, 118, 136–37,
140, 220; as Interior Appropriations chair,
133, 135–36, 139–40, 220, 225; on Israel, 28, 29,
31, 186, 191, 193, 194, 196, 197, 202, 203, 204;
on Japanese Americans, 31, 41, 45, 46–47, 48,
53; on Keith-Albee-Orpheum vaudeville circuit, 13; at Lakeview High School, Chicago, 7,
140; law practice, 8, 9, 10, 57; maiden speech,
31, 47; as Man of the Year (Jewish National
Fund), 189; marriage, 8; on Medicare, 97, 101;
name change, 7, 100–101, 211; on naturalization, 31; on NEA, 144, 164, 165, 171, 220; on
New Deal, 50, 96; newsletters, 32–33, 34, 37,
97, 129, 134, 216; on Nike-Hercules missiles
at Belmont Harbor, Chicago, 121; and organized labor, 79, 127; in Pi Lambda Phi, 7;
possible Senate campaign (1966) 113; 76–79;
Presidential Citizens Medal, 84; on radio,

33–34, 97; on Rickover, 58, 60–69, 186; on RTA, 222; Senate campaign (1962) 2, 92–93, 96, 105–6; on Social Security, 38, 96, 112; on Soviet Jewry, 191, 195–96, 205, 213; on SST, 119–21, 122–30, 220; on switchblades, 51–52, 74; at Temple Sholem, Chicago, 10; on toxaphene, 141–42; on transit, 9, 27; at United Nations Trusteeship Council, 109–10; at University of Chicago, BA in philosophy, 7; at University of Chicago School of Law, LLD, 7; U.S. Navy service, 10, 71; on veterans, 31, 112; on Vietnam War, 135; "The Washington Story" (on WJJD), 33–34, 97
Yates, Sidney Richard, on House Appropriations subcommittees: District of Columbia, 27; Foreign Operations, 133, 193; Foreign Aid, 27, 28; Interior and Related Agencies, 133, 193; Transportation, 115, 119, 124, 125–26, 193; Treasury, Post Office, and Executive Offices, 111
Yates, Stephen Richard, 9, 10, 80
"Yates Rule," 111
Yatzofsky, Louis and Ida. See Yates, Louis and Ida
Yosef, Ovadia, 194, 195
Young, Andrew J., Jr., 206
Young, James, 9
Yushakov, Yuri M., 191

Zionism, 196–97

MICHAEL C. DORF is a practicing lawyer and an adjunct professor at the School of the Art Institute of Chicago. He was Congressman Yates's Special Counsel in Washington and remained his lawyer and campaign chairman until the congressman's death.

GEORGE VAN DUSEN is Mayor of Skokie, Illinois, and an adjunct professor at Oakton Community College. He oversaw Yates's 9th District Operations for more than twenty-five years.

The University of Illinois Press
is a founding member of the
Association of University Presses.

Composed in 10.5/13 Minion Pro
with Adrianna Extended Pro display
by Lisa Connery
at the University of Illinois Press
Cover designed by Jennifer S. Fisher
Cover image: Yates with President John F. Kennedy on Air Force One
in 1962. (Sidney R. Yates Papers, Chicago History Museum)
Manufactured by Sheridan Books, Inc.

University of Illinois Press
1325 South Oak Street
Champaign, IL 61820-6903
www.press.uillinois.edu